Hans van Heeswijk
Architecture 1995–2005

Editor Hans Ibelings
Compilation Johanna Günther
Translation Robyn de Jong-Dalziel

With contributions by Mels Crouwel and Marie-Hélène Cornips

Ernst Wasmuth Verlag GmbH & Co. Tübingen/Berlin

architecture 1995–2005

Hans van Heeswijk

Body Line

PwS

KwD

NbZ

RtA

SbT

H

OhP

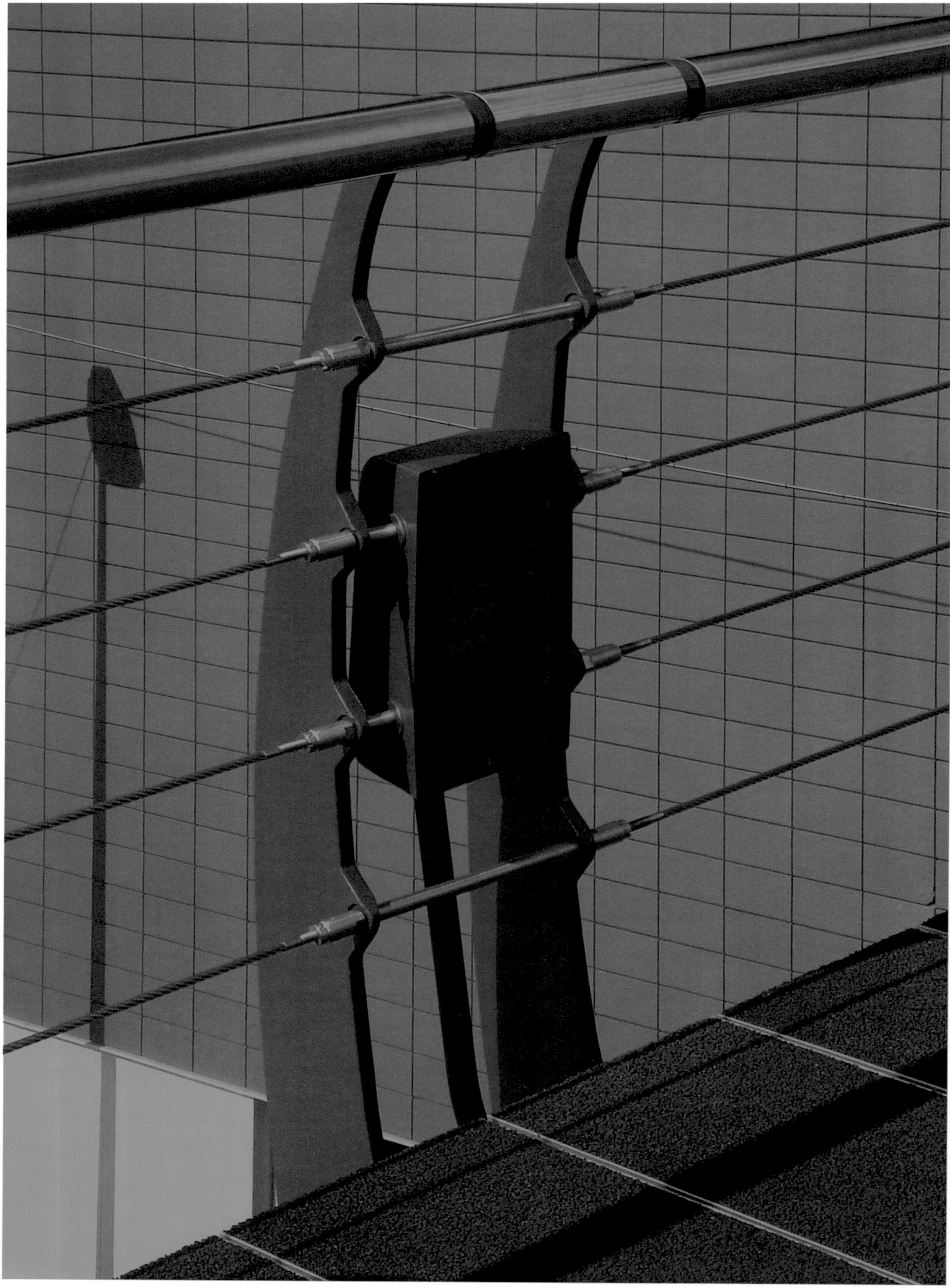

Foreword

On a warm, late summer's day I drove around Amsterdam with Hans van Heeswijk to look at some of his work in the city he now calls home. Not far from his Ertskade offices, are several projects in close proximity to one another. Six office blocks on De Rietlanden, behind them the De Schijf school and commercial premises on Oostelijk Handelskade, the IJ-tram tram stops, the bridge to the Muziekgebouw on the banks of the IJ and the bridges to the Central Station island. All these post-1997 projects bear that clinical, technical signature so characteristic of the work of Van Heeswijk.

The six metal-clad office blocks rise up out of the grass as monolithic and idiosyncratic shapes. The austere brick building containing a school and commercial spaces merges seamlessly with the surrounding dockland architecture. The meticulous detailing of the station precinct bridges and the tram stops, serves to emphasize their structural elements. The dark-coloured bridge to the Muziekgebouw rises like a gangplank between wharf and ship. Here, too, close attention has been paid to the structure, which is reminiscent of a backbone.

What is striking about all these projects is the attention to technical aspects and the exceptionally careful detailing. Nowhere does this degenerate into a pre-occupation with form or contrived constructions. The choice of materials, the care lavished on connections and technical solutions lend the work an unobtrusive presence. It is simply there.

In a way, the work of Hans van Heeswijk is typical of Dutch architecture: with limited budgets, standard materials and high design ideals, designing buildings of exceptional quality.

The same afternoon we visited the Beta Building in Sloterdijk, an office block completed in 2002. In this modest, four-storey building consisting of two disengaged office wings, added value has been achieved through clever use of the chosen materials and sophisticated detailing. On our way to the recently completed Ganzenhoef Cultural Educational Centre in Amsterdam Southeast, we passed the six former car parks on Daalwijkdreef. The end facades, which simply failed to work before the conversion, now have eye-catching projecting awnings. Here, the architectural solution is more important than the functional.

The Cultural Educational Centre, with its terracotta facade cladding and lightweight roof carried by elegant structural members, seems less technical than earlier projects. Van Heeswijk's designs, perhaps partly in response to a changing architectural climate, have become somewhat less dry and technical.

The variety of the above-mentioned projects is typical of the heterogeneous portfolio of Hans van Heeswijk architecten: new office buildings, interiors, conversions, restorations, buildings with a cultural function and infrastructural projects. That diversity of commissions owes a lot to the discreet quality of the work. Many of Van Heeswijk's designs are made for clients who enlist the advice of other architects when choosing an architect. The quality of Van Heeswijk's designs is certainly admired by colleagues: he is an architect's architect. The many commissions for bridges, viaducts and other infrastructural works that have come Van Heeswijk's way, followed from the realization in 1993 of the Verbindingsdam in the Eastern Docklands. For several years Van Heeswijk acted as consultant to the Department of Waterways and Public Works, until it became clear to him that the effect of his advice was declining.

Careful, consistent and passionate: such is the work of Hans van Heeswijk. His designs do not set a stamp on the surroundings, do not alter the context, no, they stand on their own and accept the surroundings for what they are.

A comparable carefulness, attention to detail, unobtrusiveness and passion is revealed by this book, which was designed by Irma Boom Office, compiled by Johanna Günther and edited by Hans Ibelings. As such, the book is in perfect accord with the work of Hans van Heeswijk that is displayed between its covers.

Contents

Appearance, scale, intimacy, surprise, material, colour and logistics are all important for the experience of architecture, but they cannot compare with light and space. HvH

Self-evidently modern

The architecture of Hans van Heeswijk

For Hans van Heeswijk, architecture is inseparable from its making. Thinking about architecture consequently coincides to a great extent with imagining how architecture can be made. And when it comes to making, efficiency and clarity are his first priorities, so that the question of where the design comes from is resolved in a way that provides insight into how a building is put together. For anyone with any affinity with architecture, the connections, junctions and other details in Van Heeswijk's buildings can at the very least be grasped instinctively. Van Heeswijk's architecture can be understood as a composition of elements, an assemblage in which the component parts remain recognizable. This is the result not of any enthusiasm for architectural didacticism but of a conviction that architecture should naturally reveal what it is.

This interest in the making of architecture is common to the generation of Dutch architects to which Van Heeswijk belongs. However different the work and opinions of the architects born around 1950 may be, for many members of this generation like Rudy Uytenhaak, Arne van Herk & Sabien de Kleijn, Koen van Velsen, Jan Benthem and Mels Crouwel, and Jan Pesman and Michiel Cohen of Cepezed, realization and realizability are essential to their architecture and their approach to it.

That this particular generation, which started to build in the 1980s, should be so interested in making, is rather curious in the light of the architectural production of the day where the theme of making was all but absent. In urban renewal, social aspects dominated – the 'makeability' of society figured more than the makeability of architecture. In large-scale projects and mass-produced housing, architectural makeability was certainly discussed, but the main concern was with standardization, efficiency and speed of construction rather than with architectural refinement.

The great exceptions to this were Aldo van Eyck and Herman Hertzberger who, as teachers in the architecture faculty of Delft Technical University, exerted a dual influence on an entire generation of students: as inspiring exemplars and as leading lights to rebel against. Admiration and criticism usually related to the same elements. Their determination to control every last detail of architecture and their focus on the connection between form and use were a source of inspiration. By the same token this sometimes culminated in an obsession with details and a compulsive concern with how architecture should function.

After graduating, Van Heeswijk, like several of his contemporaries, went to work for Van Eyck and his then partner Theo Bosch, a logical choice for ambitious architects who did not want to set up on their own straight after college. Van Heeswijk waited a good four years before founding his own practice in 1985, by which time he had already made his mark. His graduation plan had won the 1980 Archiprix, in 1982 he made it through to the final round of the Prix de Rome and in 1983 he was one of the 21 architects/practices presented at the first Young Dutch Architects Biennale. In the last case he was the sole exception to the rule that candidates had to have their own practice to qualify for selection.

That an exception was made for Van Heeswijk only goes to show that even before he had formally set up on his own account and had only one work (housing in Pingjum, Friesland) and a few competition designs to his name, he had already found his own way in architecture. The inspiration of his teacher and employer Aldo van Eyck is recognizable in the earliest designs. In the Pingjum housing scheme (1977–1980), designed before he went to work for Van Eyck & Bosch, there are 'thresholds' and transitions between inside and outside that reveal an unmistakable structuralist influence. And the way circular elements are incorporated into the 1984 competition design for an Architecture Museum Holland could also be connected with Van Eyck. The extent to which Van Heeswijk has continued to draw inspiration from Van Eyck's ideas is difficult to determine. This is chiefly due to the fact that Van Heeswijk approaches architecture as an architectural construction rather than as a vehicle for abstract ideas or as the representation of an all-embracing world view.

Van Heeswijk's architecture is made from the knowledge and, increasingly over the years, the experience of how buildings are put together. With this kind of architecture, you see what you get and you get what you see. Occasionally it will have a striking form, like the design for the Papendorp Bridge in Utrecht or the office towers in Amsterdam's Rietlandpark, but generally speaking Van Heeswijk's work does not advertise its presence unless specifically required to do so by the client. If not, his architecture is largely or wholly free of eye-catching elements, usually to its advantage.

The straightforward nature of this architecture, which is what it is, also finds expression in Van Heeswijk's habit of emblazoning a building's function or name in giant letters on a glazed facade. The effect is twofold: you read the lettering and at the same time you can see with your own eyes that what is going on behind the glass accords with what you read.

Van Heeswijk's best work has an unemphatic self-evidence owing to the logic it displays, the restraint and the discreet perfection of the details. 'Remarkably unremarkable and through its self-evidence, evident,' as Herman Hertzberger described it in 1995, words that are still true today. It is simply there, without any conspicuous authorial signature. Despite the great consistency in his work, Van Heeswijk's designs are not recognizable from a distance as Genuine Van Heeswijks. The care and reflection that have gone into the design and making do not obtrude. Indeed, at its best his architecture looks like a completely logical response to a question, matter-of-fact and seemingly free from caprice, as if it really could not be otherwise. Form, spatial composition, routing, organization: on none of these points are you ever misled or confused. To say that it could not be otherwise is of course untrue, for even the simplest of designs entails dozens of individual choices. Nonetheless, Van Heeswijk's choices generally seem logical. Apart from the clarity of the spatial layout, this is very much bound up with his idiom which, thanks to a century-long tradition in the Western world, and especially in the Netherlands, has by now achieved the status of a modern vernacular.

Within the modern tradition there has always been a small, critical tendency made up of thinkers and designers who take the friction between architecture and modernity as their starting point. According to Hilde Heynen, author of Architecture and Modernity, A Critique (Cambridge Mass. 1999), their ambition is to make an architecture that 'gives structure to daily life while at the same time embodying the contradictions of modernity' and as such 'adopts a critical attitude to modernity'.

The mainstream of the modern tradition is not, however, made up of individuals keen to show the problematical and contradictory aspects of modernity, but of designers who want to produce solutions for this. Though this approach may very occasionally produce the promise of a better world for tomorrow, ambitions are usually confined to the more realistic endeavour to create the best possible world for today.

Modern architecture that is aimed at making the best possible world here and now, has a technical aspect that manifests chiefly as an innovative development and application of production methods, constructions, techniques and materials. Hans van Heeswijk has an undeniable affinity with this tendency, which brings together such diverse figures as Joseph Paxton, Charles and Ray Eames, Jean Prouvé, Renzo Piano and Future Systems. The affinity with these experimenting seekers lies in a shared view that experiments should not be one-off affairs, but part of a continuous project of improvement. Van Heeswijk's body of work reveals not only a like-minded continuous experimental quest, but also a conviction, untainted by postmodernist relativism, that change is or can be an improvement. In his work to date, one can recognize all manner of ongoing developments in the construction and composition of the facades, frames, stairs and balustrades.

The curved noise barrier in Dordrecht, the heightening of apartment buildings in Amsterdam-North, the conversion of car parks to business premises in Amsterdam's Bijlmermeer: it is in such commissions in particular that his approach manifests itself, an approach in which elegance is not, and certainly not solely, a matter of aesthetics, but is the product of ingenuity and efficiency. Beauty plays a role in this, but outward show is not what it is about.

The second aspect of the endeavour to make the best possible world for today is socio-cultural: architecture is seen as a means of giving optimal form to the current, existing social constellation. Although this approach is free from the unrealistically high expectation that architecture could change society, it does harbour an ambition, based on a pragmatic optimism, that it lies within the power of an architect to improve the built environment and so render society a service. This is most apparent in Van Heeswijk's public buildings which by their very nature have a social dimension, such as the Ganzenhoef cultural-educational centre, the Piet Hein School or the extension of the Heerhugowaard town hall or museums like De Beyerd in Breda and the Hermitage in Amsterdam. The bringing together of people and the promotion of interchange obviously play a role in such projects. But the same is true of Van Heeswijk's offices where, even when they have been dictated by the standards of commercial viability, the central circulation area is always dedicated to social interaction and there is maximum engagement between the internal world and what is going on outside. The transparency and openness of Van Heeswijk's buildings are not purely aesthetic; they also have social implications. If there is any carry-over of Van Eyck's ideas, it is in this.

The modernist idiom Van Heeswijk employs is so familiar that it has an affirmative effect. Modern forms are so well established that they no longer cause any 'shock of the new'. While undeniably contemporary, Van Heeswijk's idiom is so much part of a tradition that is firmly rooted in the Netherlands, that it has in some degree become everyday, or at any rate non-confrontational. This reinforces the self-evidence of Van Heeswijk's architecture, one intended aim of which is to contribute directly to a more harmonious social intercourse. What Hans van Heeswijk makes is unarguably new, but not unsettling. This is true of all the works in the sphere of infrastructure and traffic, where functional and structural expressiveness is generally accepted. But it is equally true of work environments, where his functional austerity accords with what is expected. And it is also true of conversions and extensions of heritage buildings where the clear contrast between old and new has long been accepted as a way of treating history with respect. In only very few instances does a work by Van Heeswijk confound expectations. The clearest example of this is the urban renewal infill in Amsterdam's Dapperbuurt, where elements from office construction were transferred to housing. Suddenly, there is an awkwardness about the work. Despite its undeniable qualities, this project lacks the capacity of his other architecture to be self-evidently modern.

The Netherlands is one of the (European) countries where an architectural King Midas appears to rule, turning nearly everything in the built environment into architecture or into spatial or graphic design, urbanism or landscape architecture. Designers can never escape completely from this condition without renouncing their own discipline. In his best work, Hans van Heeswijk succeeds in making architecture that does not immediately prompt even a dyed-in-the-wool architecture critic to wonder who designed it. By the very nature of their profession, architects, architecture critics and architectural historians know the names of the designers of many buildings. Many towns and districts are consequently personalized for them, consisting in part at least of buildings associated with a particular architect. This is also true in my own case. Before starting to work on this book, I was already familiar with various 'Van Heeswijks' scattered around the Netherlands, just as I am with the work of a number of other architects. However, while working on this book, I discovered that I was acquainted with nearly all Hans van Heeswijk's work, albeit without knowing that he and his associates had designed it. In some cases, such as the small buildings at the ends of Amsterdam's bus and tram routes, I can recall wondering who the designer was. But I also realized that by no means all his buildings had provoked this automatic speculation. Even the knowledge that every artefact is one way or another designed by people did not prompt this Amsterdam resident to wonder who had designed the elegant balustrades of the bridge on Piet Heinkade, the fine stairs in the renovated Zuiderkerk, the interior of the premises of the Netherlands Foundation for Fine Arts, Design and Architecture or the end facades of the converted car parks on Daalwijkdreef. This certainly says something about me, but probably also about the work that Hans van Heeswijk makes, which has the remarkable capacity to be completely absorbed into modern everyday life.

effectiveness

clarity

intelligible

self-evident

restraint

perfection

consistency

meticulous

well thought-out

logical

businesslike

free from caprice

ingenuity

efficiency

transparency

openness

functional and structural expressiveness

practical austerity

'The Dapperstraat' from 1946 by J.C. Bloem is the poem
on the facade facing the street it celebrates:

Nature is for the contented or the empty
Besides, what does nature amount to
  in this country?
A patch of woodland, the size of a newspaper
A hill with a few villas clinging to its sides?

Give me the grey, urban streets
The water corseted by riveted quays
The clouds, never more beautiful than when,
  framed
By attic windows, they drift across the sky.

Anything is a lot for those who expect so little.
Life keeps its wonders hidden
Only to reveal them, suddenly, at their finest.

These things I pondered to myself
Soaked through, one drizzly morning
Simply happy, in the Dapperstraat.

DpA.

name
Dapperbuurt Housing Blocks

project code
DpA

place
Linnaeusstraat
Commelinstraat
Dapperstraat
Von Zesenstraat
Amsterdam

client
Woningstichting Lieven de Key, Amsterdam

construction
1992–1995

design team
Hans van Heeswijk
Paul Seuntjens
Jurgen van Tiggelen

On three locations in Amsterdam's Dapperbuurt, a total of 53 dwellings were built by Hans van Heeswijk architecten. In terms of construction, detailing and materialization, the architecture has more in common with utilitarian than with conventional residential construction. To afford urban dwellers a measure of privacy, the facades are predominantly closed. In compensation, the lift shafts and staircases are glazed and the ground floor has been made as transparent as possible. A striking feature of the buildings are the lines of verse by Dutch poets Nescio and J.C. Bloem that grace the facades. The typography is by graphic designer, R.D.E. Oxenaar.

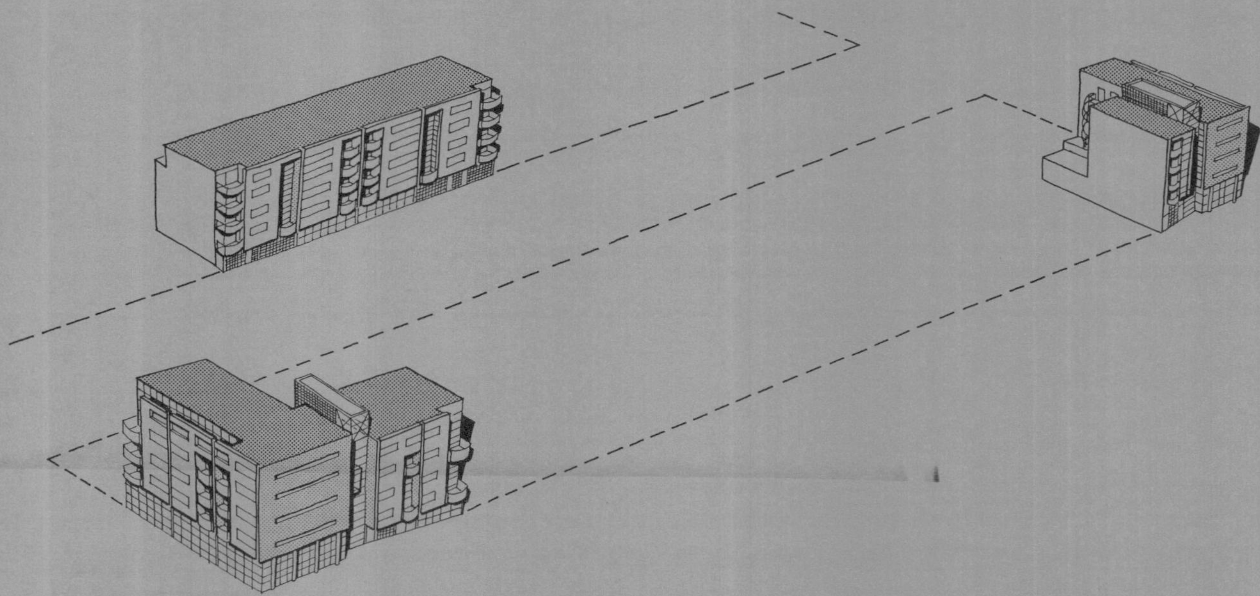

The project consists of two corners and a street front.

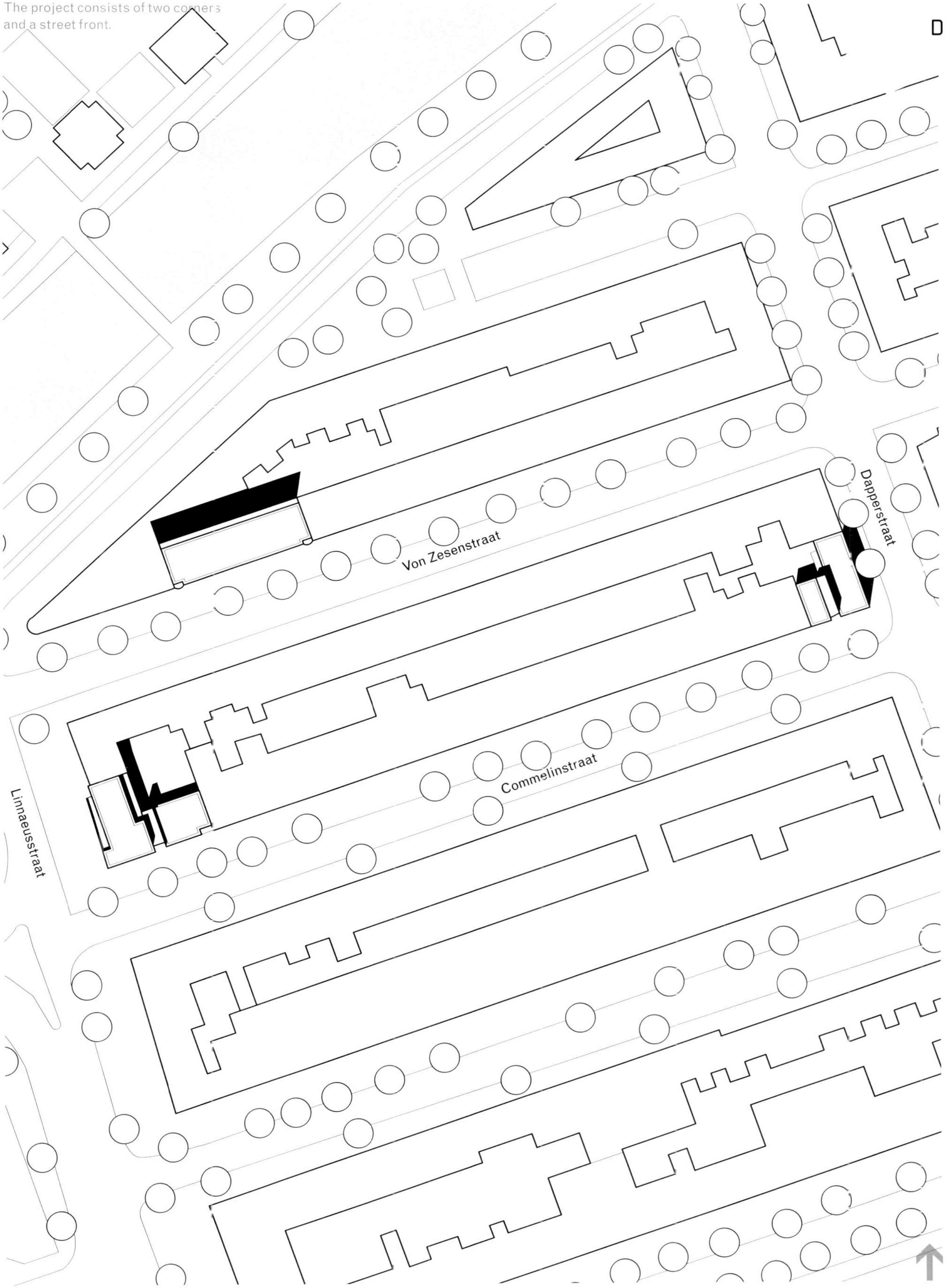

DpA.block Dapperstraat 12.JP

DpA.facade Dapperstraat 06.JP

DpA.facade Dapperstraat 04.JP

DpA.courtyard Dapperstraat 09.JP

DpA.stairs interior Dapperstraat 15.JP

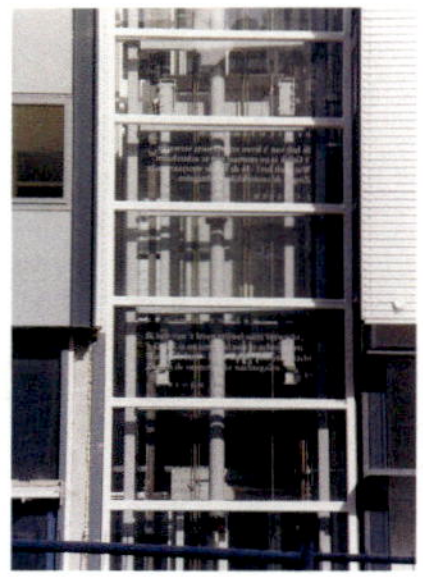

DpA.elevator exterior Dapperstraat 17.JP

DpA.block Linnaeusstraat 13.JP

DpA.facade Linnaeusstraat 07.JP

DpA.facade Linnaeusstraat 03.JP

DpA.court facade Linnaeusstraat 11.JP

DpA.court facade Linnaeusstraat 08.JP

DpA.courtyard Linnaeusstraat 10.JP

DpA.block Von Sezenstraat 14.JP

DpA.facade Commelinstraat 01.JP

DpA.facade Commelinstraat 02.JP

DpA.facade Commelinstraat 05.JP

DpA.stairs exterior Commelinstraat 16.JP

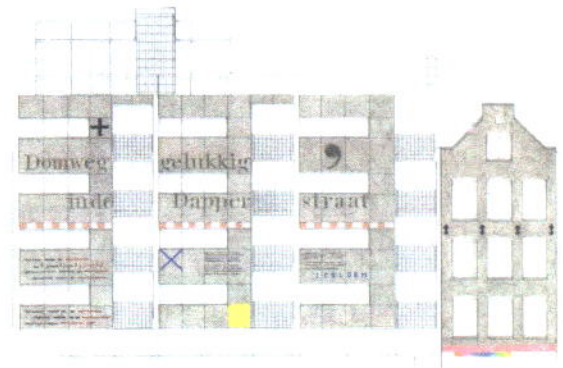

DpA.sketch facade Dapperstraat 18
R.D.E. Oxenaar

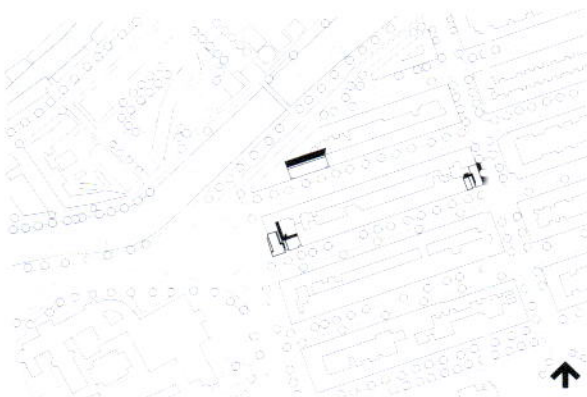

DpA.situation

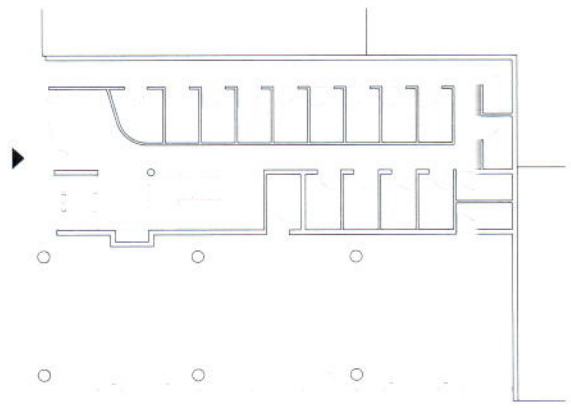

DpA.ground floor – 50

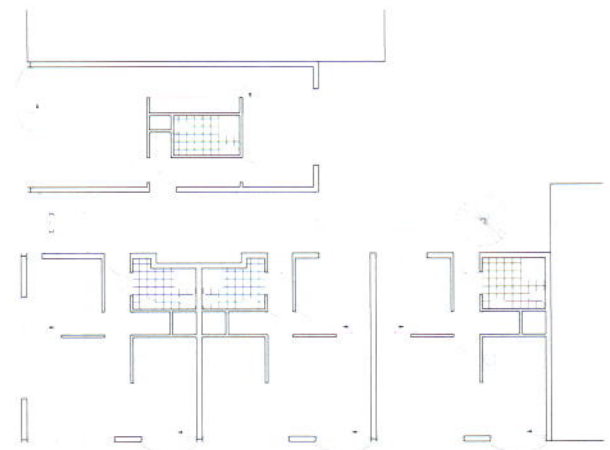

DpA.first floor – 50

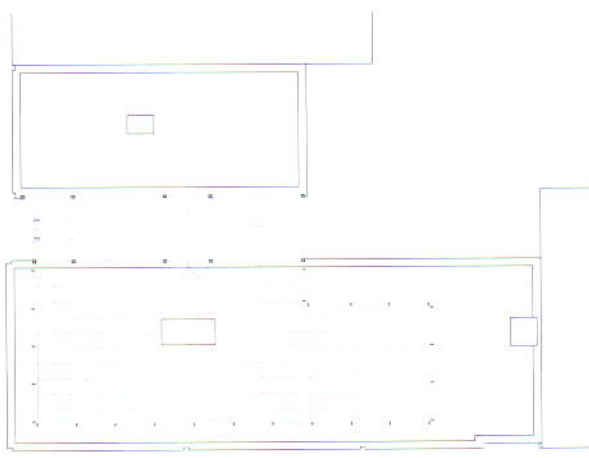

DpA.roof – 50

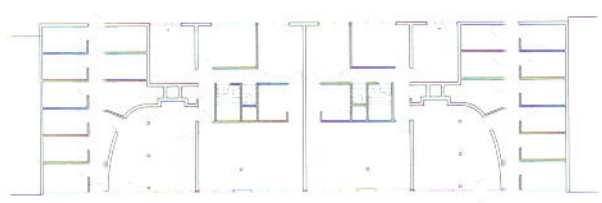

DpA.ground floor – 51

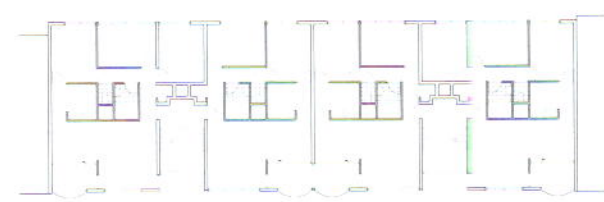

DpA.first floor – 51

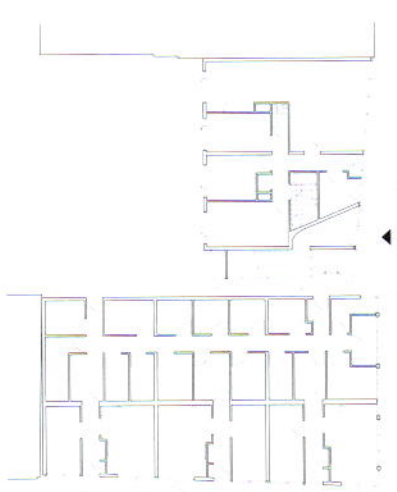

DpA.ground floor – 52

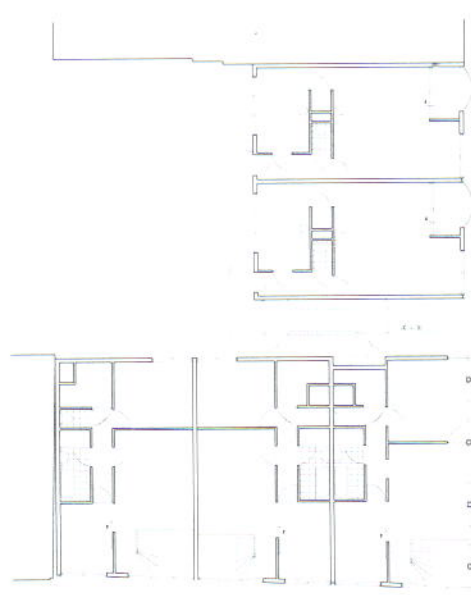

DpA.first floor – 52

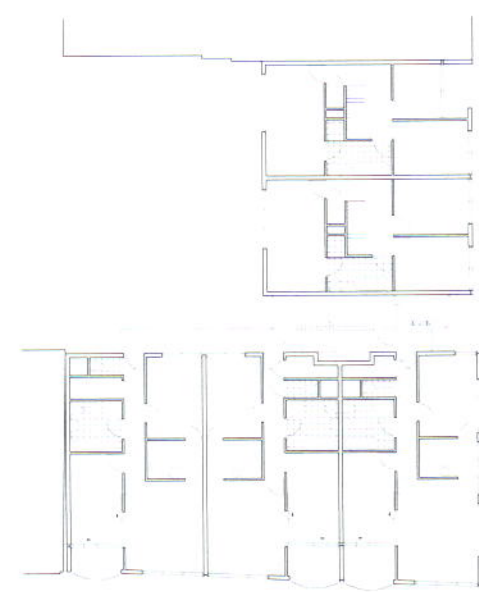

DpA.second floor – 52

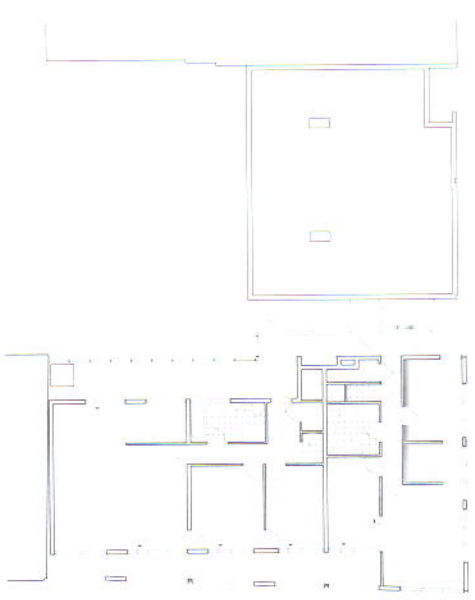

DpA.top floor – 52

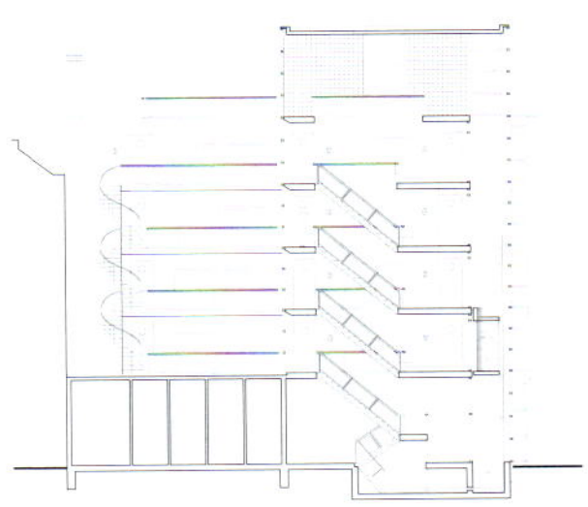

DpA.section – 50

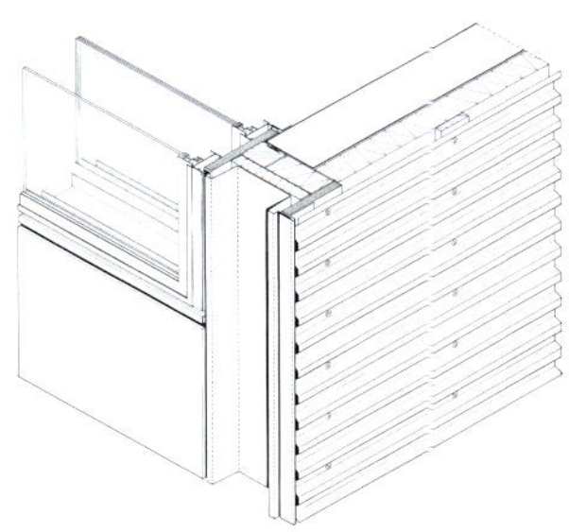

DpA.detail

38.D

In the two buildings on the corner, the front elevations have a strict grid composition, the scale of which is determined by the original plot widths. The side elevations have a simple composition with horizontal strips of fenestration.

40.D

..DpA

As is usual in non-residential construction, the floors and outer walls consist of precast concrete elements. The facade cladding is of cement-bonded panels and aluminium. Secondary structures like the staircases are in steel, wood and glass.

E D

The glazed lift shafts and staircases point up the division between servant and served spaces.

TAXI
SG-26-ZJ
JX-VL-20
PH-55-DK

DE NACHTEGALEN
Ik heb van 't leven vrijwel niets verwacht,
't Geluk is nu eenmaal niet te achterhalen.
Wat geeft het? - In de koude voorjaarsnacht
Zingen de onsterfelijke nachtegalen.
J.C. BLOEM

50.D

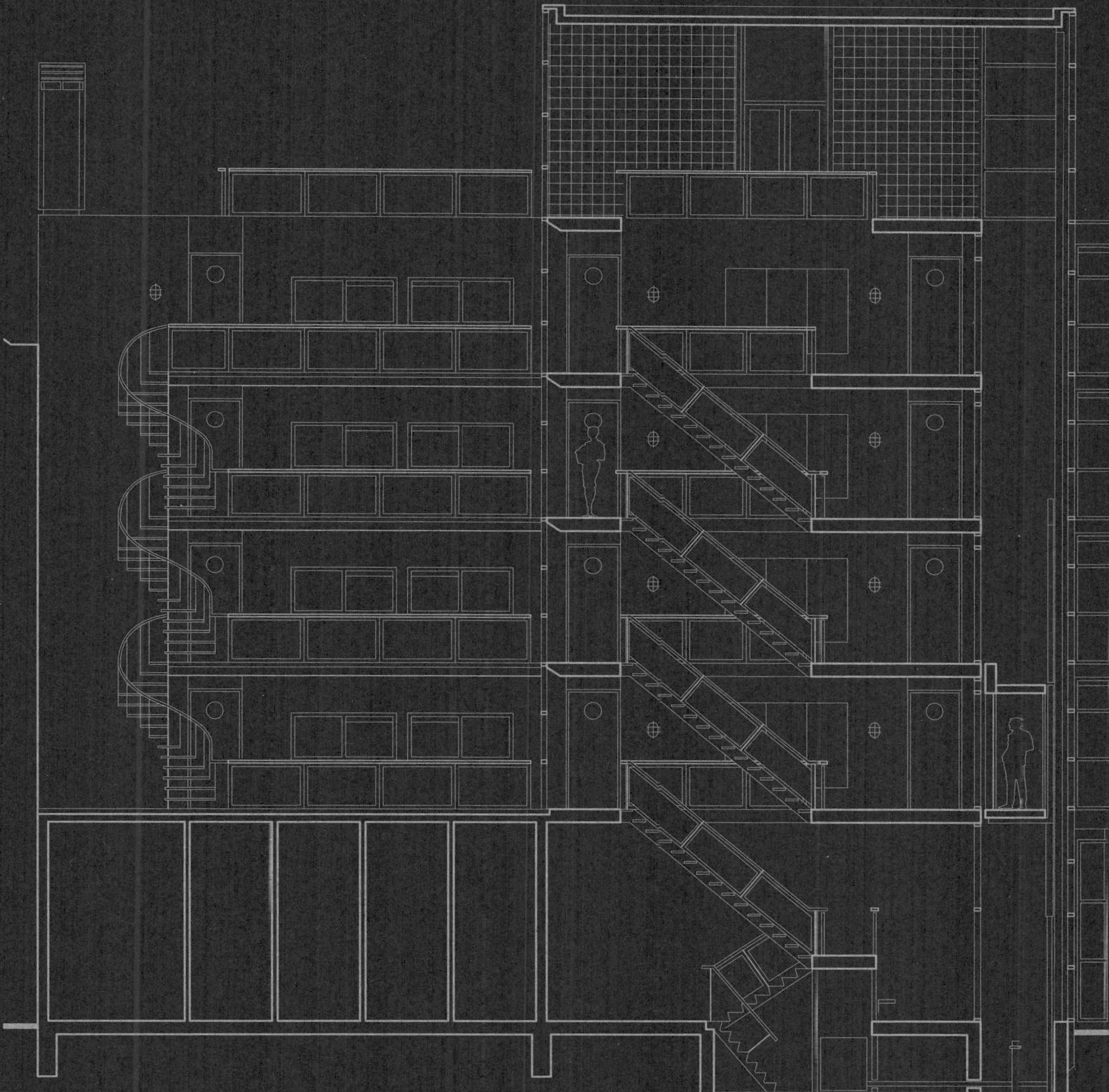

Section
1:120

Floor plans corner Dapperstraat-Commelinstraat

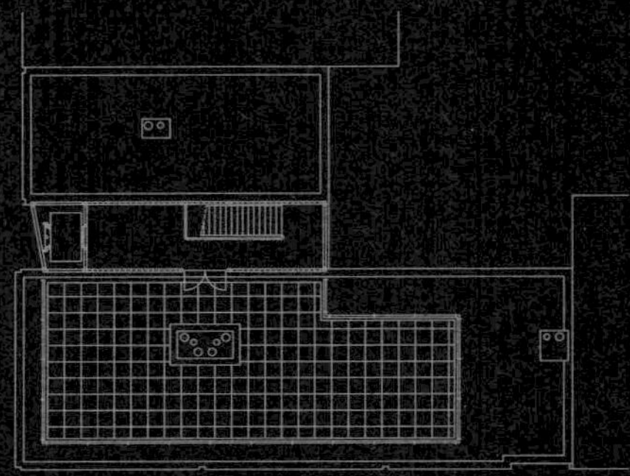

Roof

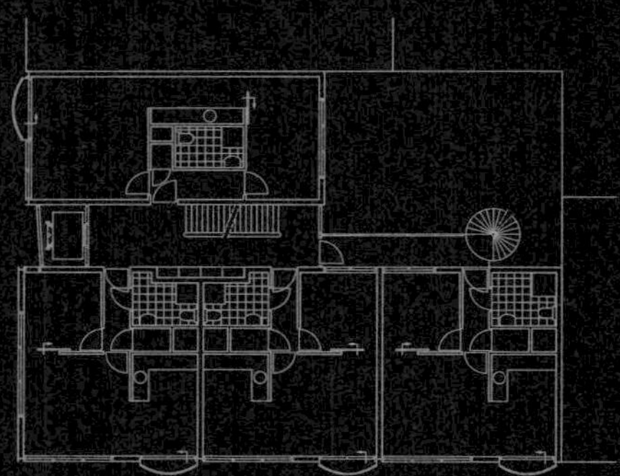

First floor

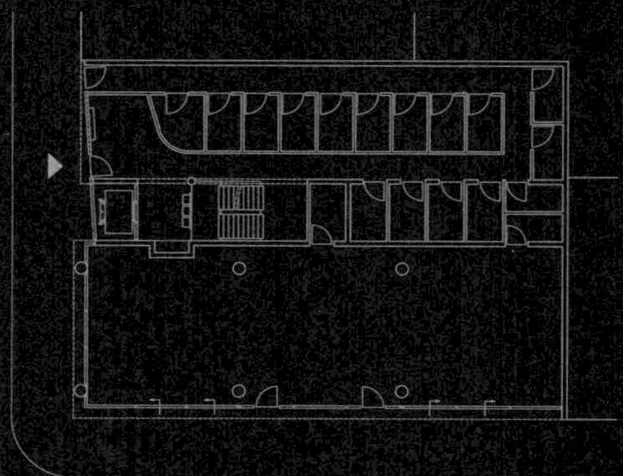

Ground floor
1:400

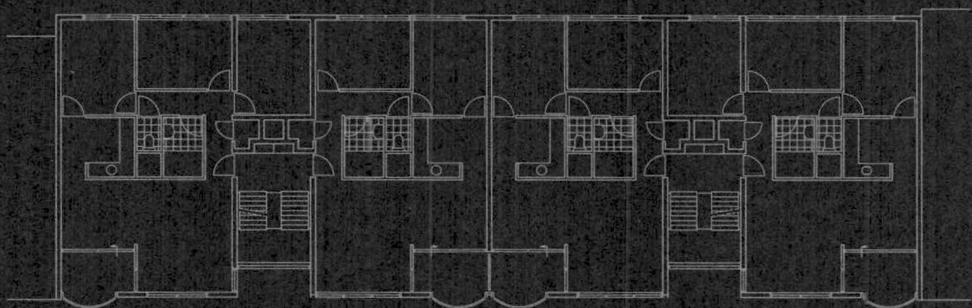

First floor

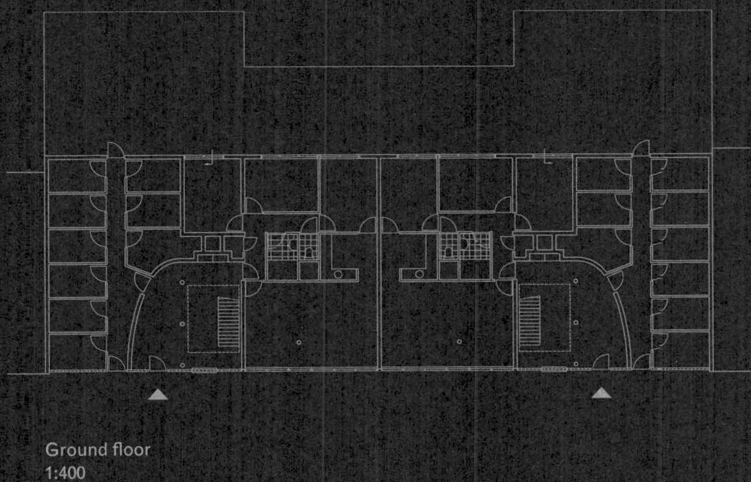

Ground floor
1:400

Floor plans corner Linnaeusstraat-Commelinstraat

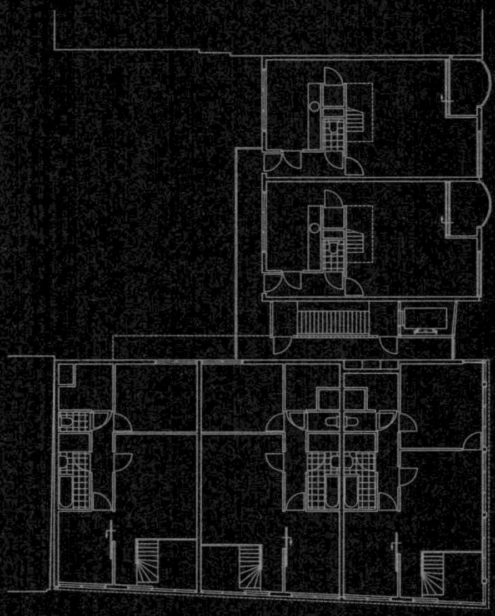

First floor

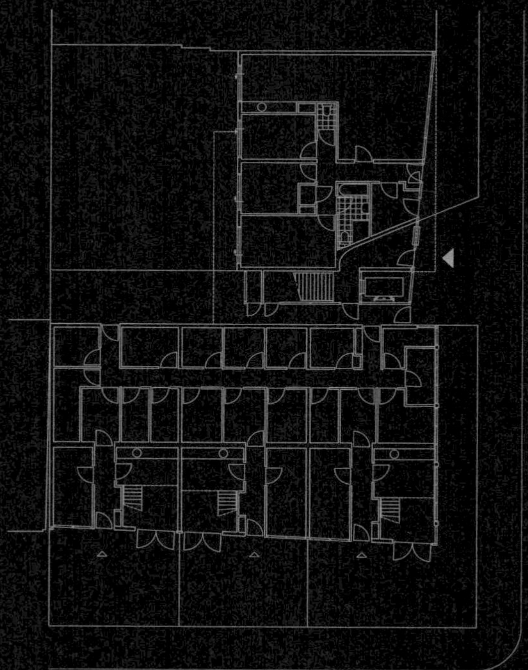

Ground floor
1:400

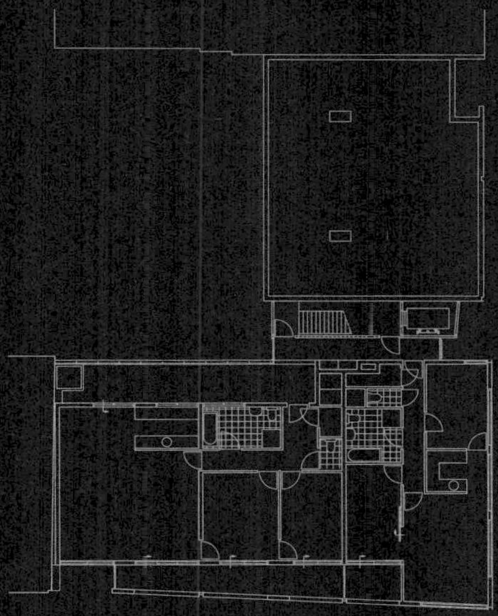

Roof

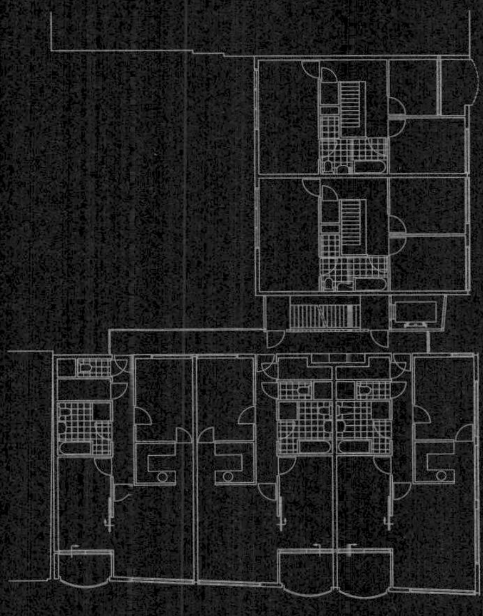

Second floor

Veritas Komet sports car, 1950
Designers Georg Meier, Lorenz Dietrich
and Ernst Loof

GsD. GsT.

name
Wielwijk and Krispijn
Noise Barriers

project code
GsD/GsT

place
Rijksweg 16 ter hoogte
van de wijken Wielwijk
en Krispijn, Dordrecht

client
Bouwdienst Rijkswater-
staat Tilburg en
Dordrecht

design
1994 (Wielwijk)
2004 (Krispijn)

construction
1996–1997 (Wielwijk)
2006–2007 (Krispijn)

design team
Dick de Gunst
Hans van Heeswijk
Rob Hulst
Arjen Honig

The noise barrier that curves over two lanes of traffic along the A16 near Dordrecht is a striking feature of the motorway landscape between Rotterdam and Breda. The level of noise nuisance for houses in Wielwijk, right beside the motorway, was such that an ordinary vertical screen was judged to be inadequate. Hence this curved design. A second noise barrier similar in form and material will be built along the same road where it passes Krispijn, another Dordrecht suburb.

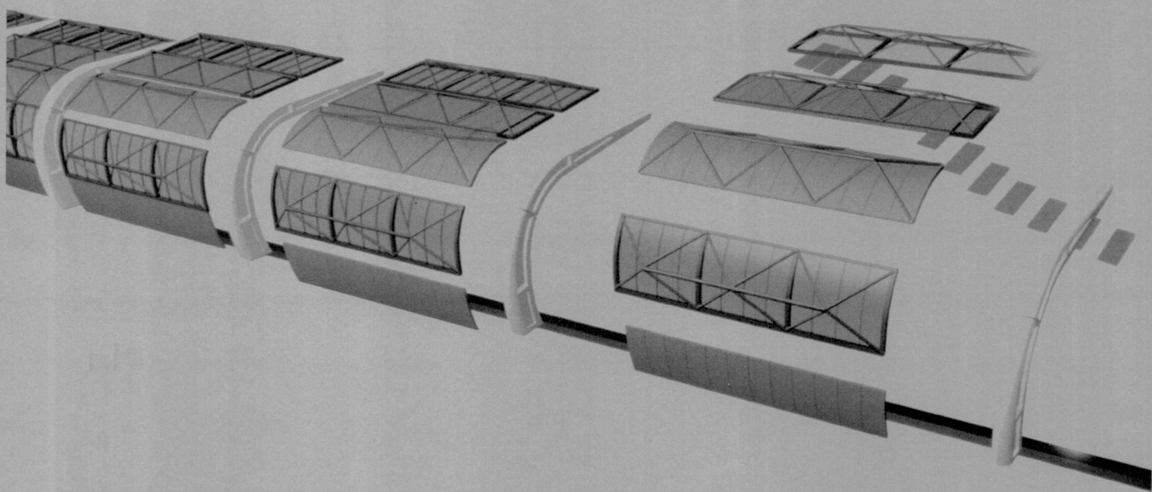

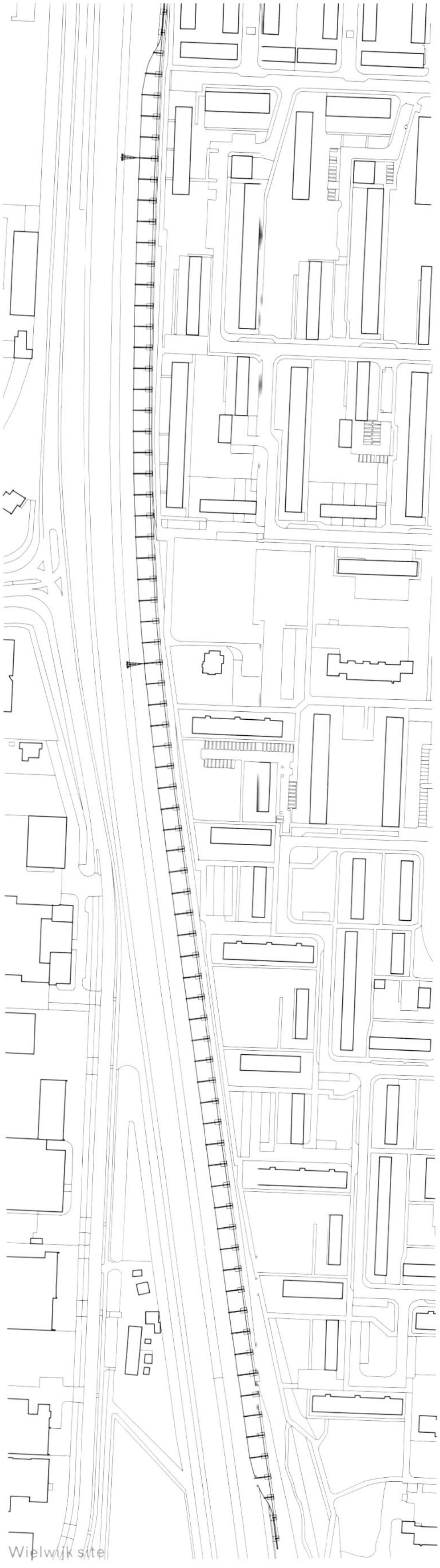

Wielwijk site

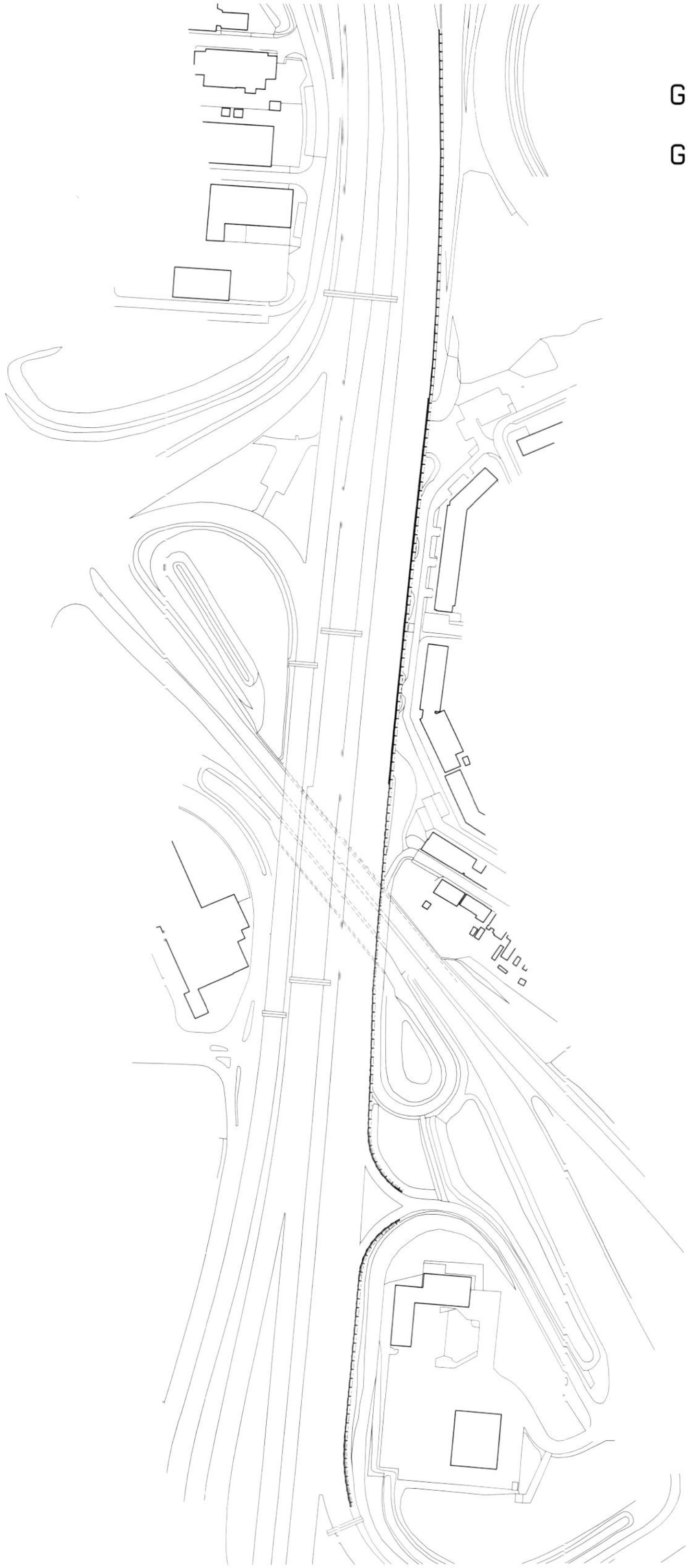

The Wielwijk barrier s one kilometre long,
the Krispijn barrier 840 metres.

Krispijn site

GsD.arial view 13.HvH

GsD.Wielwijk 19.JP

GsD.Wielwijk driving side 06.JP

GsD.Wielwijk at night 12.HvH

GsD.Wielwijk driving side 08.JP

GsD.Wielwijk driving side 07.JP

GsD.Wielwijk 18.JP

GsD.Wielwijk 16.HvH

GsD.Wielwijk start 09.HvH

GsD.Wielwijk 17.HvH

GsD.Wielwijk living side 04.JP

GsD.Wielwijk living side 05.HvH

GsD.Wielwijk living side 03.JP

GsD.Wielwijk living side 02.HvH

GsD.Wielwijk 15.HvH

GsD

GsT

GsD.Wielwijk detail 01.HvH

GsD.situation Wielwijk

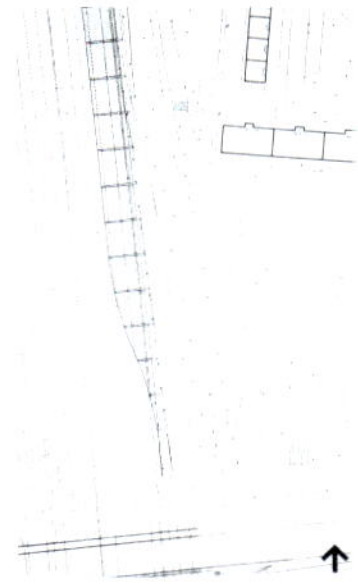

GsD.Wielwijk southside

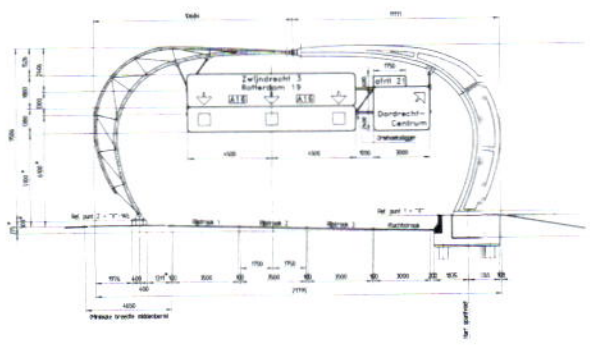

GsD.Wielwijk total frame

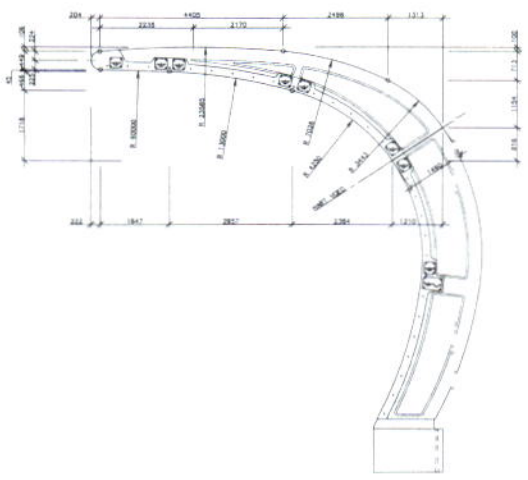

GsD.Wielwijk concrete frame

GsT.Krispijn living side 10.HvH

GsD.Krispijn driving side 11.HvH

GsT.Krispijn 14.HvH

GsT.situation total

GsT.situation Krispijn

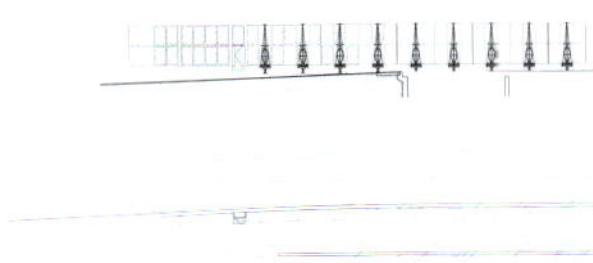

GsT.Krispijn elevation

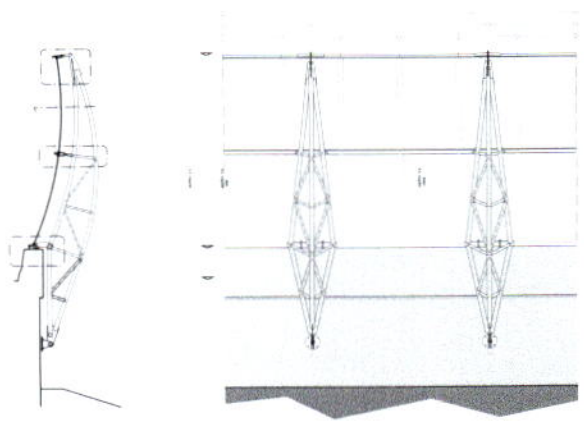

GsT.Krispijn fragment

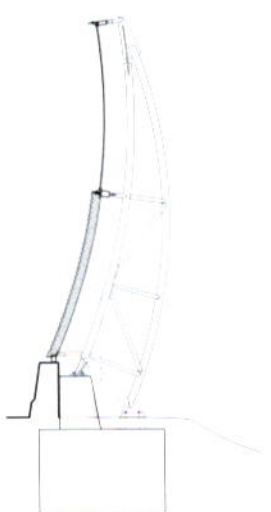

GsT.Krispijn frame

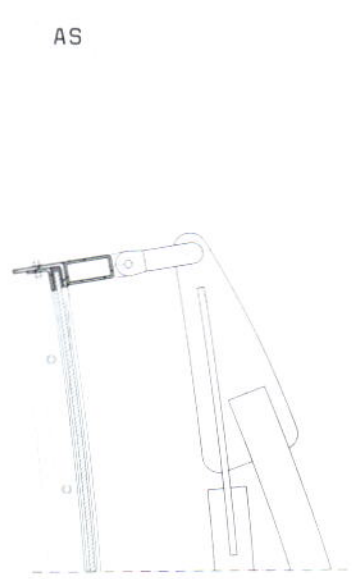

GsT.Krispijn detail frame top

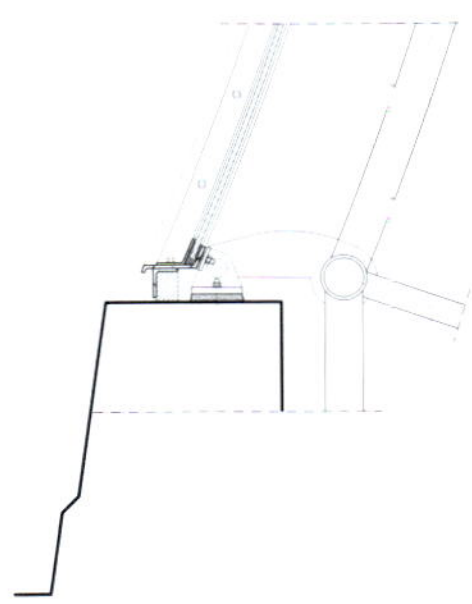

GsT.Krispijn detail frame bottom

.GsD
GsT

52.G

Some of the houses in Wielwijk stand no more than ten metres from the motorway.

GsD

66.G

ndrecht 3
erdam 19
A 16
afrit 21
Dordrecht-
Centrum

The slender main trusses are of precast concrete. Between them are steel lattice girders filled with panels of clear acrylic. The bottommost strip is of precast concrete panels, except where the barrier abuts the street behind, where it, too is transparent.

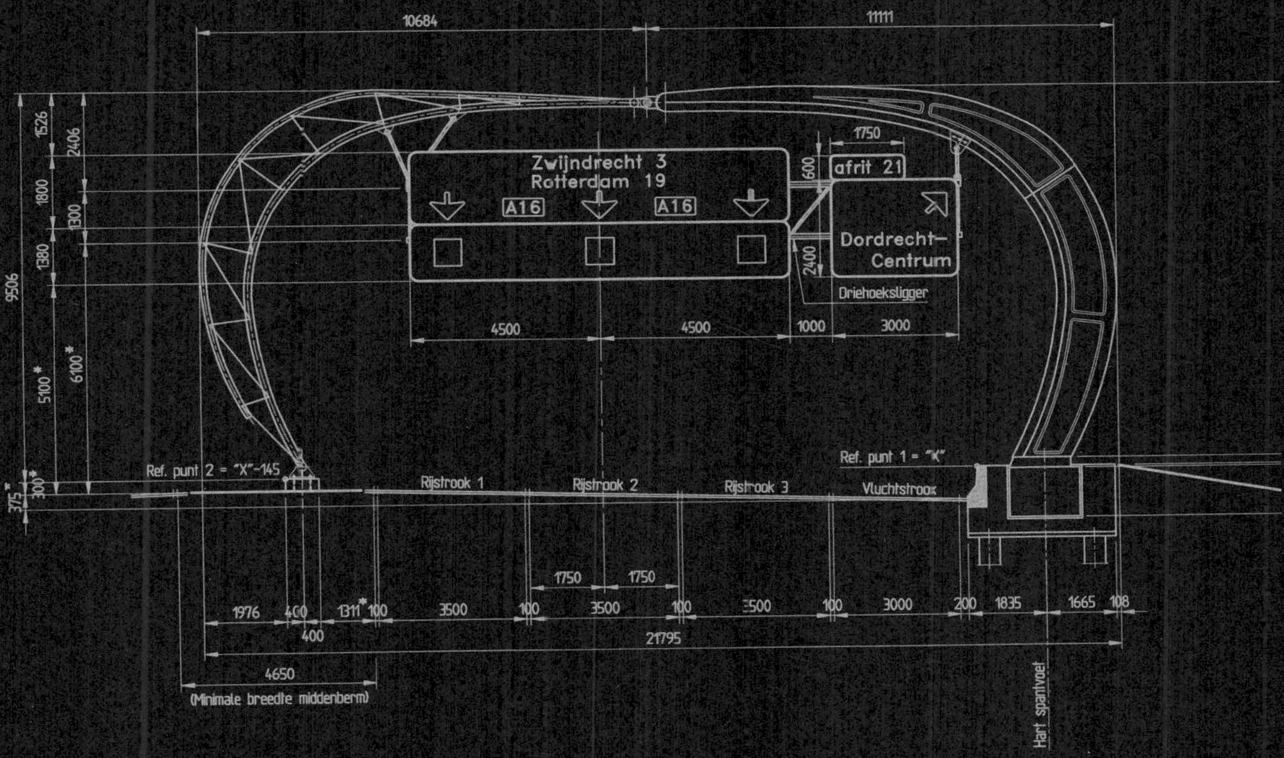

Wielwijk: whole truss

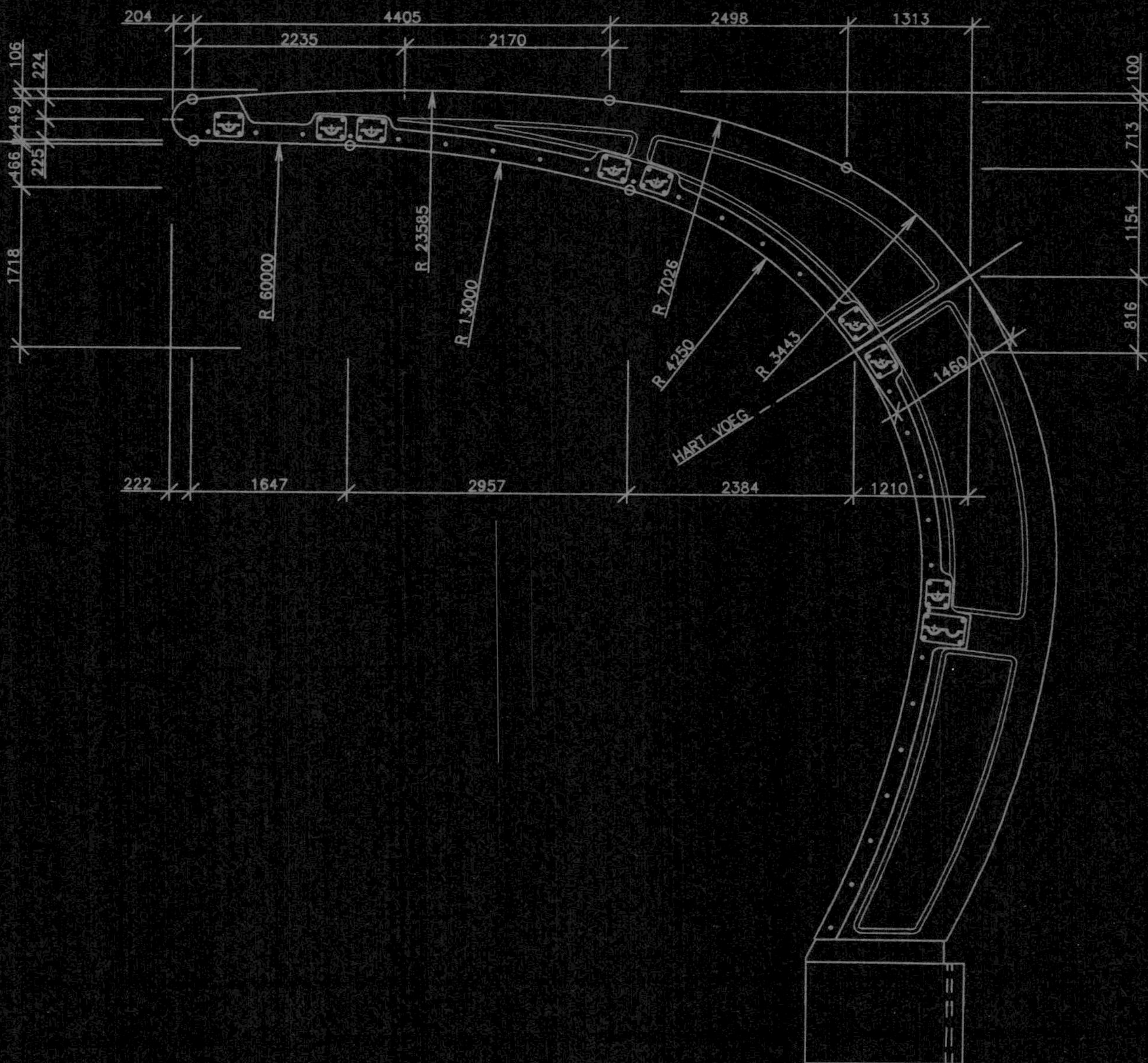

Wielwijk: concrete truss

The straight trusses of the Krispijn barrier are derived from the curved trusses of the Wielwijk barrier. The 6.5-metre-high barrier will stand on top of a 4-metre-high retaining wall.

76.G

GsT

Detail top side Krispijn truss
1:20

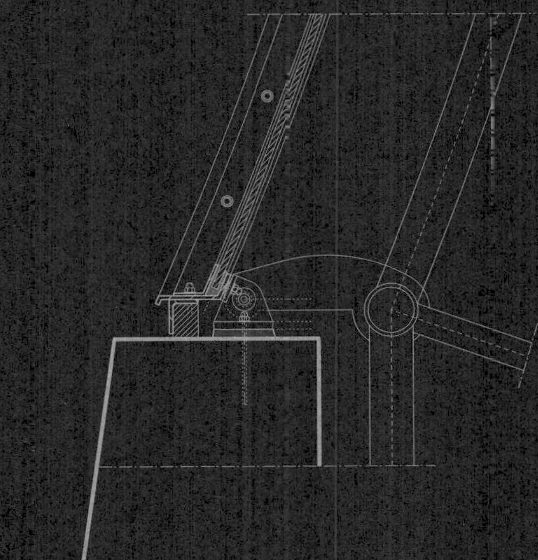

GsT

Detail underside Krispijn truss
1:20

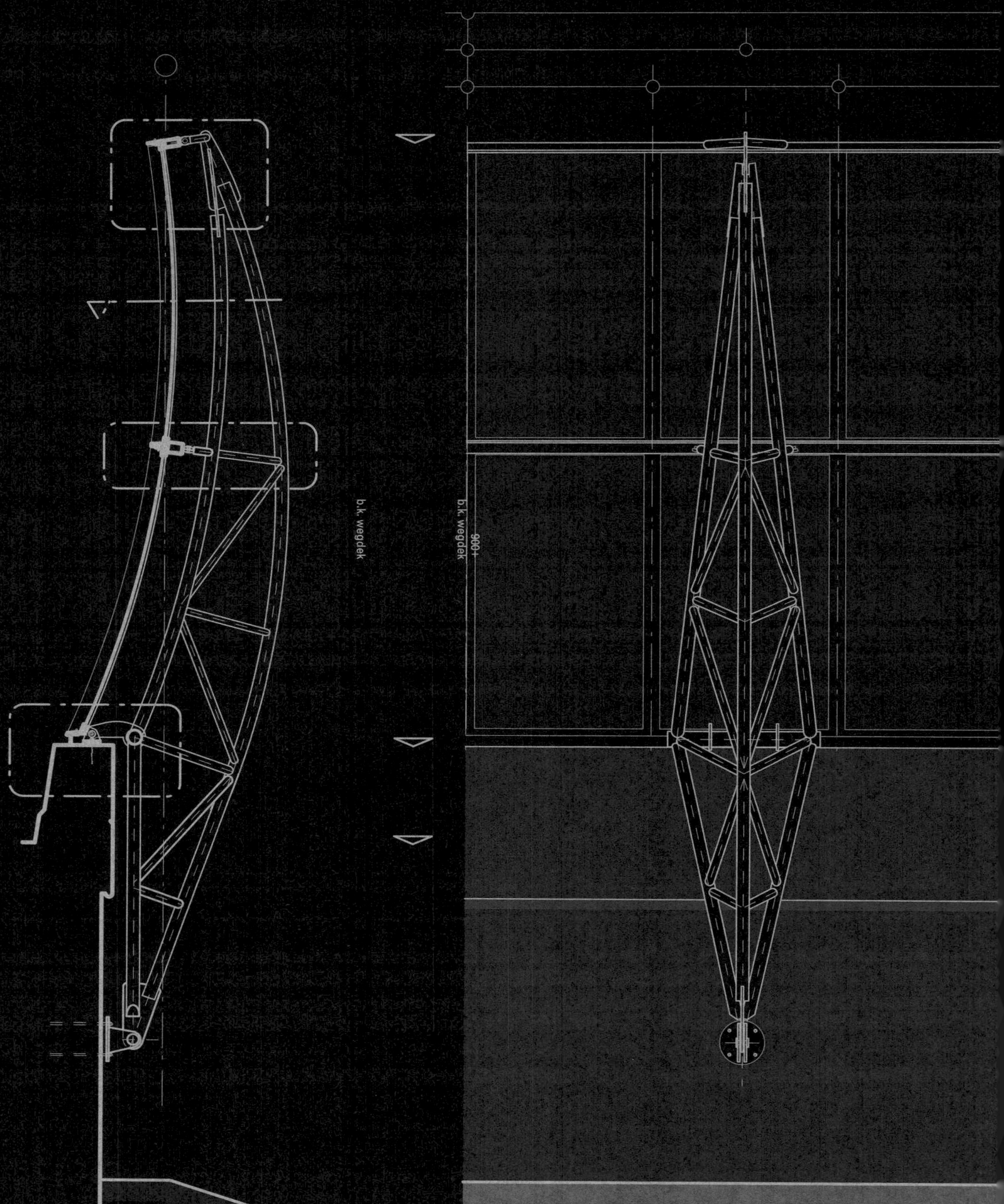

Section and view Krispijn noise barrier
1:50

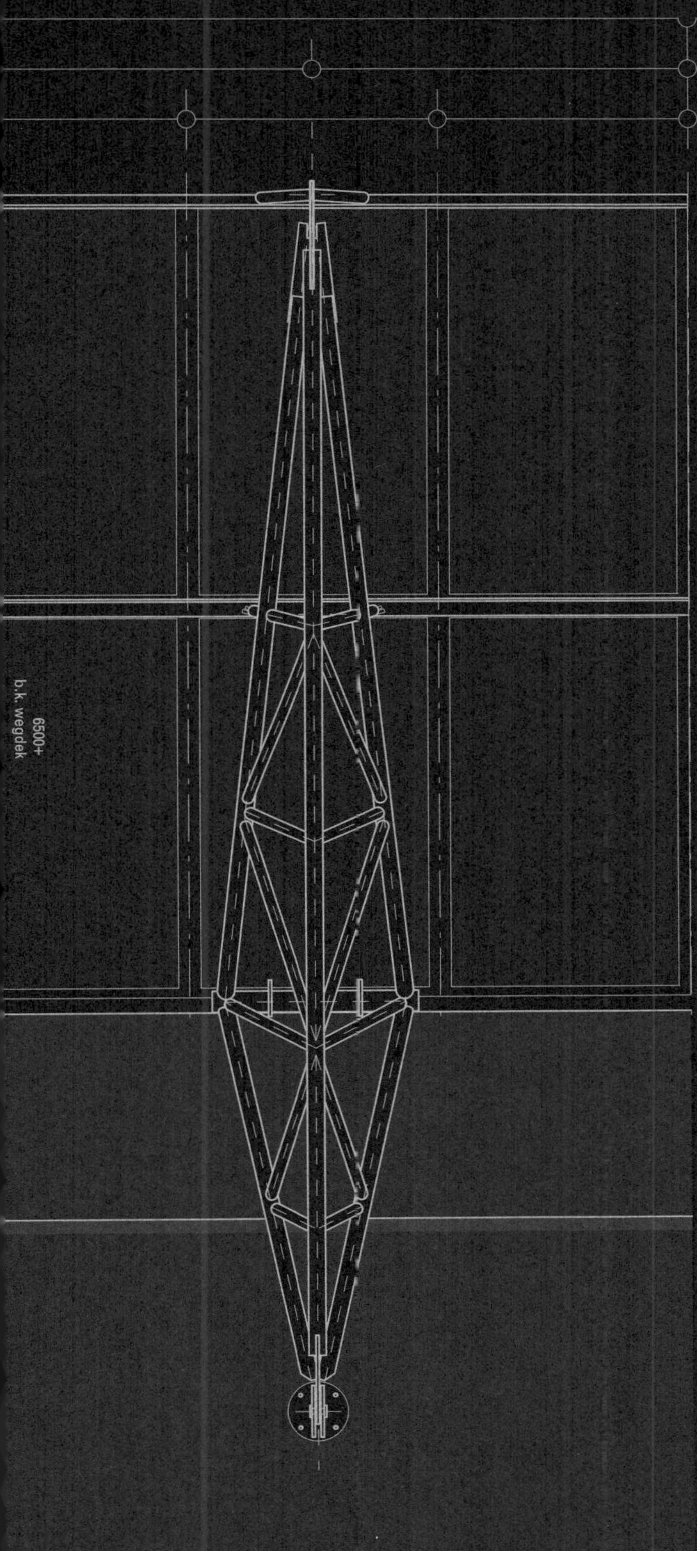

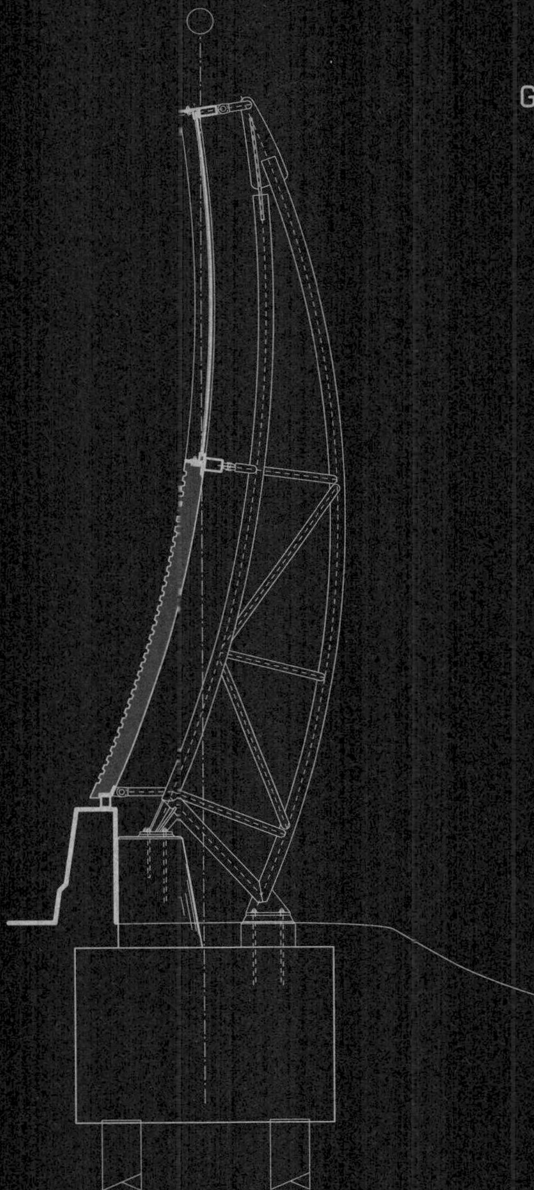

Section Krispijn truss
1:50

Nighthawks, Edward Hopper, 1942

PwS.

name
Parkweg Metro Station

project code
PwS

place
Burgemeester Honnerlage
Gretelaan, Schiedam

client
RET Gemeentelijk
Vervoerbedrijf
Rotterdam

design
1994

construction
2002

design team
Hans van Heeswijk
Paul Seuntjes
Jurgen van Tiggelen

In the late 1990s, the Rotterdam metro network was expanded with a new, 12.5 kilometre line. This Caland Line connects the Marconiplein station, the western end of the current east-west line, to the Hoogvliet/Spijkernisse station, the southern end of the north-south line. From the Marconiplein station the Caland Line runs first westwards through Schiedam and then southwards through the Benelux Tunnel via Pernis to Spijkenisse. To bring variety to the six metro stations along the Caland Line, each station was designed by a different architect.

For most of its route, the Caland Line runs above ground. The only underground station, Parkweg, was designed by Hans van Heeswijk architecten. The main aim of the design was to provide the platform with as much light as possible. Above ground, therefore, the station consists of four glazed pavilions, elliptical in plan, the first and last of which contain the station entrances. The two other pavilions act as huge dome lights.

Above ground, the metro station differs in form, material and transparency from the surrounding buildings. Below ground it differs from traditional metro stations by virtue of its brightness and transparency. Both entrances afford travellers a good view of the platform below. Thanks to the good visibility of the column-free platform and the daylight streaming in from above, the station strikes users as a safe and pleasant place to be.

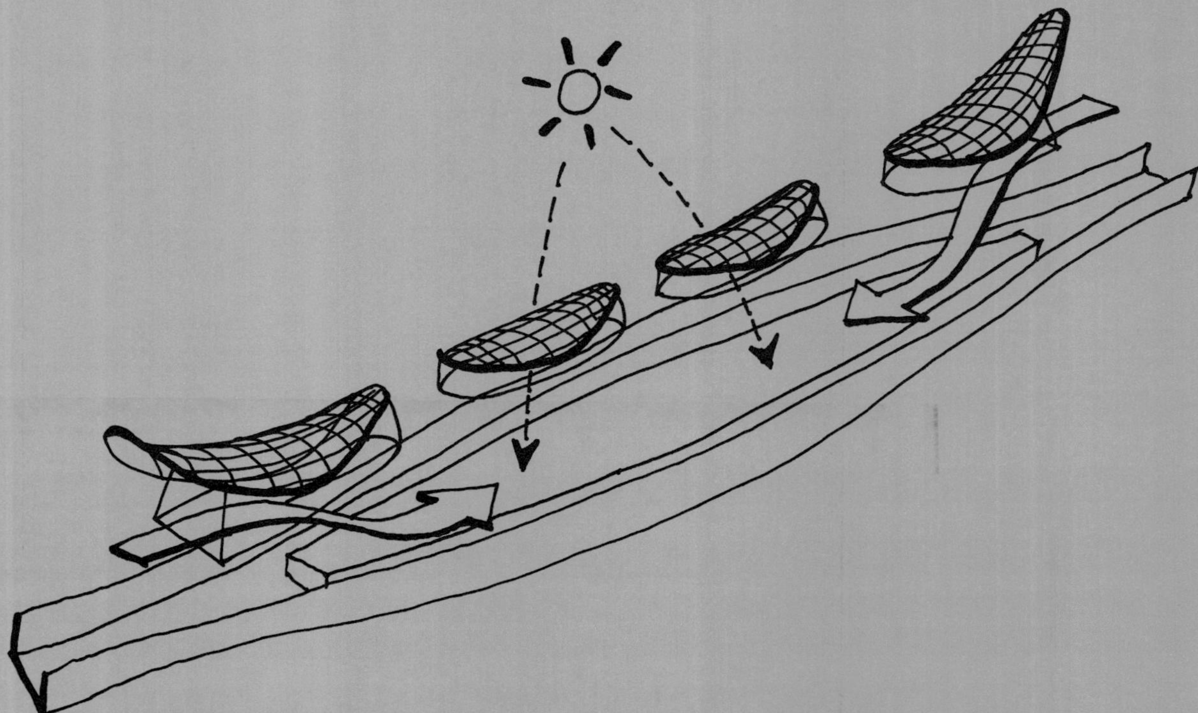

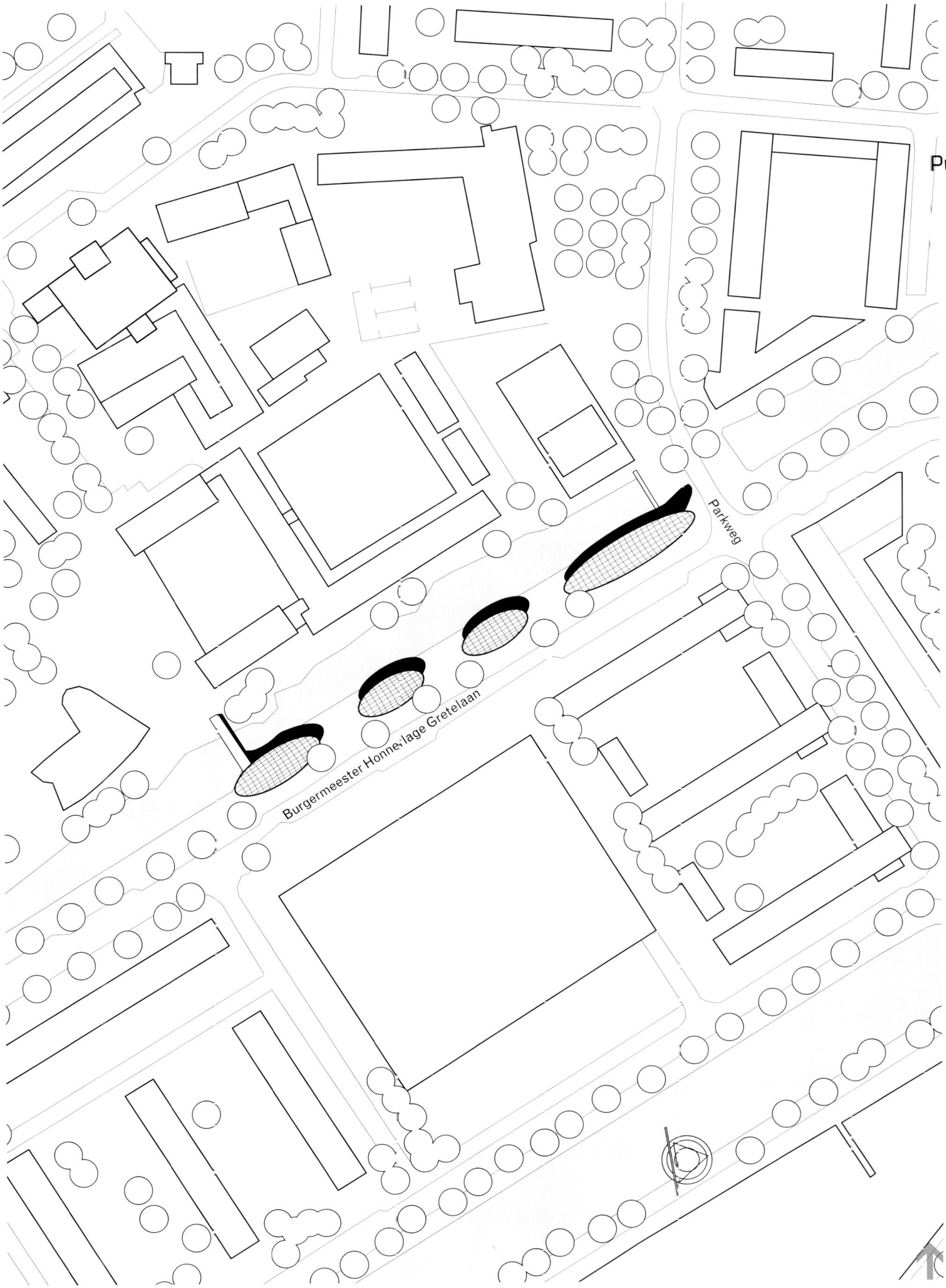

PwS

. PwS

PwS.overview 05.CR

PwS.exterior 17.CR

PwS.exterior 18.CR

PwS.entrance 01.HvH

PwS.entrance 02.CR

PwS.entrance 21.CR

PwS.entrance 20.CR

PwS.entrance 19.CR

PwS.entrance skylight 13.HvH

PwS.entrance skylight 08.CR

PwS.entrance skylight 10.CR

PwS.entrance skylight 07.CR

PwS.entrance skylight 11.CR

PwS.entrance skylight 12.HvH

PwS.interior entrance 98.CR

PwS

PwS.entrance 22.CR

PwS.detail skylight 15.HvH

PwS.detail skylight 16.HvH

PwS.detail skylight 13.HvH

PwS.detail skylight 14.HvH

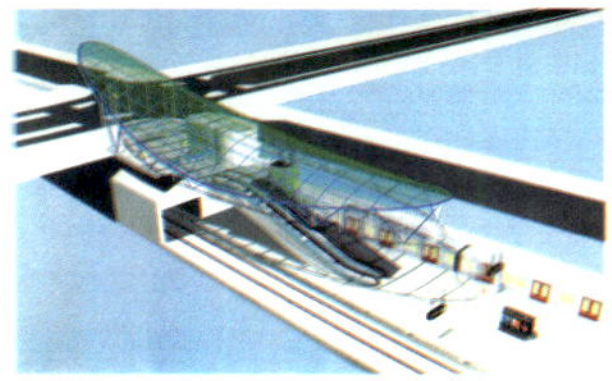

PwS.construction 06.HvH

PwS.model 03.CR

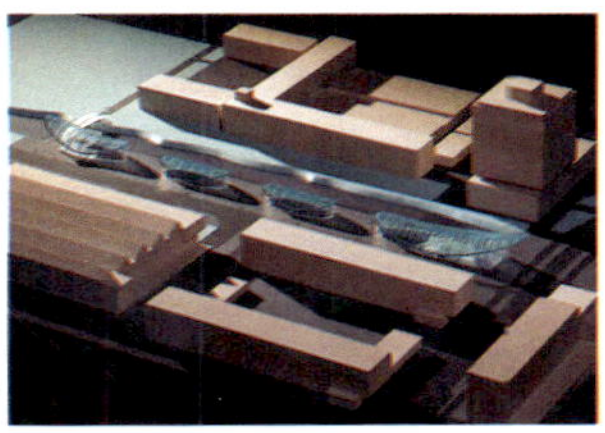

PwS.model 04.CR

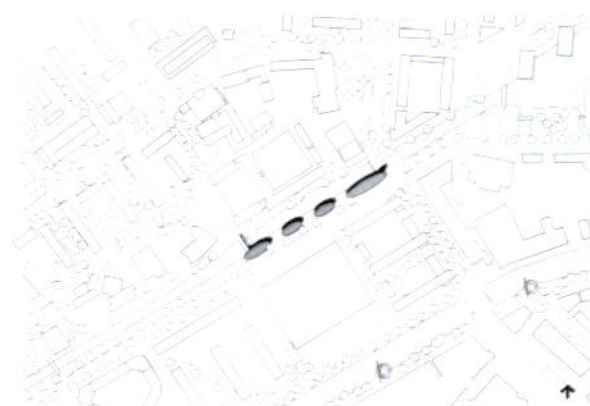

PwS.situation

PwS. floor plan -1

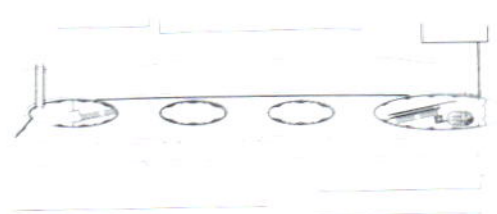

PwS. floor plan street level

PwS.section

.PwS

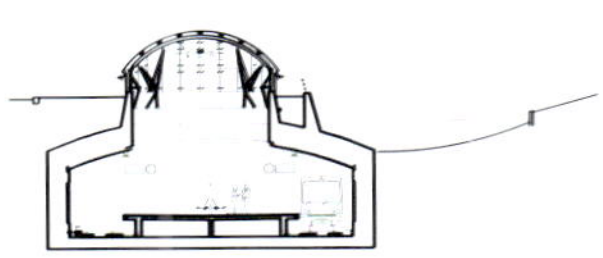

PwS.section 1

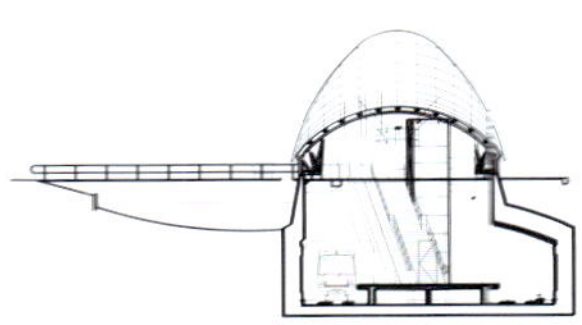

PwS.section 2

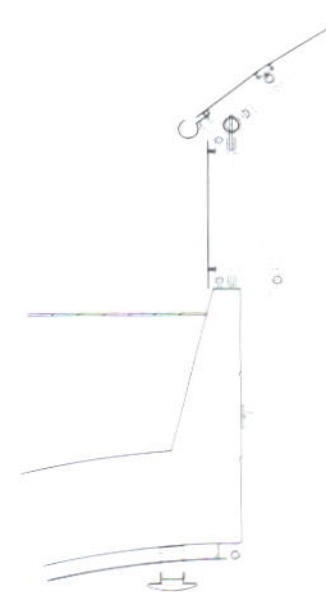

PwS.detail

The exterior of Parkweg station consists of four elliptical, glazed pavilions that are in marked contrast to the surrounding housing.

PwS

Entrance at the end of the metro station. The curved roof truss accentuates the shape of the roof. The big awning projects out into the street, so that users can see the station from a distance.

PwS

9.PwS

The entrance is directly connected with the platform below.

.PwS

The column-free platform receives light through the glazed entrance pavilions and the two big glazed domes in between. The station has gently curved side walls that make it possible to see the full length of the platform.

PwS

Calandlijn
Beurs · Zevenkamp · richting Oost
Ommoord · Capelle a/d IJssel ·
Tussenwater · richting
Spijkenisse ·
SOS

.PwS

The glass roof panels are fixed with a spider-like steel construction to the purlins, which in turn rest on curved roof trusses. These tubular purlins also serve as sub-diagonals for the roof trusses and rest on an elliptical edge beam that is supported by cruciform spider constructions attached to and against the concrete edge of the light opening.

5.PwS

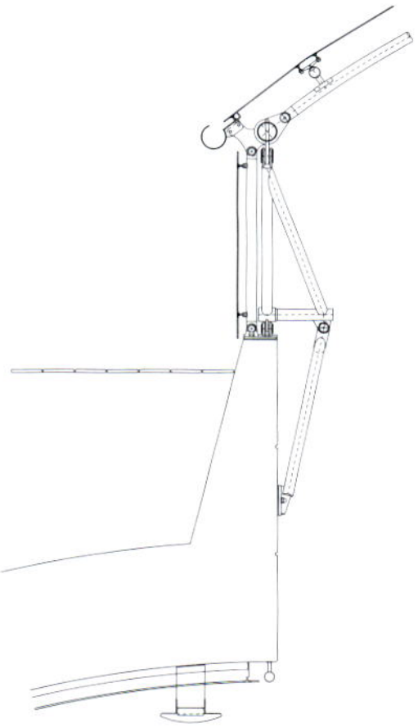

1:120

Detail roof light edge

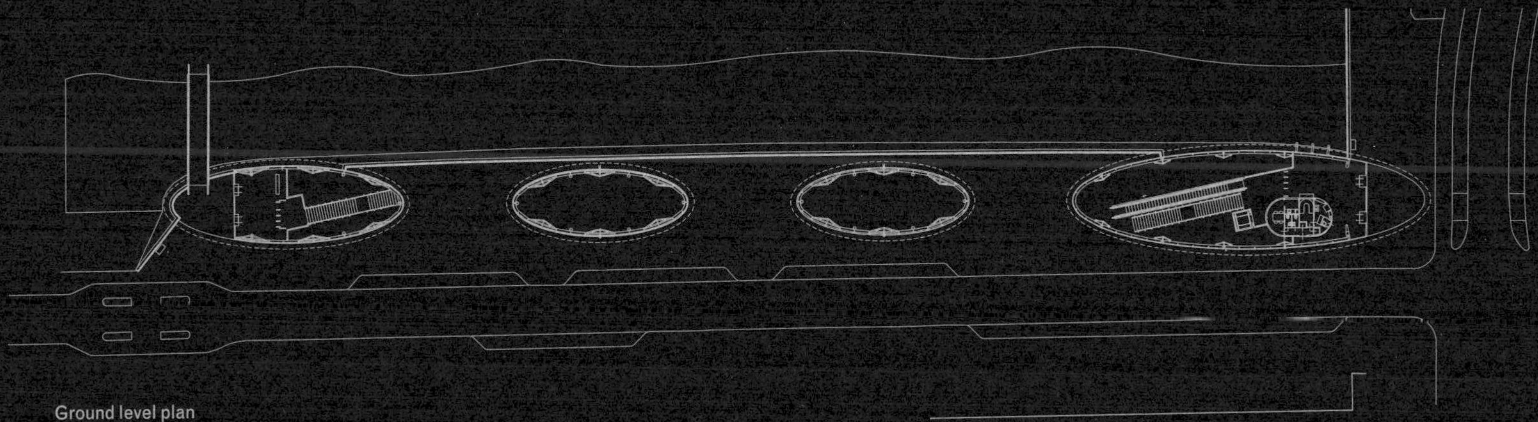

Ground level plan
1:1000

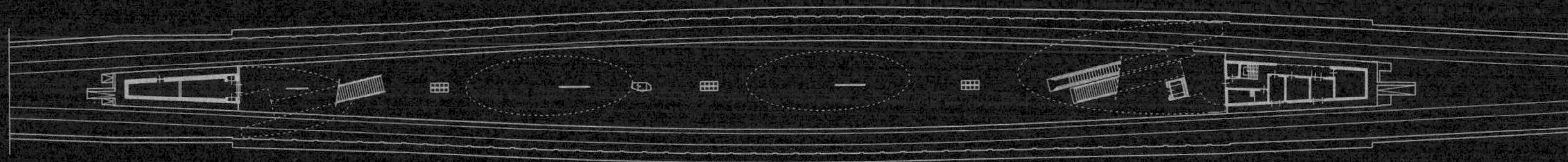

Floor plan -1
1:1000

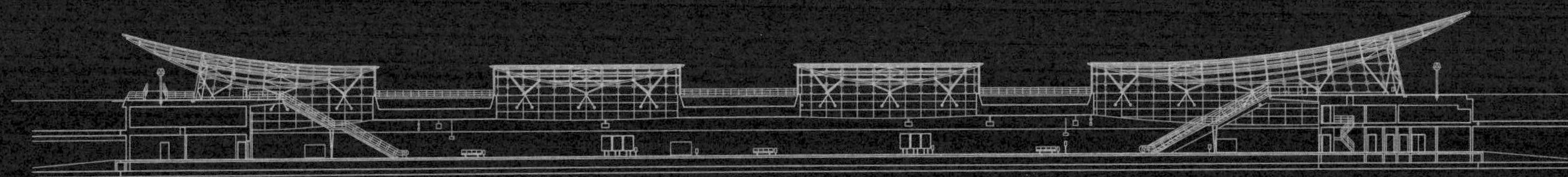

Longitudinal section
1:1000

Designing an apparently simple building is disproportionately more difficult than designing a complex one. Simply because organizing takes a lot more energy than designing. The more lucid the building, the better it is. In that respect, Mies is virtually unsurpassable. HvH

BrA.

name
Conversion of Fonds BKVB offices

project code
BrA

place
Brouwersgracht 276, Amsterdam

client
Fonds voor Beeldende Kunsten, Vormgeving en Bouwkunst, Amsterdam

design
1995

construction
1996–1997 (eerste fase)
1999–2002 (tweede fase)

design team
Ellen Baan
Marieke Bekirov
Dick de Gunst
Hans van Heeswijk
Derk-Jan Wentink

garden design
Lodewijk Baljon

The Netherlands Foundation for Visual Arts, Design and Architecture (Fonds BKVB) is housed in a former customs house on Brouwersgracht in Amsterdam. The building, a national monument dating from 1889, had undergone several renovations over the course of time so that little remained of the original layout. The building had inefficiently high-ceilinged offices and poor acoustics. This has been resolved by extending the mezzanine floor to cover most of the space. The result is a lucid and spacious interior organized around a skylit hall.

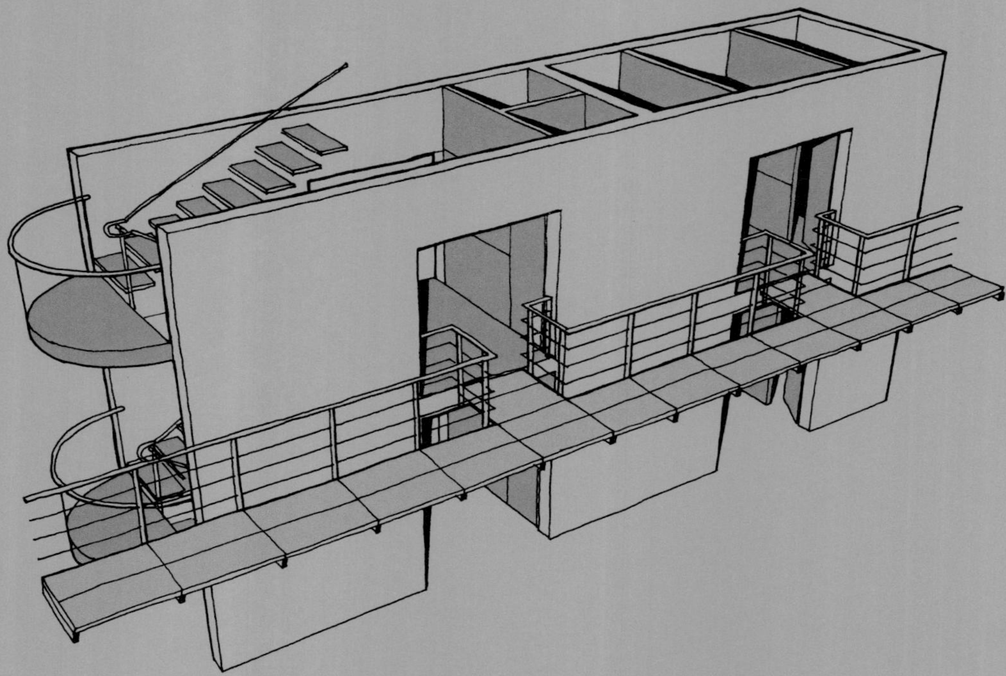

102.8

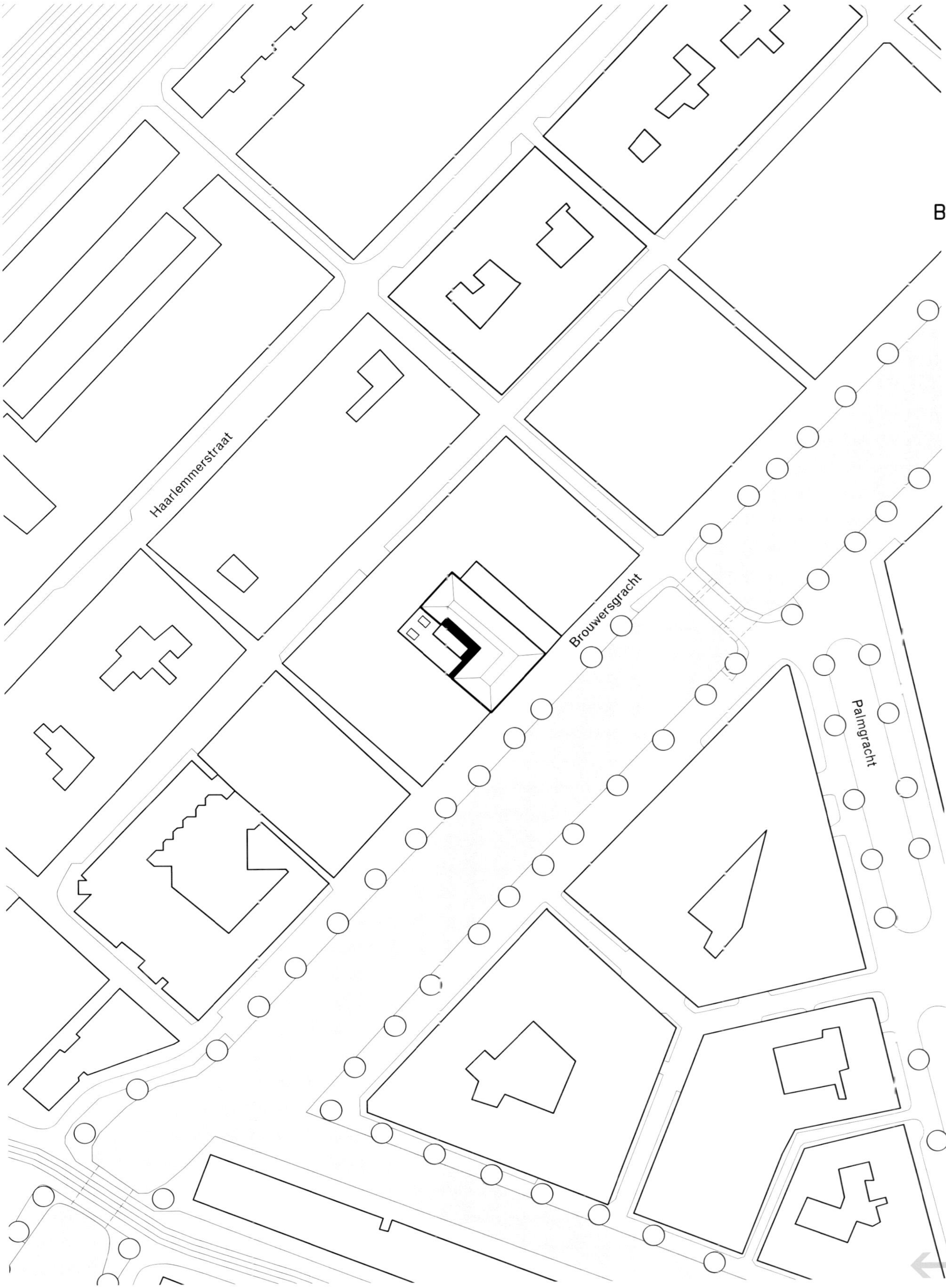

BrA

BrA.front elevation 06.JP

BrA.front elevation 14.LK

BrA.entrance 07.LK

BrA.central hall 02.JP

BrA.central hall 16.JP

BrA.exhibition space 10.LK

BrA.central hall 03.JP

BrA.gallery 11.LK

BrA.stairs 04.LK

BrA.stairs 05.LK

BrA.interior 22.HvH

BrA.interior 17.JP

BrA.interior 18.JP

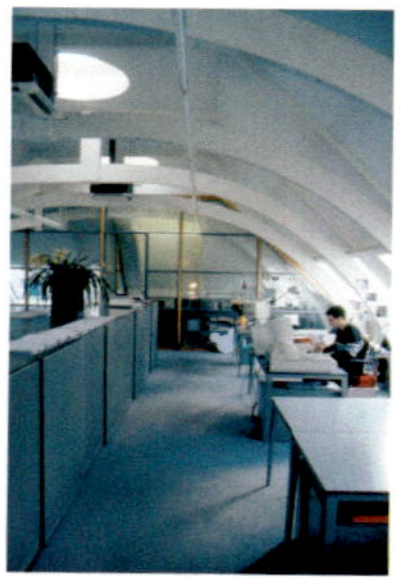

BrA.top floor 19.JP

BrA.top floor 08.JP

BrA.top floor 09.LK

BrA.top floor 15.JP

BrA.desk 12.HvH

BrA.desk 21.HvH

BrA.patio 13.JP

BrA.garden 20.JP

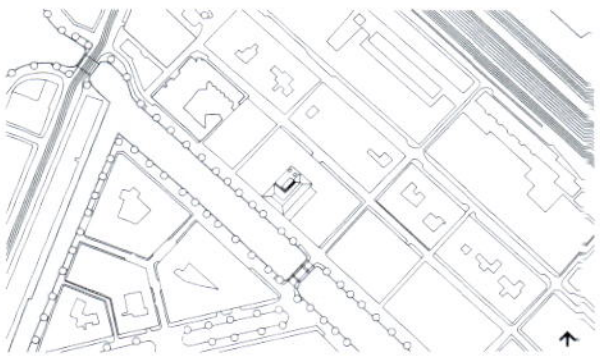

BrA.situation

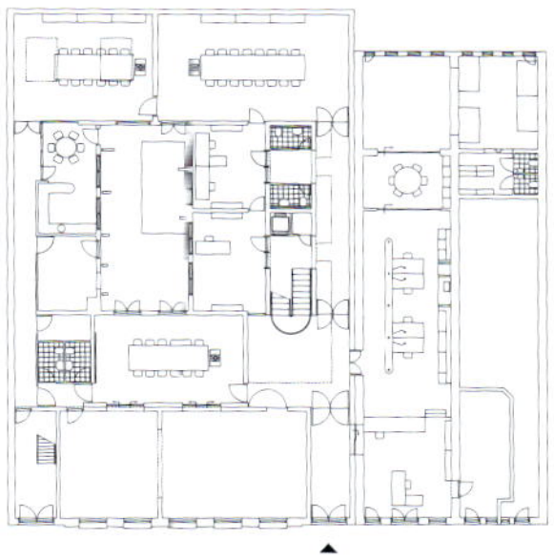

BrA.ground floor

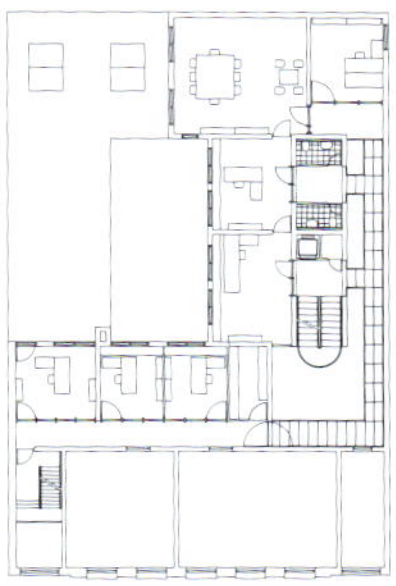

BrA.first floor

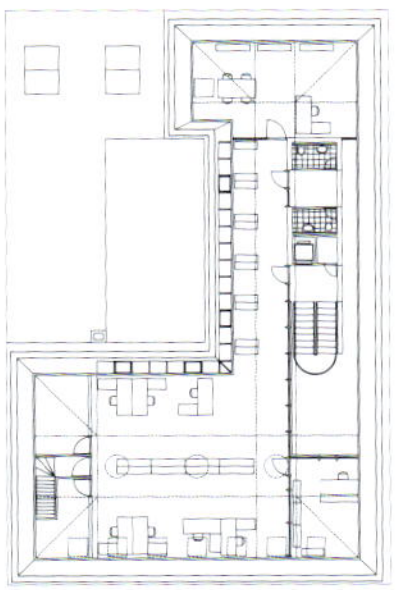

BrA.top floor

In the heart of the building is a light-filled hall created by removing sections of the floors and installing skylights. All the rooms in the building open onto this central space.

.1.BrA

Glass and light colours have turned the previously dark and poky interior into a bright and airy space, creating long sight lines and vistas.

A glass wall on the attic floor admits extra light and provides a view down into the central hall from the attic.

BrA

BrA

Garden design Lodewijk Baljon

The ground floor is occupied by publicly accessible spaces that include conference rooms and exhibition space. Staff workplaces are on the mezzanine floor while the administrative section and archives are housed on the attic floor.

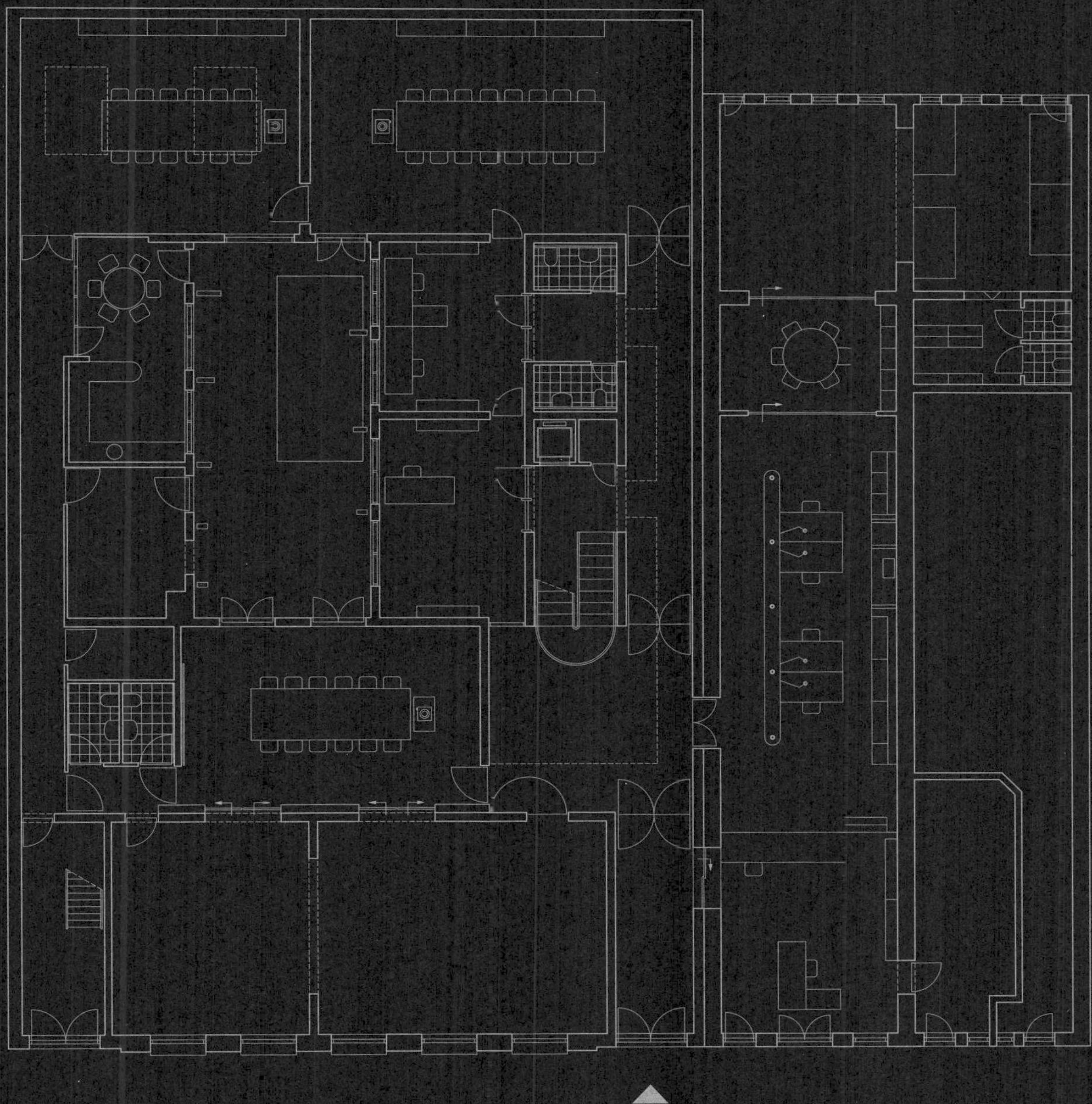

Ground floor
1:200

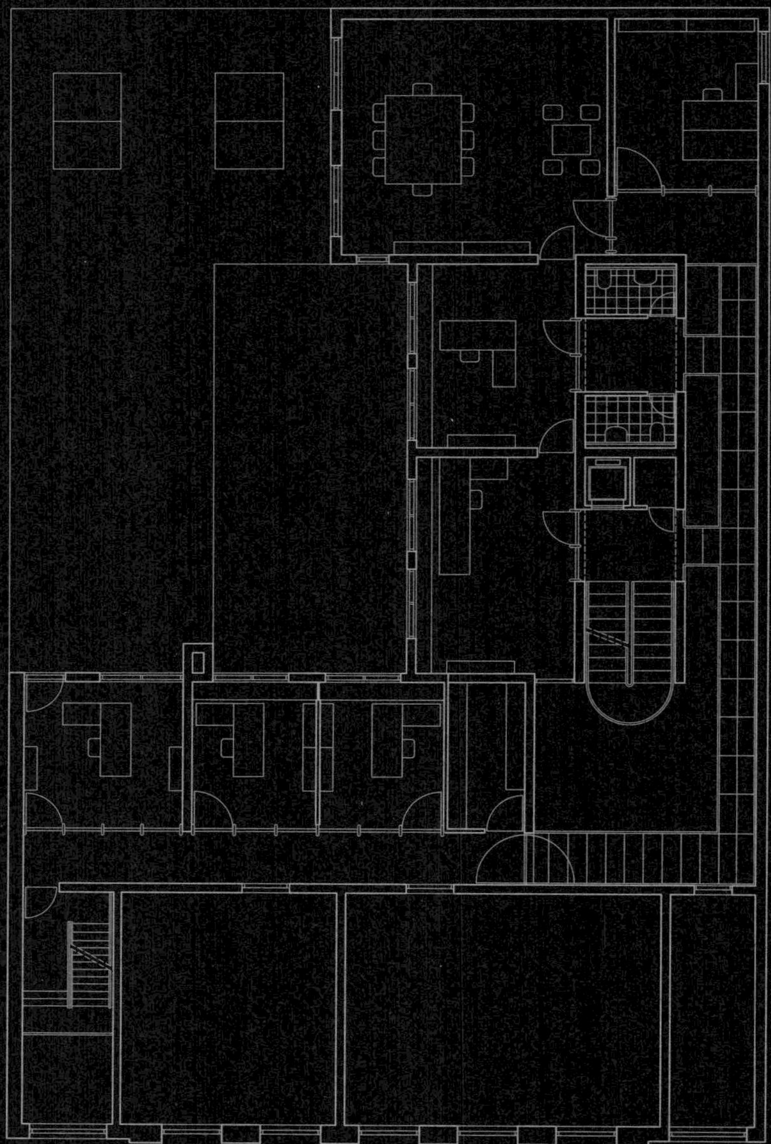

First floor
1:200

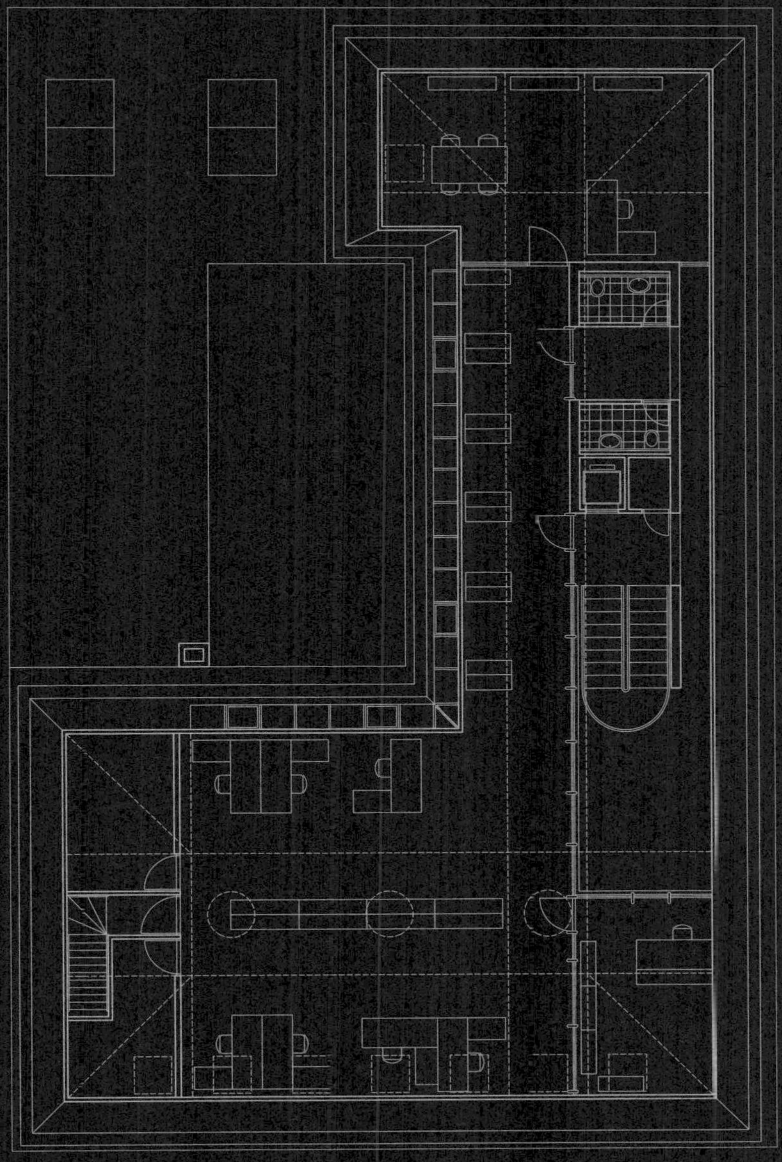

Attic
1:200

Cellular office interior in Jacques Tati's
Playtime, 1967

KwD.

name
New premises for Geo-information and ICT Department

project code
KwD

place
Derde Werelddreef, Delft

client
Rijksgebouwendienst, Directie Programma's en Projecten, Den Haag

design
1995–1998

construction
1999–2003

design team
Jerome Adema
Ellen Baan
Jens Böhm
Marieke Bekirov
Niki Carman
Rob van Dam
Andrew Dawes
Helene Gros
Dick de Gunst
Hans van Heeswijk
Remko van Heummen
Mirjam Heymann
Remco de Hoogh
Rob Hulst
Maartje Kaper
Thijs Postma
Jeroen Rademaker
Ton Span

garden design
Lodewijk Baljon

This large office building in Delft houses the Geo-information and ICT Department, an information and consultation centre operated by Rijkswaterstaat (Directorate-General for Public Works and Water Management). Behind the horizontal ribbon glazing lies a flexible, well-appointed office machine, as befits a large service organization. It is a building with a complex spatial programme and a high level of technical services.

The building has a clear, symmetrical layout. On a rectangular base containing the entrance and service areas stand seven floors of office space. This volume has deep recesses which reveal the interior. In plan the building consists of two L-shaped wings either side of a central core. This core is a transparent hall that links the floors to one another.

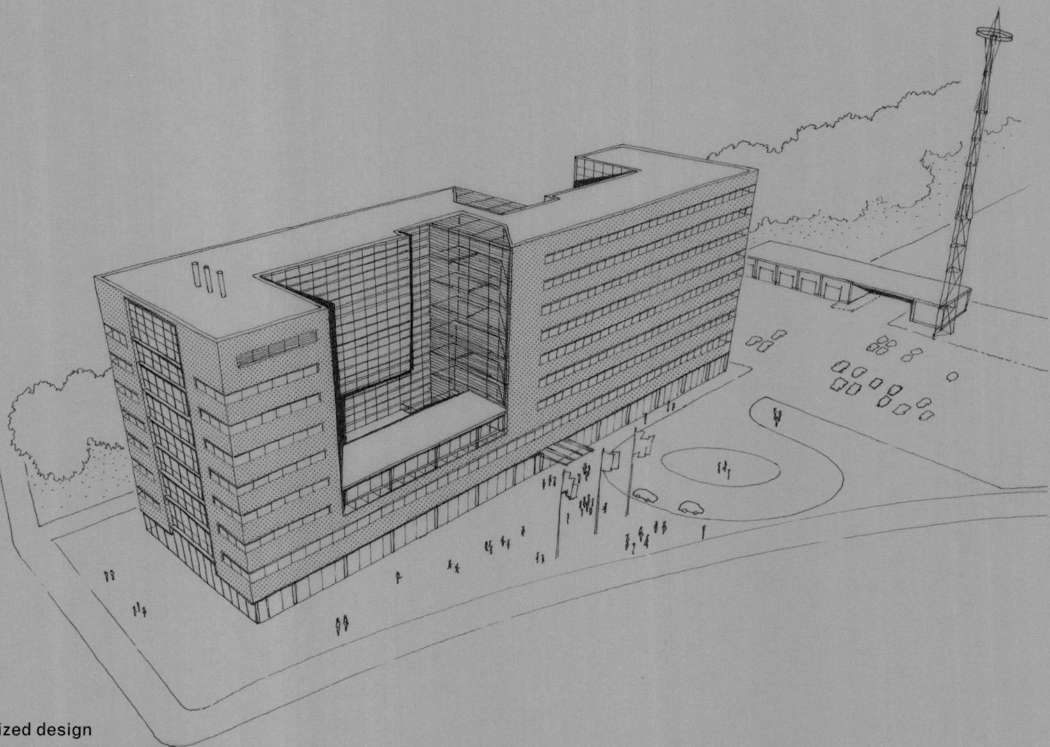

Realized design

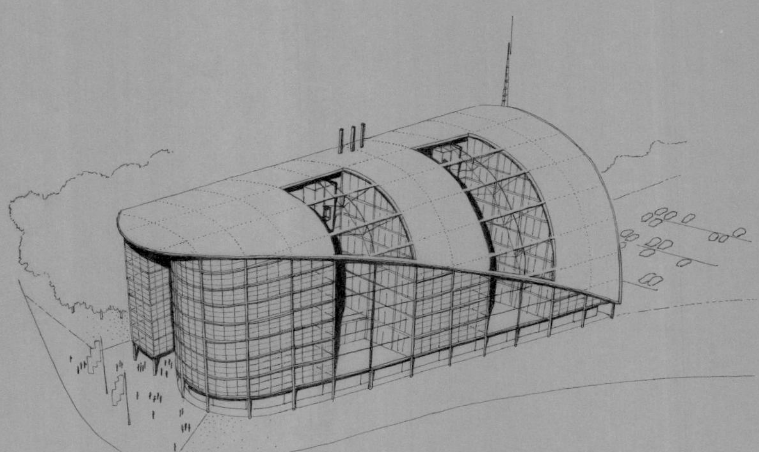

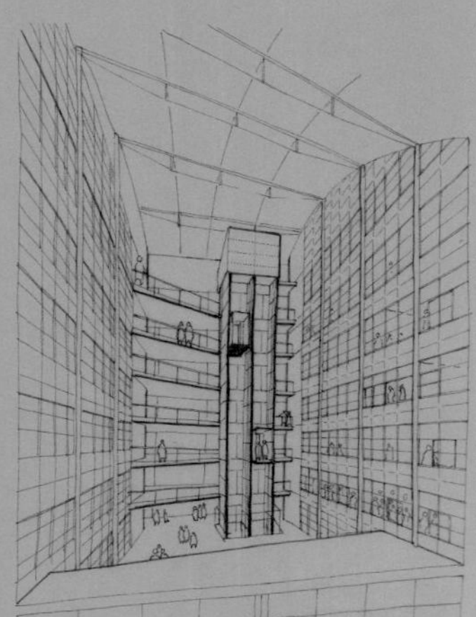

First design

KwD

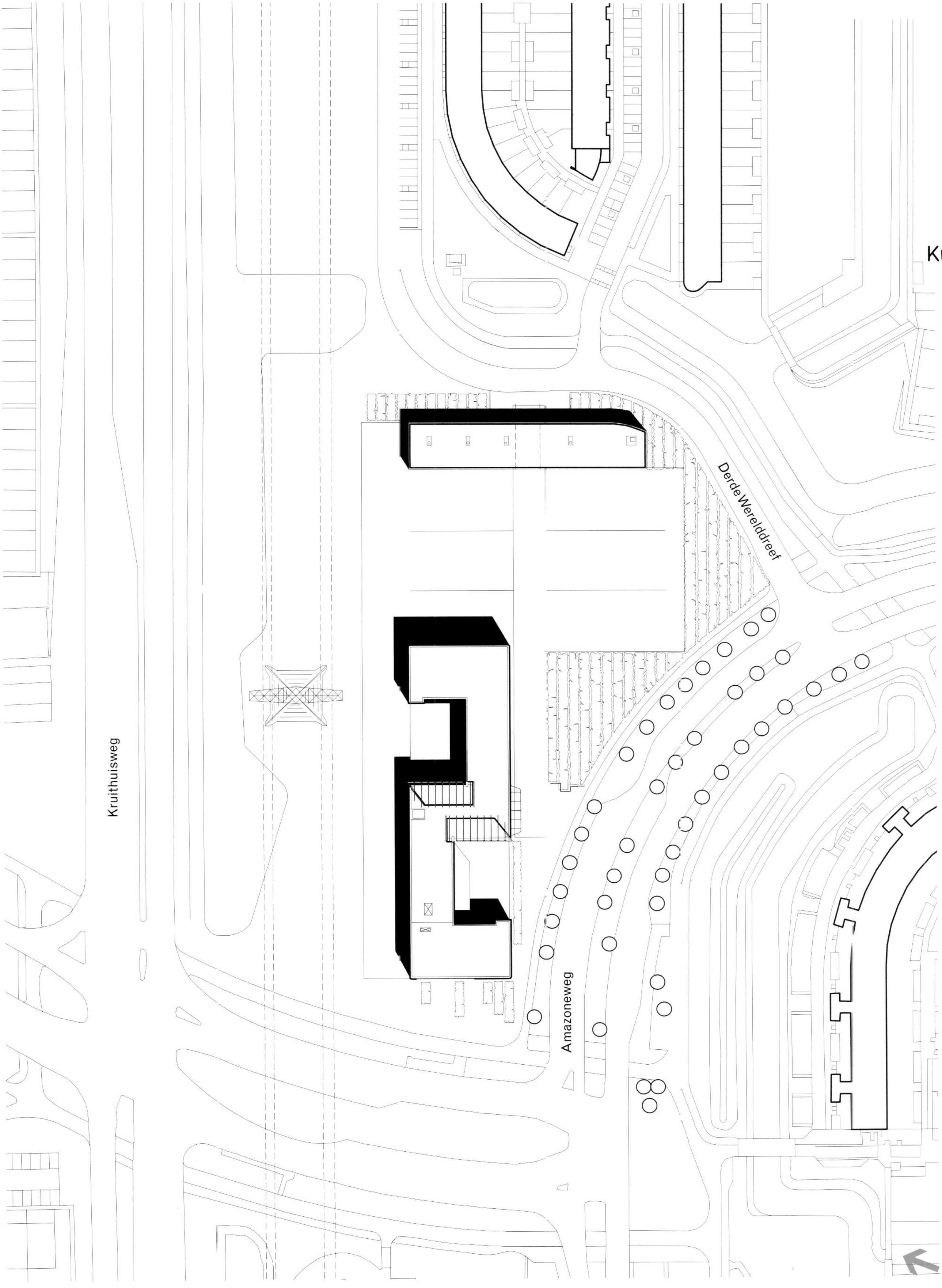

. KwD

KwD.overview 02.HvH

KwD.overview 01.CR

KwD.overview 04.LK

KwD.overview 06.RGD

KwD.overview 05.LK

KwD.glass facade 09.LK

KwD.void 64.CR

KwD.exterior 07.LK

KwD.void 66.LK

KwD.corner 14.CR

KwD.corner 17.CR

KwD.corner 15.LK

KwD.entrance 11.LK

KwD.entrance 12.LK

KwD.central hall 14.CR

KwD.central hall 15.CR

KwD.central hall 17.LK

KwD.central hall 21.RGD

KwD.corridor 29.LK

KwD.corridor 28.LK

KwD.corridor 33.RGD

KwD.elevator 70.LK

KwD.glass facade 10.LK

KwD.stairs 67.LK

KwD.interior 41.LK

KwD.interior offices 42.LK

KwD.interior 39.LK

KwD.interior offices 43.LK

KwD.interior offices 54.LK

KwD.interior offices 80.LK

KwD.interior offices 51.RGD

KwD.interior offices 45.LK

KwD.interior offices 49.LK

KwD.interior offices 46.LK

KwD.interior offices 82.RGD

KwD.interior offices 53.RGD

KwD.interior offices 47.LK

KwD.interior offices 81.LK

KwD.restaurant 55.LK

KwD.restaurant 56.LK

KwD.terrace 61.LK

KwD.terrace 58.LK

KwD.services building.LK

KwD.services building 02.LK

KwD.detail 74.HvH

KwD.detail 71.HvH

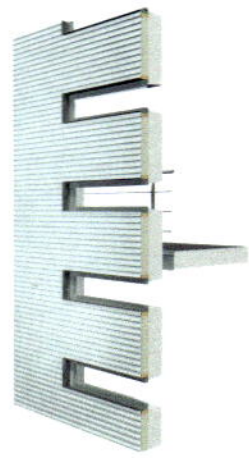

KwD.detail 72.HvH

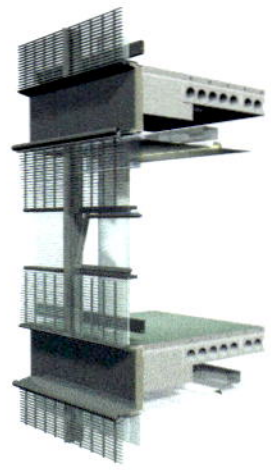

KwD.detail 73.HvH

KwD.interior 40.HvH

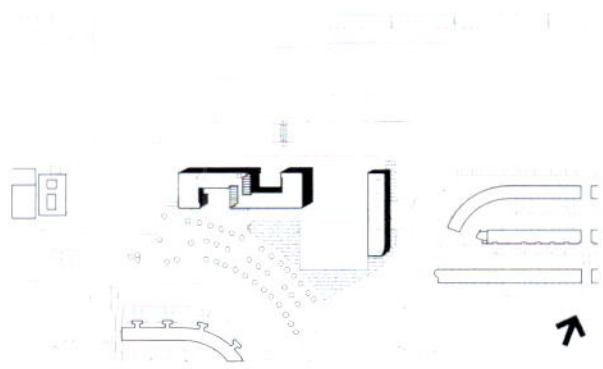

KwD.situation

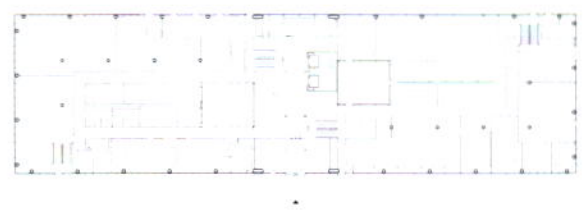

KwD.ground floor

KwD.first floor

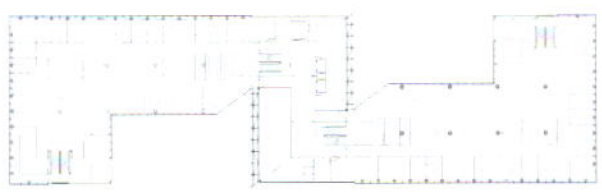

KwD.2nd–6th floor

KwD.7th floor

KwD.service building

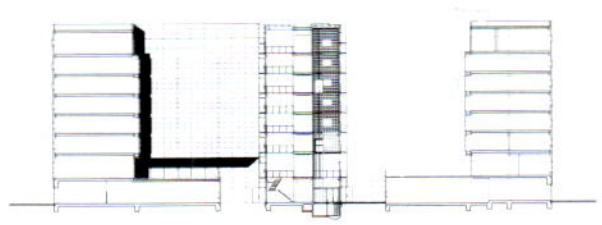

KwD.section

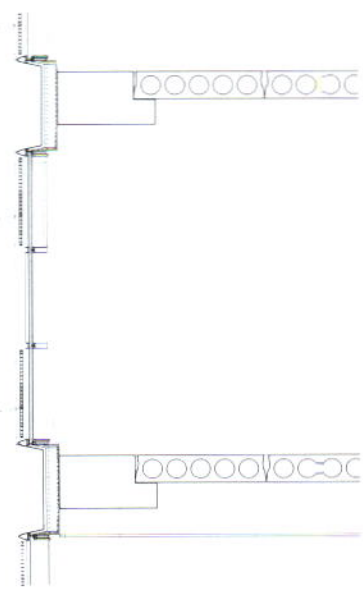

KwD.detail facade 1

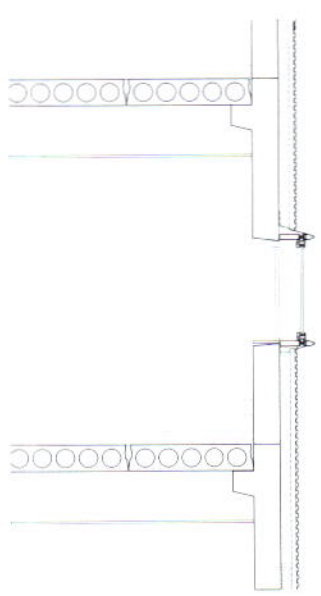

KwD.detail facade 2

KwD.detail facade 3

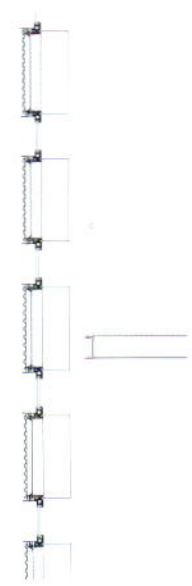

KwD.detail facade 4

informatie en ICT Rijkswaterstaat

KwD

The staircase in the hall is the only element in the building to eschew the symmetrical, orthogonal organization. The stairs follow the line of travel from the entrance to the conference centre on the first floor. The staircase has an open-work steel truss structure; the treads are of glass.

The two wings are linked by a central hall that is constructed of steel. The facade is suspended from a storey-high lattice girder. Any vertical movement caused by thermal expansion is absorbed by the junctions at the bottom.

The lifts, like the hall facades, are suspended from the roof. They are situated in an open void behind a fully glazed shaft face and glass doors.

On the ground floor, either side of the entrance hall, is a patio that brings daylight into the building, turning the hall into a light, airy and inviting space.

138.K

The L-shaped office wings are divided into three parallel zones. The middle zone contains all the service functions, while the various types of office space are arranged along the outer walls.

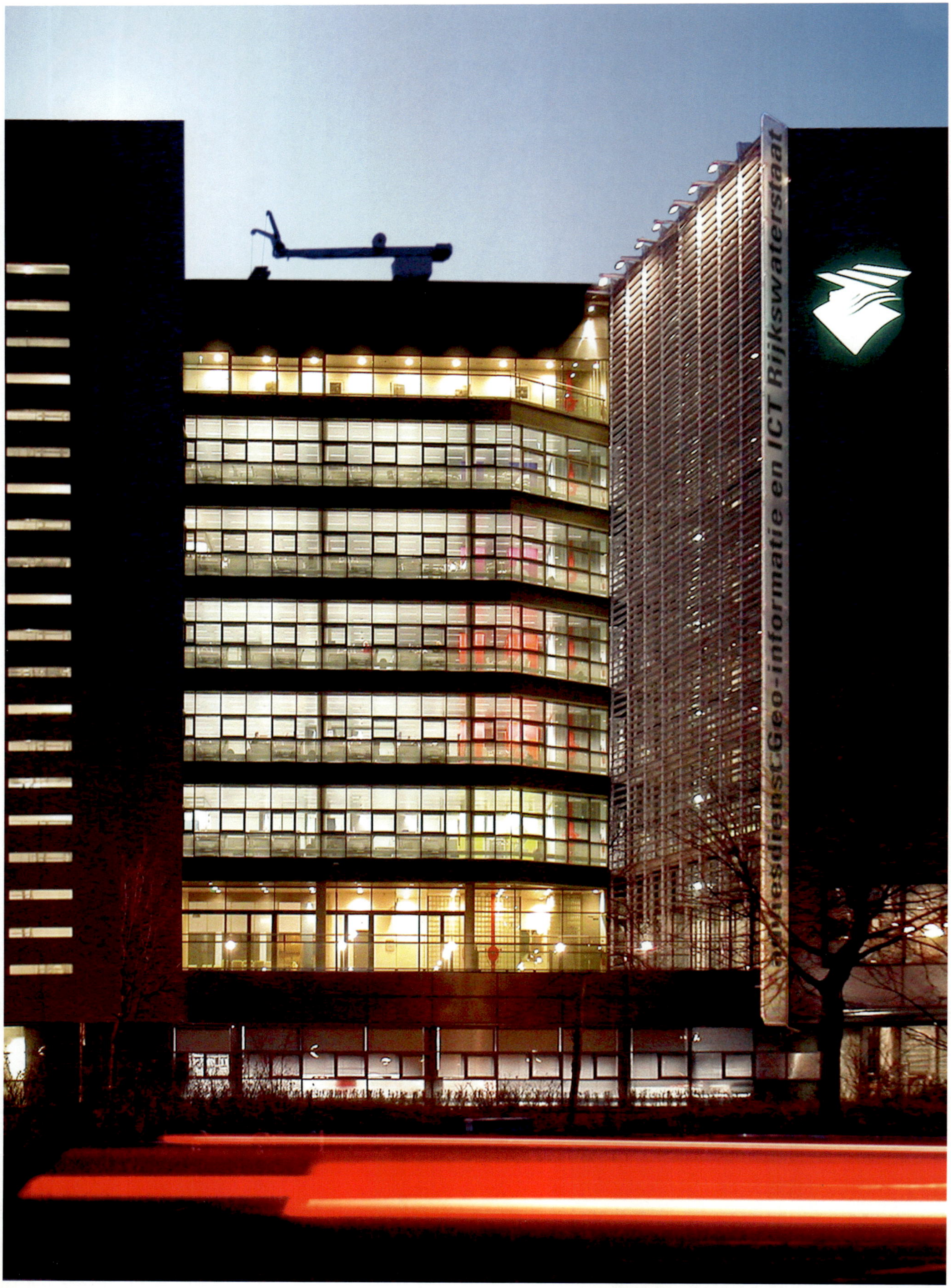
Geo-informatie en ICT Rijkswaterstaat

In the middle zone of every floor, close to the entrance, is a brightly coloured service unit containing a pantry, pigeon holes, lockers and cloakroom. The colour of the service units differs from floor to floor. At a central location in the office wings is a second service block containing printers and photocopiers.

Between the two service units in the middle zone are short-term work-spaces and consultation areas. The concentrated-work cubicles and interview rooms are along the outer facade with the narrow ribbon windows. The open-plan offices are mainly behind the glazed facades of the recessed parts of the building.

The layout, materials and colours of the office areas underpin the division into zones. The facade zones are open and light while the middle zone is more sheltered and darker in colour.

KwD

Adviesdien
B

KwD

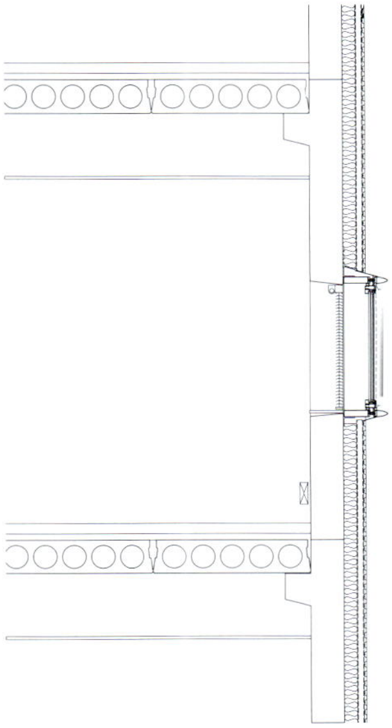

1:50

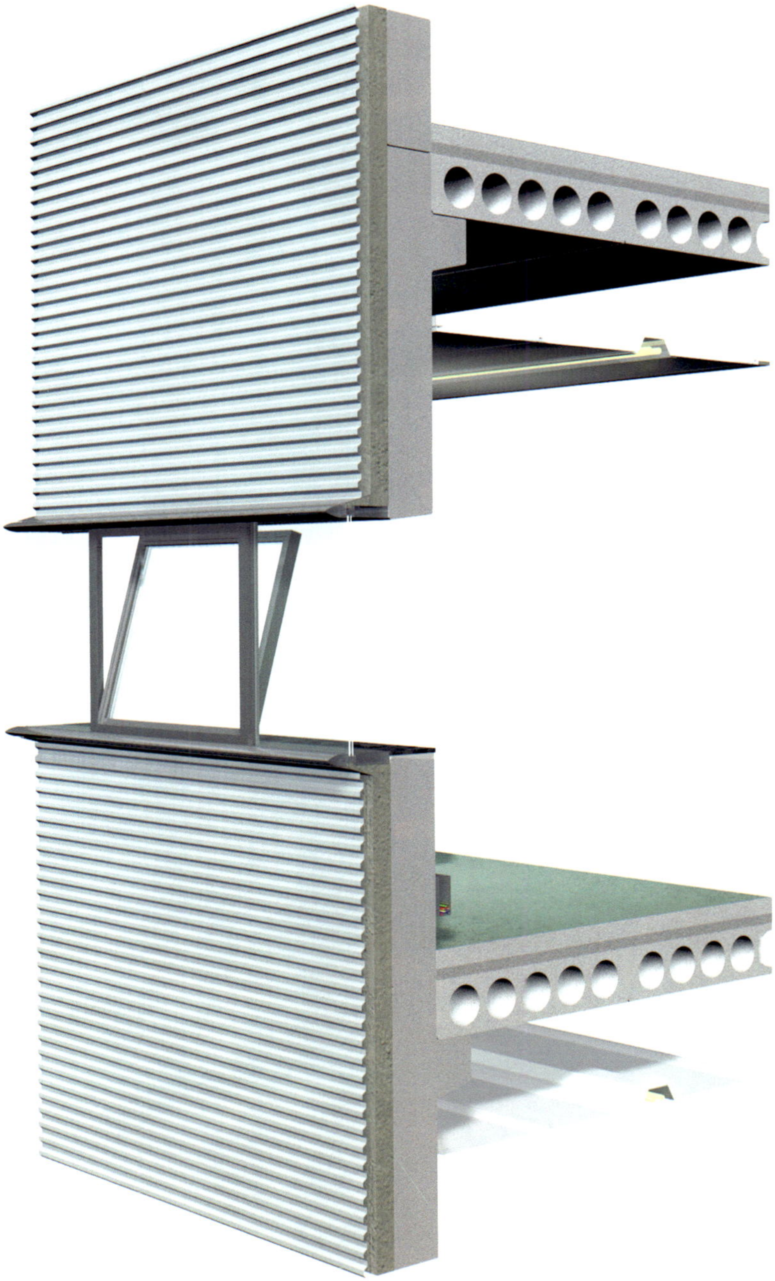

Detail facade with wide window bands

Where the outer walls coincide with the building line, the building is relatively closed. By contrast, the facades of the recessed sections are three-quarters glass. The facades of the core are all glass.

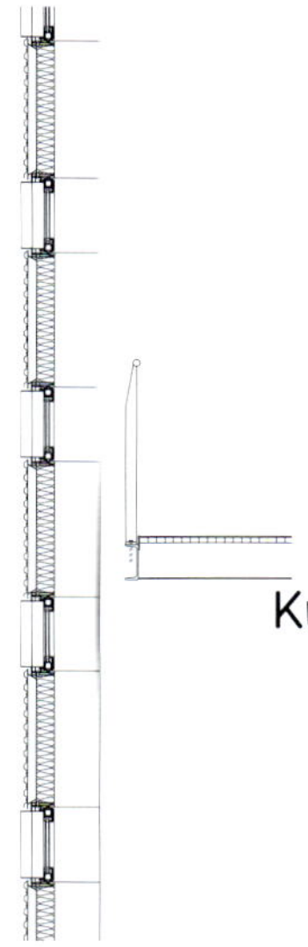

KwD

1:50

Detail facade with narrow window bands

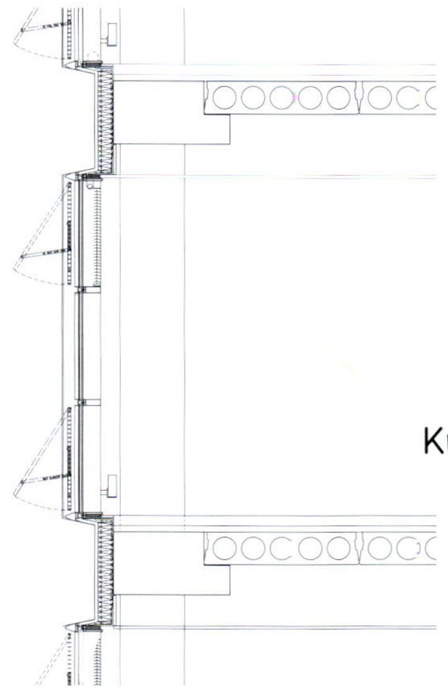

1:50

.KwD

Detail facade recessed section

The central hall has a double facade consisting of glass on the inside and aluminium slats on the outside. Between the two facades on each floor is a platform with a lattice girder in the floor which transfers the wind load to the building's core.

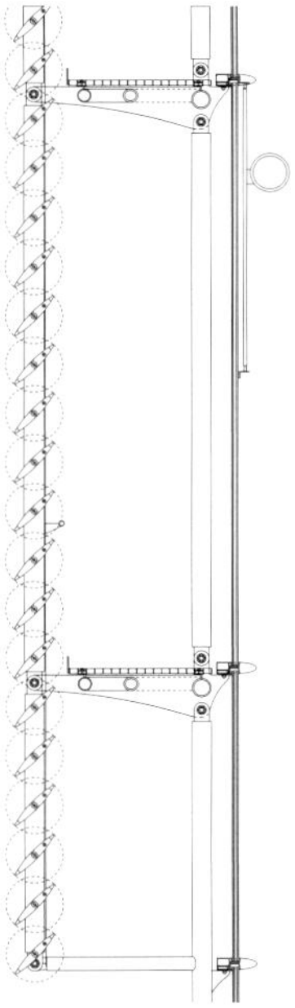

1:50

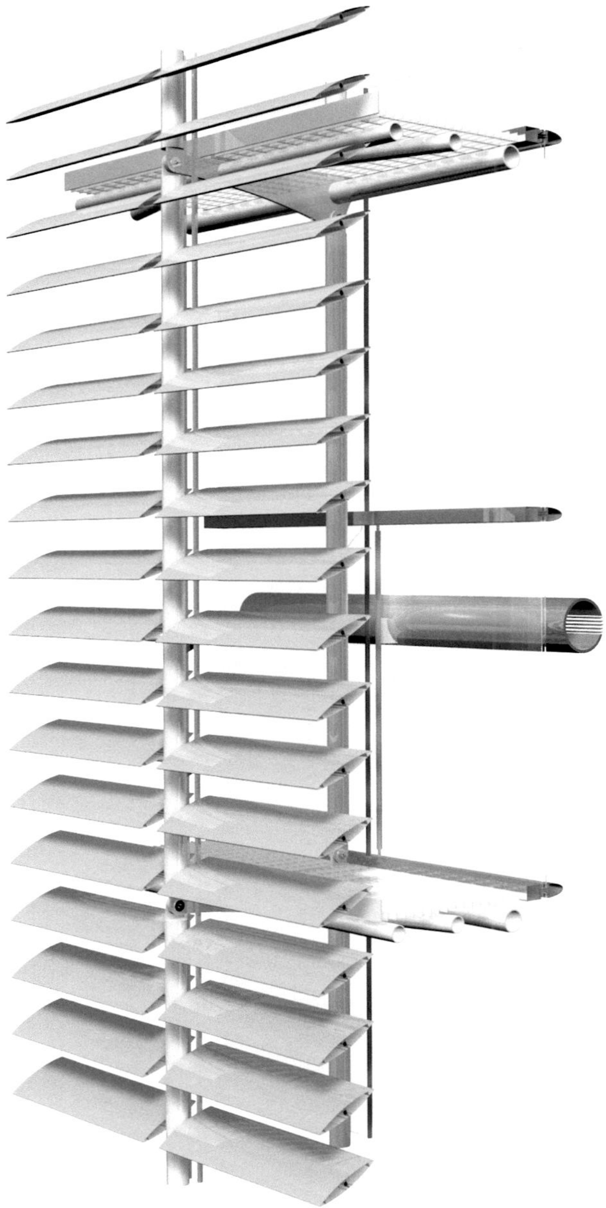

Detail facade core with slats

On the first floor, in addition to the conference centre, is a cafeteria that opens out onto a large, south-facing terrace overlooking the polder landscape between Delft and Vlaardingen.

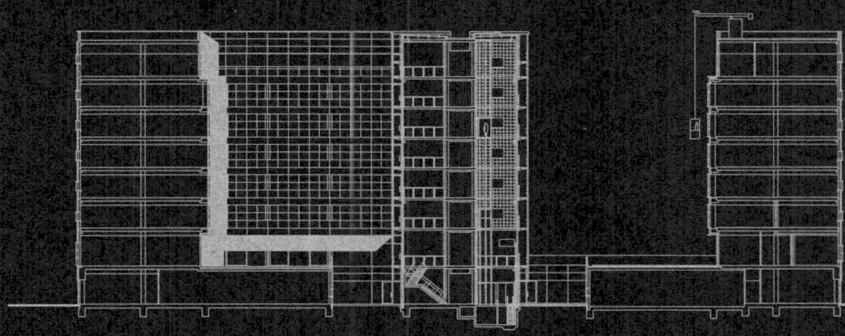

Section
1:1000

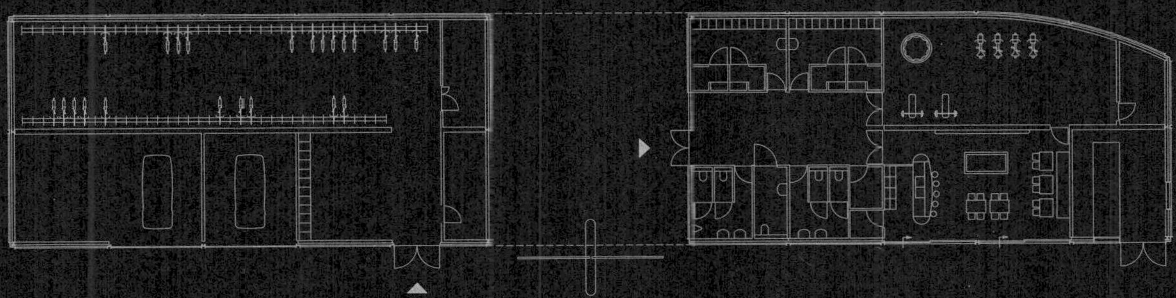

Service building
1:400

Floor plans page 162/163
Building services, cable ducts and other services have been so arranged that the office floors can be subdivided in different ways, with open workstations and cubicles for concentrated work, depending on the organization concerned and the requirements of the moment. In the interests of optimal flexibility the plans are deeper than usual (14.4 instead of 12.6 metres) and the grid is narrower than usual (1.2 instead of 1.8 metres).

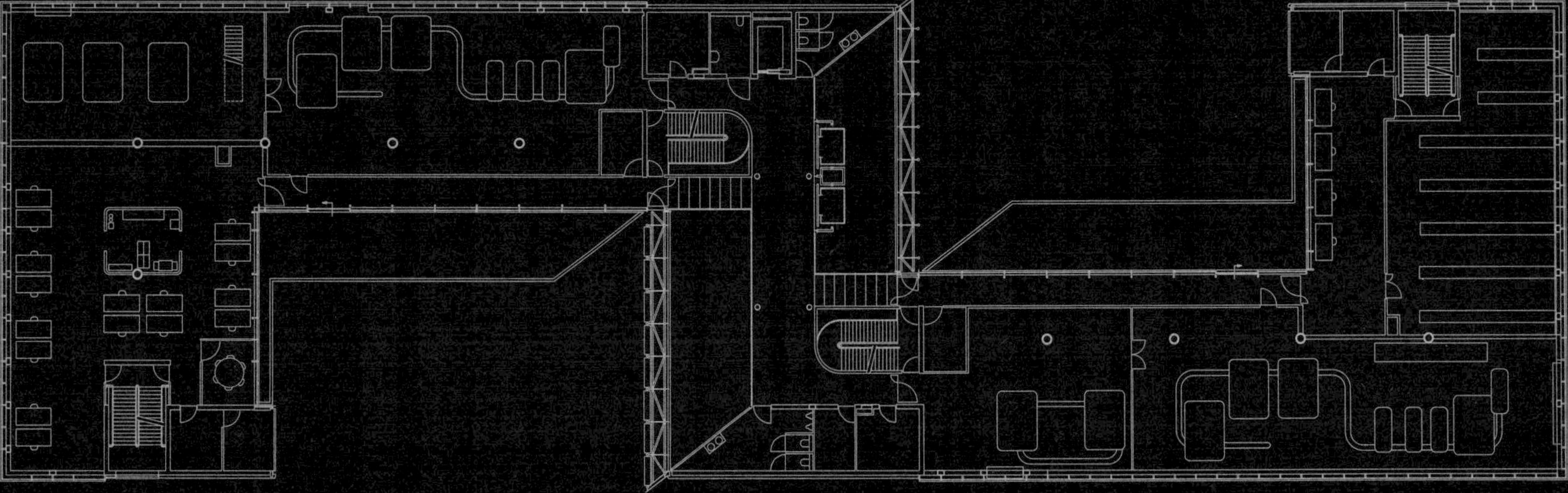

Seventh floor

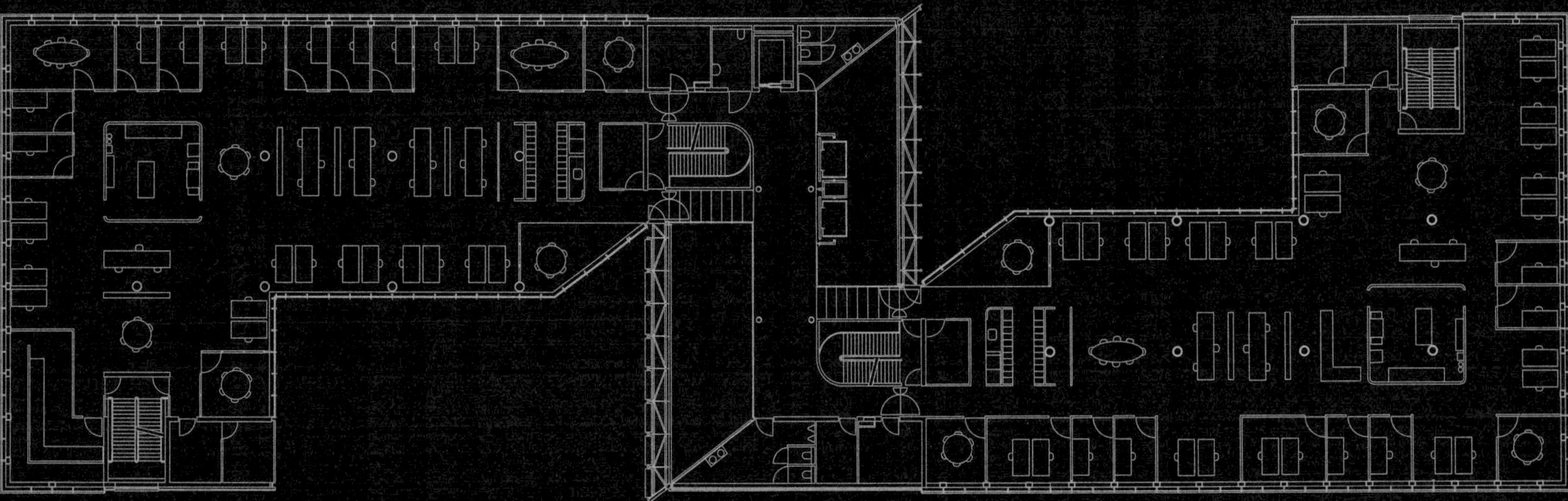

Second to sixth floor

KwD

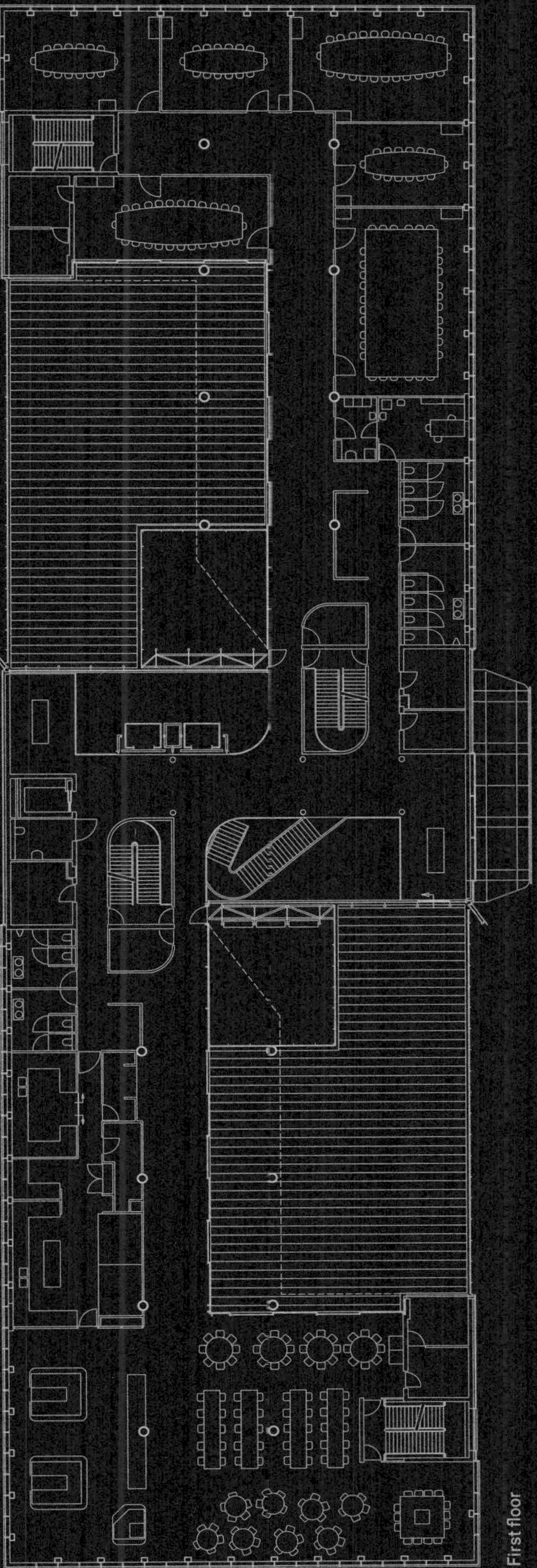

First floor

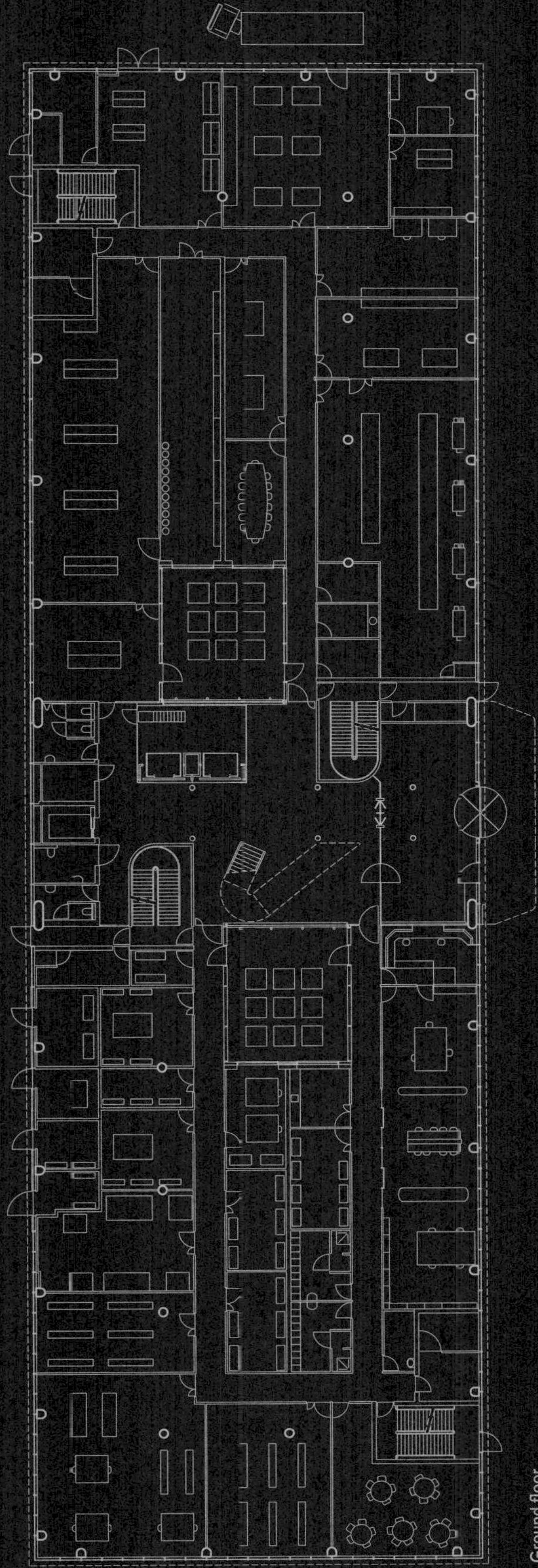

Ground floor
1:400

North Sea oil platform, 1985

KeA.

name
Interior of De Key office

project code
KeA

place
Loods 6, KNSM eiland
Amsterdam

client
Woonstichting De Key,
Amsterdam
(de Principaal)

design
1996

construction
1996–1997

design team
Marieke Bekirov
Dick de Gunst
Hans van Heeswijk

The development division of De Principaal Housing Corporation used to be accommodated in a Hans van Heeswijk-converted office on the Veemarkt in Amsterdam. When more space was needed after a merger, the company, now called De Key, relocated to Loods 6 on KNSM Island in the Eastern Docklands area of Amsterdam. The new offices are in a former building of the Royal Dutch Steamship Company dating from around 1900; it is now a multi-occupancy building containing offices, studios and exhibition space. The De Key offices were renovated and fitted out with specially designed furniture.

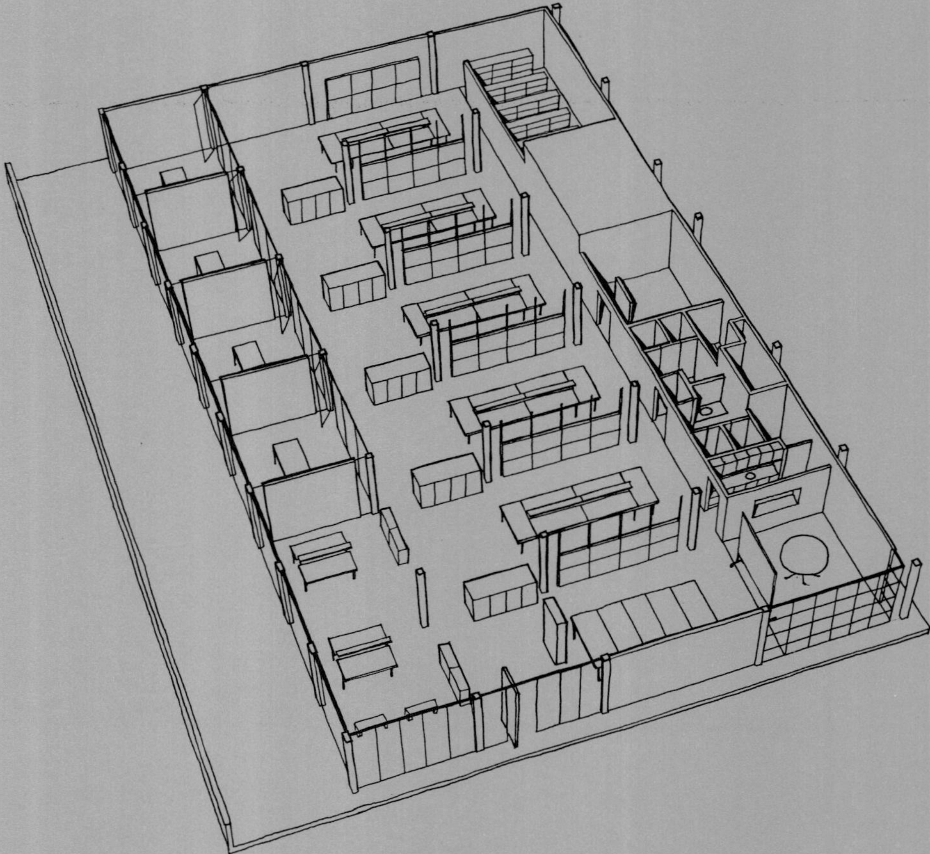

The office is on the first floor on the quay side of the building. It has a long terrace overlooking the waters of the IJ.

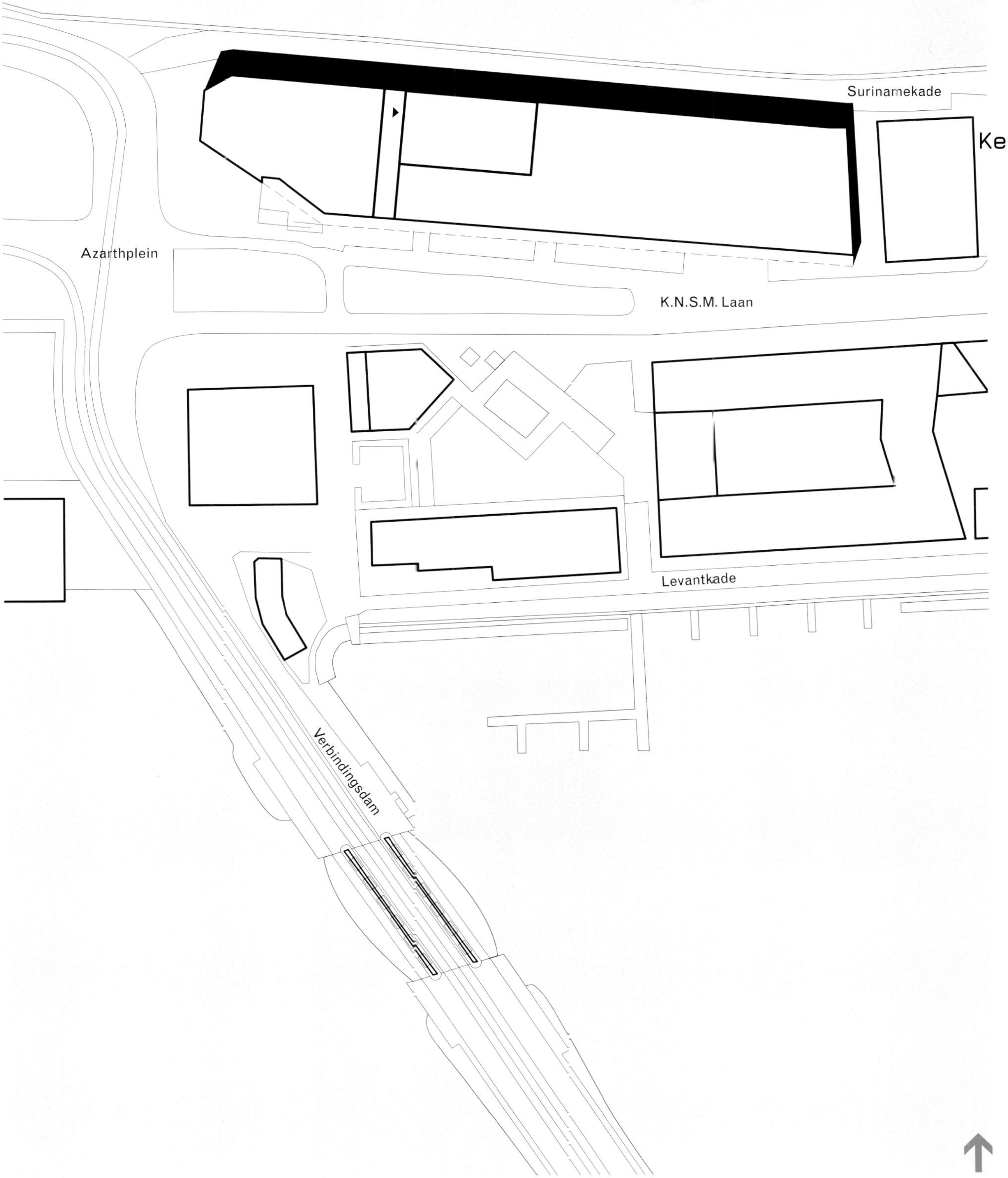

KeA.presentations 01.JP

KeA.workspace 02.JP

KeA.meeting room 03.JP

KeA.pantry 04.JP

KeA.interior 05.JP

KeA.corridor 06.JP

KeA.meeting room 15.JP

KeA.workspace 08.JP

KeA.hallway 14.JP

KeA.workspace 10.JP

KeA.workspace 12.JP

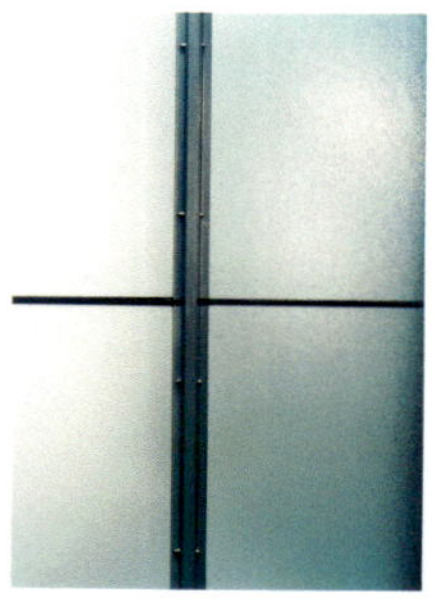

KeA.detail screen 07.JP

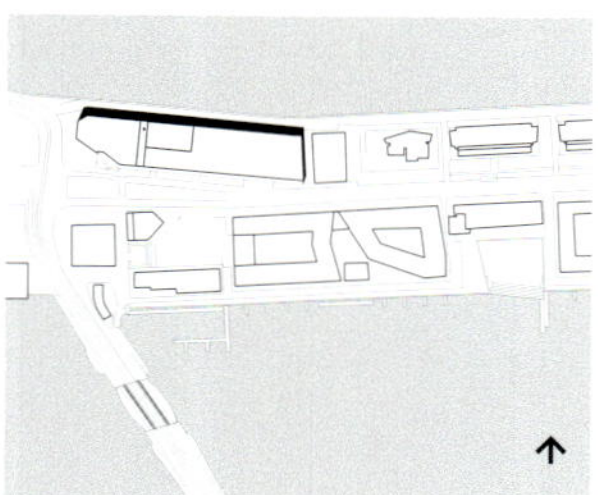

KeA.situation

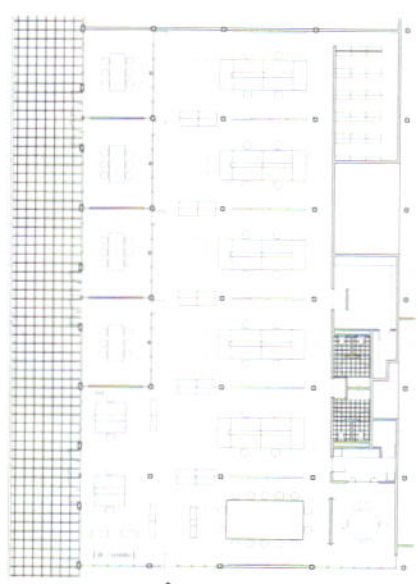

KeA.floor plan

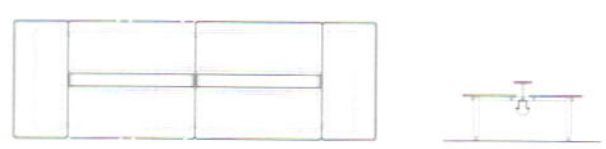

KeA.table top view

Loods 6 is one of the few remnants of the industrial past of what is now a residential area. It is a multi-occupancy building containing offices and shops.

With its concrete floors and columns, tall spaces and old hangar doors, the building has retained an industrial ambience.

KeA

Glass walls separate the meeting rooms from the rest of the office. The individual workstations are divided by cupboards and acoustic partitions.

KeA

[illegible] specially for De Key. They consist [illegible] linked together to form one big [illegible] beneath the table tops.

The floor plan has a linear arrangement. Along the outer wall are the secretarial office and several meeting rooms. Behind these is an open-plan office with workstations for all the staff members. At the back are service spaces – archives, photocopying room, washrooms and a pantry/lunchroom.

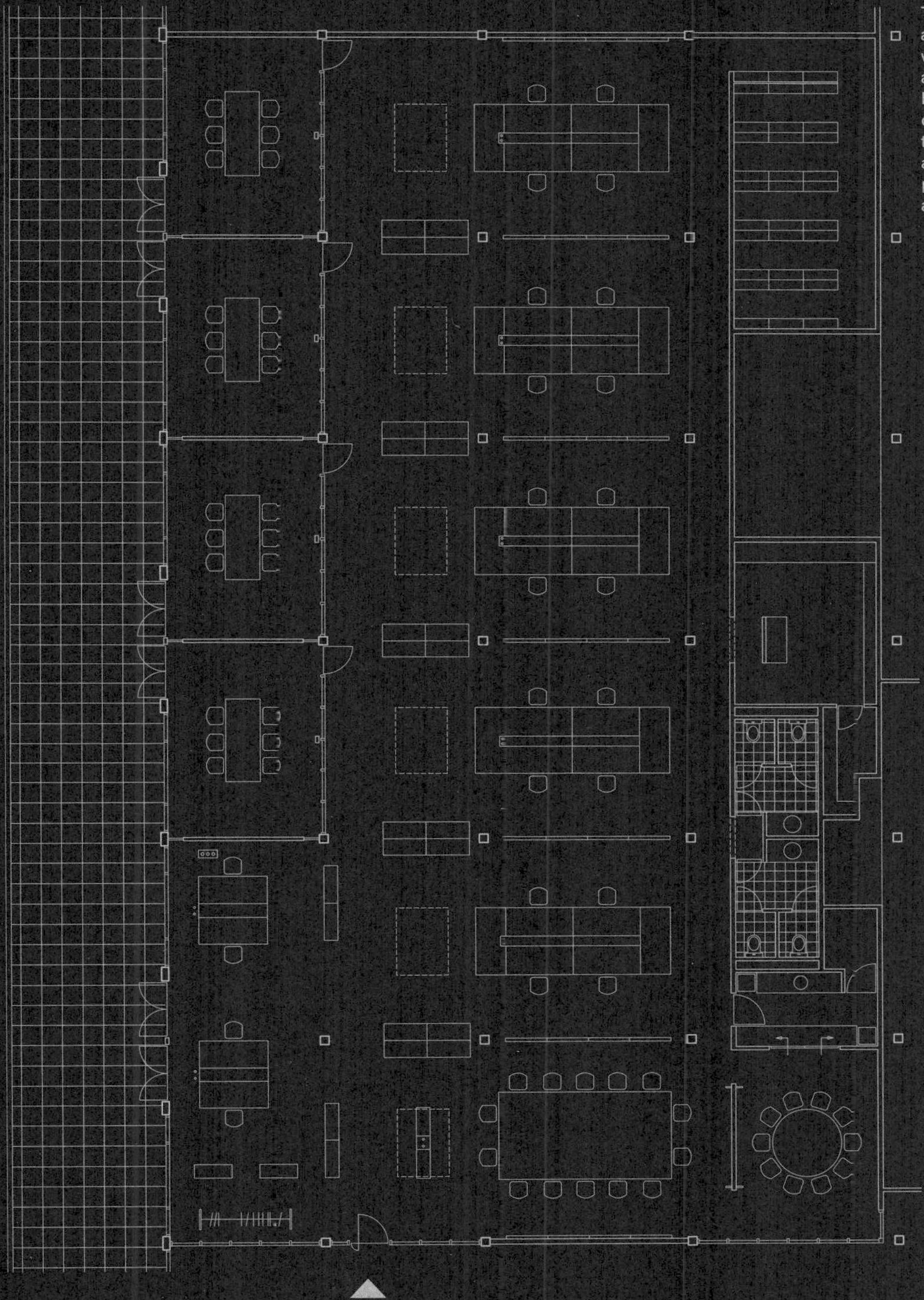

Floor plan
1:200

Table: top view and section
1:50

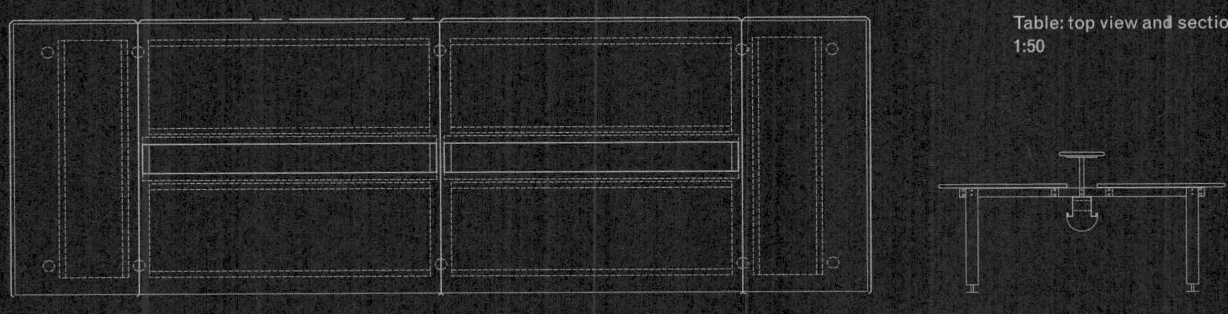

The Strip, Las Vegas

PdD.

name
Conversion of 6 car parks on Daalwijkdreef

project code
PdD

place
Daalwijkdreef,
Amsterdam Zuidoost

client
Gemeente Amsterdam

design
1995

construction
1997–2000

design team
Peter de Bruin
Dick de Gunst
Hans van Heeswijk
Maartje Kaper
Jochem van der Spek
Derk Jan Wentink

Part of the comprehensive redevelopment of Amsterdam's Bijlmer, the vast modernist housing estate of the 1960s and '70s, is the conversion of the ends of six vacant car park buildings on Daalwijkdreef into multi-occupancy buildings providing affordable office and work space for small start-up businesses. A key aim of the design was to counteract the anonymous character of the car park buildings.
The expressiveness of the renovated buildings is due mainly to the added awnings and advertising masts. The robust and crisp awnings, consisting of die-cast gratings in a steel frame, give the buildings a distinctive face on the avenue. Companies can use the masts placed alongside the buildings for modest self-advertisement. Each building has an awning and mast in a different colour so that the six buildings differ slightly from one another. The names of the buildings are etched in large, sandblasted letters in the glass at the corners of the buildings
The six multi-occupancy buildings have the same layout: a double-height central hall flanked left and right by the business premises. Behind the hall is a zone containing the stairs and washrooms and behind that again is what is left of the garages.

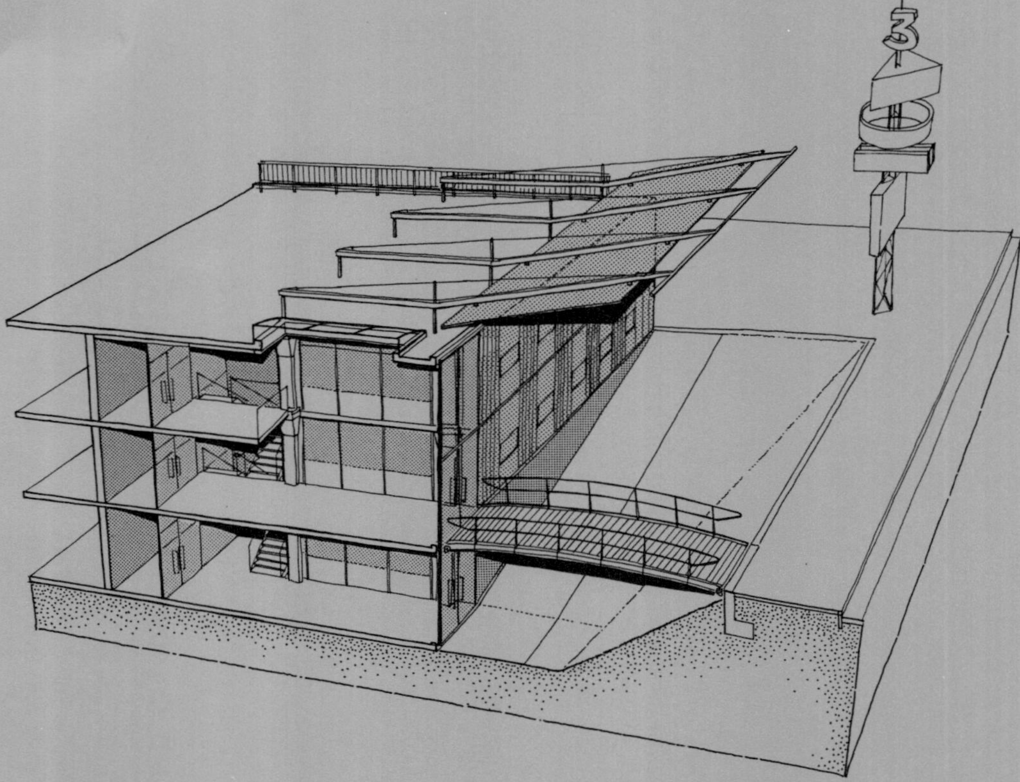
3

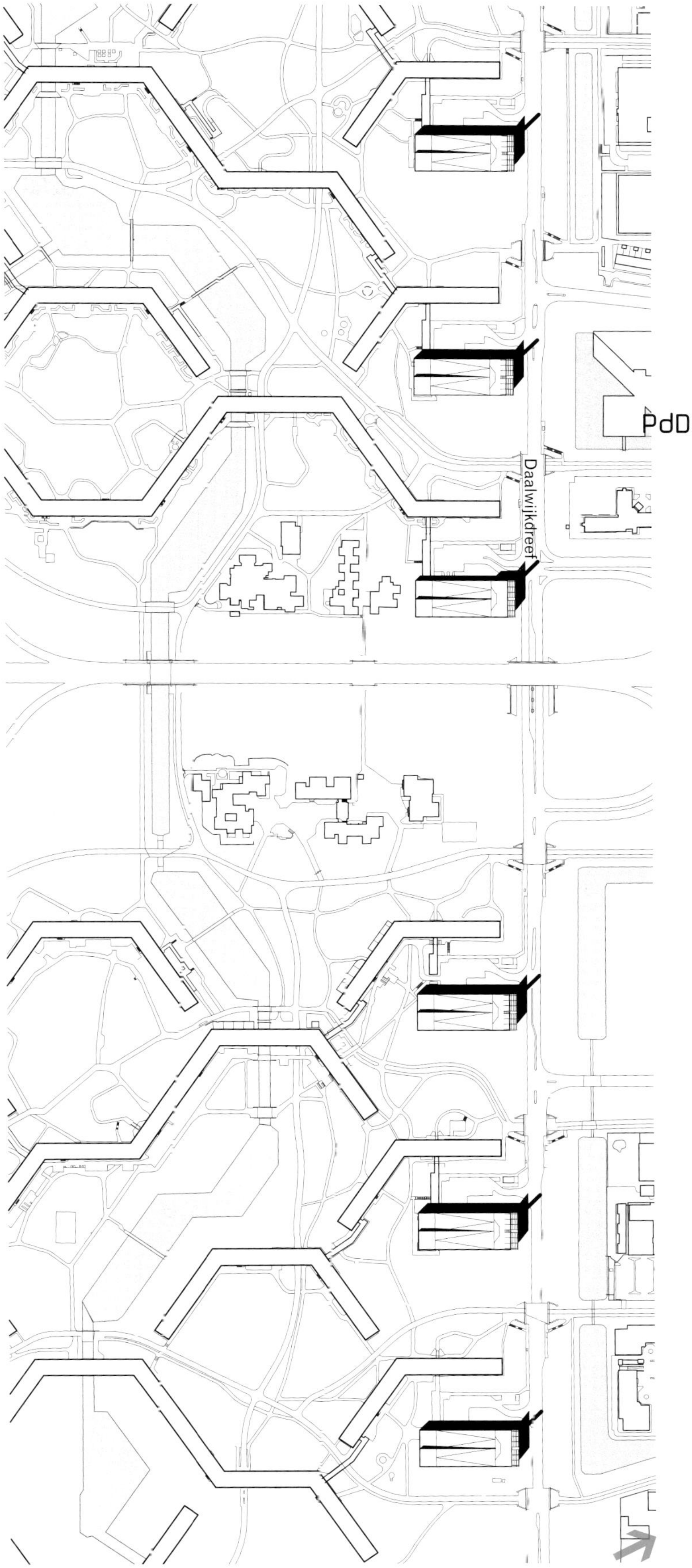

. PdD

PdD.overview 04.CR

PdD.street elevation 02.CR

PdD.side elevation 03.CR

PdD.facade and roof 05.CR

PdD.entrance 13.CR

PdD.facade and roof 06.CR

PdD.facade and roof 07.CR

PdD.facade and roof 10.CR

PdD.detail facade 08.HvH

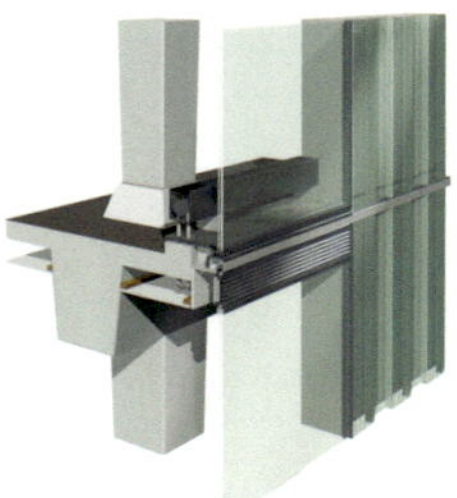

PdD.detail facade 09.HvH

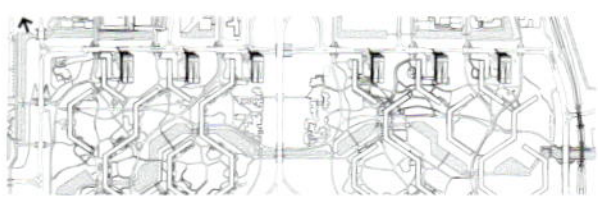

PdD.situation

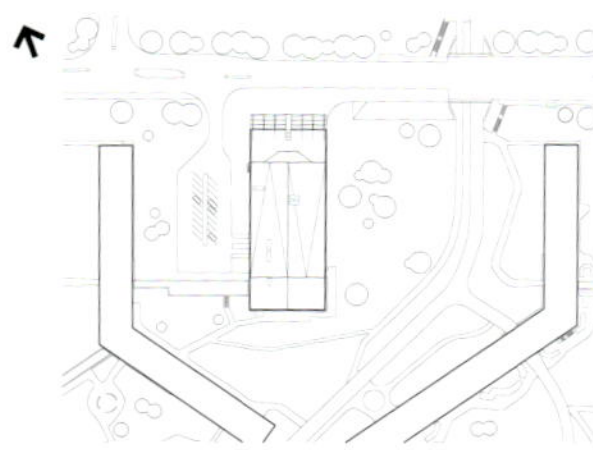

PdD.situation fragment

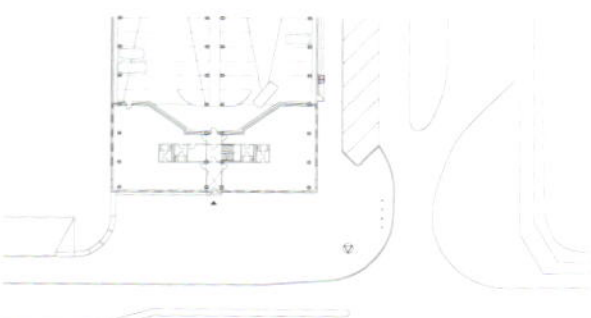

PdD.floor plan

PdD.noord facade

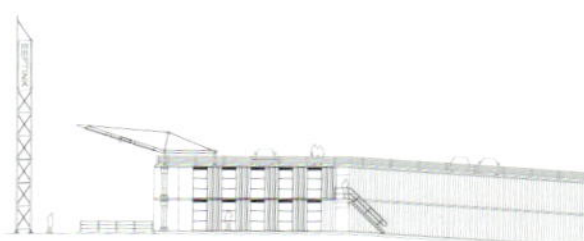

PdD.west facade

EGELDONK

The steel awning above the central entrance is filled with glass. Strip lighting and spotlights in the awning soffit illuminate the facade and accentuate the horizontal line along Daalwijkdreef.

PdD

The facades are made up of the existing frosted glass U-sections supplemented by an insulated sand-lime brick inner leaf and new vertical fenestration in which insulated glass panels are glued in thin steel frames. The module is 1.2 metres. At the corners, structurally glued toughened glass panels were added.

Detail Daalwijkdreef facade

PdD

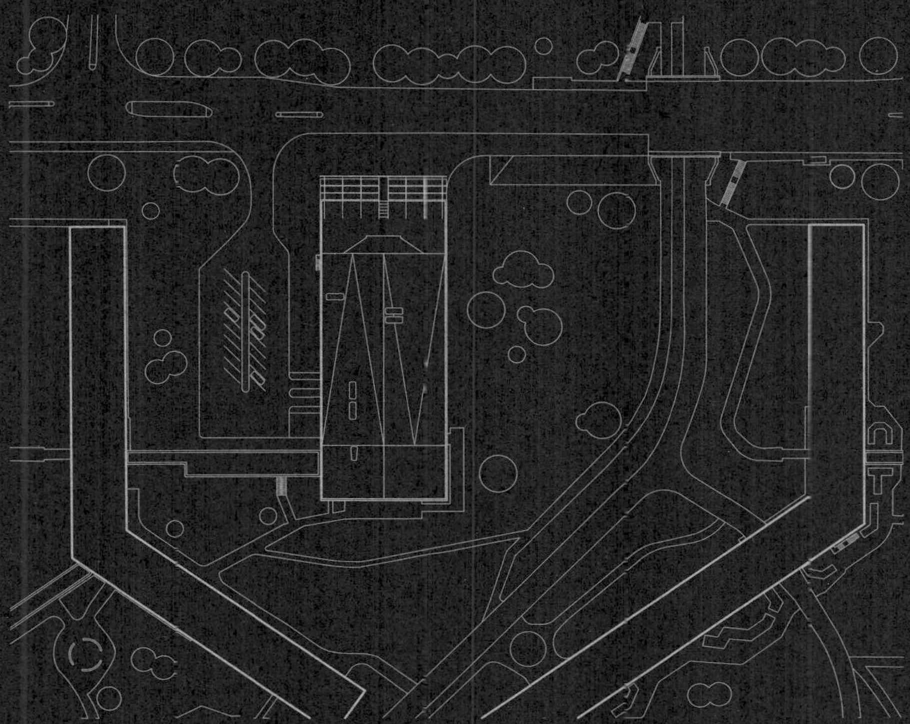

Situation
1:2000

Ground floor. The business premises are at the front end; behind is the pre-existing garage.

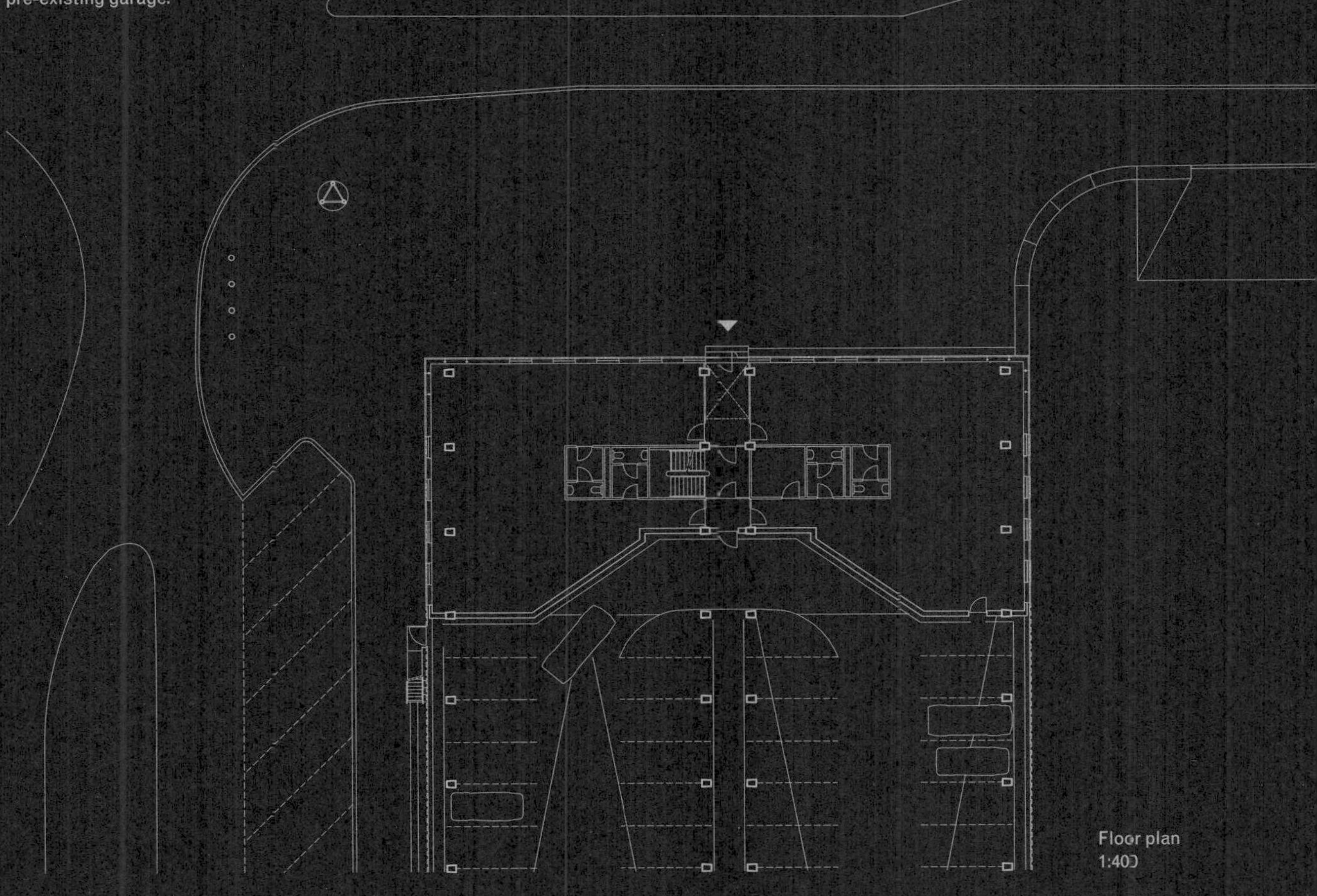

Floor plan
1:400

North elevation
1:200

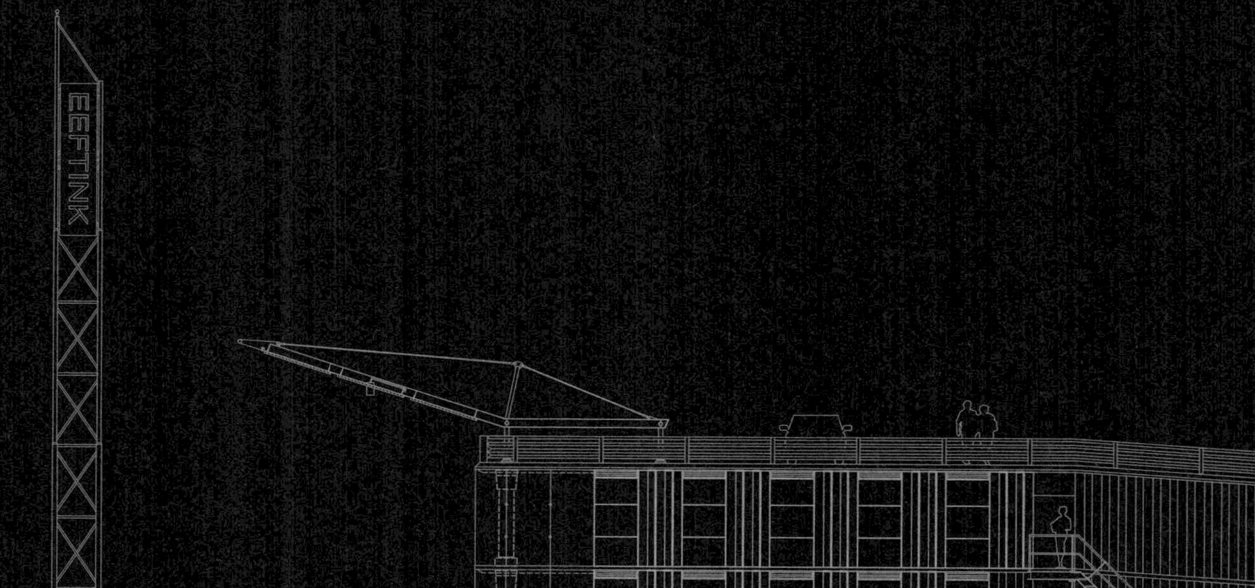

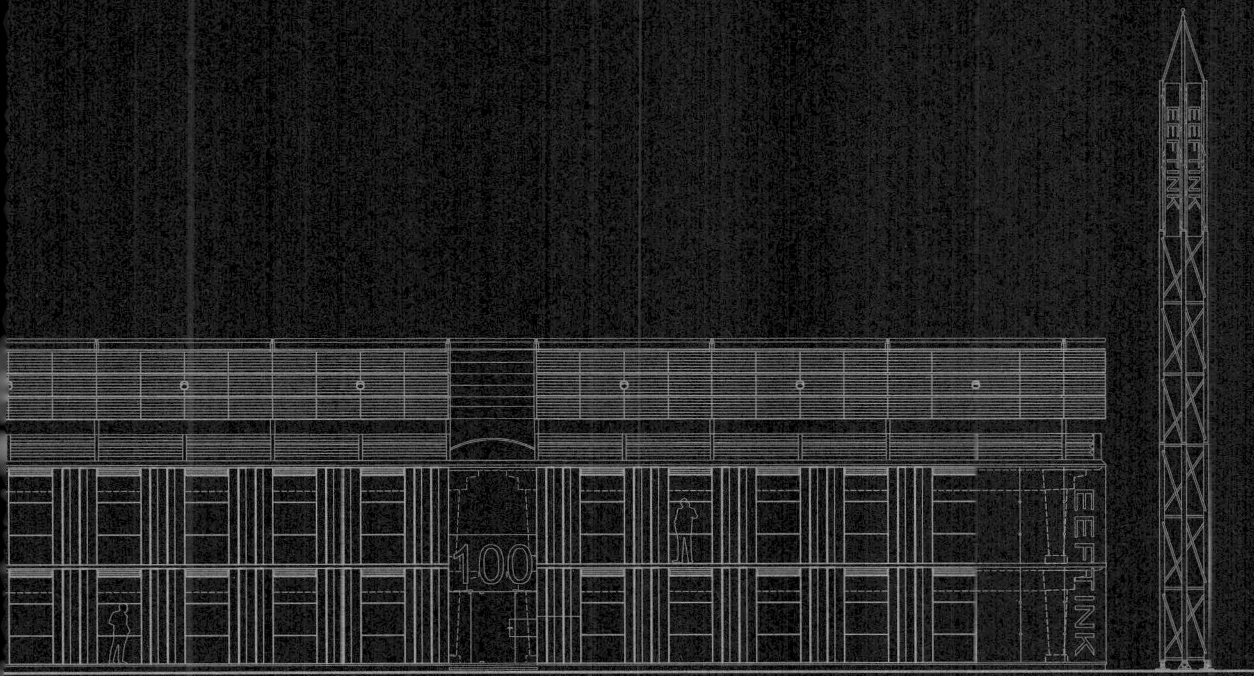

PdD

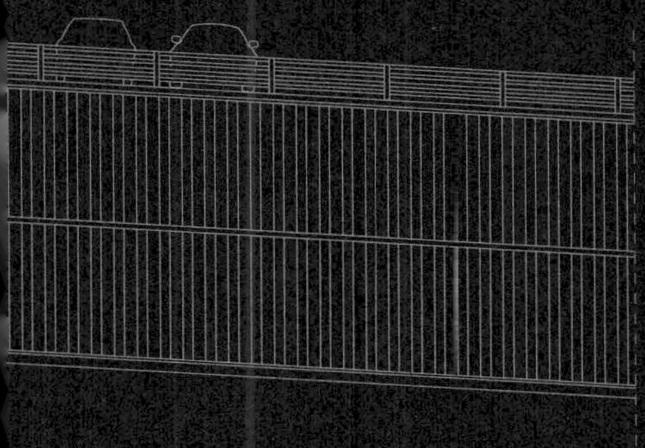

West elevation
1:200

.PdD

Even relatively new buildings in the Netherlands are prone to being altered, renovated and re-painted quite soon after completion. Why is it that the Dutch are unable to recognize the cultural value of buildings and cannot keep their hands off the buildings in which they live or work? HvH

IJdL.

name
Heightening housing blocks and construction of new dwellings

project code
IJdL

place
IJdoornlaan, Amsterdam Noord

client
Algemene Woningbouwvereniging

design
1996–1999

construction
2001–2003

design team
Joris Berger
Peter de Bruin
Dick de Gunst
Hans van Heeswijk
Arjen Honig

As part of a programme aimed at increasing the density of 1960s residential areas in Amsterdam-North, two storeys were added to two apartment blocks in an ensemble of five. In addition, an eleven-storey housing block was built at the short ends of both buildings.
The two porch-access buildings acquired an additional two floors of gallery-access flats. These galleries are linked to glass staircases between the old block and new tower. The composition of the 1960s porch-access flats, with their alternation of balcony/blank wall, was maintained in the added storeys. The use of prefabricated units speeded up construction and minimized inconvenience to existing residents.

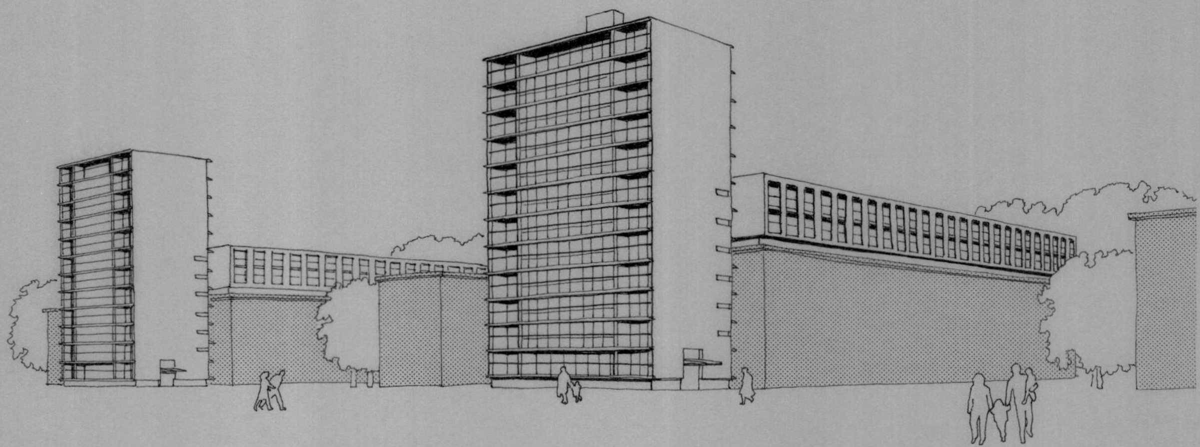

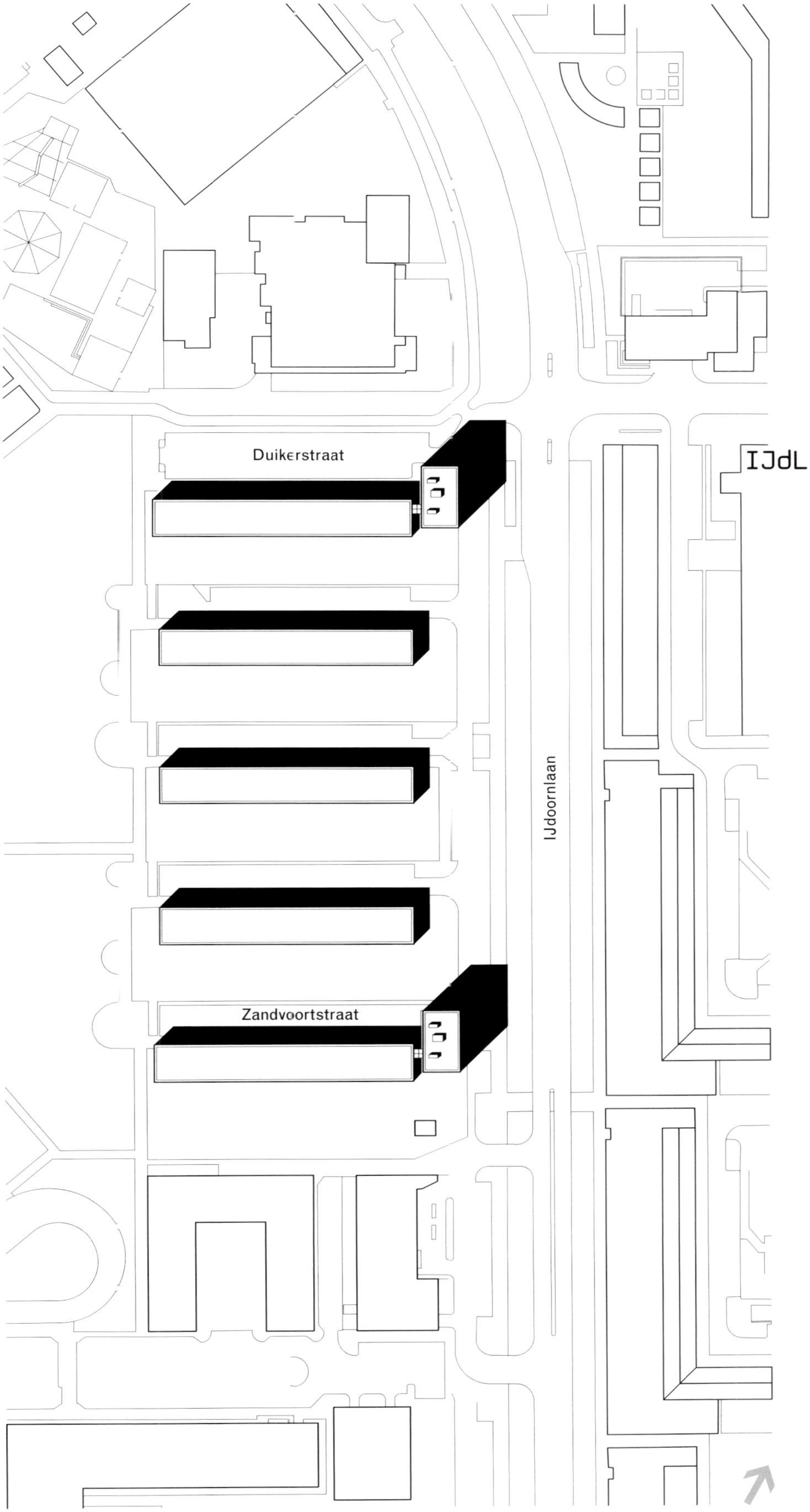
Duikerstraat
Zandvoortstraat
IJdoornlaan
IJdL

IJdL.block 05.LK

IJdL.block 06.LK

IJdL.block 08.LK

IJdL.block 09.LK

IJdL.block 04.LK

IJdL.block 03.LK

IJdL.side elevation 21.LK

IJdL.side elevation 24.LK

IJdL.street elevation tower 28.LK

IJdL.linking volumes 10.LK

IJdL.street elevation tower 29.LK

IJdL.side elevation 22.LK

IJdL.side elevation 23.LK

IJdL.linking volumes 11.LK

IJdL.linking volumes 12.LK

IJdL.street elevation tower 27.LK

IJdL.ground floor tower 18.LK

IJdL.elevation top up 15.LK

IJdL.gallery 16.LK

IJdL.gallery 17.LK

IJdL.stairs between building parts 26.LK

IJdL.placing topup unit 20.HvH

IJdL.placing top up unit 19.HvH

IJdL.3D block 01.HvH

IJdL.3D entrance 02.HvH

IJdL.detail loggia 13.HvH

IJdL.detail street facade tower 14.HvH

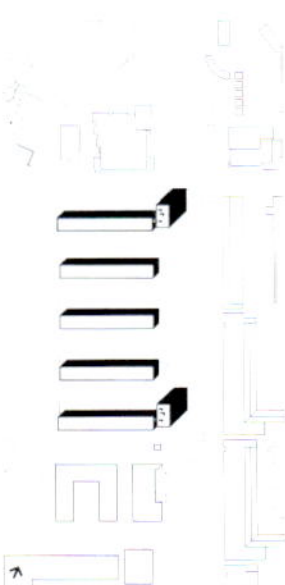

IJdL.situation

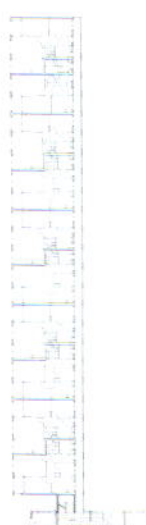

IJdL.floor plan

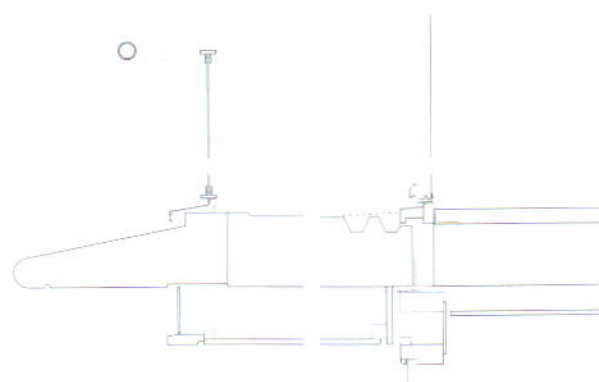

IJdL.detail loggia facade

IJdL

202.I

IJdL

204.1

6
5
4
3
2

The two extra storeys contain rental apartments. Each tower contains 19 owner-occupied dwellings: 18 apartments of 92 m² and a live-work unit consisting of a ground-floor workspace almost four metres high with its own street-level entrance, and a 110 m² living space on the first floor.

The original flats were so frugally constructed that the extra storeys could only be of very limited weight. Hence the choice of lightweight timber units with a flat aluminium cladding. The units rest on a steel structure that distributes the weight evenly. The space in between is used for all necessary pipes, wiring and building services.

The apartments in the towers look out onto IJdoornlaan through wide panorama windows and glassed-in verandas. From the higher floors there is a view of the IJsselmeer.

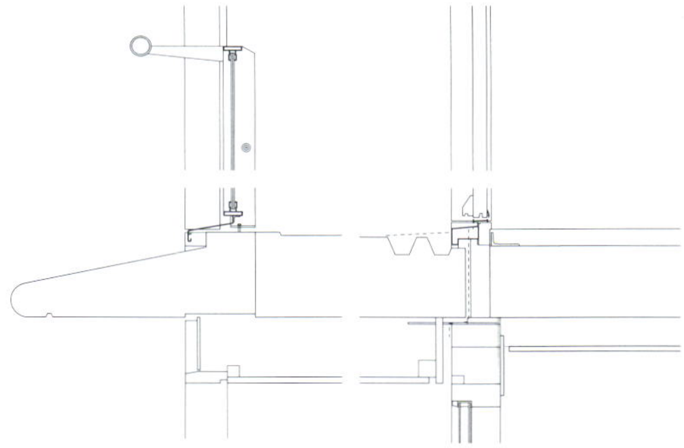

1:20

IJdL

Detail facade

02/41
44-FP-TV

Floor plan
1:400

Ship's cranes at Malaga, 1990

P1R.

name
Papendorp Bridge

project code
P1R

place
Amsterdam Rijnkanaal, Utrecht

client
Gemeente Utrecht

design
1997–1998

In collaboration with ABT, Schlaich Bergerman und Partner and West 8

design team
Andrew Dawes
Hans van Heeswijk
Ton Span
Jochem van der Spek

Between Nieuwegein and Diemen, the Amsterdam-Rhine canal is sleek and straight, with sheet pile walls for quays: a motorway for inland shipping. The Papendorp Bridge, designed by Hans van Heeswijk architecten for an invited competition, links two districts of Utrecht: Kanaleneiland and the new Papendorp district in Leidsche Rijn. As well as providing a traffic link for cyclists, trams and cars, the bridge was also required to symbolize the unity of the two districts.
The design of the Papendorp Bridge is characterized by a curved shell construction with reptilian connotations. This particular reptile makes a giant leap from Papendorp over the water to Kanaleneiland; its snout and tail extend beyond the banks.
The construction is asymmetrical in both elevation and section and it is this that gives the bridge its direction. The deck is split into three, for the different types of traffic, allowing light to penetrate below the bridge.
The structure, a combination of arch and shell, is new to the Netherlands. The main supporting structure is designed in steel, the bridge deck is a combination of steel and concrete. The materials and colours reinforce the expression of the general shape and the spatial and structural principles.

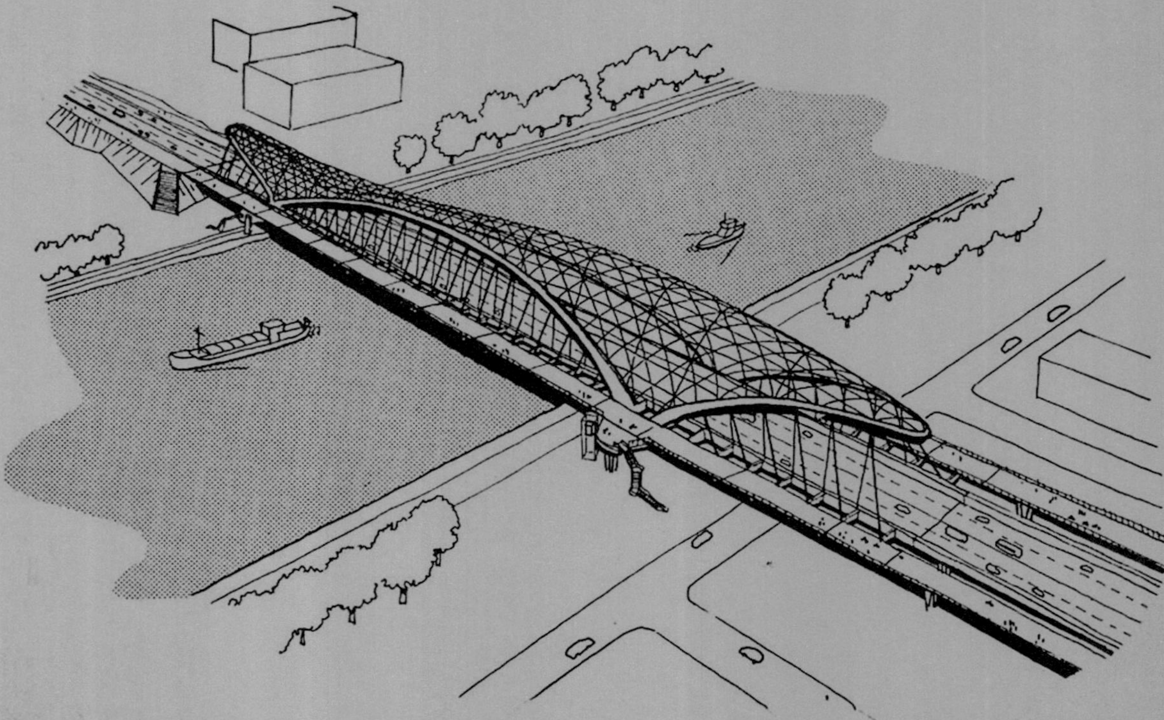

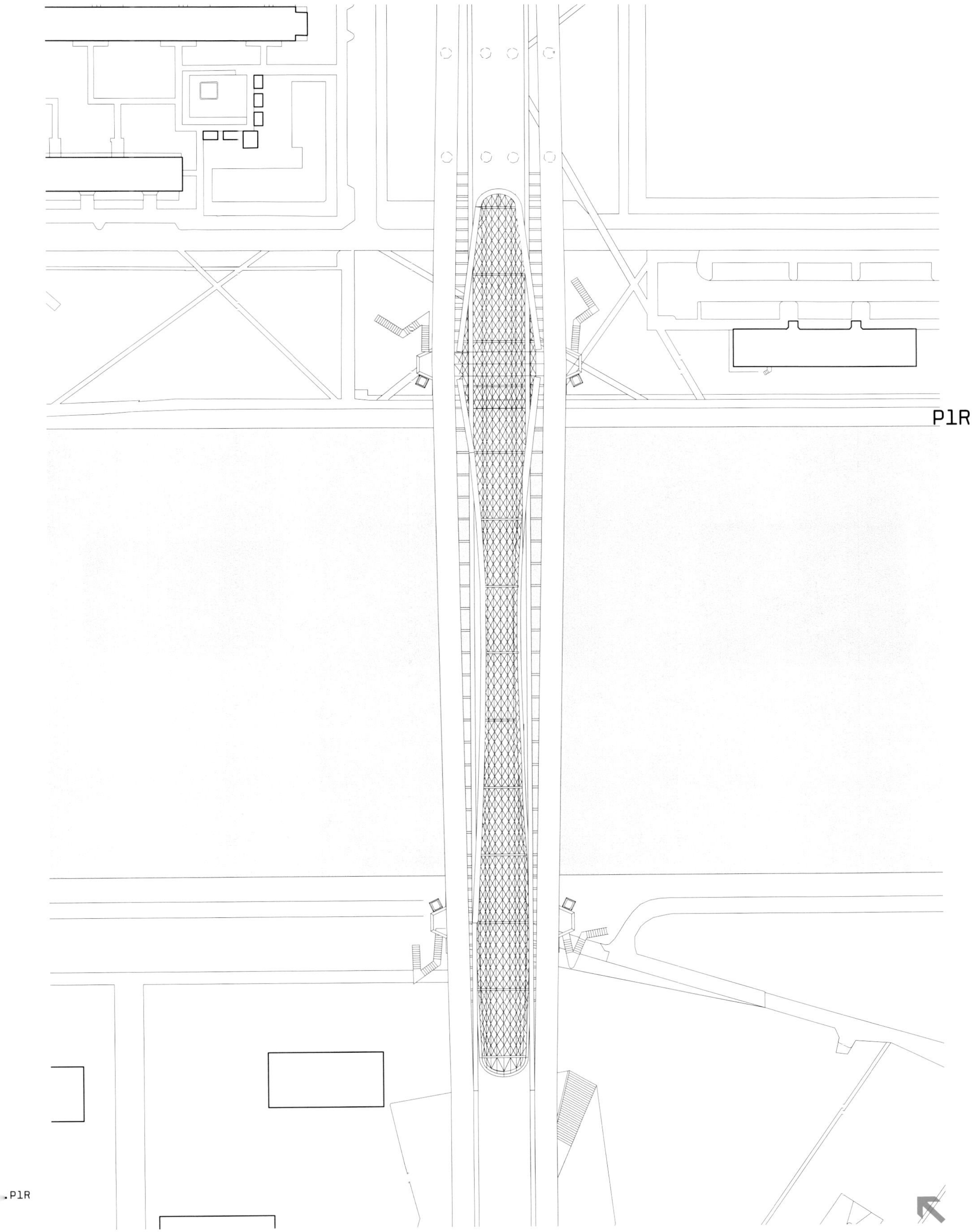

P1R
P1R

P1R.day view.PB

P1R.day view 2.PB

P1R.night view.PB

P1R.sunset.PB

P1R.fragment side.PB

P1R.fragment under.PB

P1R.fragment.PB

P1R.cross section.PB

P1R.model.HvH

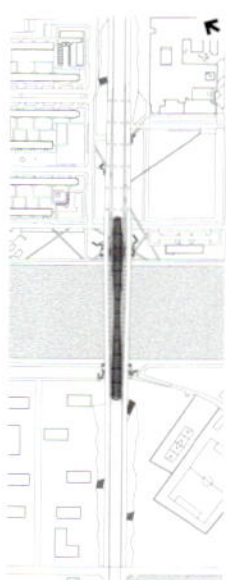

P1R.situation

P1R.elevation

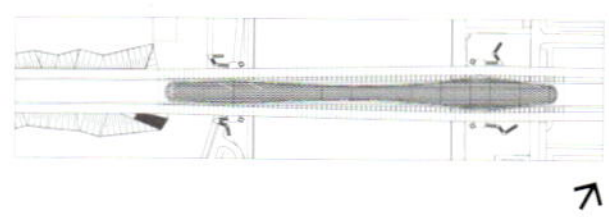

P1R.top view

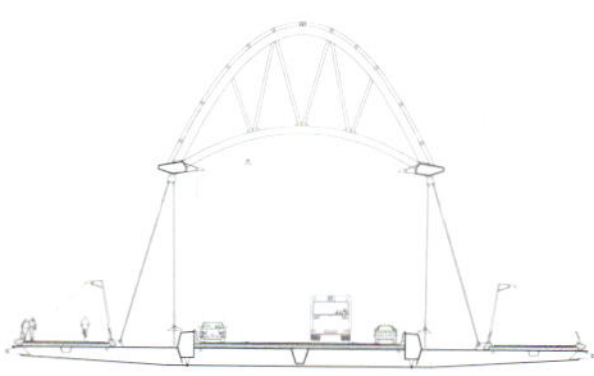

P1R.section 1

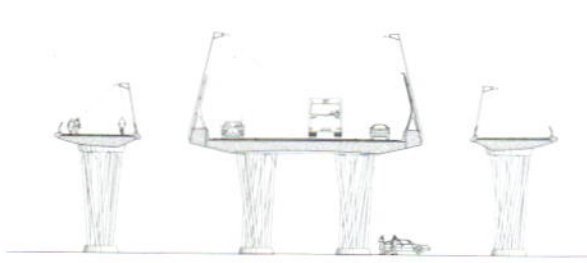

P1R.section 2

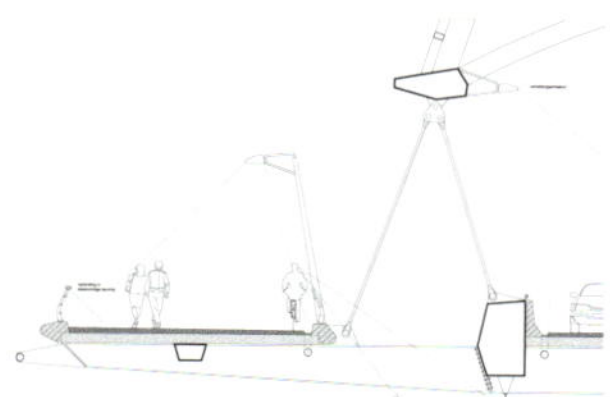

P1R.section fragment

P1R

P1R

The three-dimensional structure is formed by latticework shells made up of box sections with tubular edge girders. The deck hangs from the edges of the shells on steel rods.

P1R

.P1R

P1R

P1R

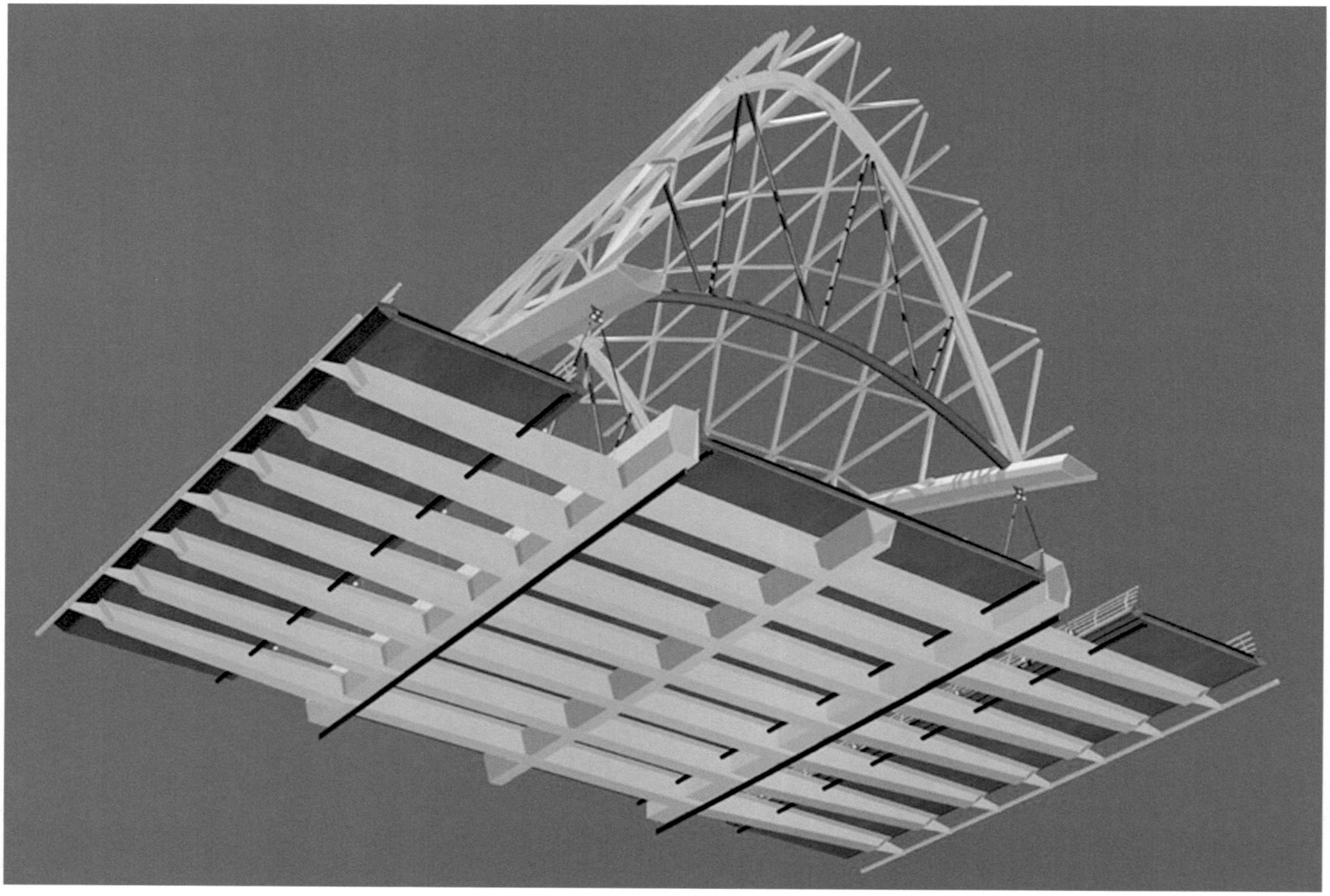

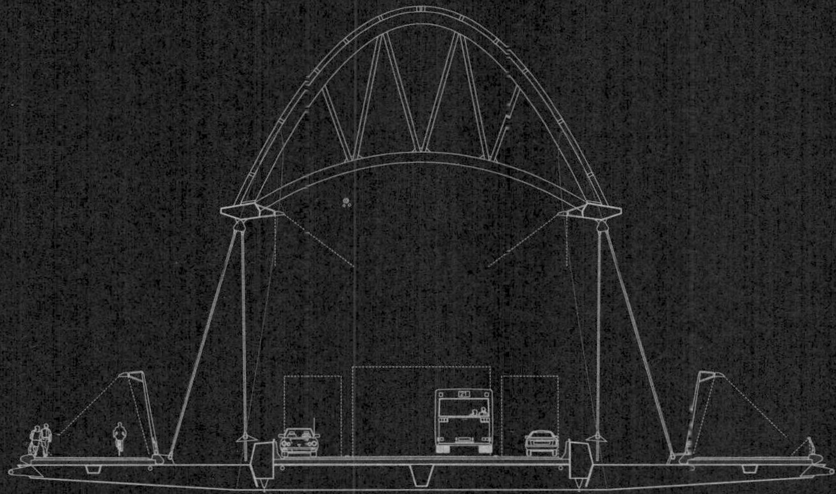

Section main supporting structure
1:400

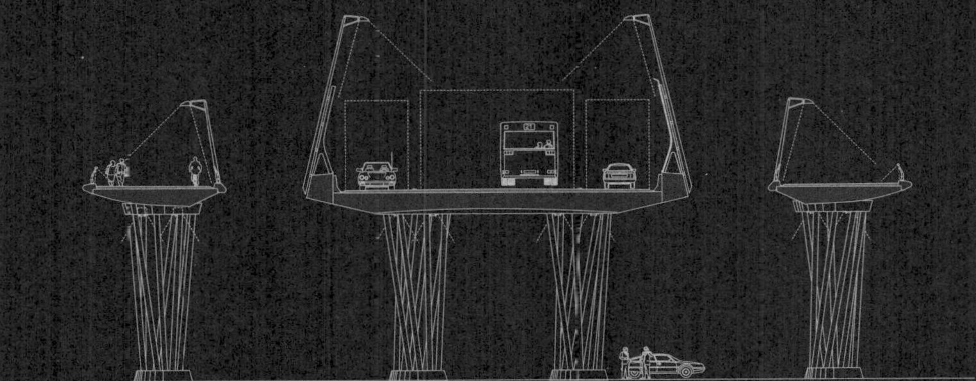

Section bridge beginning
1:400

The main span is over 150 metres long; the road deck is 33 metres wide.

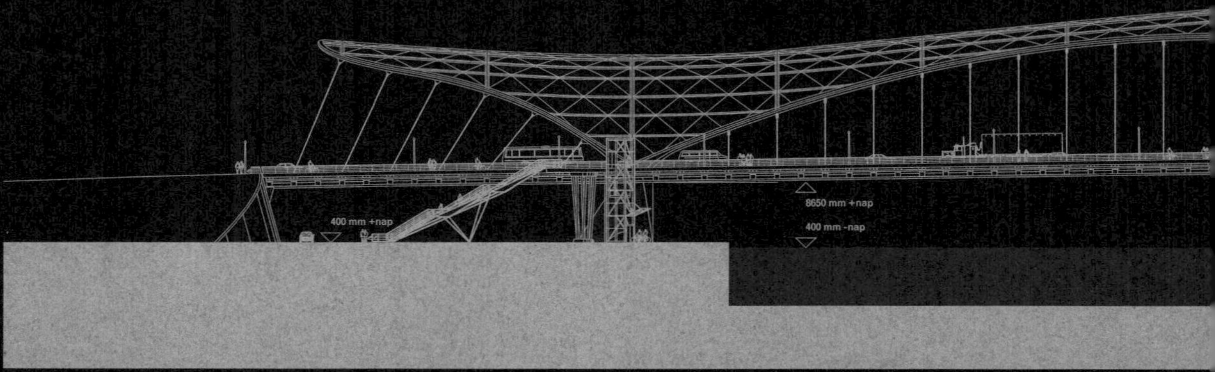

Side view
1:1000

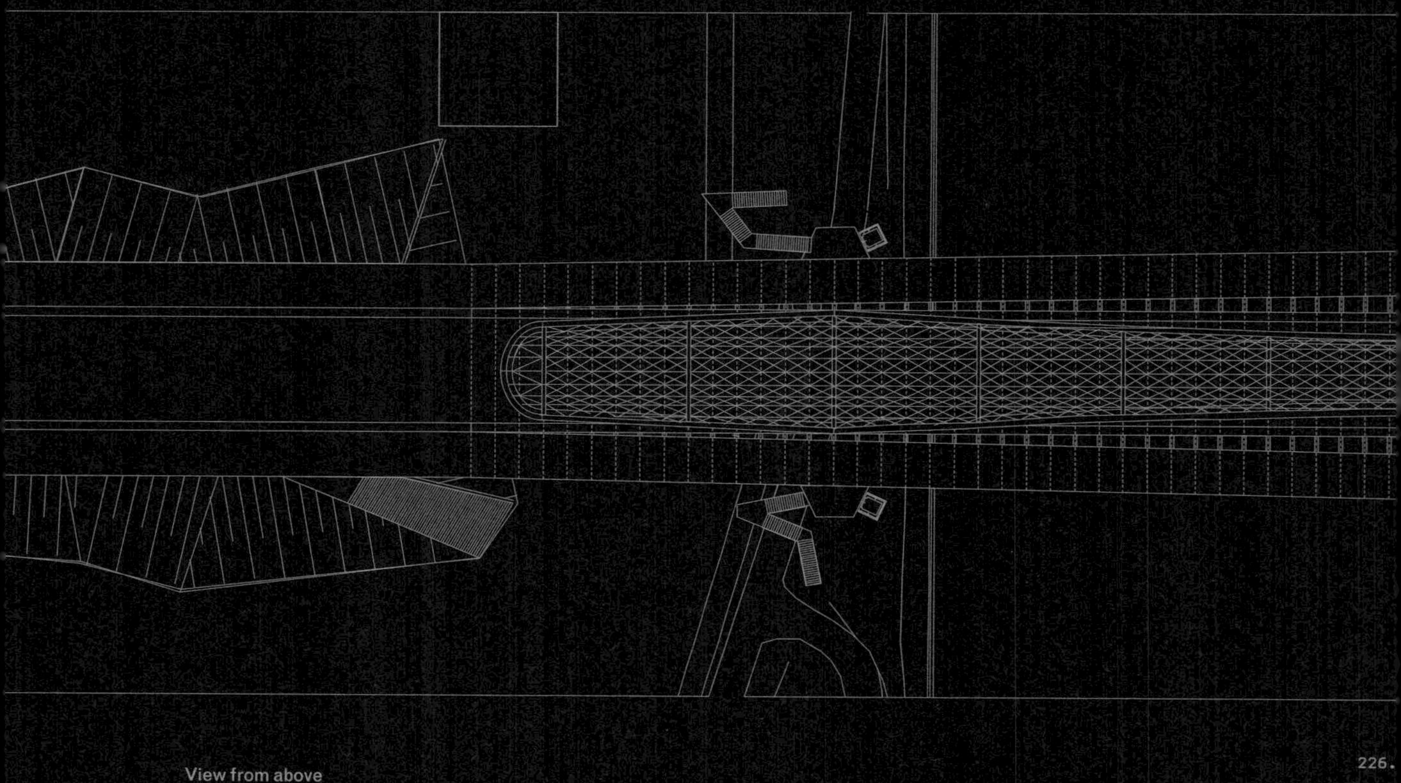

View from above
1:1000

P1R

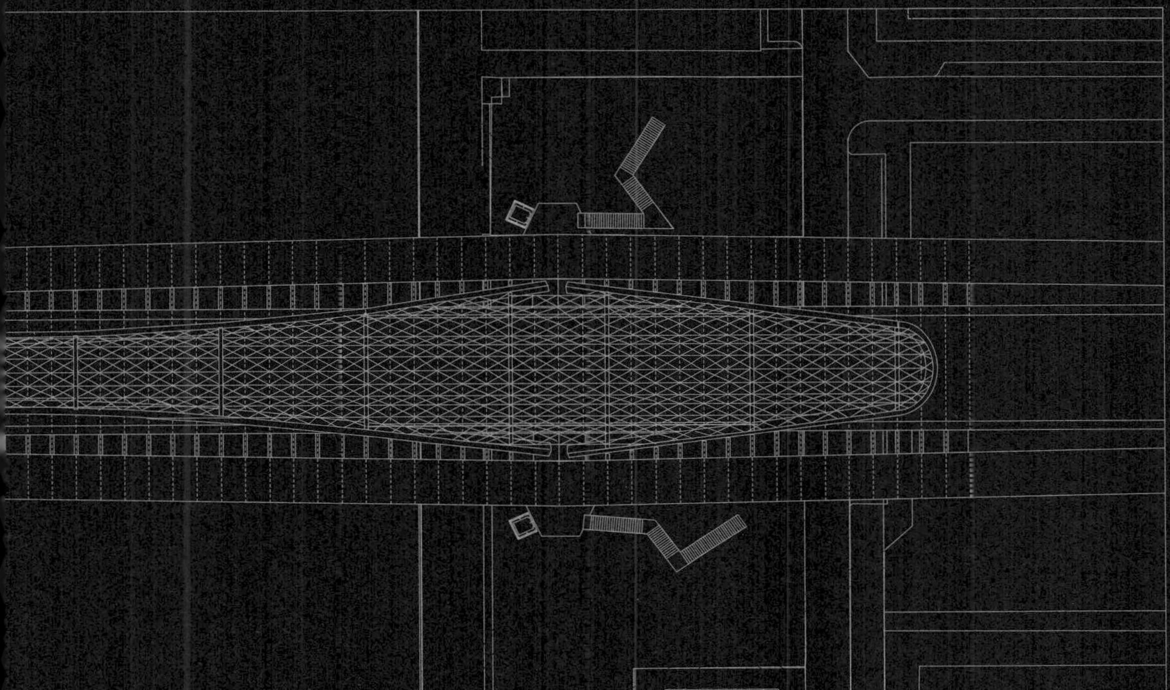

.P1R

Ship's superstructure

OkD.
OkT.

name
Bolkestein Bridge/
Snipperling Bridge,
Deventer

project code
OkD/OkT

place
Overijssels Kanaal,
Deventer

client
Gemeente Deventer

design
1999

construction
2000 – 2001

design team
Dick de Gunst
Stephanie Haumann
Hans van Heeswijk

The City of Deventer commissioned two bridges over the Overijssel Canal: the Bolkestein Bridge in the Vijfhoek district, and the Snipperling Bridge at Snipperlingsdijk.
The Bolkestein Bridge is a concrete and steel arch bridge for motorized traffic. Cyclists and pedestrians use an adjacent bascule bridge. The one inbound/three outbound lane arrangement is reflected in an unevenly divided bridge deck. The main arch is placed at an angle in the opening between the two sections. This arch supports the bridge together with a smaller, oblique side arch on the side of the wide deck section. The narrow section cantilevers out from the main arch.
The separation of traffic is even more rigorous with the Snipperlings Bridge. This bridge consists of two concrete bridges for motorized traffic, one for each direction. Alongside is a separate steel bridge for cyclists and pedestrians. This bridge is based on the same principle as the Bolkestein Bridge. The cambered bridge deck has a span of 27 metres and is divided into a cycle and a pedestrian section. The arch of this bridge stands structurally separate between the two sections of the bridge deck. Cross girders in the deck supply the structural link between the pedestrian and cyclist sections and transfer the load via hangers to the arch. The combination of the slightly angled arch and the tie rods of solid round-bar steel gives the bridge a distinctive appearance.
The division of the bridges into multiple decks creates voids that expose the structure and the water below, underscoring the nature and function of bridges.

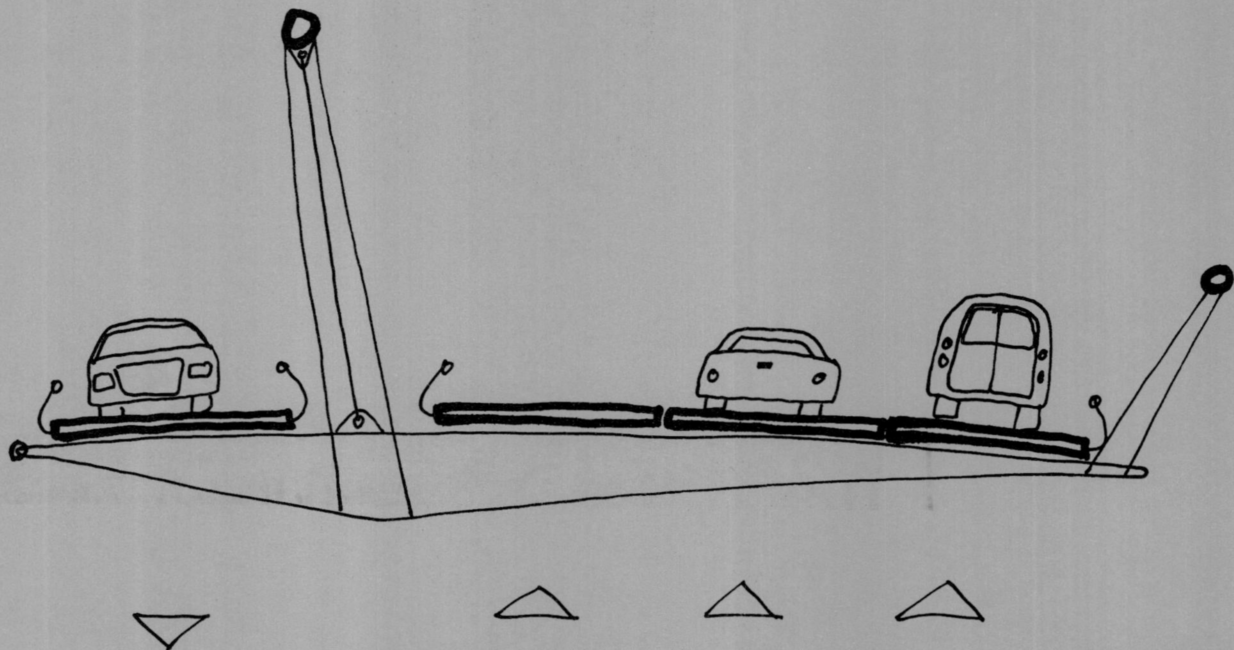

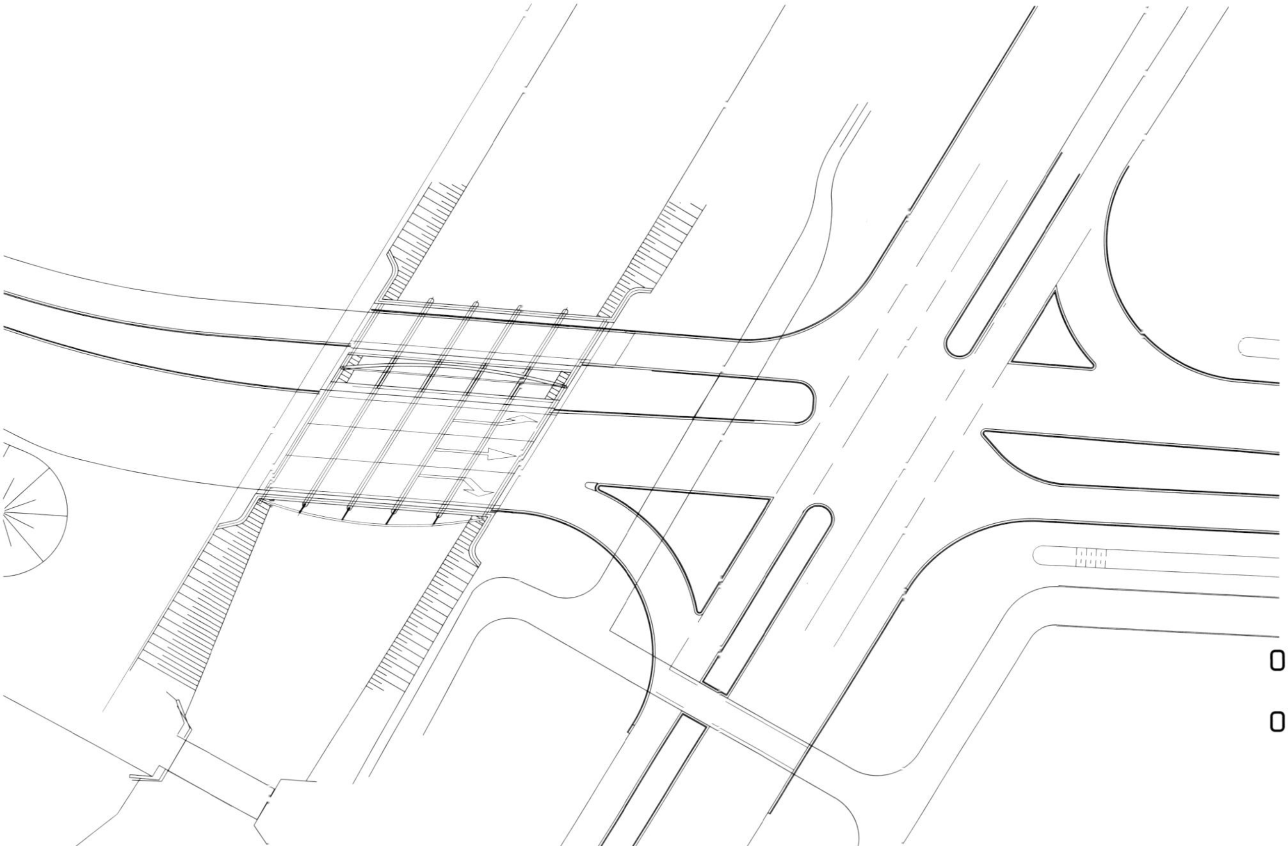

Site plan Bolkestein Bridge

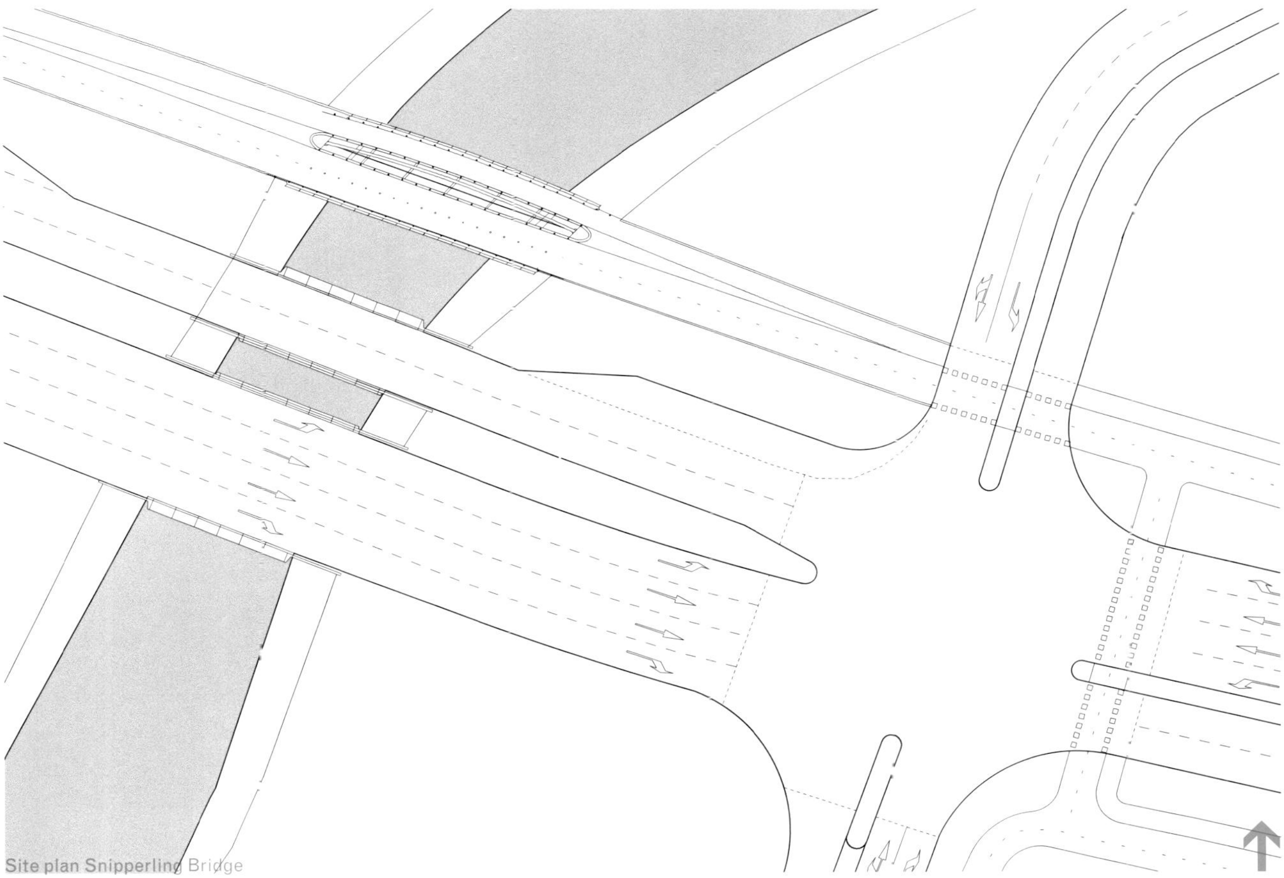

Site plan Snipperling Bridge

OkD.Bolkesteinbrug overview 06.LK

OkD.Bolkesteinbrug overview 22.LK

OkD.Bolkesteinbrug railing 10.LK

OkD.Bolkesteinbrug void 07.LK

OkD.Bolkesteinbrug span 23.LK

OkD.Bolkesteinbrug construction 20.HvH

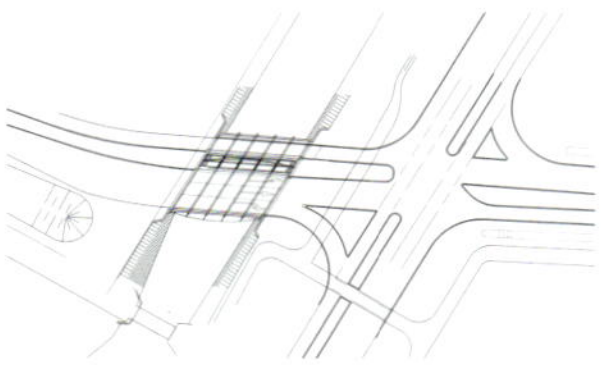

OkD.situation Bolkesteinbrug

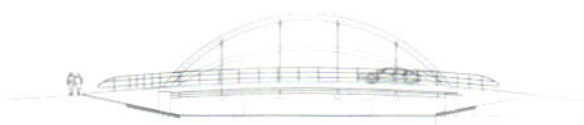

OkD.elevation Bolkesteinbrug

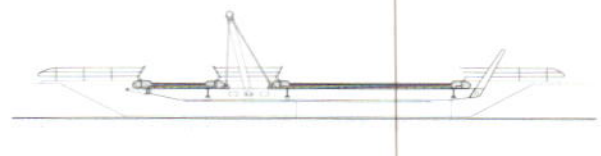

OkD.section Bolkesteinbrug

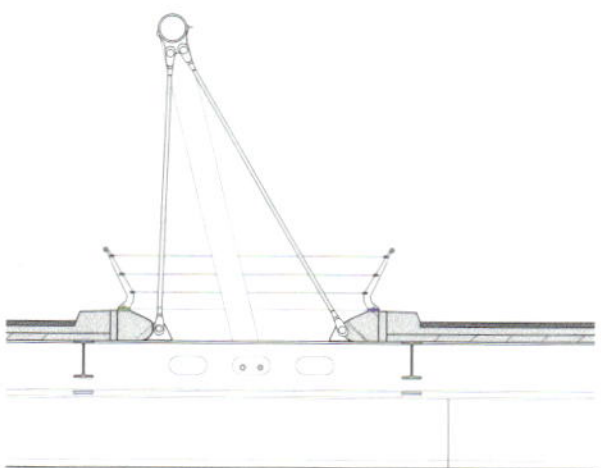

OkD.section detail Bolkesteinbrug

OkT.Snipperlingsbrug overview 01.RR

OkT.Snipperlingsbrug overview 02.RR

OkT.Snipperlingsbrug overview 03.HvH

OkT.Snipperlingsbrug overview 04.RR

OkT.Snipperlingsbrug overview 05.RR

OkT.Snipperlingsbrug railing 12.DG

OkT.Snipperlingsbrug railing 13.DG

OkT.Snipperlingsbrug void 21.RR

OkT.Snipperlingsbrug void 11.RR

OkT.Snipperlingsbrug railing 14.DG

OkT.Snipperlingsbrug railing 15.DG

OkT.Snipperlingsbrug void 08.DG

OkT.Snipperlingsbrug void 09.DG

OkT.Snipperliongsbrug detail 16.DG

OkT.Snipperlingsbrug construction 17.PB

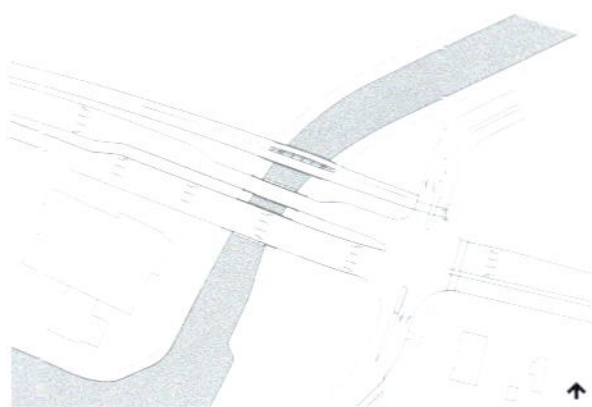

OkT.situation Snipperlingsbrug

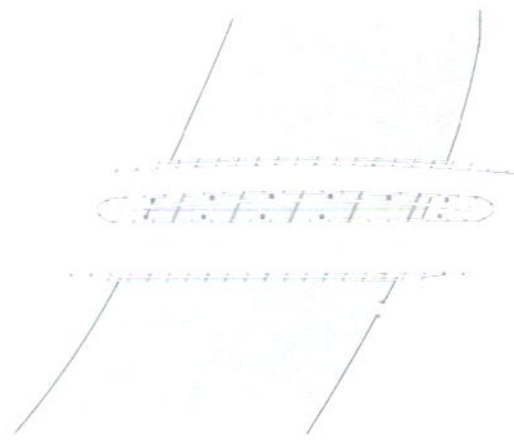

OkT.plan Snipperlingstrug cyclists

OkT.section 3 bridges Snipperlingsbrug

OkT.elevation carbridge Snipperlingsbrug

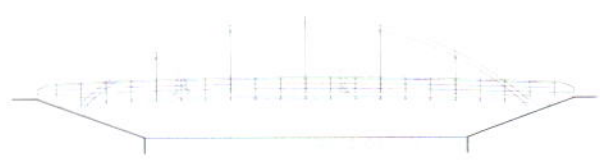

OkT.elevation cyclebridge Snipperlingsbrug

Bolkestein Bridge. The main span is 22 metres long.

Bolkestein Bridge

Colmschaterstraatweg
huisnummers
34-36-38-40
bereikbaar

The 3.7-metre-high central arch of the Bolkestein Bridge consists of a thick-walled tube approximately 40 centimetres across. The arch is stabilized by four pairs of hangers consisting of solid round bars. These hangers are connected by cross girders in the bridge deck. The 2.3-metre-high side arch is a thick-walled tube with a diameter of 35 centimetres.

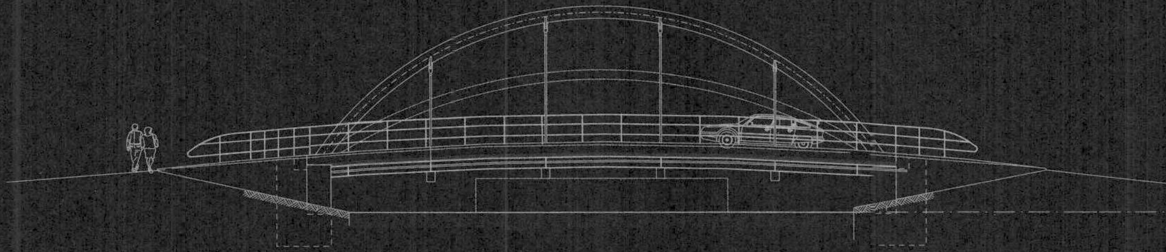

Side view Bolkestein Bridge
1:200

OkD

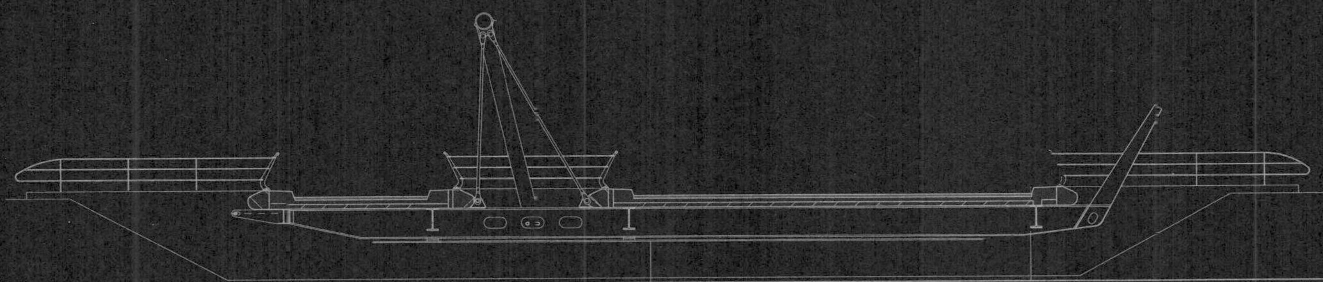

Section Bolkestein Bridge
1:200

Part section Bolkestein Bridge
1:50

Snipperling Bridge. The main span is 27 metres long.

OKT

Snipperling Bridge

Snipperling Bridge

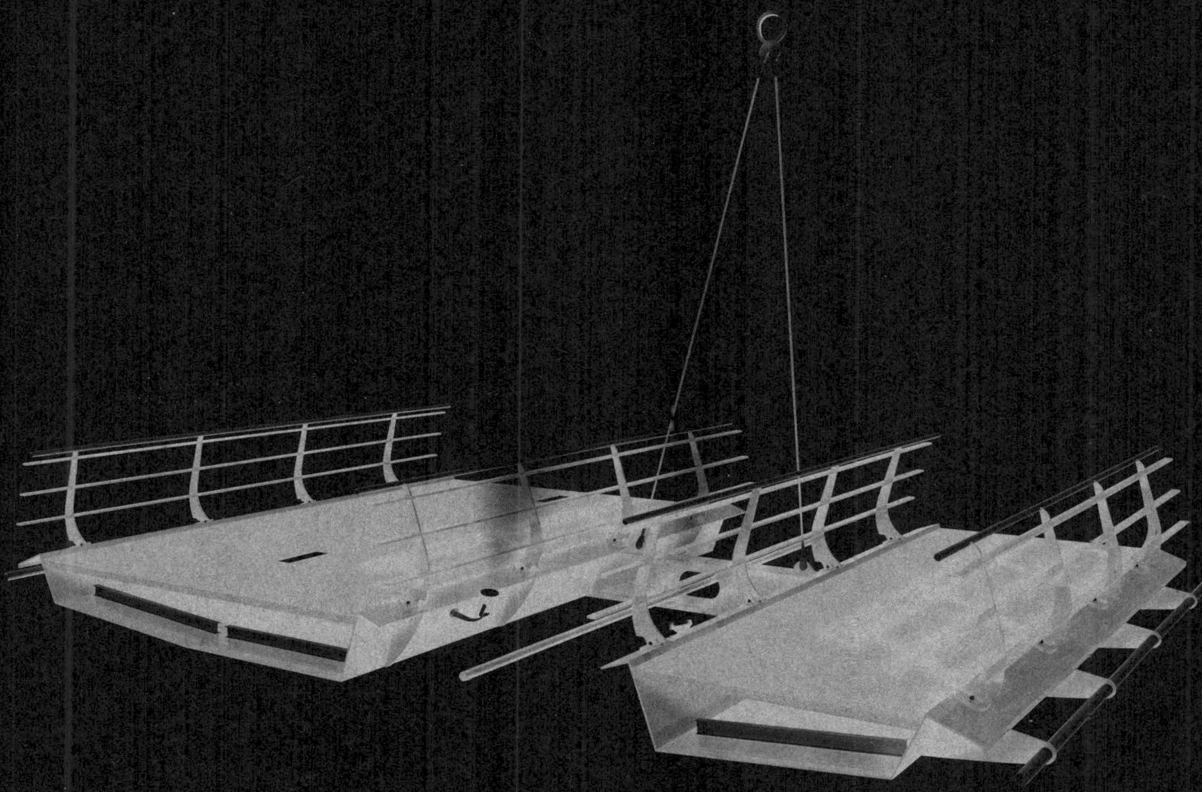

OkT

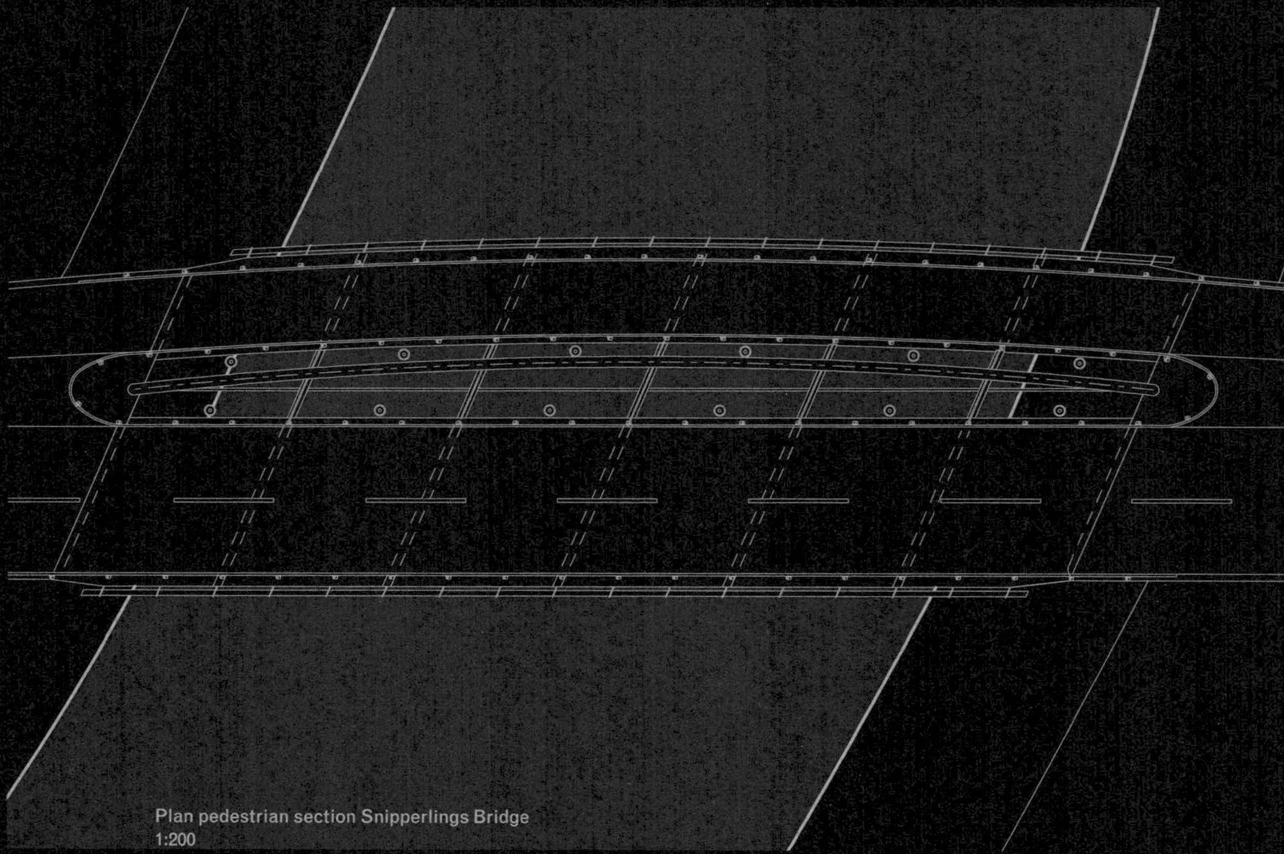

Plan pedestrian section Snipperlings Bridge
1:200

The three sections of the Snipperlings Bridge
1:400

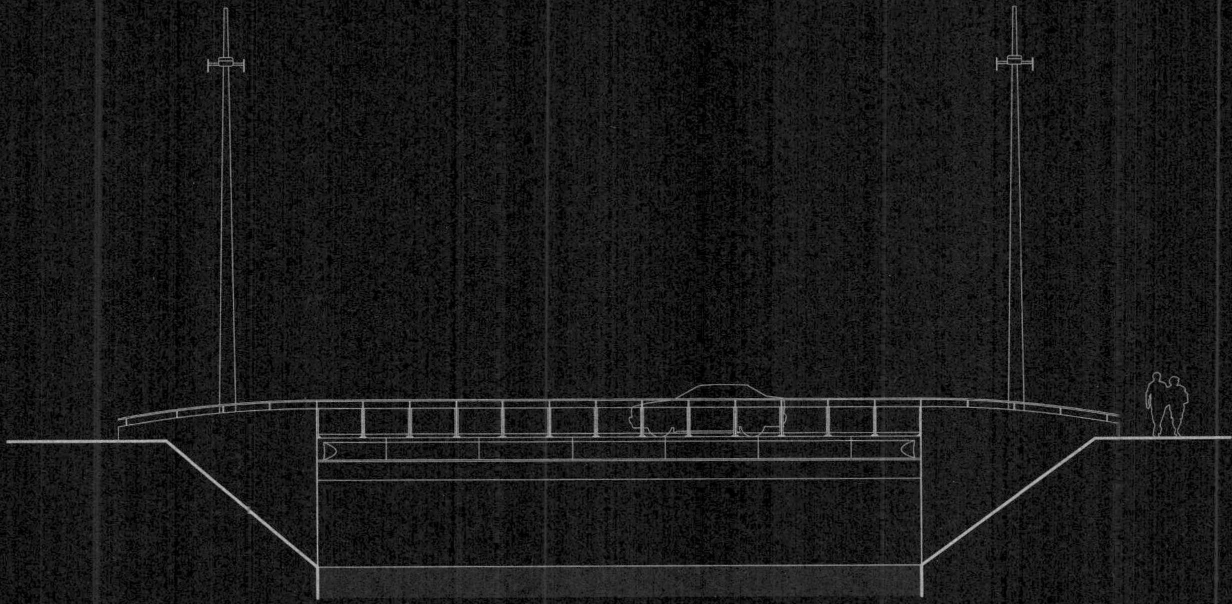

Side view motorized section Snipperlings Bridge
1:200

OkT

Side view pedestrian secticn Snipperlings Bridge
1:200

Het Kanaal sea platform, 1978

NbZ.

name
Alteration and renovation of Noordwachter, Brandaris and IJdoorn

project code
NbZ

place
Hoogaarslaan, Javazee en Noordzee, Zaandam

client
Woningstichting Patrimonium Amsterdam/Zaandam

original building
1969

design
1997

construction
1998–1999

number of dwellings
163 in Noordwachter
192 in IJdoorn
363 in Brandaris
744 dwellings in total

design team
Dick de Gunst
Stephanie Haumann
Hans van Heeswijk
Ton Span
Jochem van de Spek

Noordwachter, IJdoorn and Brandaris are three large apartment buildings which stand, together with two other blocks of flats, along the A8 motorway in Zaandam. Plans for a much-needed noise barrier and a major overhaul of the 744 flats in the three buildings were combined, with the noise barrier budget being invested in a sound-insulating facade. As a result, inhospitable balconies were turned into congenial glassed-in verandas.
The flats were built in the late 1960s using large precast concrete elements. The lack of load bearing internal walls made it fairly easy to carry out quite radical alterations. Because sun reflecting off the glazed facade would have posed a danger to motorway traffic, the glass facade on each floor is canted outwards. This also serves to reduce reflection from within, as well as enhancing the spaciousness of the former balcony and the view.
The renovations were seized upon as an opportunity to increase the buildings' sustainability and to reduce their energy consumption. The most visible evidence of this are the solar collectors and sustainable energy information centre on the roof of Brandaris.

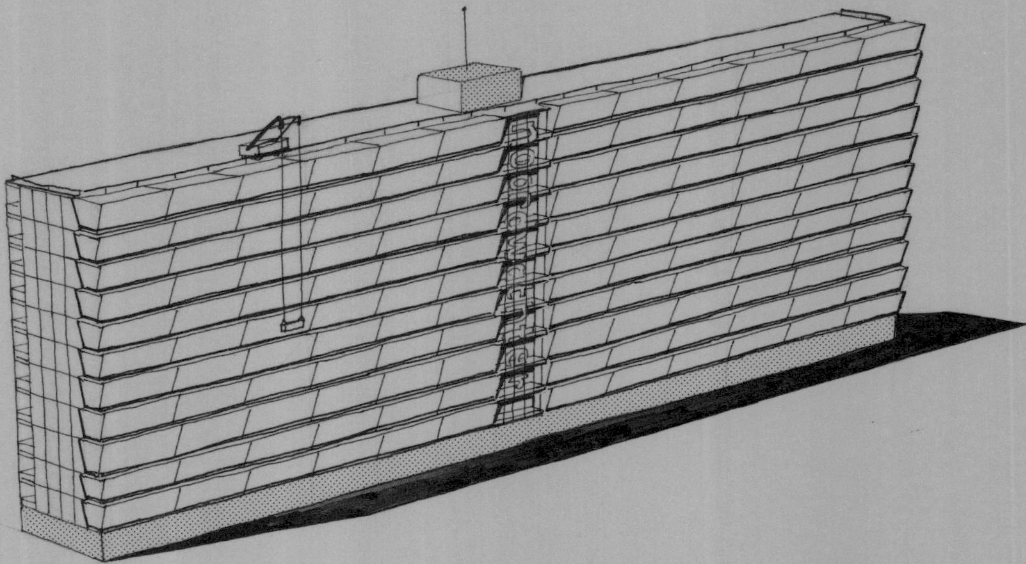

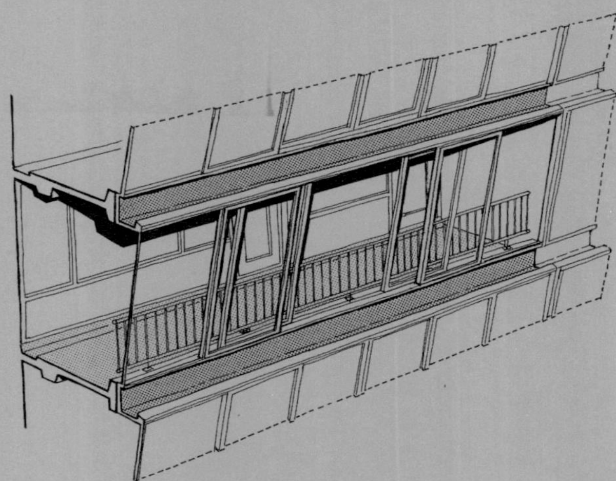

6.NbZ

NbZ.existing flat 1.HvH

NbZ.existing flat 3.HvH

NbZ.view highway 04.LK

NbZ.view highway 03.HvH

NbZ.elevation 05.LK

NbZ.entrance 08.LK

NbZ.entrance 09.LK

NbZ.entrance dwelling 10.LK

NbZ.veranda elevation 11.LK

NbZ.veranda corner 12.HvH

NbZ.veranda corner 13.LK

NbZ.roof pavilion 24.HvH

NbZ.roof 22.LK

NbZ.roof 23.LK

NbZ.roof pavilion 25.LK

NbZ.roof pavilion 25.LK

NbZ.roof pavilion 27.DG

NbZ.street 20.DG

NbZ.veranda detail 15.HvH

NbZ.veranda detail 16.HvH

NbZ.veranda detail 17.HvH

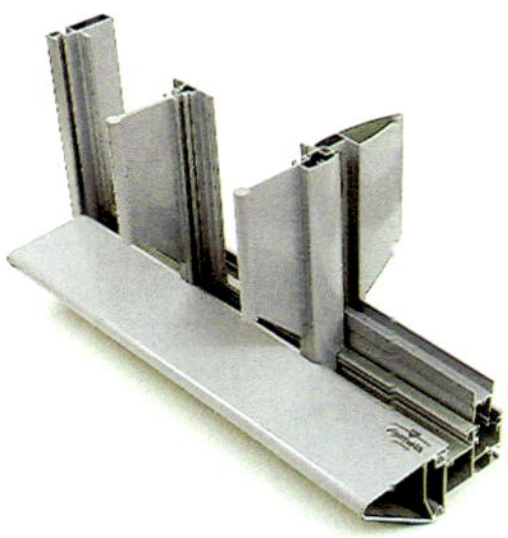

NbZ.veranda detail 14.HvH

NbZ.situation

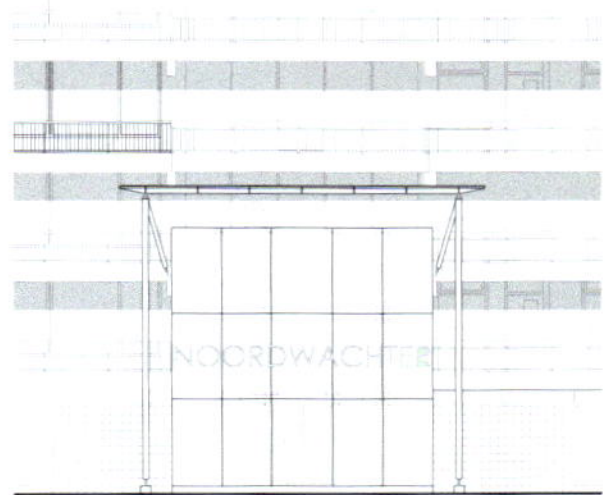

NbZ.entrance facade

NbZ

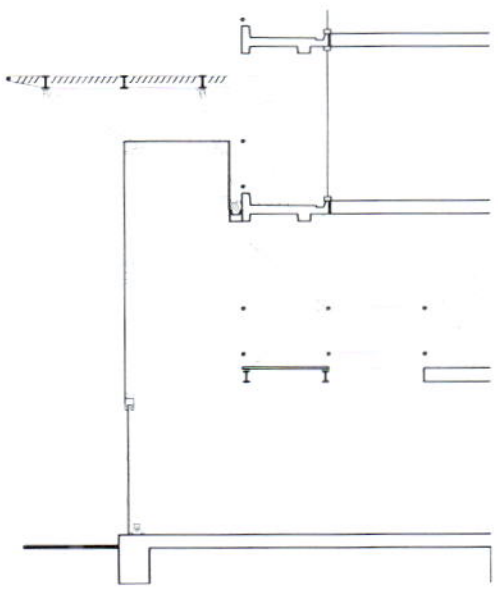

NbZ.section entrance

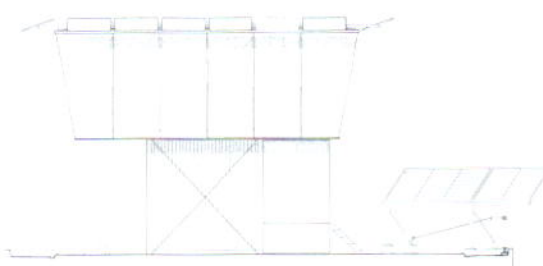

NbZ.elevation pavilion south

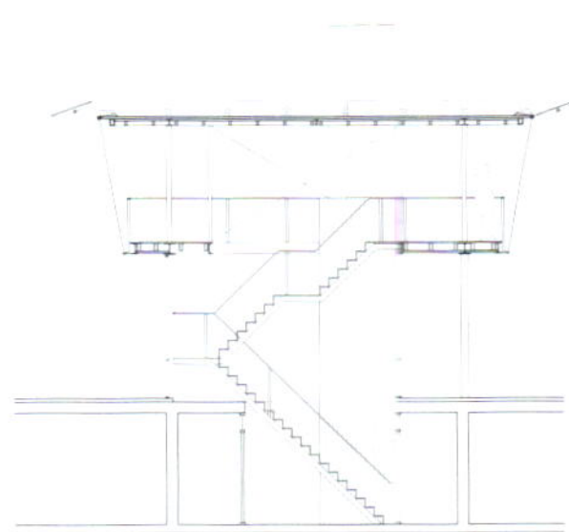

NbZ.section pavilion

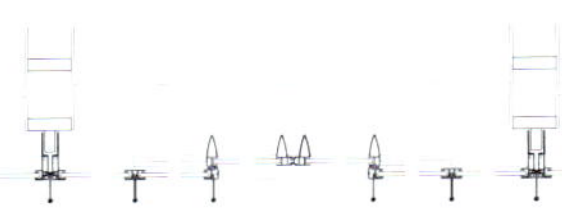

NbZ.horizontal detail serre

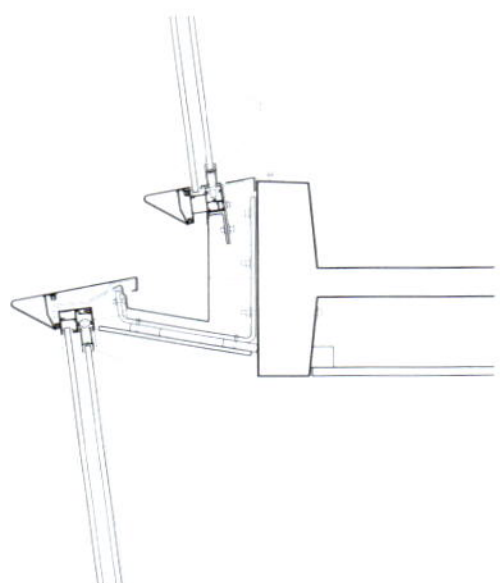

NbZ.vertical detail serre

NbZ.section serre

.NbZ

NbZ

The smooth surface of the end elevation accentuates the building's size whereas the jagged rhythm of the angled verandas reintroduces the human scale.

NbZ

The entrances were renovated as well. The new entrances have a slender steel construction that guarantees optimal transparency.

3.NbZ

The verandas have floor-to-ceiling sliding doors that allow 33 per cent of the glass surface to be opened. This means that residents can enjoy the sun while, with sliding doors closed, the cavity created between the single glazing of the outer facade and the existing balcony wall muffles traffic noise and reduces heat loss.

NbZ

At the corners of the balconies, the glass of the veranda facade is joined with structural glue. This, together with the continuous, sharp-edged rail of the storey-high glass front delivers crisp, open corners with a panoramic view.

New window frames that impact as little as possible on the view were developed in collaboration with a manufacturer of aluminium frames. The slender junctions, which have an elliptical cross-section, derive their strength from the depth of the frame. A special mounting ensures that the sliding doors open and close smoothly and silently.

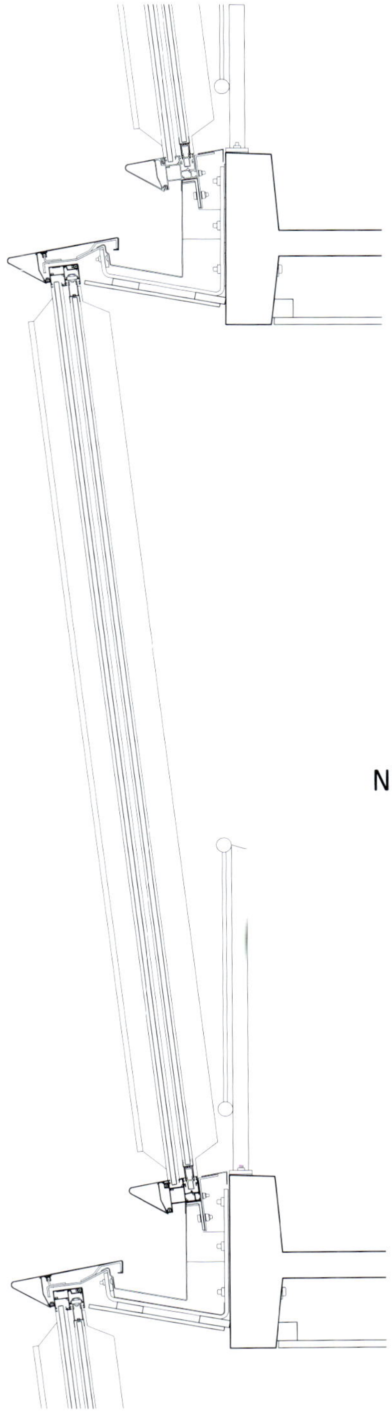

1:20

NbZ

Detail veranda facade

Detail veranda facade

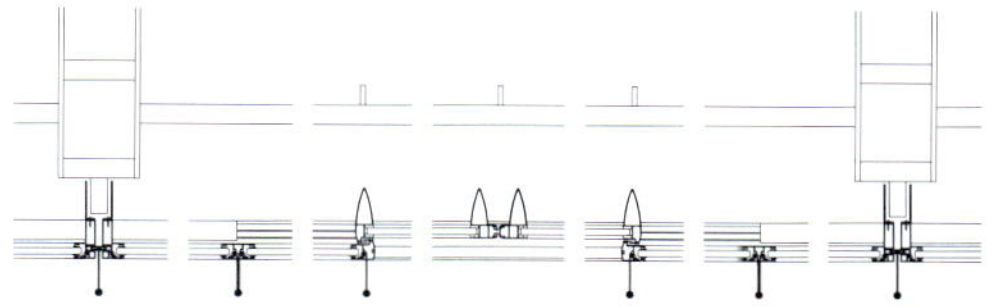

1:20

NbZ

1:20

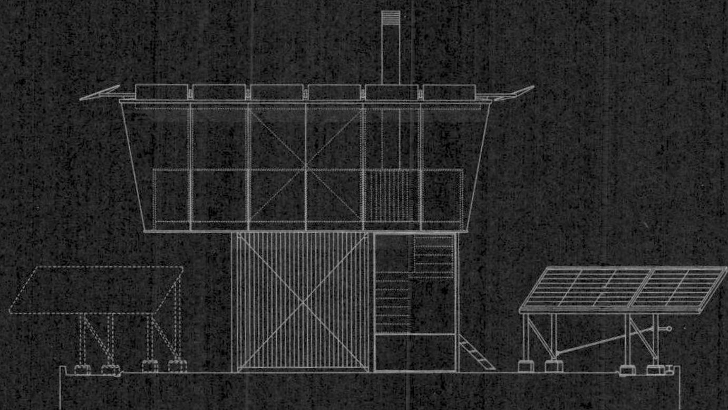

Information centre on the roof of Brandaris, elevation
1:120

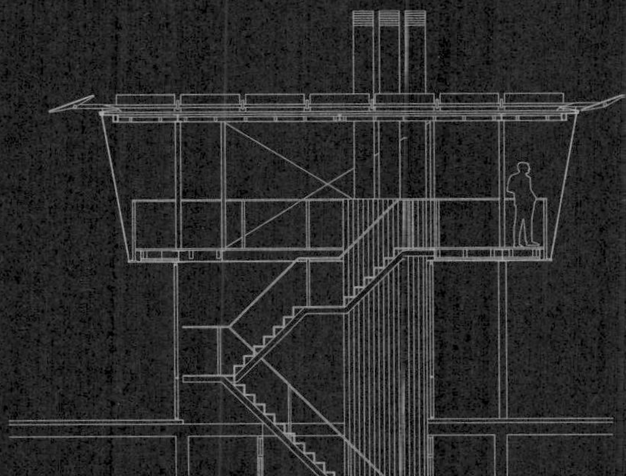

Information centre on the roof of Brandaris, section
1:120

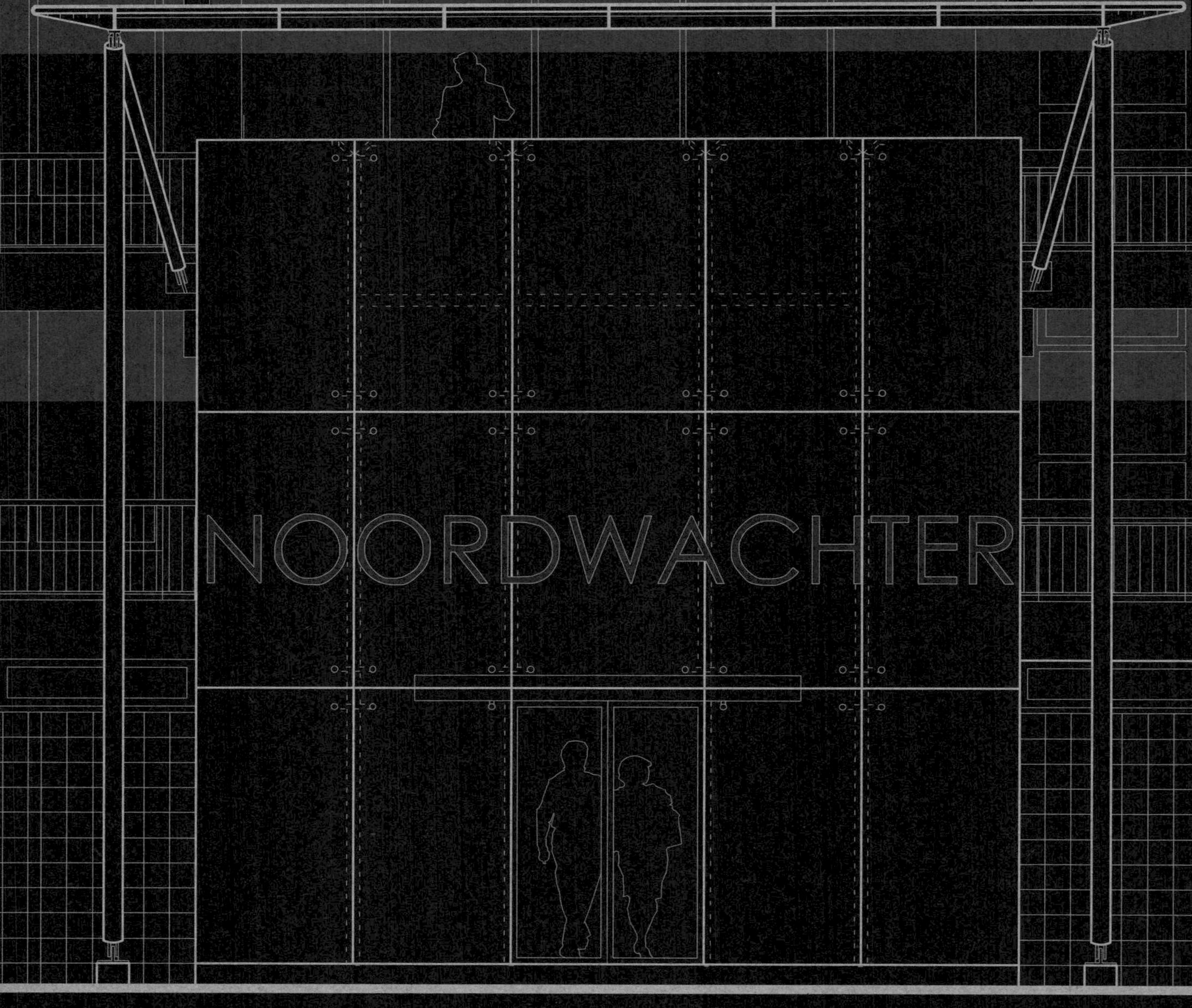

Facade main entrance

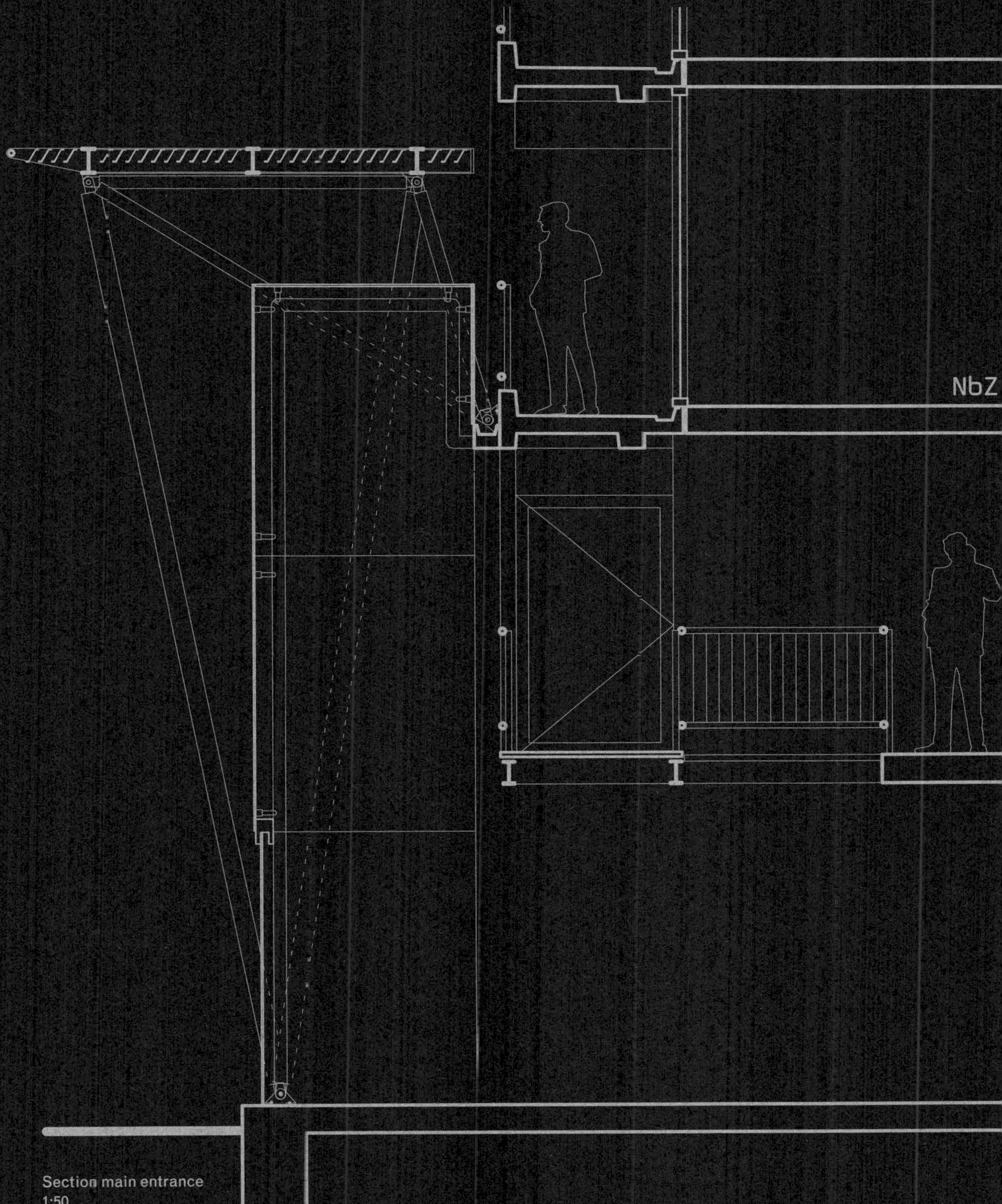

Section main entrance
1:50

Ertskade with view of Ersthaven, 1930

SpA.

name
Office premises and gymnasium on Sporenburg

project code
SpA

place
Ertskade 105–111, Amsterdam

client
Ontwikkelingsmaatschappij New Deal bv, Amsterdam

design
1997

construction
1999–2000

design team
Ellen Baan
Floris van Gennep
Hans van Heeswijk
Ton Span
Meike Stoetser
Joost Woertman

On the corner of Ertskade, on the north side of the Sporenburg quay in Amsterdam's Eastern Docklands, a building containing a gymnasium and office space stands in the middle of low-rise housing. In the spatial master plan for Sporenburg, a leftover plot of land measuring 17 by 34 metres was earmarked for a gymnasium for a nearby school. The stipulated building envelope offers more cubic metres than were required for the gym. The rest was turned into office space and subsequently occupied by Hans van Heeswijk architecten. The gymnasium, which required a closed space, follows the dictates of the master plan and is executed in brick to match the closed facades of the neighbouring housing. The office section eschews this solution and has a glazed facade composed of a timber frame filled alternately with transparent and frosted sheets of glass. Thanks to the transparency of the facade, office users are treated to an impressive view of the open waters of the Ertshaven and the IJ and the cloudscapes above. At night the building is a beacon in the area.

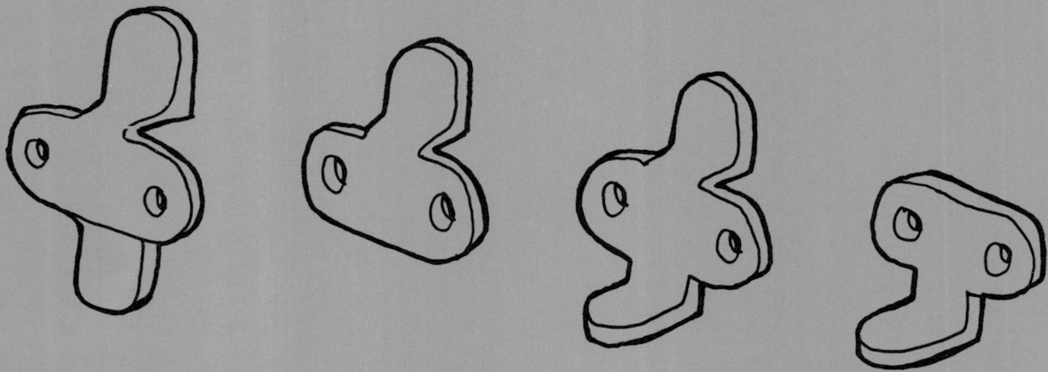

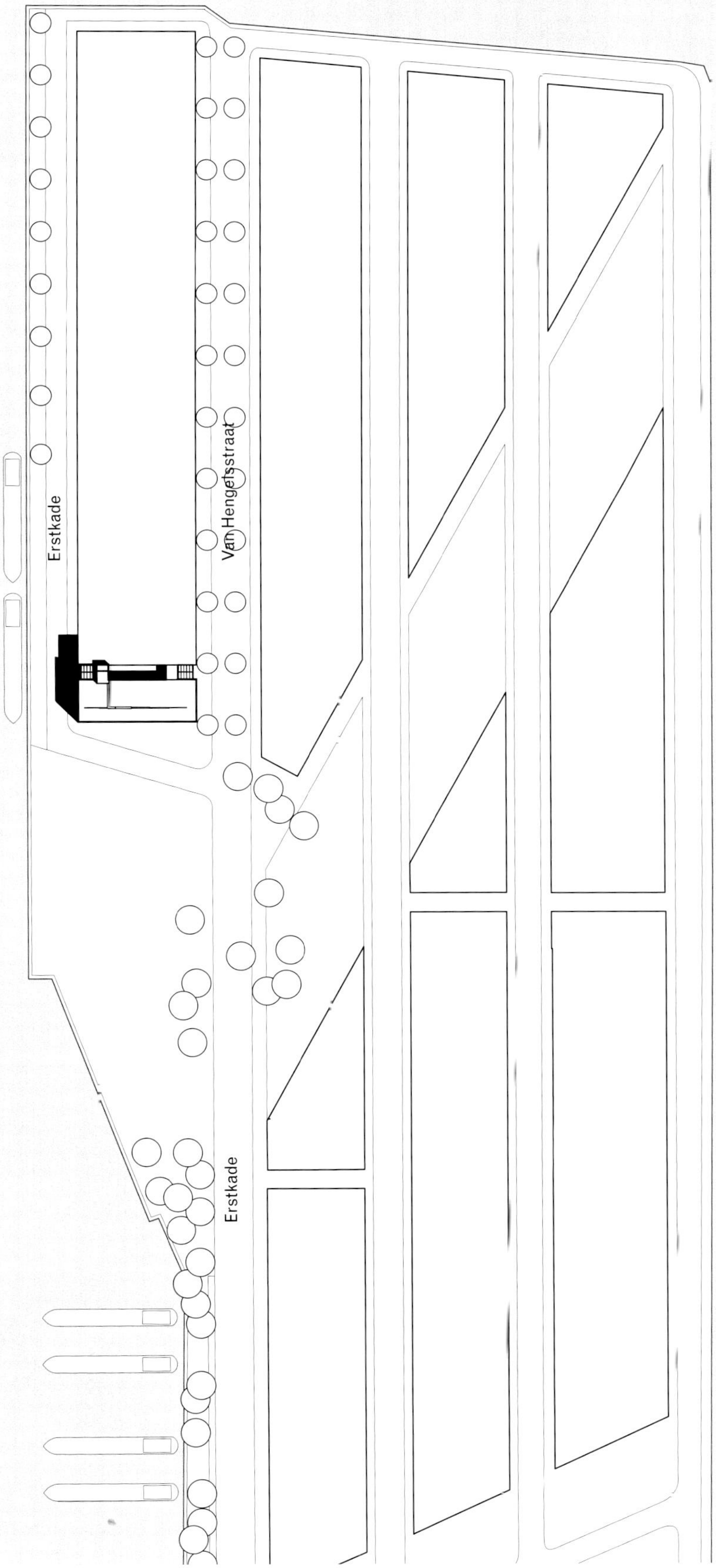

SpA

.SpA

SpA.overview 01.HvH

SpA.side facade 02.HvH

SpA.corner 03.HvH

SpA.side facade 04.HvH

SpA.corner 21.HvH

SpA.entrance 05.LK

SpA.facade 19.LK

SpA.corner 06.HvH

SpA.interior 18.LK

SpA.interior 16.LK

SpA.interior 14.LK

SpA.interior 17.LK

SpA.interior 15.LK

SpA.interior 11.LK

SpA.interior 12.LK

SpA.interior 13.LK

SpA.interior 07.LK

SpA.interior 09.LK

SpA.interior 02.LK

SpA.interior 10.LK

SpA.detail 19.HvH

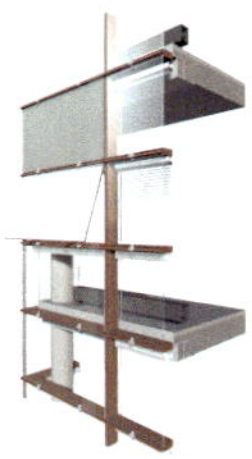

SpA.detail 20.HvH

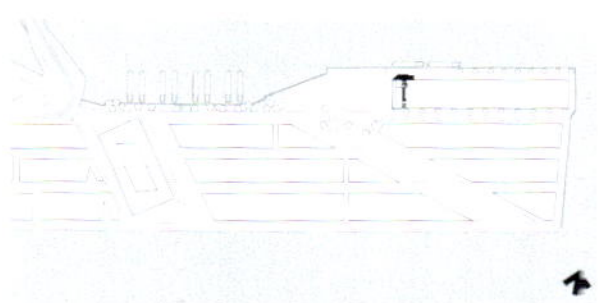

SpA.situation

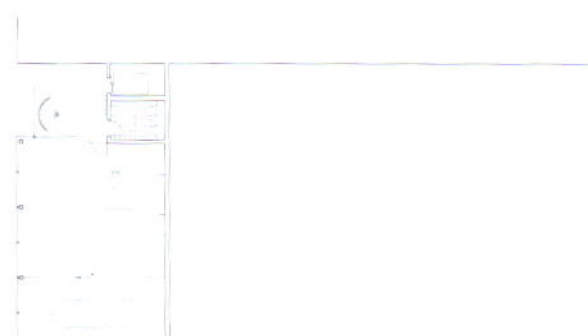

SpA.ground floor/basement

SpA

SpA.ground floor/first floor

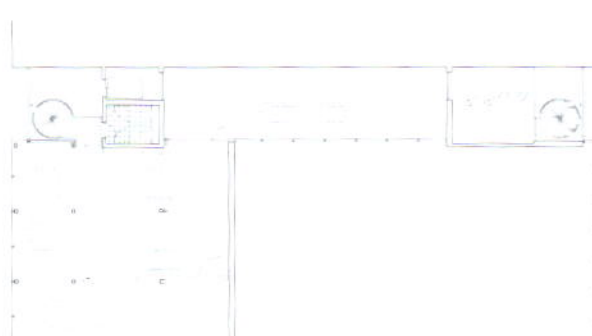

SpA.second floor

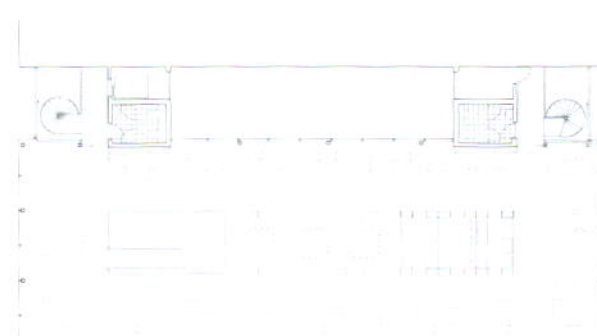

SpA.third floor

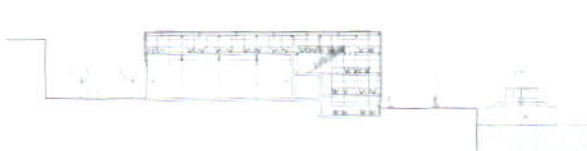

SpA.section offices

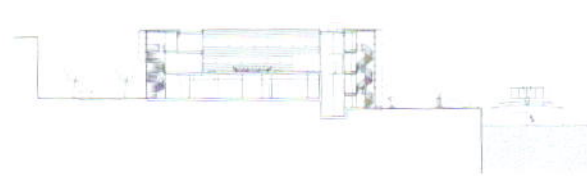

SpA.section stairs

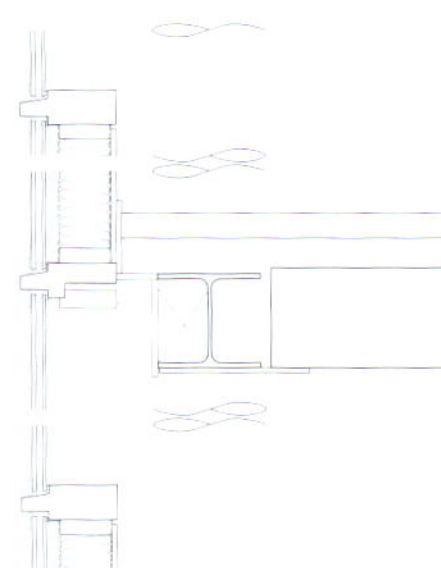

SpA.detail facade

SpA

3.SpA

SpA

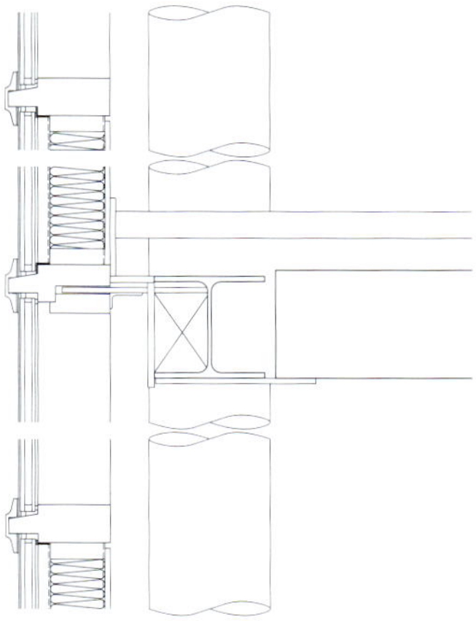

1:20

SpA

Detail facade

Kaarten van Amsterdam
ArchiLab
BrO
HVH

SpA

The office of Hans van Heeswijk architecten is organized as an open studio. All the workstations are located along the facades; the central area is a service zone.

SpA

9.SpA

The meeting/archives area is directly connected to the floor above.

SpA

, SpA

Third floor

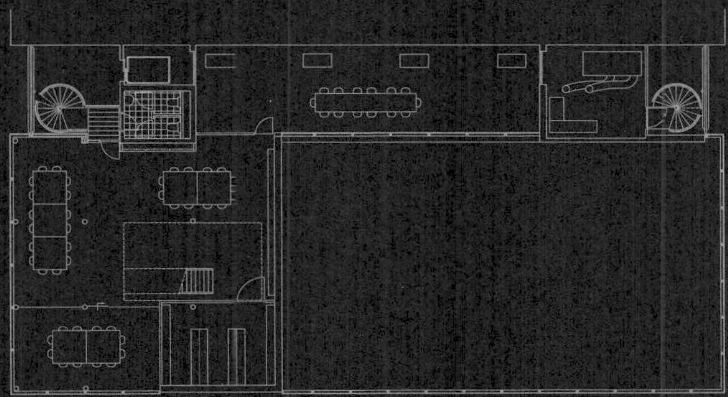

Second floor

SpA

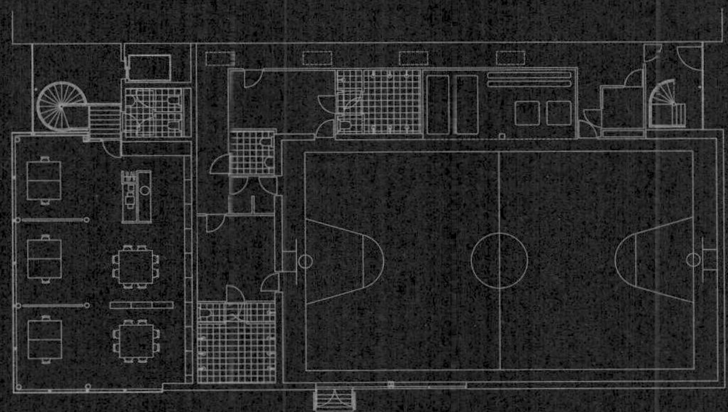

Ground floor/first floor

.SpA

Ground floor/basement
1:400

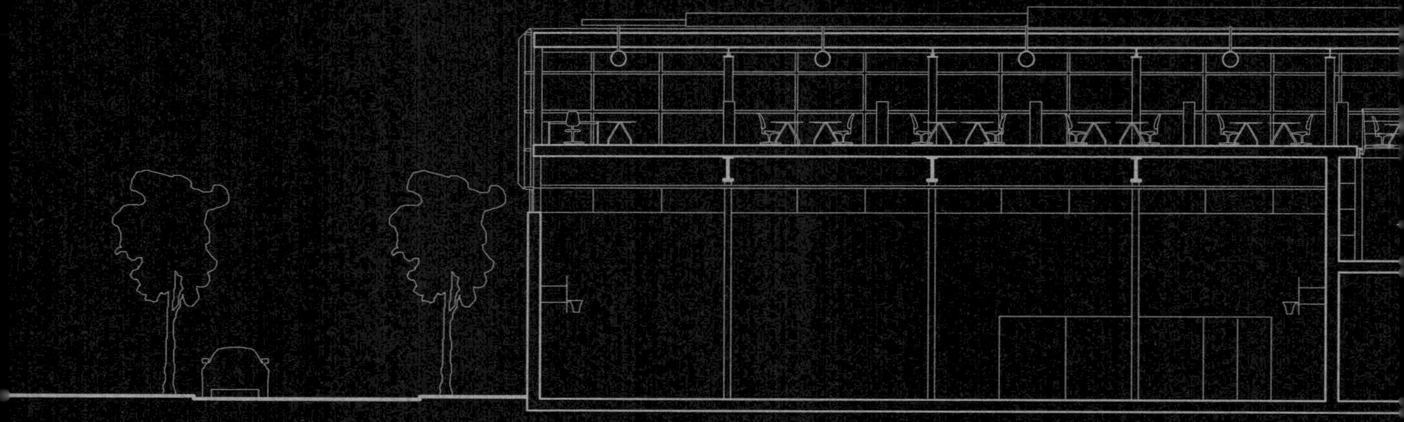

Section office
1:200

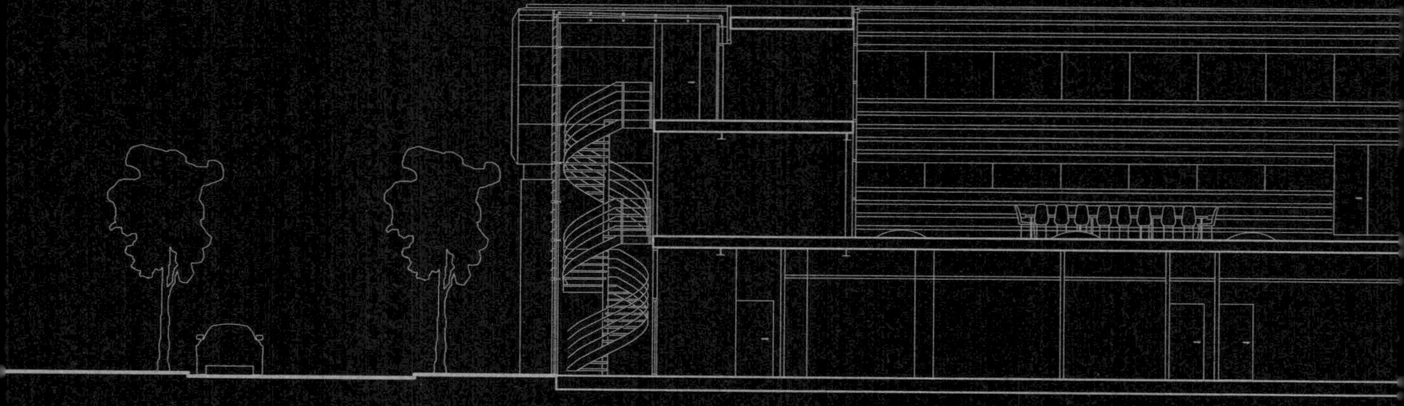

Section staircase
1:200

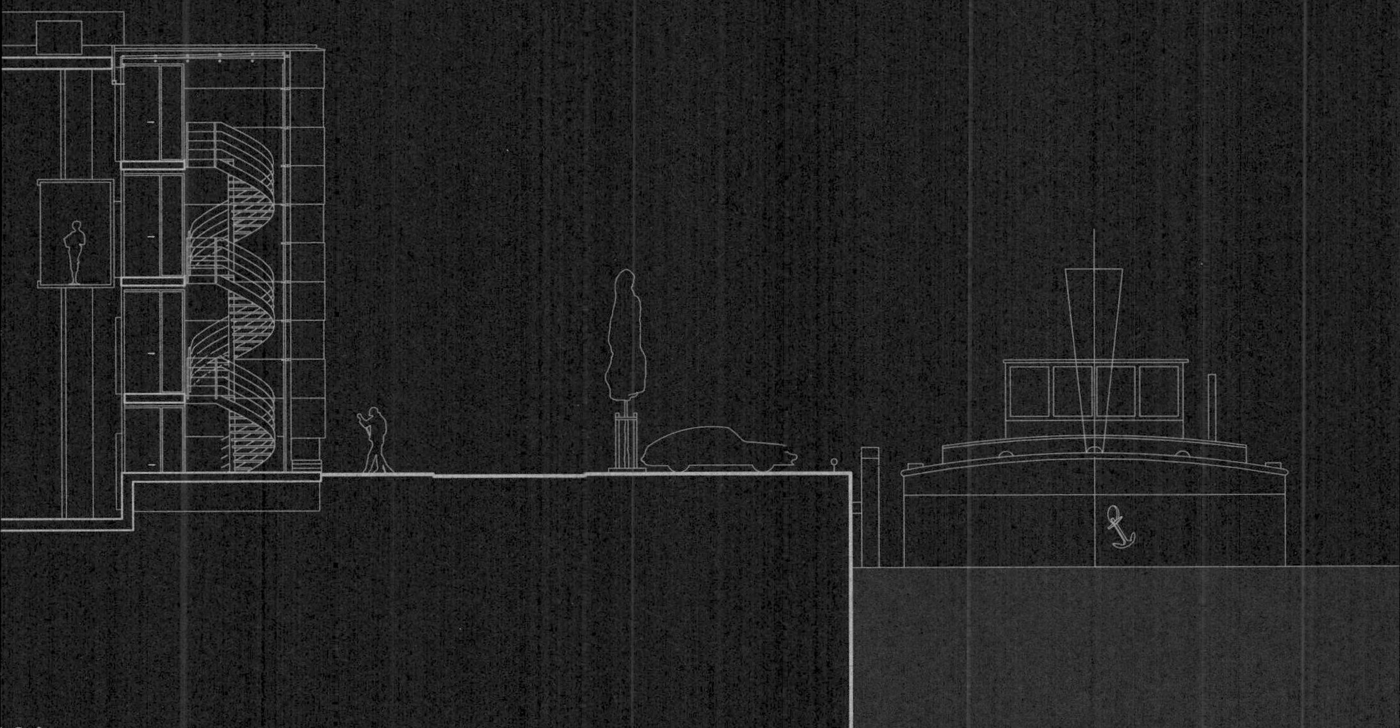

.SpA

Fitting a building into a context consists in first instance of mending the urban fabric as seamlessly as possible. That done, the question of what role the building plays in the city will determine whether or not it should have a striking appearance. HvH

RtA.

name
Rietlandpark Offices

project code
RtA

place
Rietlandpark, Amsterdam

client
Amplan Vastgoed BV

design
1993–1999

construction
2000–2001

design team
Bart Commandeur
Hans van Heeswijk
Remco de Hoogh
Jeroen van Nieuwenhuizen
Jeroen Rademaker
Arjan van Ruyven
Leen Stapper
Wilbert Swinkels

The office towers in Rietlandpark were the first of several related projects by Hans van Heeswijk architecten in Amsterdam's Oostelijk Havengebied (Eastern Docklands). The five office blocks are metal-clad volumes on a carpet of grass. The towers, each with a slightly different articulation, stand on a long, narrow underground car park. The buildings consist of freely subdivisible office floors which can be leased out in a variety of configurations.

The towers' appearance is determined by contrasts: between the volumes, between light and dark, between straight, flat facades and rounded, grooved facades and between protruding and flush ribbon glazing. Each building has one large window, in each case in a different position, which frames a unique view.

The five buildings share three central entrances that connect directly with the car park. Right next to the entrance zones, which contain lifts and open steel stairs, are the concrete cores of the buildings containing the vertical shafts and washrooms. The facades of the buildings are perforated by the emergency staircases which, together with the concrete cores, provide structural stability.

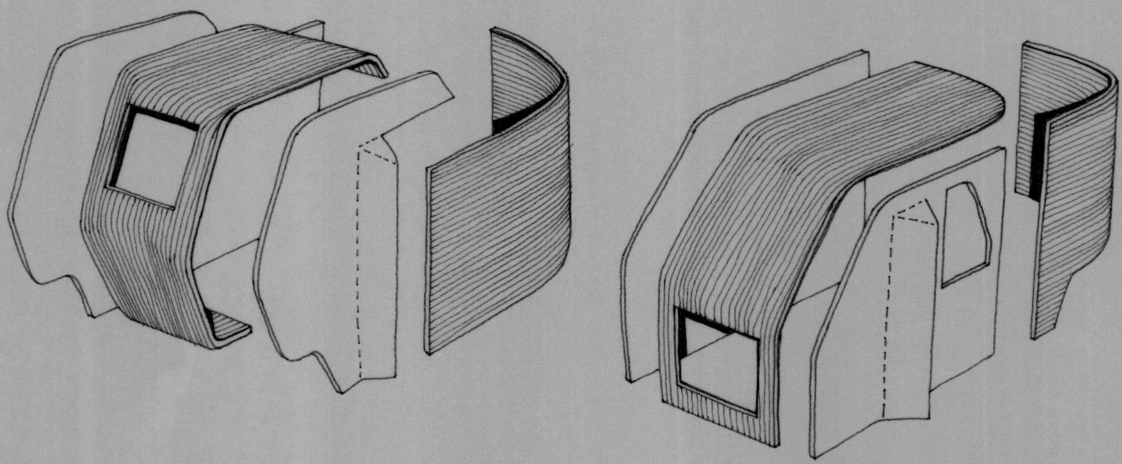

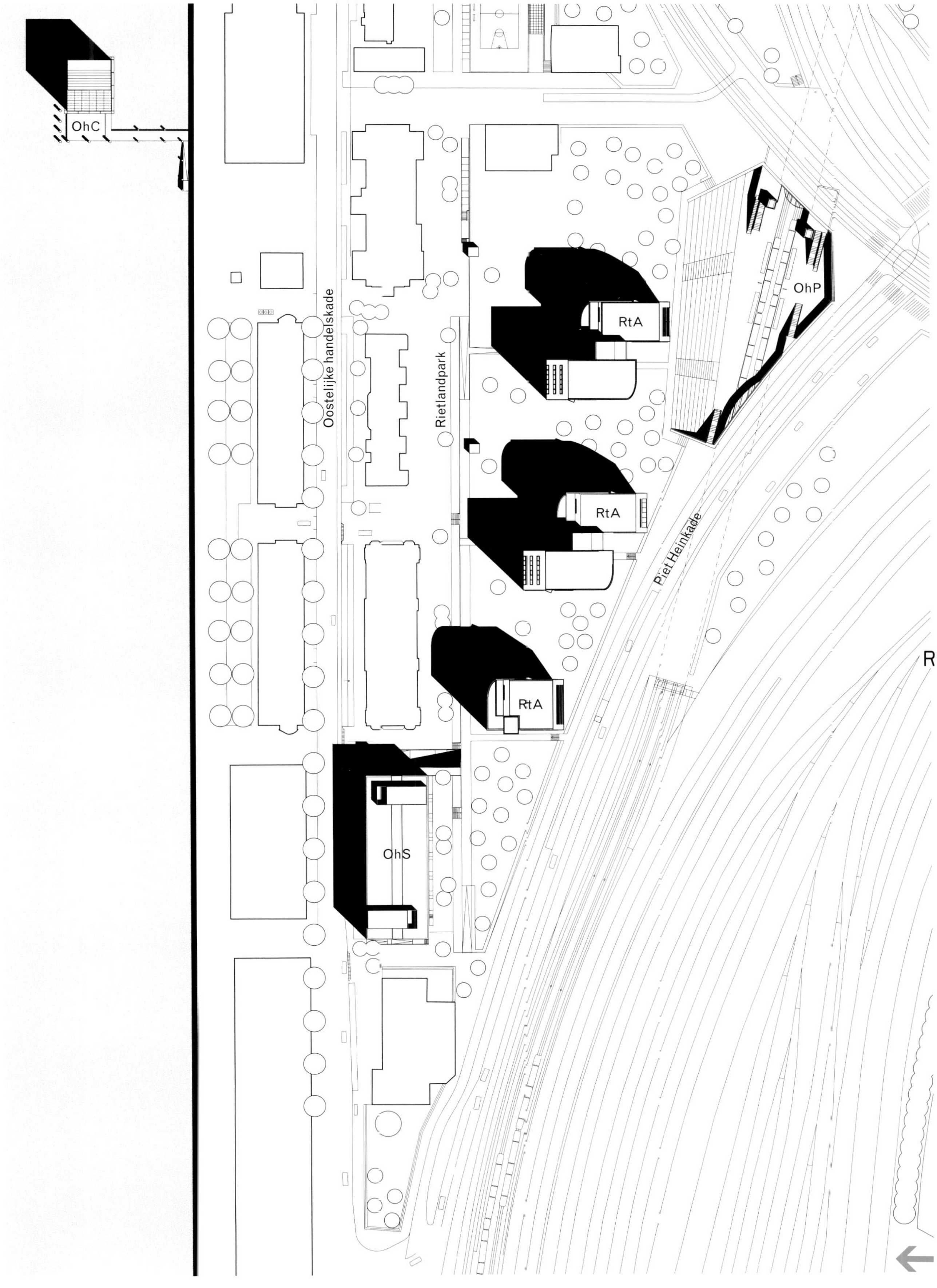
OhC
OhP
RtA
RtA
RtA
OhS
Oostelijke handelskade
Rietlandpark
Piet Heinkade

RtA

.RtA

RtA.overview 01

RtA.exterior 09.HvH

RtA.exterior 07.LK

RtA.overview 0343.JG

RtA.exterior 11.LK

RtA.exterior 04.LK

RtA.exterior 05.HvH

RtA.exterior 06.LK

RtA.exterior 10.LK

RtA.exterior 12.LK

RtA.facade 24.LK

RtA.facade 21.HvH

RtA.facade 22.HvH

RtA.entrance 14.LK

RtA.entrance 15.LK

RtA.entrance 18.LK

RtA.entrance 20.LK

RtA.interior 27.LK

RtA.interior 25.LK

RtA.interior 34.LK

RtA.interior 32.LK

RtA.detail 35.HvH

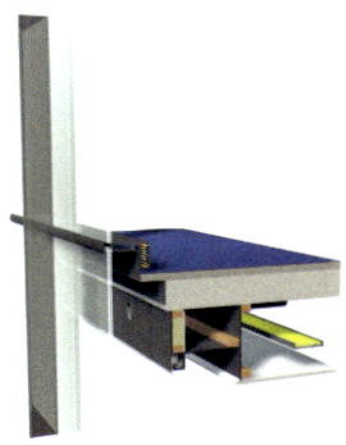

RtA.detail 36.HvH

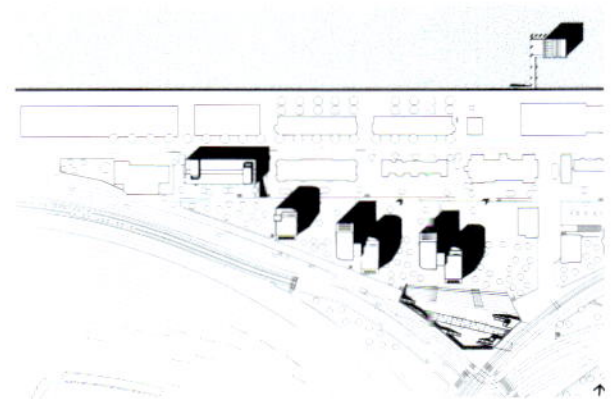

RtA.situation

RtA

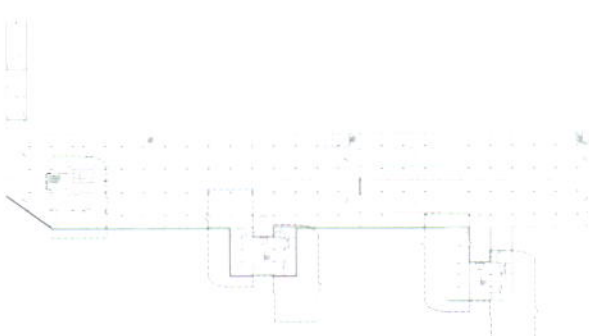

RtA.parking garage

RtA.ground floor

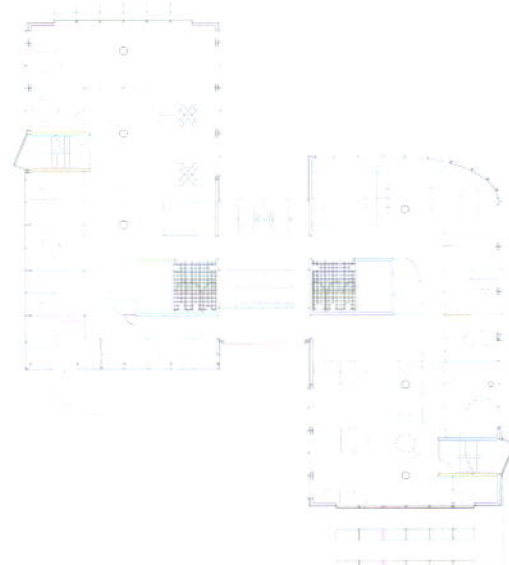

RtA.typical floor

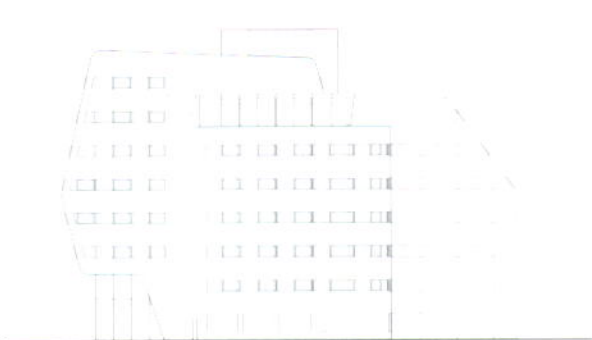

RtA.elevation

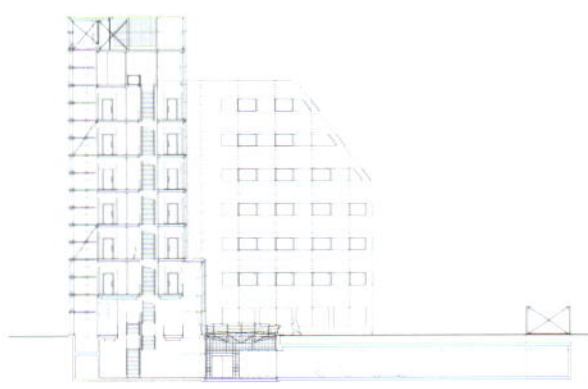

RtA.section

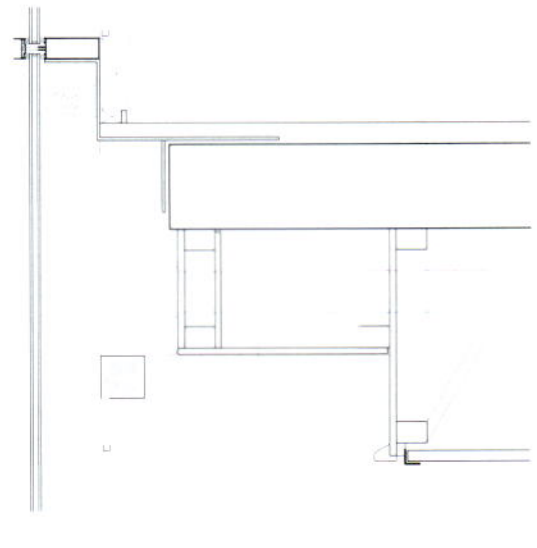

RtA.detail facade

..RtA

RtA

.RtA

The spatial master plan drawn up by the Department of Physical Planning (dRO), called for freestanding, monolithic volumes clad in metal sheet.

RtA

The main entrances to the office buildings lie on the north side of the park. They also contain a door leading directly to the basement car park.

RtA

The glass elevations take the form of 'curtain' climate-control facades. These consist of clear glass on the outside and cloth solar shading on the inside. The cloth reflects part of the heat. The cavity between curtain and glass window is mechanically ventilated. The two combine to prevent the glass facade from overheating.

RtA

Car park entrance

RtA

Entreehal

RtA

.RtA

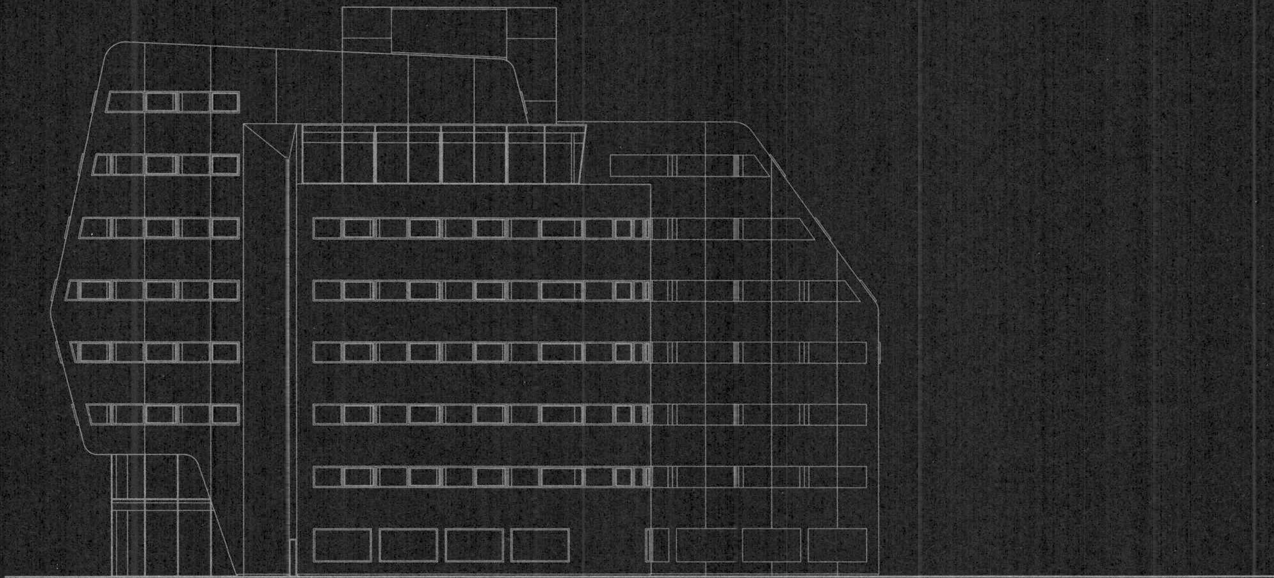

Facade
1:400

RtA

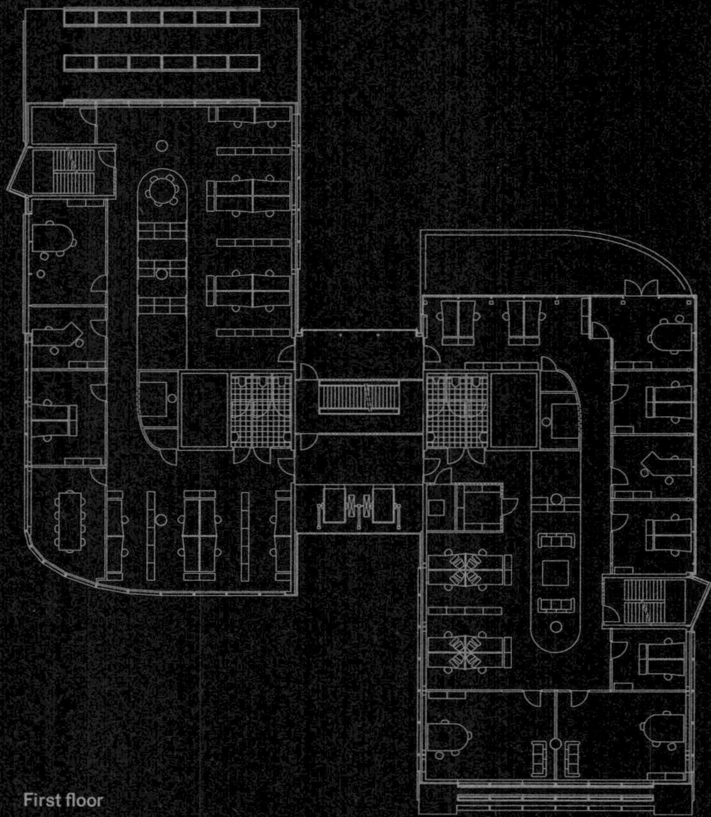

First floor

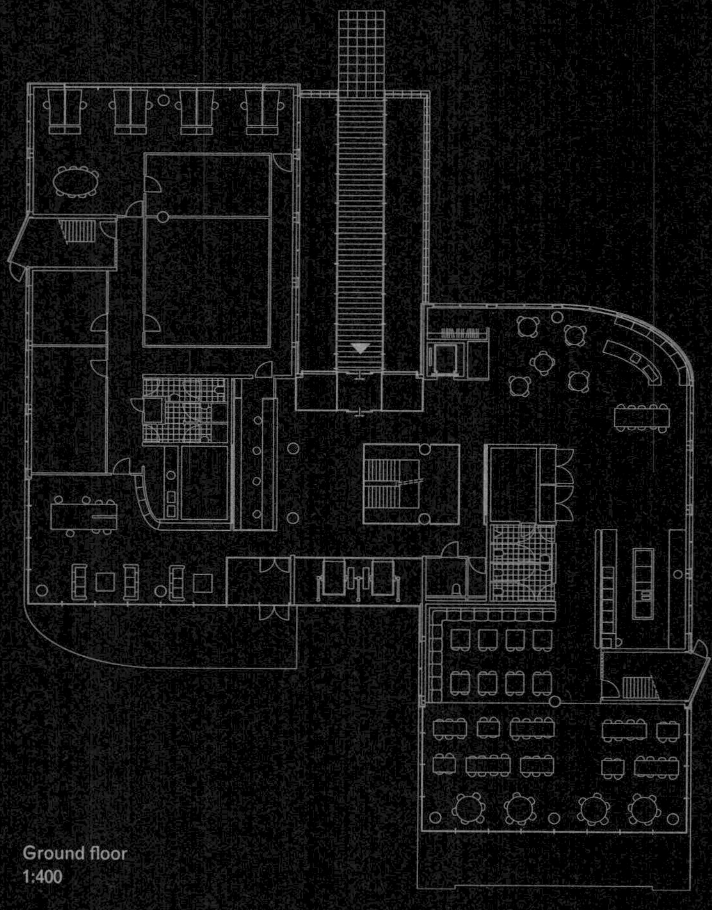

Ground floor
1:400

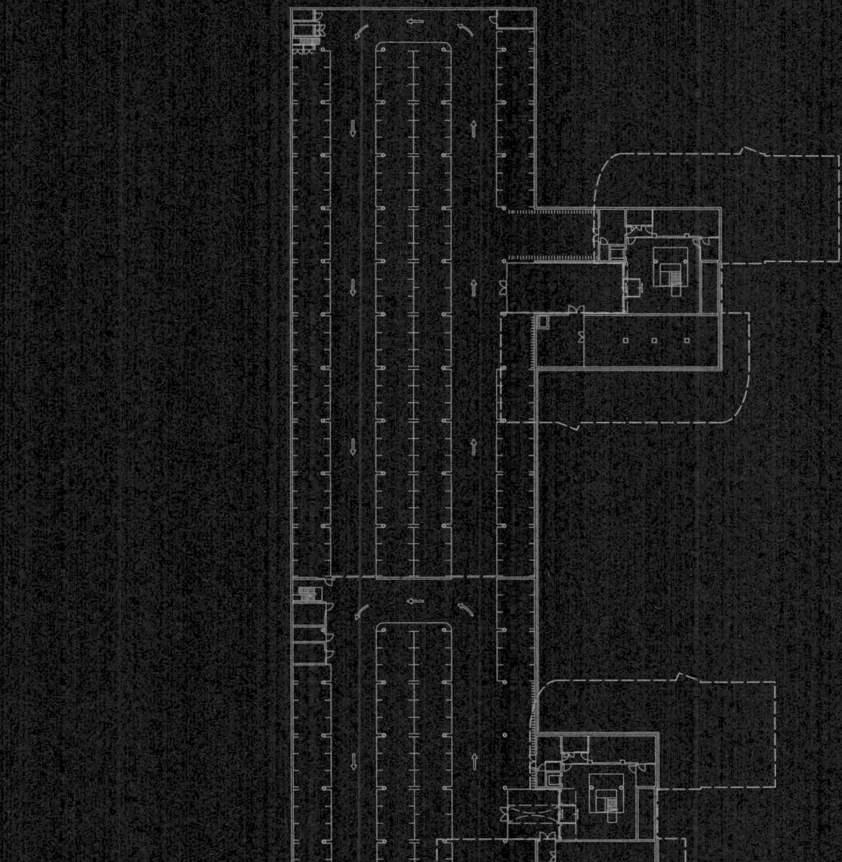

Parking
1:1000

You usually come up with a concept for a building not long after receiving the commission or during your first visit to the site. After that you may spend years elaborating, materializing and detailing that concept before the design becomes a finished building. It follows that the major part of your ambition and professional enjoyment should lie in that process of elaboration. HvH

GhH.

name
Heerhugowaard Town Hall
and Library

project code
GhH

place
Parelhof 1,
Heerhugowaard

client
Gemeente Heerhugowaard

design
2003–2004

construction
2004–2006

design team
Eelco Braakman
Jens Böhm
Stephanie Haumann
Hans van Heeswijk
Arjen Honig
Rob Hulst
Rirke Kluwer
Holger Mührmann

The renovation and extension of the town hall is part of the redevelopment of the centre of Heerhugowaard. The town hall will be augmented with an art lending library, public library and an underground car park. The building is intended to become a modern urban emporium where citizens drop in for information, an exhibition, a book, a passport, a wedding, a meeting or a cup of coffee and a read in the library's coffee corner.

The town hall, built in 1982, is an introverted building. By contrast, the additions, which stand in front of the existing building on the new city square, are extravert and inviting, thanks to their transparency and front-line position, and they emphasize public accessibility. The new office wing for the town hall, the library and the wedding room are all housed in separate volumes. Together with the existing building, they form a composition in which each element has its own separate identity, expressed in differences in material and elaboration. The different parts come together in a ten-metre-high hall, the heart of the building, from where there is direct access to all the public functions.

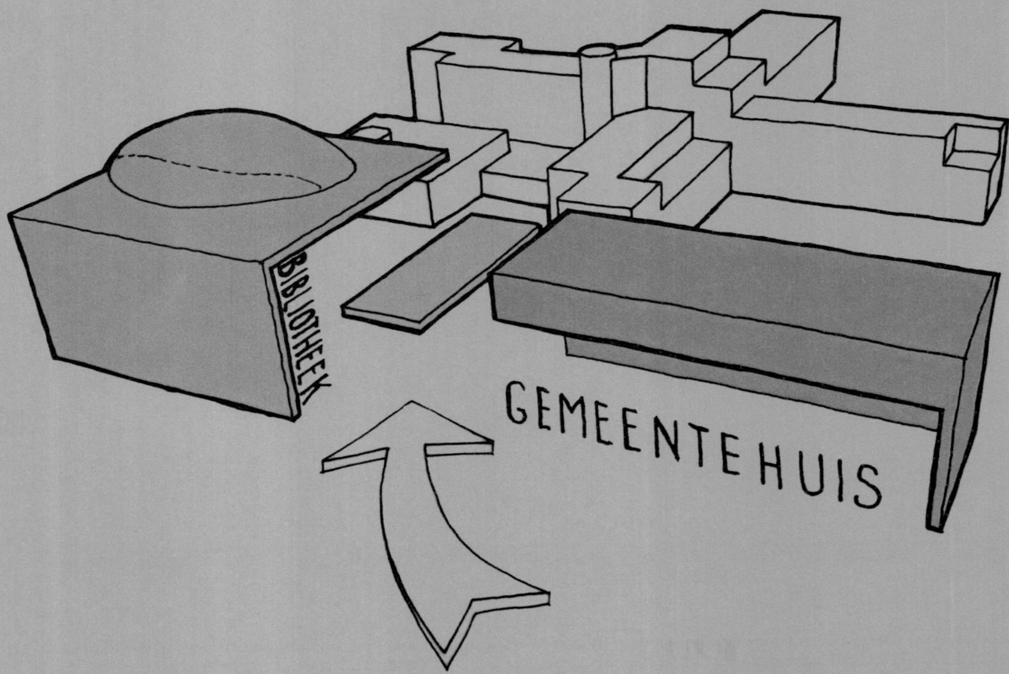
BIBLIOTHEEK
GEMEENTEHUIS

Kraaijvanger Urbis's spatial master plan for the centre of Heerhugowaard creates a new city core by extending and renovating the shopping centre, redeveloping the city park and constructing a congenial city square.

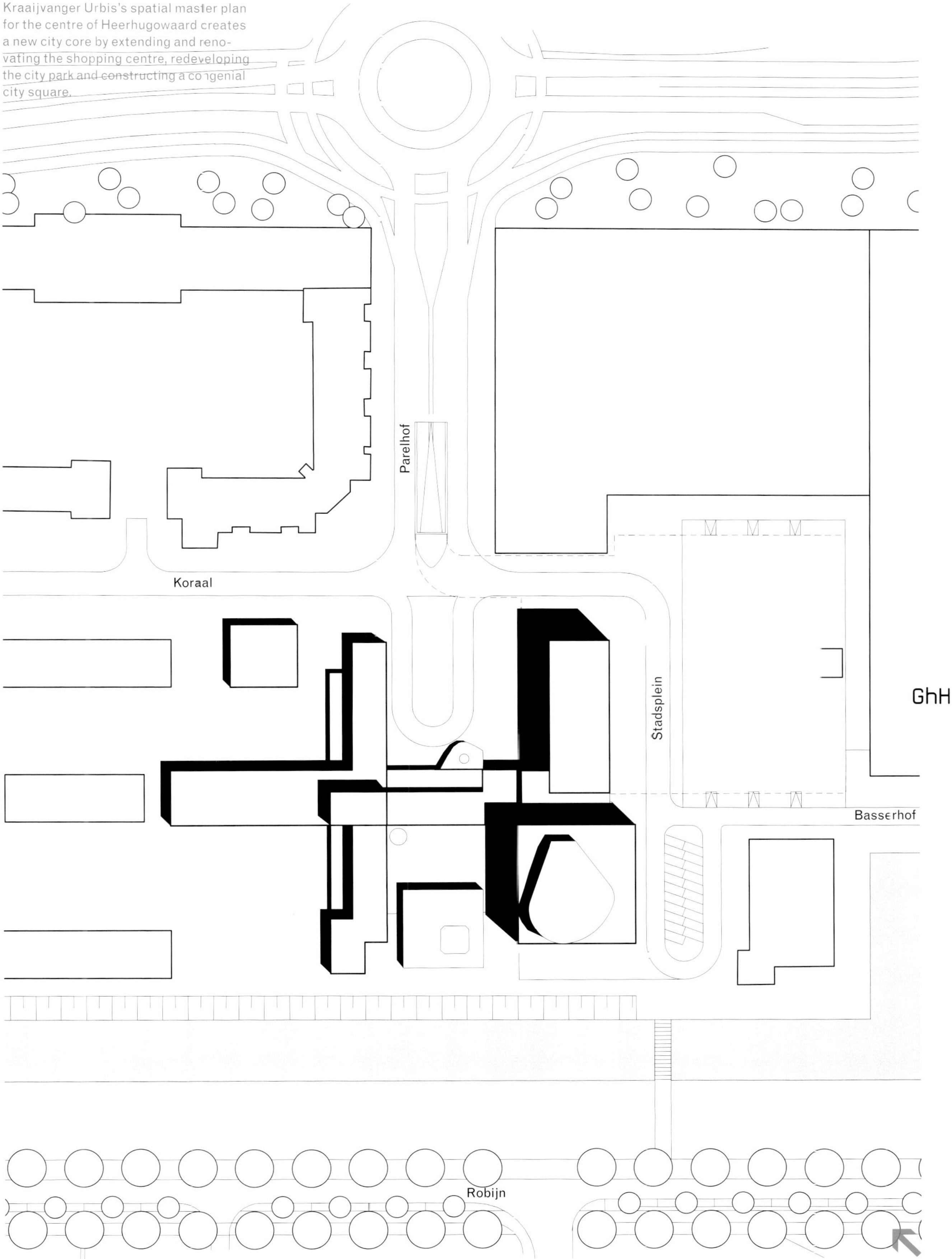

GhH

GhH.old front elevation 07.HvH

GhH.exterior 01.PB

GhH.central hall 02.PB

GhH.central hall 03.PB

GhH.patio 04.PB

GhH.entrance court 05.PB

GhH.library 06.PB

GhH.first pile 11.HvH

GhH.first pile 10.HvH

GhH.building site 11.HvH

GhH.building site 12.HvH

GhH.building site 13.HvH

GhH.building site 14.HvH

GhH.building site 15.HvH

GhH.building site 16.HvH

GhH.detail facade 08.HvH

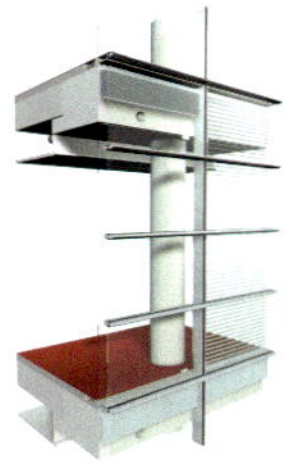

GhH.detail facade 09.HvH

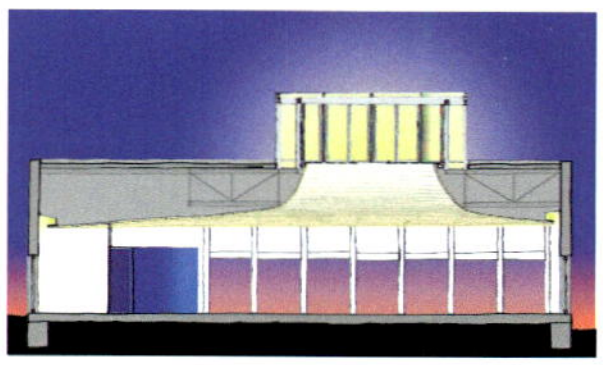

GhH.sketch council hall 12.HvH

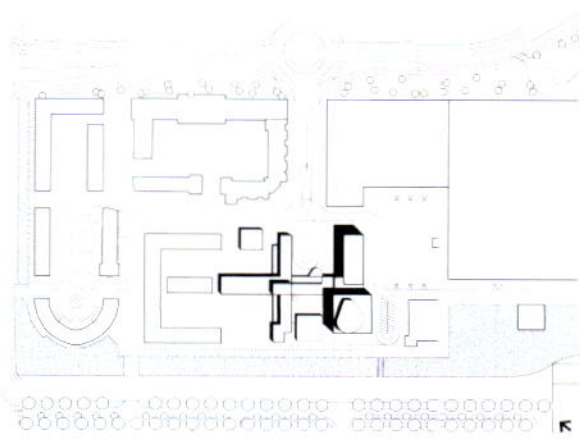

GhH.situation

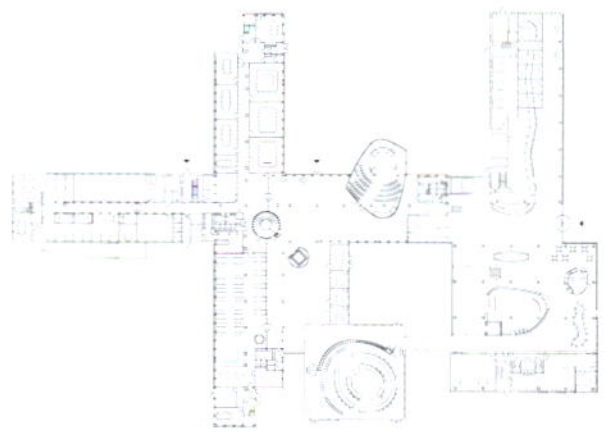

GhH.ground floor

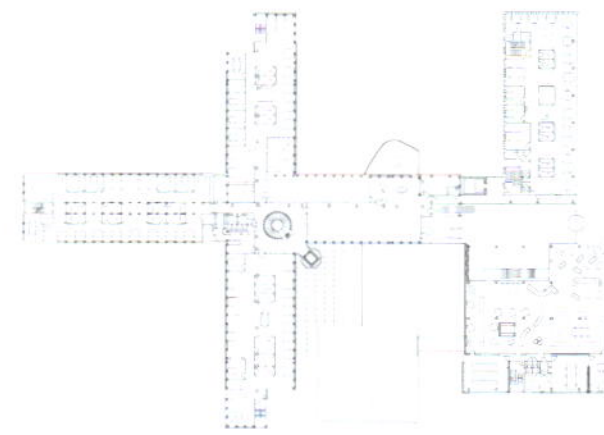

GhH.first floor

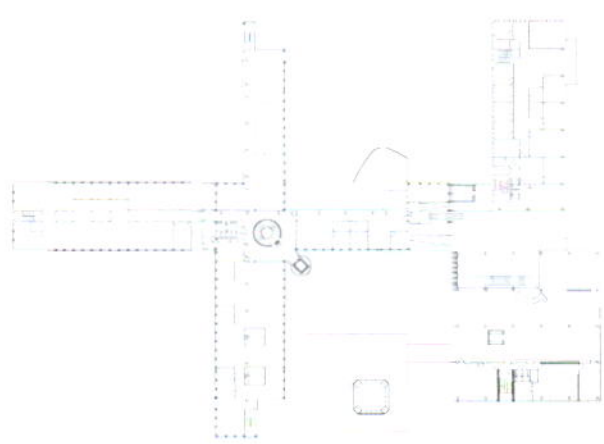

GhH.second floor

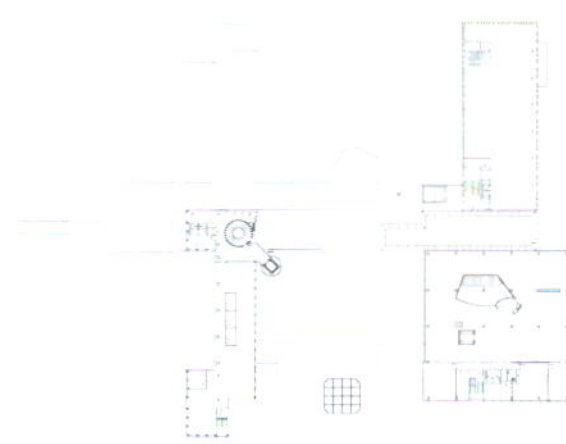

GhH.third floor

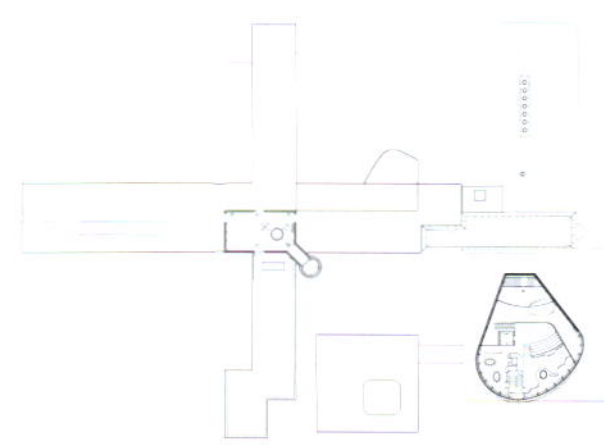

GhH.forth floor

GhH

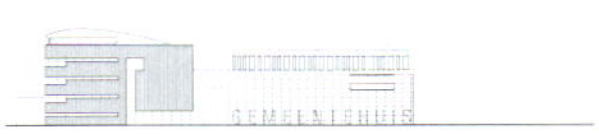

GhH.elevation

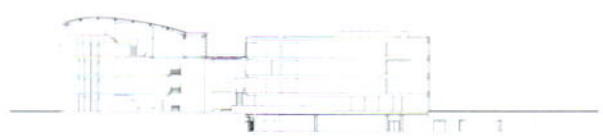

GhH.section 1

GhH.section 2

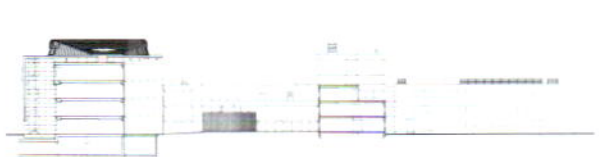

GhH.section 3

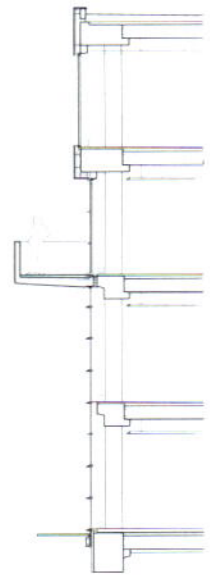

GhH.section facace

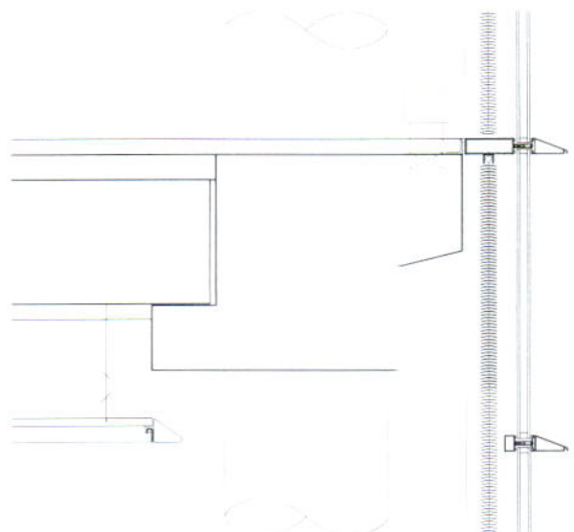

GhH.detail facade

.GhH

The new volumes, each consisting of two closed and two open sides, interlock and converge at the corner in the central hall. The facades of the new section of the town hall are stone-clad while the library has a timber facade. The existing building is in dark brick.

GhH

The entrances to all the public functions are in a tall, light-filled hall. The openness and the simple routing make it easy for users to find their way around.

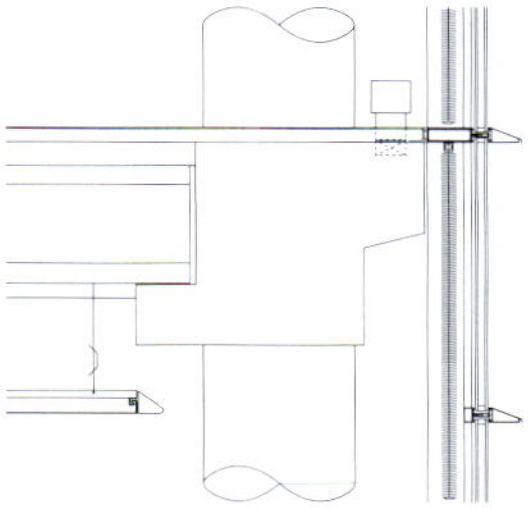

1:50

Detail city square elevation

ABN-AMRO
makelaardij
Wouters Sijkerman
DRUKWERK

Between the library and the existing building is a patio that allows daylight to penetrate directly into all the public areas.

The wedding room, with facades of glass blocks, is on the north-west side of the complex. It has its own entrance on a separate court so that weddings are not disrupted by the everyday activities inside and around the building.

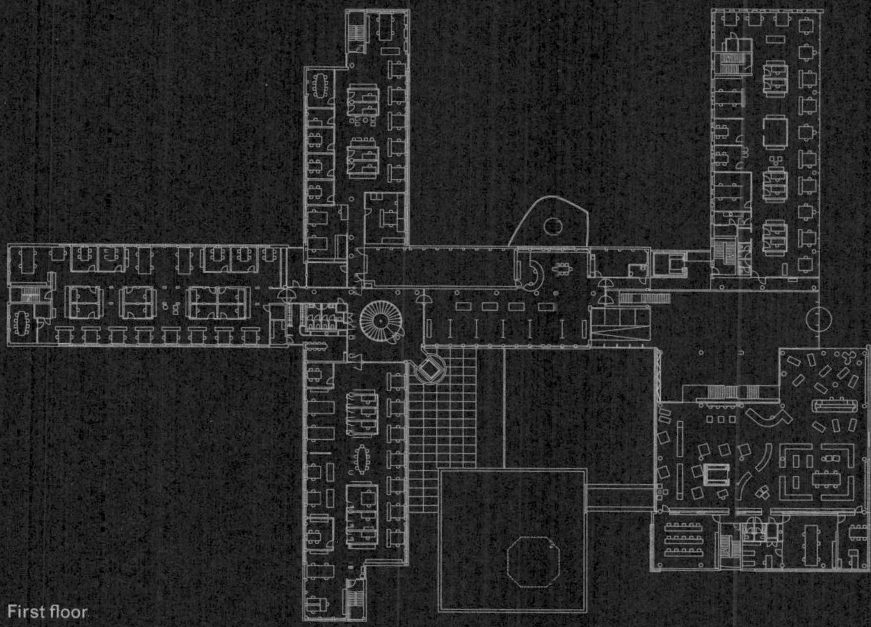

First floor

On the ground floor, a gallery connects all the public areas: the town hall service counters, the library with coffee corner and Internet café, the council chamber, the wedding room and the art lending library.

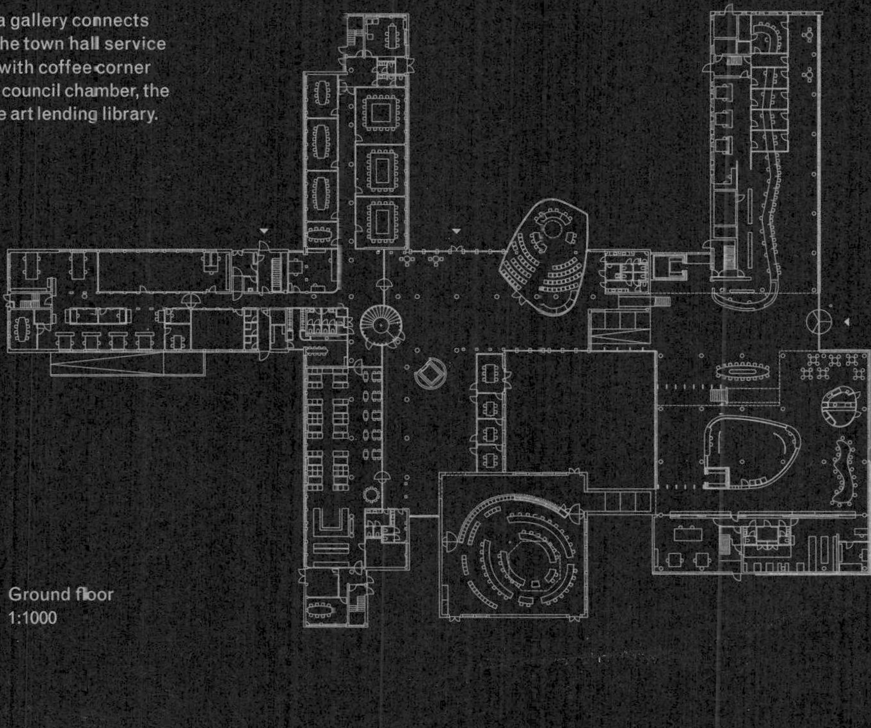

Ground floor
1:1000

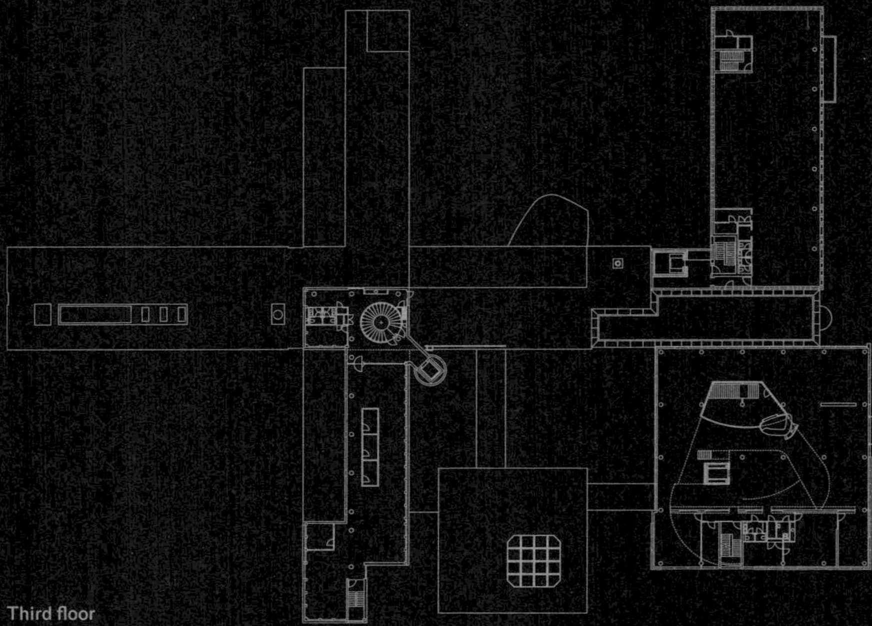

Third floor

In the interests of efficient use, the offices have flexible workstations. The new building is an open, column-free space that can easily be reconfigured.

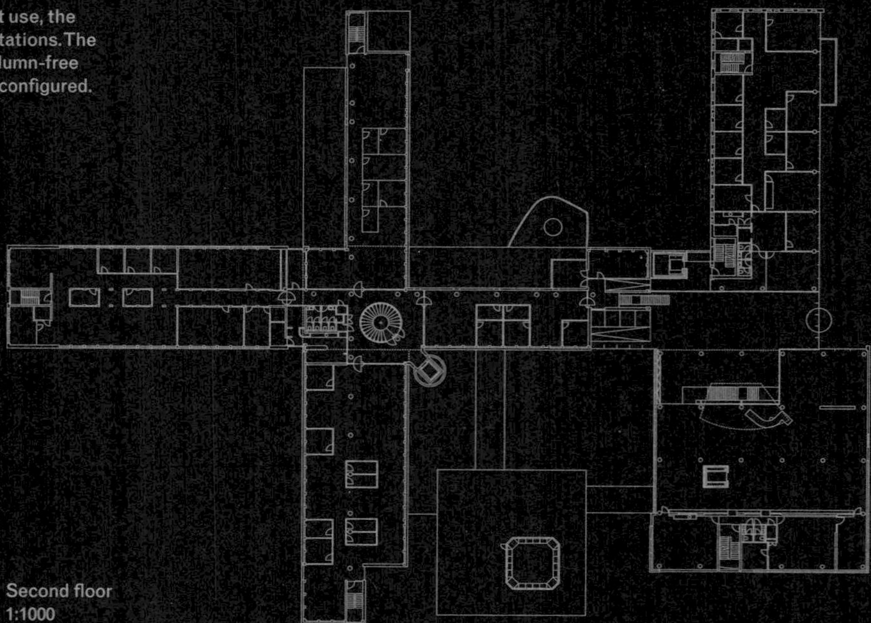

Second floor
1:1000

The children's section of the library has a mezzanine 'attic' with a dome-shaped roof. The dome looks out over the revamped city park.

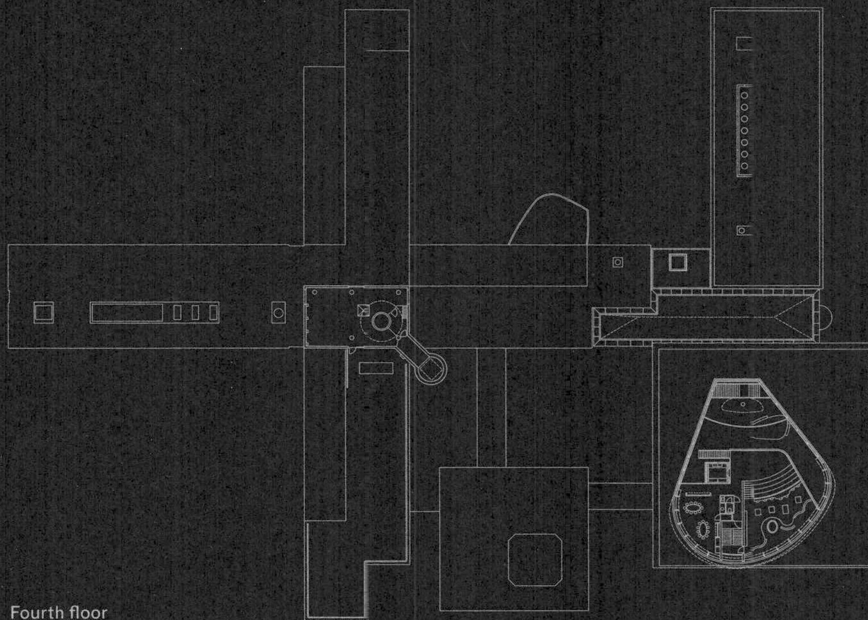

Fourth floor

GhH

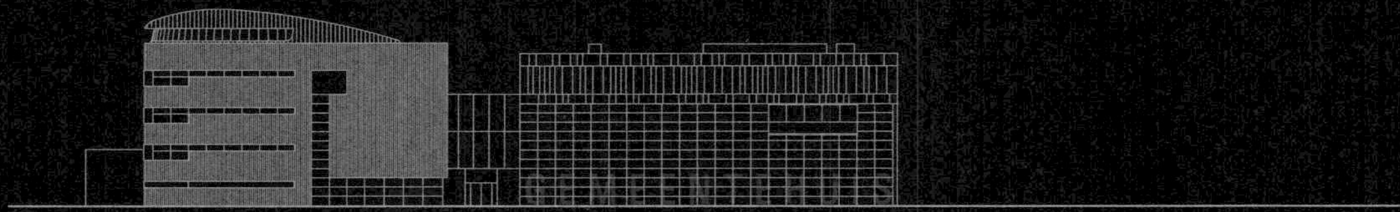

Facade
1:1000

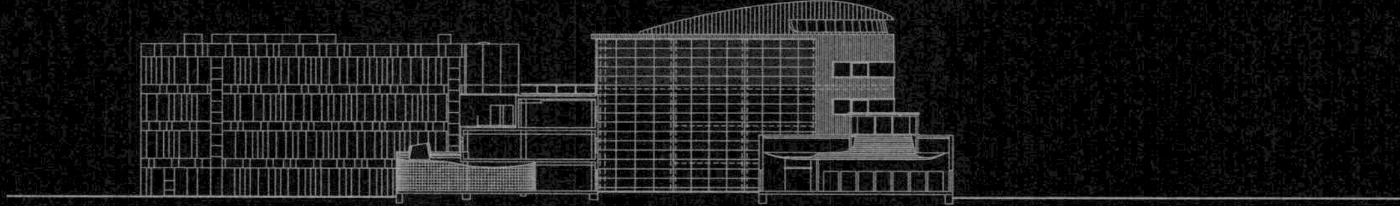

Section 1
1:1000

Section 2
1:1000

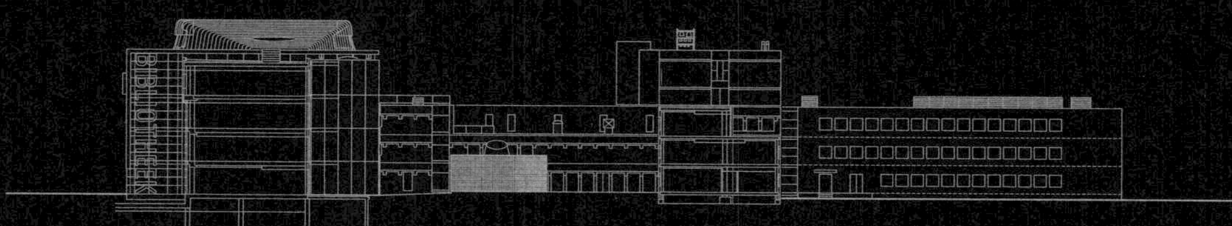

Section 3
1:1000

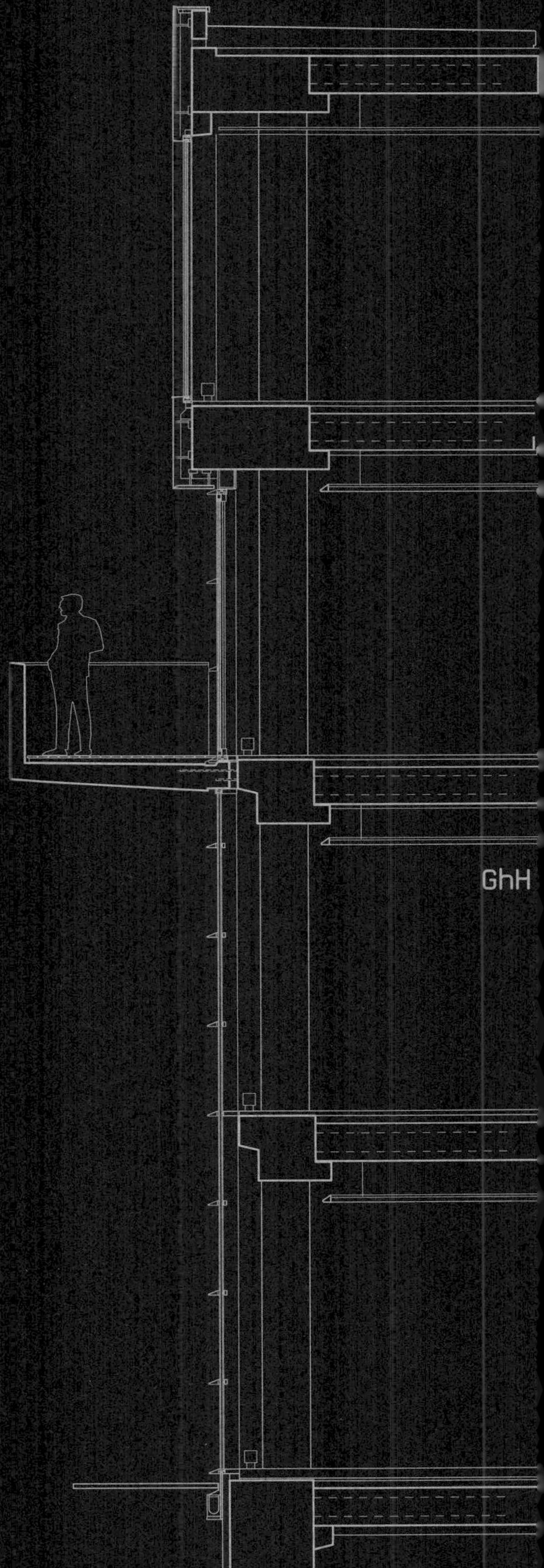

Section facade

MV Kalakala, the world's first streamlined Art Deco ferry, Seattle, 1935

ScB. SbT.

name
Convair Building

project code
ScB

place
Stationsplein, Schiphol

client
Schiphol Real Estate en
KLM Facility Services

design
1996

construction
1999–2000

design team
Milos Dimitrijevic
Hans van Heeswijk
Jeroen Rademaker
Ton Span
Jochem van de Spek
Rick Thani

name
Constellation Building

project code
SbT

place
Stationsplein, Schiphol

client
Schiphol Real Estate

design
1997

construction
1998–1999

design team
Hans van Heeswijk
Jeroen Rademaker
Ton Span
Jochem van de Spek

The big demand for office and commercial space around Schiphol Airport has resulted in the development of a number of sites in the vicinity. One such is Schiphol-Oost, where the arrivals and departures hall stood until 1967. Hans van Heeswijk architecten realized two office buildings here.
All the offices on this site are named after famous commercial aircraft types. The Convair Building stands on a plaza near the old control tower, at the end of the main road into Schiphol-Oost. The slightly earlier Constellation Building is the last in a series of office and company buildings along the same route. The entrances of both buildings are prominently located in the main elevation.
Convair and Constellation are based on the same principle: two office wings linked by a tall central hall of steel and glass containing the impressive-looking entrance.
The Convair Building has an orthogonal plan. The Constellation Building follows the curve of the road and its entrance hall consequently has a curved glass facade. The metal-clad facades of the office wings curve upwards, a movement that enhances the resemblance to the Constellation aircraft. Part of the rear elevation is staggered and transparent, giving the offices a spectacular view of the take-off and landing runways

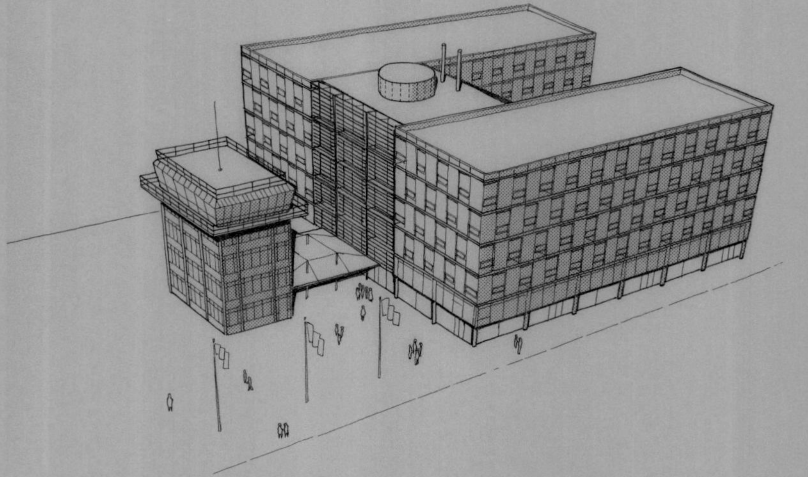

Constellation Building (top) and Convair Building on Stationsweg in Schiphol-Oost.

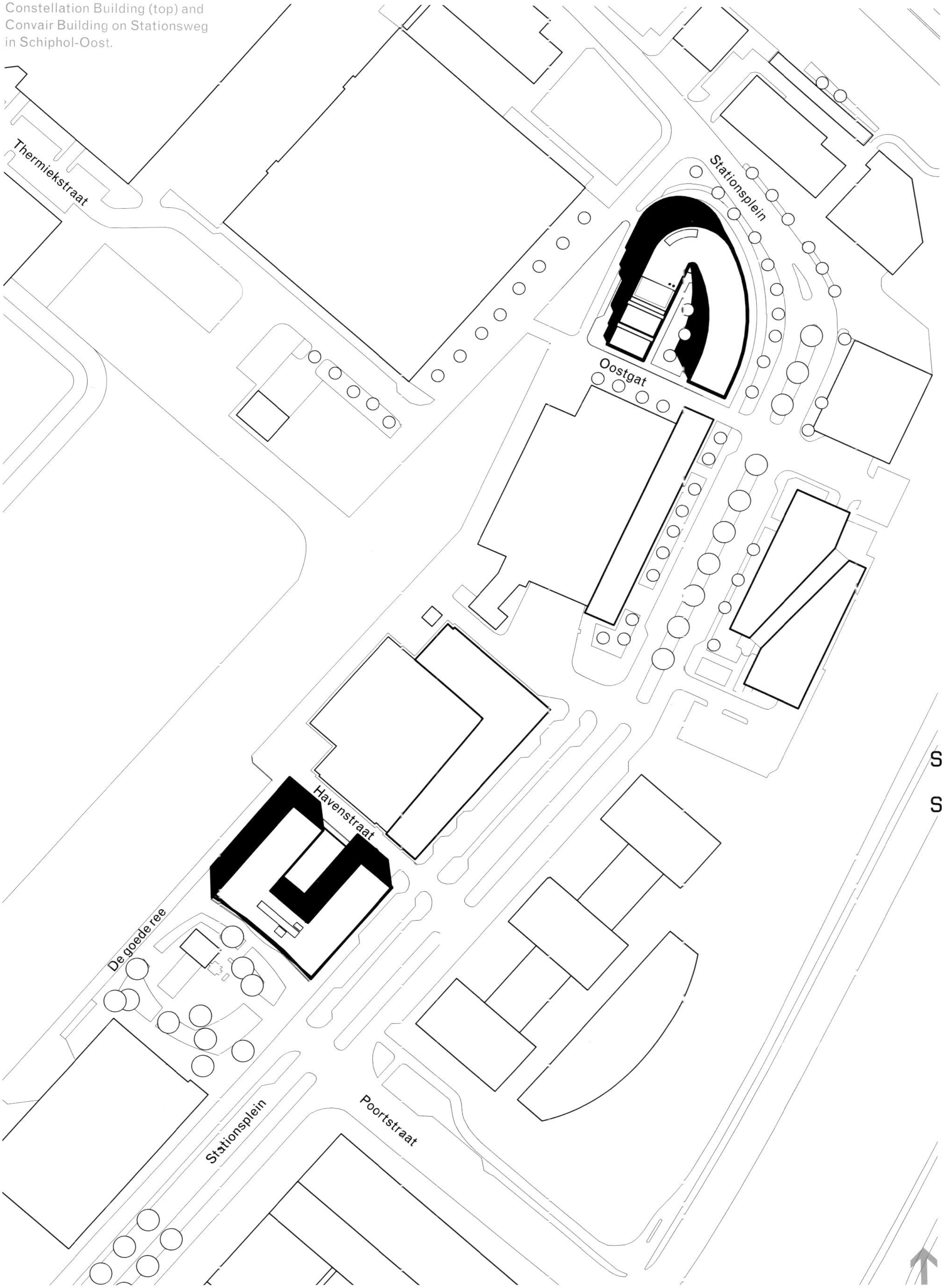

ScB.block back 03.LK

ScB.overview 21.LK

ScB.block front 02.LK

ScB.front facade 06.LK

ScB.front facade 05.LK

ScB.front facade 07.LK

ScB.front facade 04.LK

ScB.court 10.LK

ScB.court 20.LK

ScB.front facade 08.LK

ScB.front facade 09.LK

ScB.front facade 18.LK

ScB.entrance 11.LK

ScB.corridor 12.LK

ScB.corridor 13.LK

ScB.stairs 14.LK

ScB.stairs 15.LK

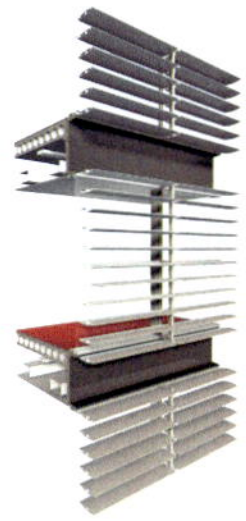

ScB.detail 16.HvH

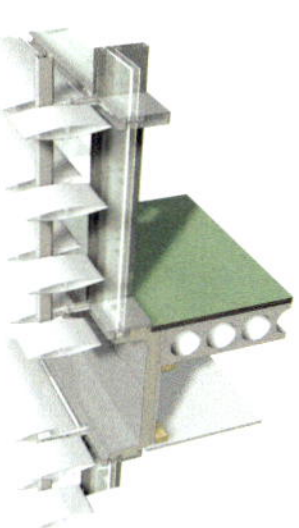

ScB.detail 17.HvH

ScB.3d 16.HvH

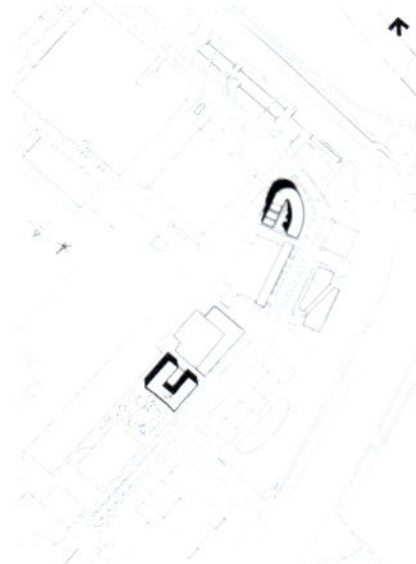

SbT.situation

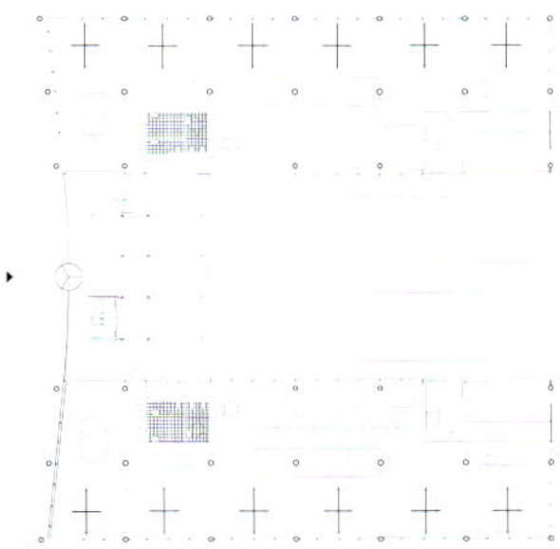

ScB.ground floor

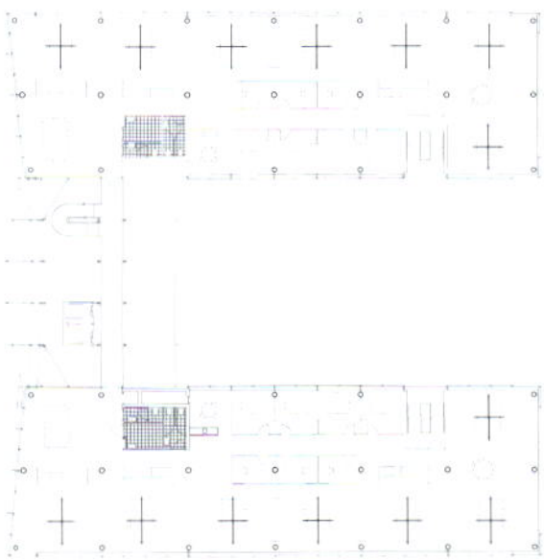

ScB.first floor

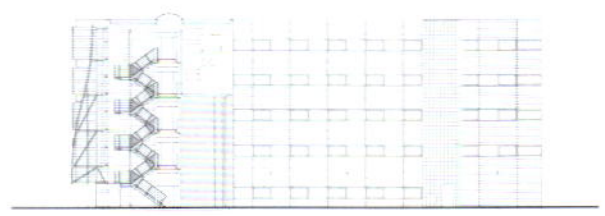

ScB.elevation

ScB

SbT

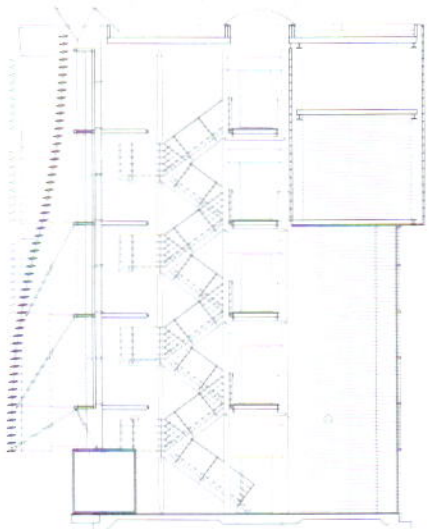

ScB.section

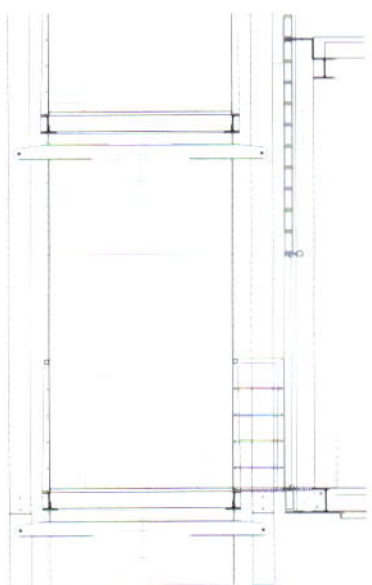

ScB.fragment section

Sbt.overview 03

SbT.front elevation 04.CR

SbT.front elevation 05.CR

SbT.front elevation 06.CR

SbT.side elevation 09.CR

SbT.side elevation 10.CR

SbT.side elevation 08.CR

SbT.side elevation 07.CR

SbT.court 11.CR

SbT.stairs 12.CR

SbT.stairs 13.CR

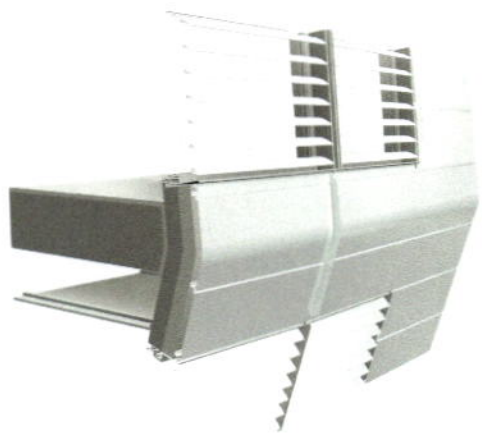

SbT.detail 14.HvH

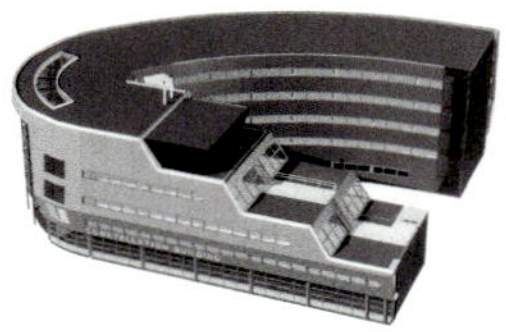

SbT.3d 15.HvH

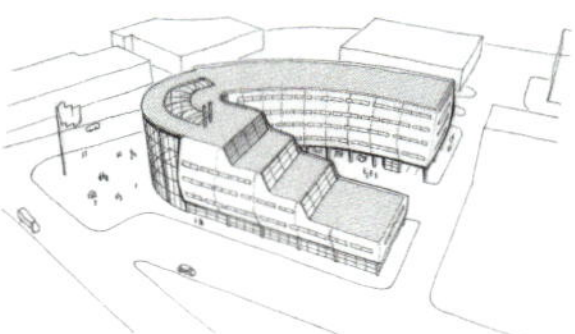

SbT.sketch 01.HvH

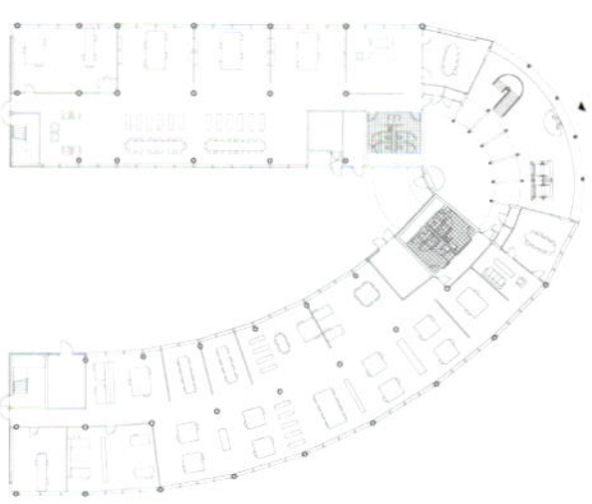

SbT.ground floor

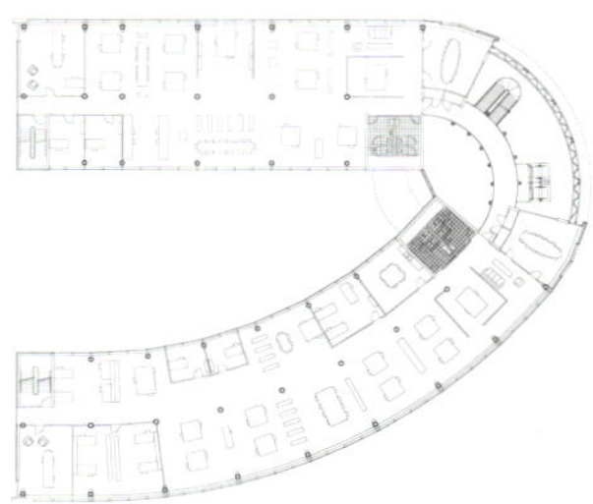

SbT.first floor

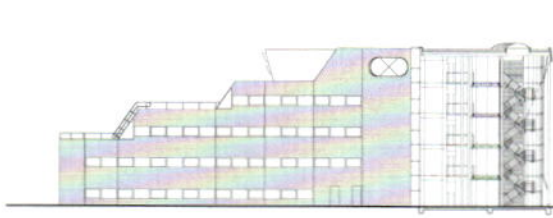

SbT.section

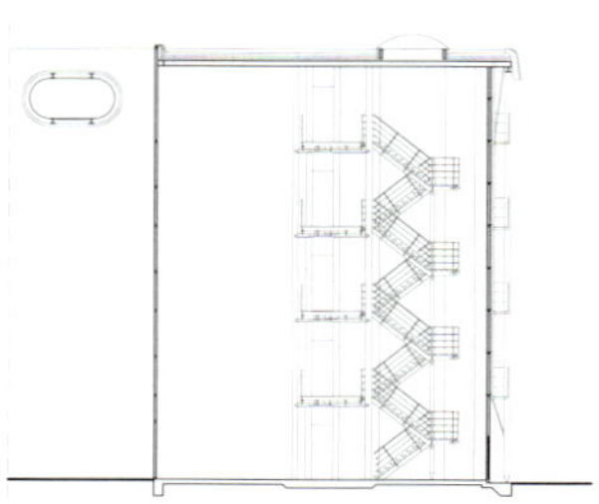

SbT.section hall

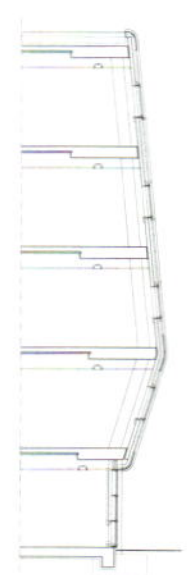

SbT.section facade

ScB

.ScB

Front facade with entrance hall of Convair Building

ScB

.ScB

The elevations of both buildings are an assemblage of metal cladding and glass curtain walls.

ScB

3.ScB

354.9

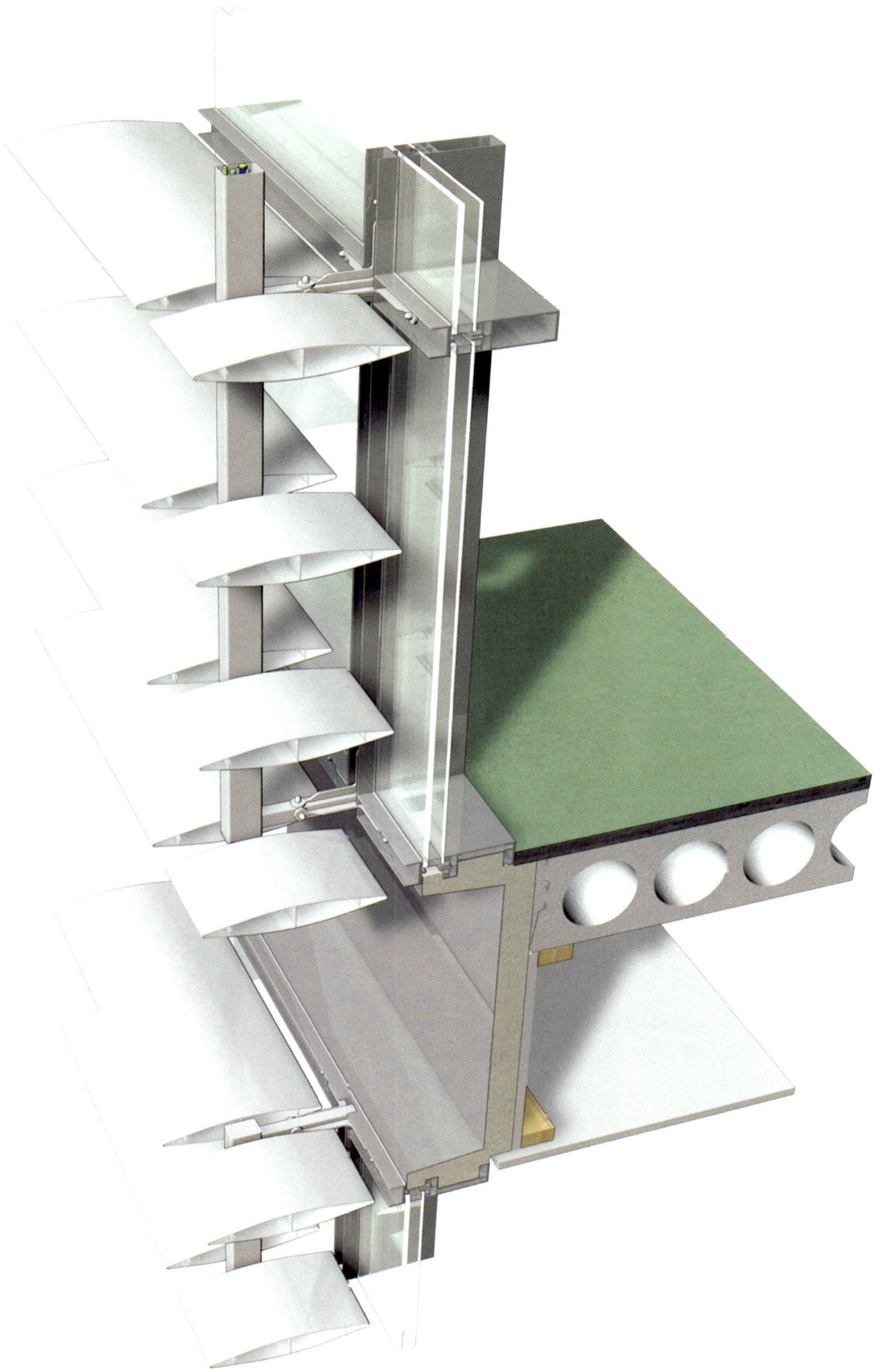

SScB

.ScB

Detail façade

Inner courtyard of Convair Building. The glass-block volume above the entrance foyer contains the building services.

ScB

Entrance hall Convair Building

ScB

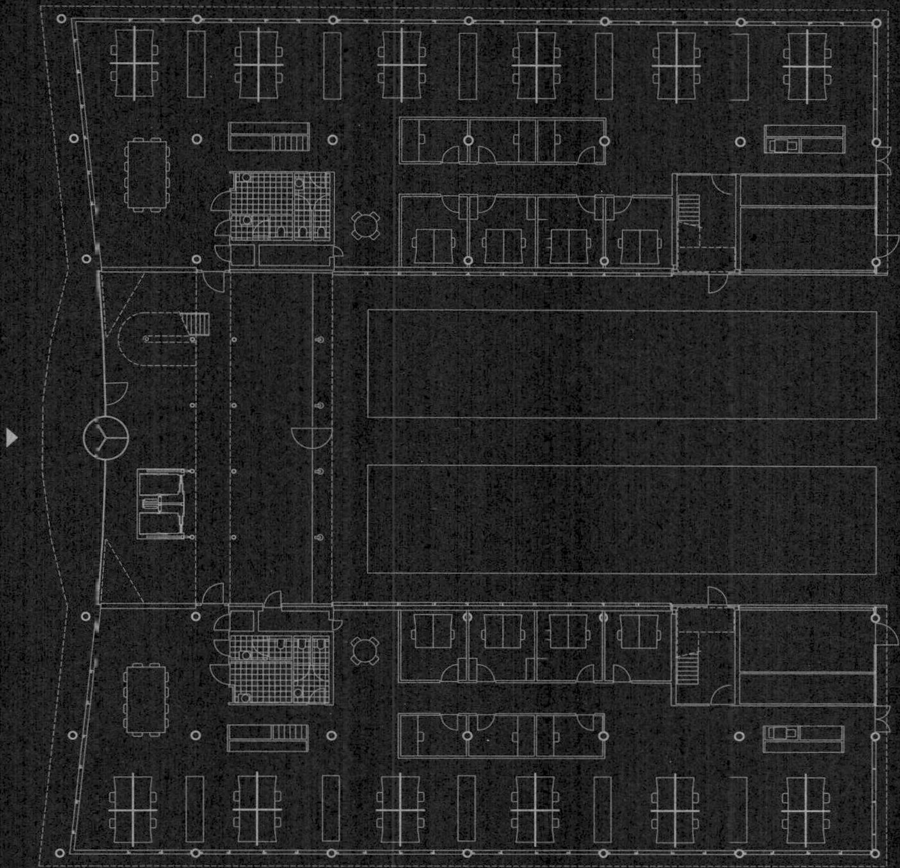

Grounc floor
1:400

ScB

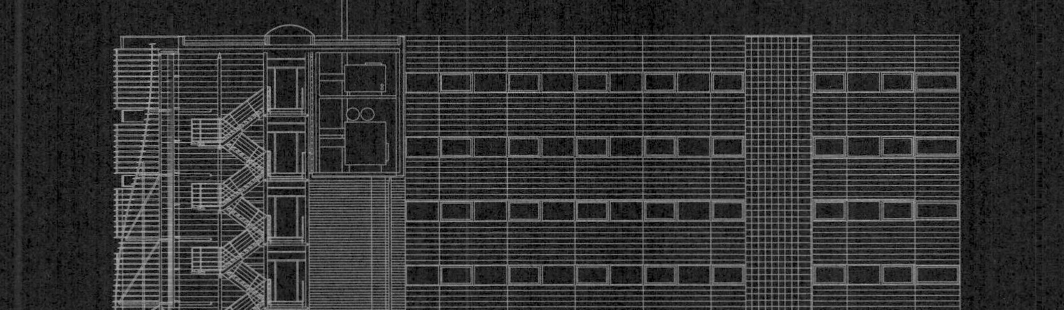

Facade
1:400

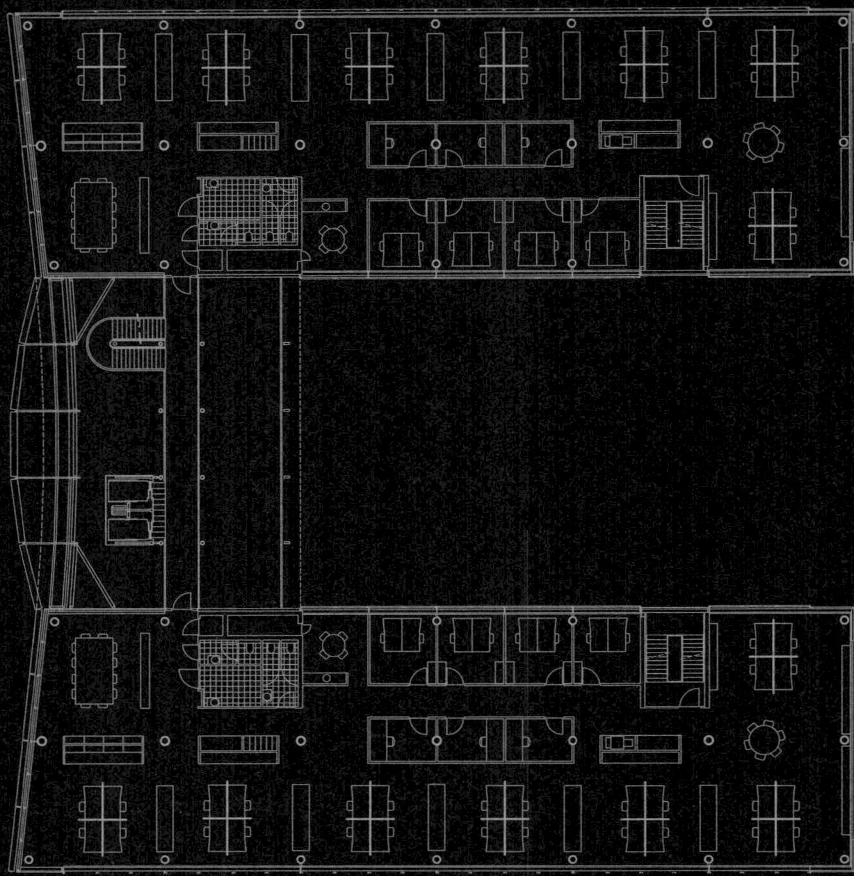

First floor
1:400

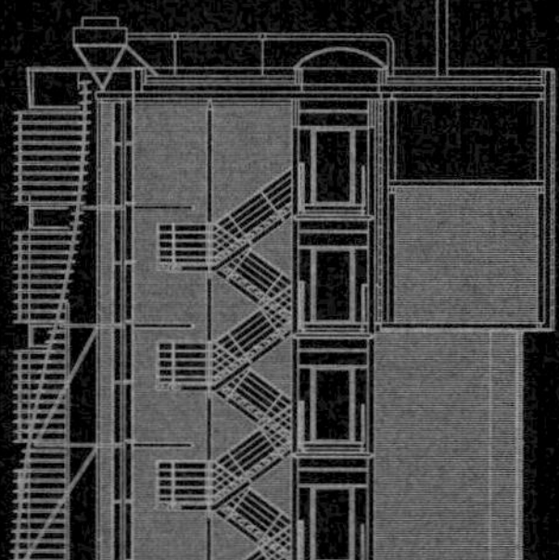

Section
1:400

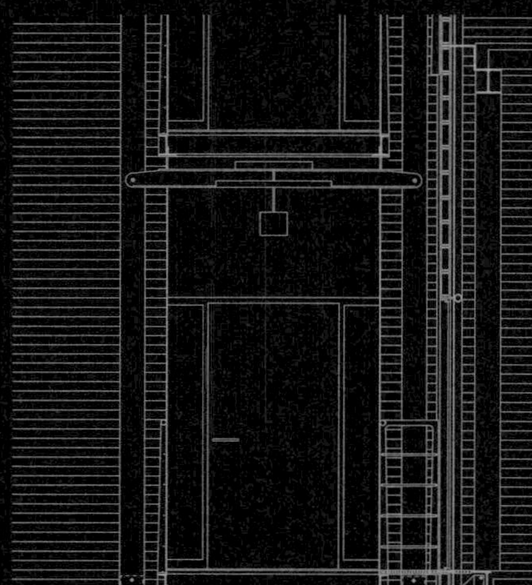

Part section
1:50

ScB

.ScB

Front facade with entrance hall of Constellation Building

.SbT

SbT

The gently curved side elevations of the Constellation Building allude to the aerodynamic shape of the aircraft after which the building is named. One wing is straight, the other is staggered. At the ends, the wings have huge panorama windows.

SbT

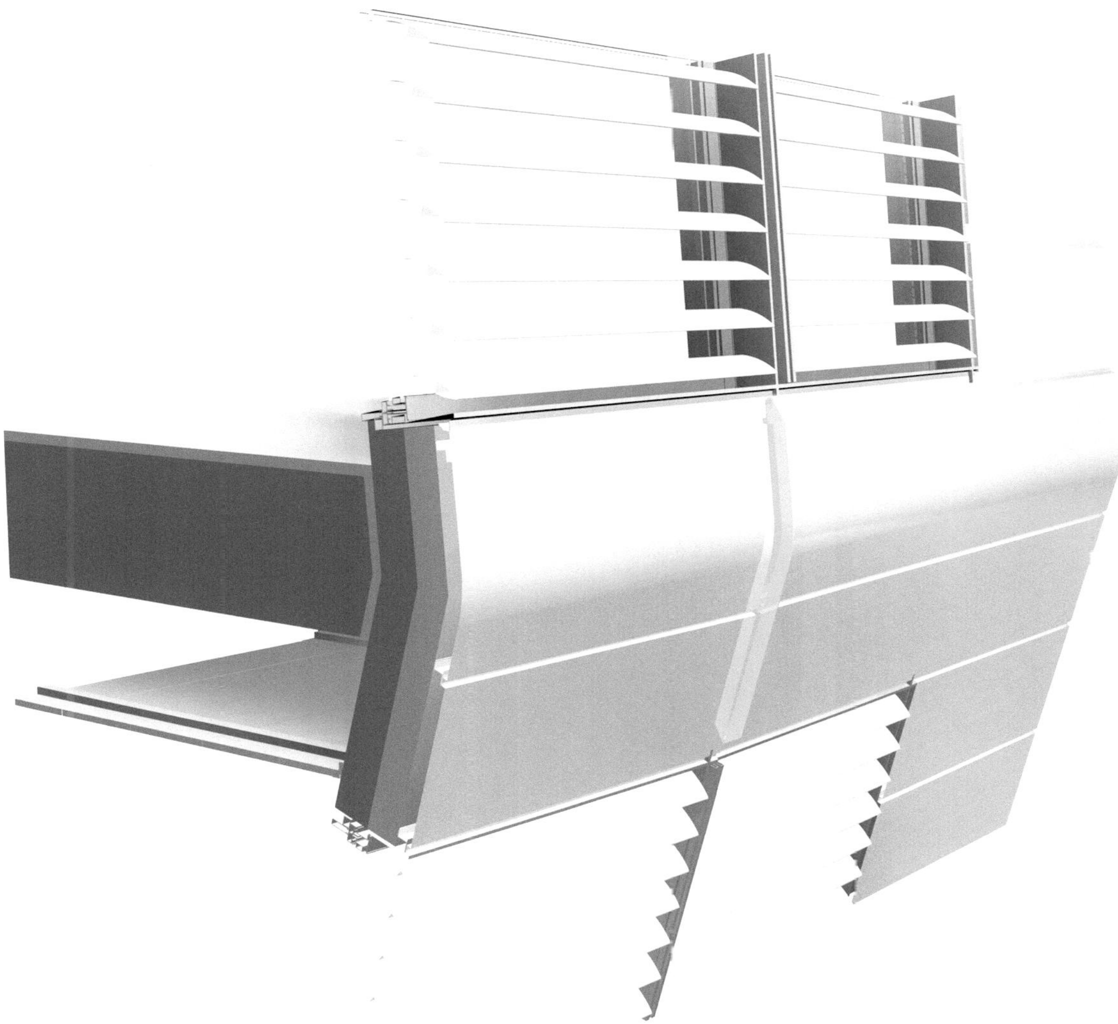

SbT

.SbT

Detail facade

Inner courtyard of Constellation Building

SbT

.SbT

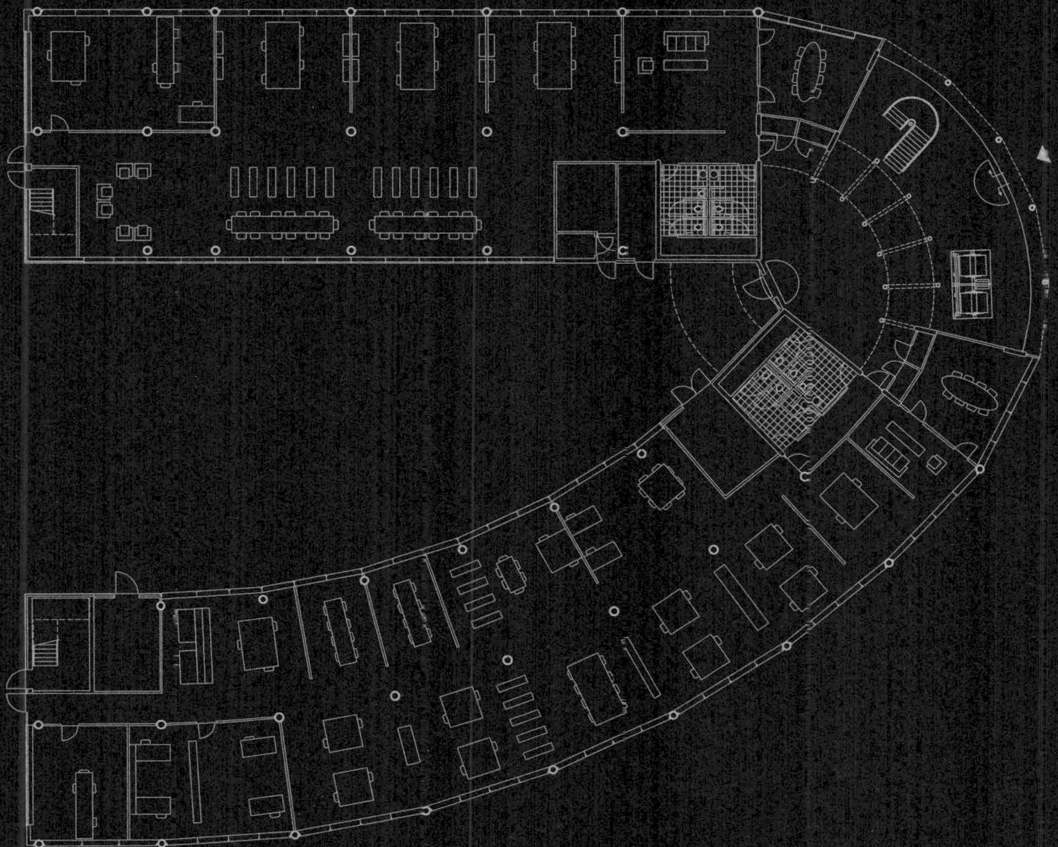

Ground floor
1:400

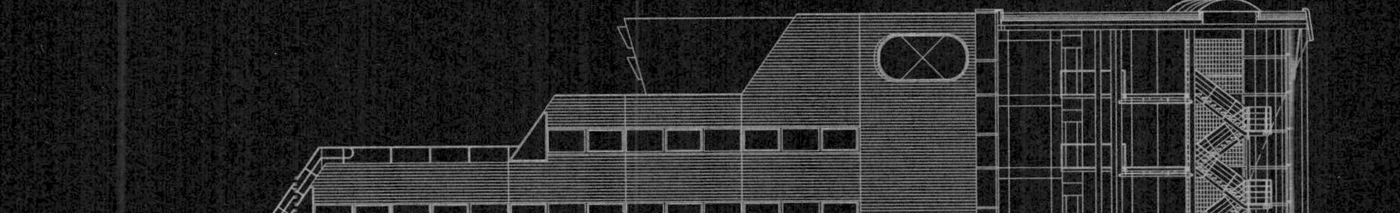

Section
1:400

SbT

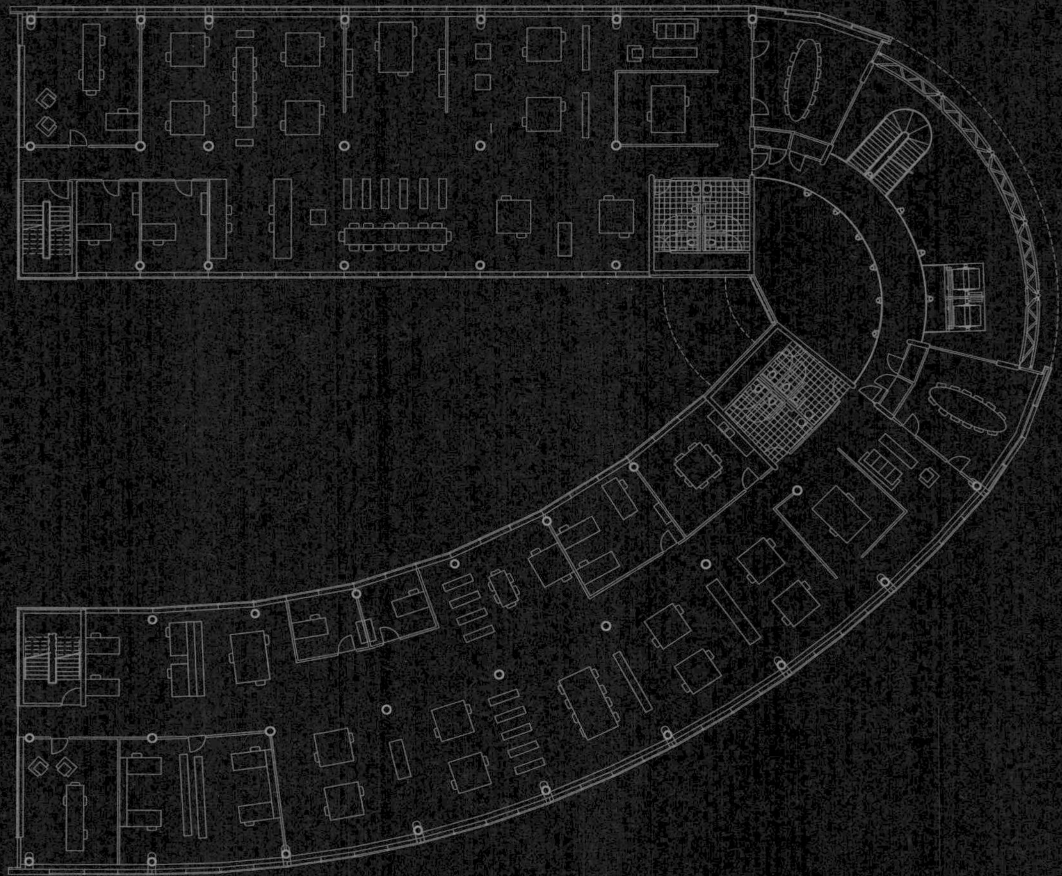

First floor
1:400

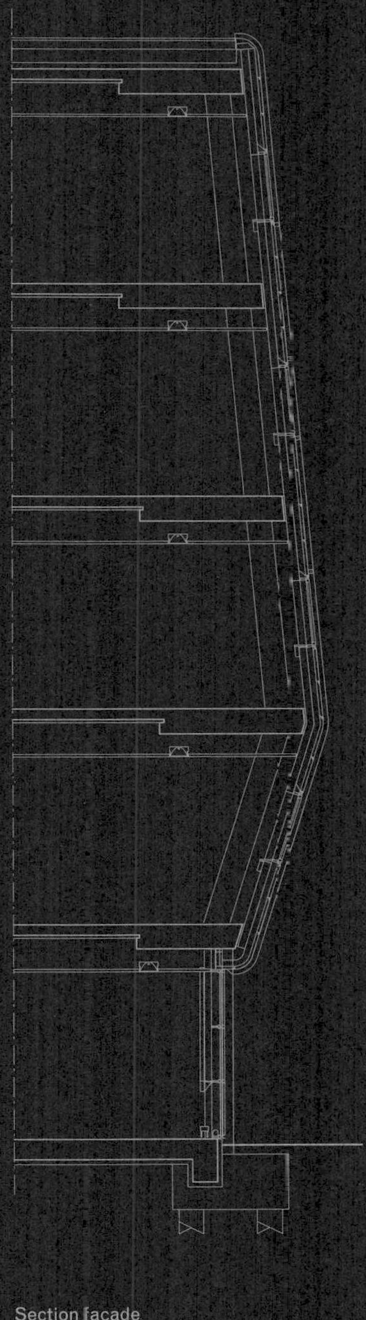

Section facade
1:120

Every building has a structure and connections between the different building parts and materials. It usually makes more sense to detail these as carefully as possible than to clad everything and hide it from sight. HvH

ZdK.

name
Renovation of Zuiderkerk

project code
ZdK

place
Gravenmakersplein,
Amsterdam

client
Stedelijke Woningdienst,
Amsterdam

design
1998 – 2000

construction
1998 – 2000

design team
Floris van Gennep
Hans van Heeswijk
Rutger van der Meer
Meike Stoetser
Joost Woertman

Zuiderkerk was completed in 1630 to a design by Hendrick de Keyzer. Deconsecrated early in the twentieth century, it was for many years used as a storage depot by the public works department. In 1980, the heyday of urban renewal, it became a studio for full-scale housing models. Since the 1990s, the Department of Physical Planning (dRO) has used the church building for exhibitions and symposia. Since the renovation by Hans van Heeswijk architecten, Zuiderkerk also houses the information centre of the Municipal Housing Agency (Stedelijke Woningdienst).
The renovation was seized on as an opportunity to reveal the original interior, which successive interventions had increasingly hidden from sight. The nave is once again a large, open space suitable for events, lectures and temporary exhibitions. The aisles accommodate an enquiry desk, call centre, a small auditorium and ancillary functions. A mezzanine floor inserted in the aisles provides space for permanent exhibitions.

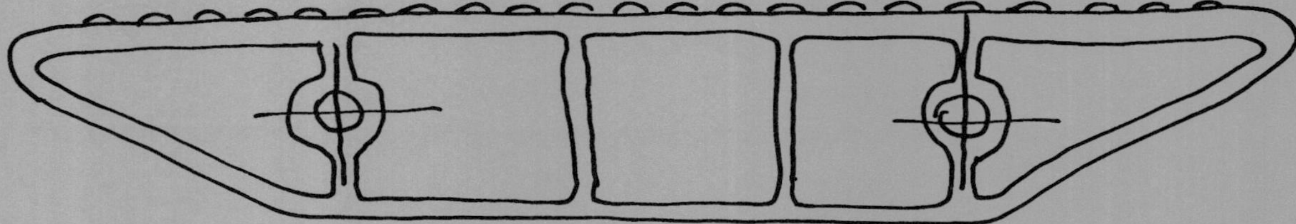

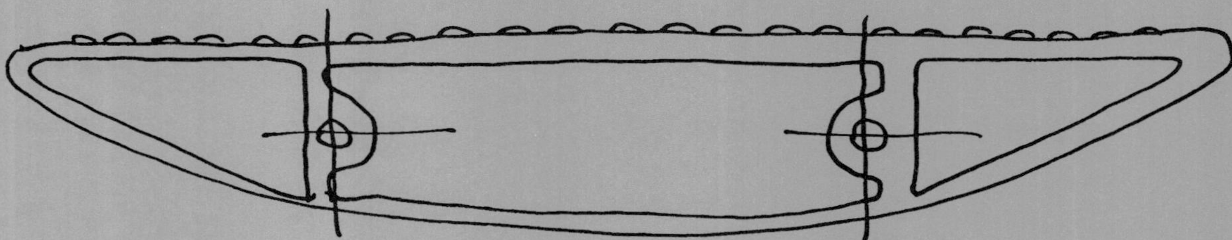

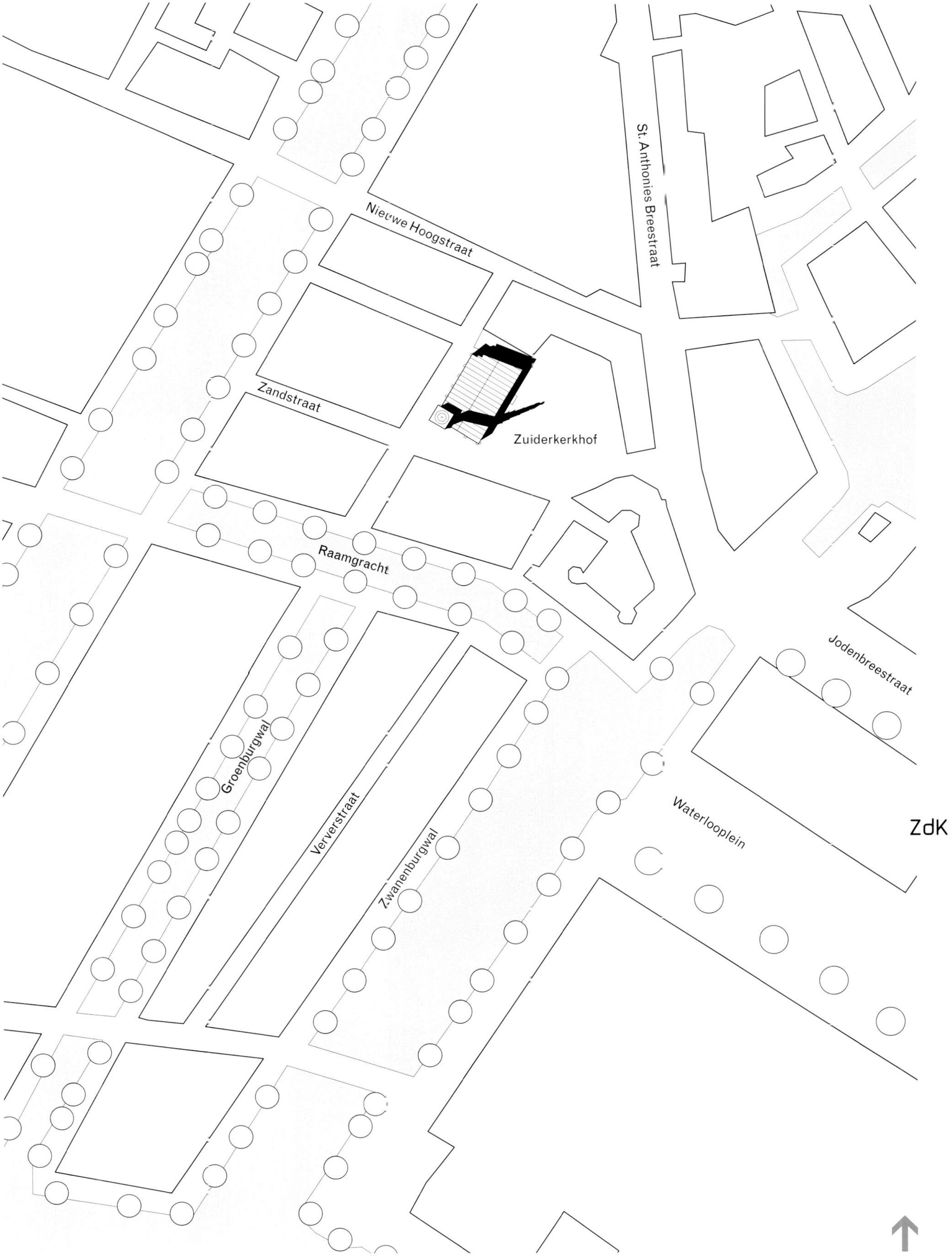

Nieuwe Hoogstraat
St. Anthonies Breestraat
Zandstraat
Zuiderkerkhof
Raamgracht
Jodenbreestraat
Groenburgwal
Ververstraat
Zwanenburgwal
Waterlooplein
ZdK

.ZdK

ZdK.former church 03

ZdK.former church 04

ZdK.street 01.HvH

ZdK.street 02.HvH

ZdK.main hall 05.LK

ZdK.main hall 06.LK

ZdK.main hall 07.LK

ZdK.detail 27.LK

ZdK.kiosk 20.LK

ZdK.kiosk 21.LK

ZdK.desk area 13.LK

ZdK.main hall 10.HvH

ZdK.desk 30.LK

ZdK.detail 25.LK

ZdK.stairs 15.LK

ZdK.stairs 16.LK

ZdK.stairs 17.LK

ZdK.stairs 18.LK

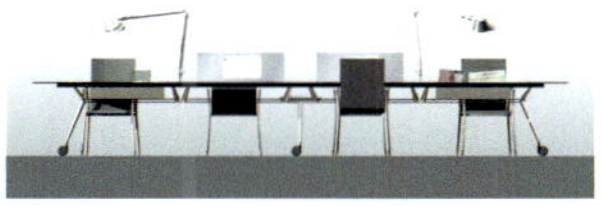

ZdK.furniture 23.HvH

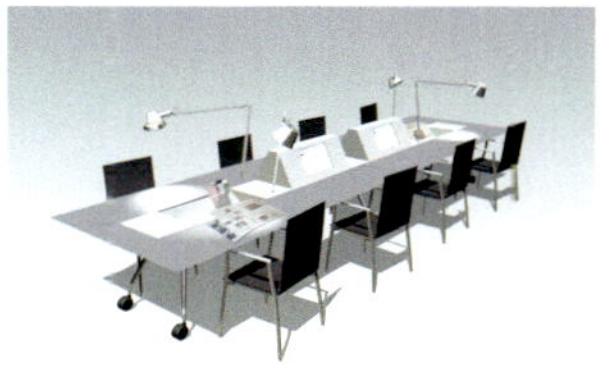

ZdK.furniture 24.HvH

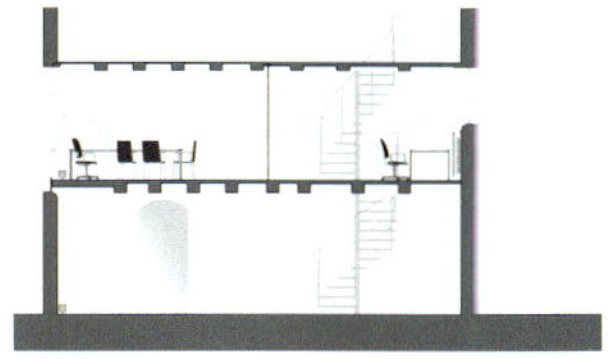

ZdK.sketch offices 29 HvH

ZdK.detail 28.HvH

ZdK.detail 29.HvH

ZdK.detail 26.HvH

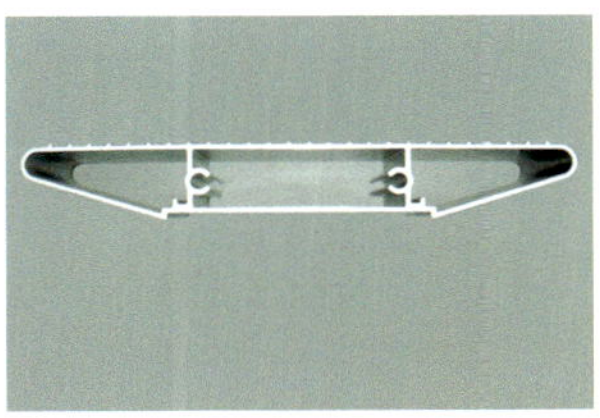

ZdK.stairs 19.HvH

ZdK.situation

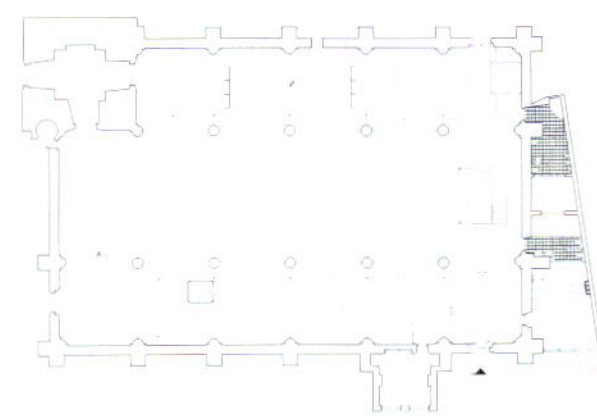

ZdK.ground floor

ZdK

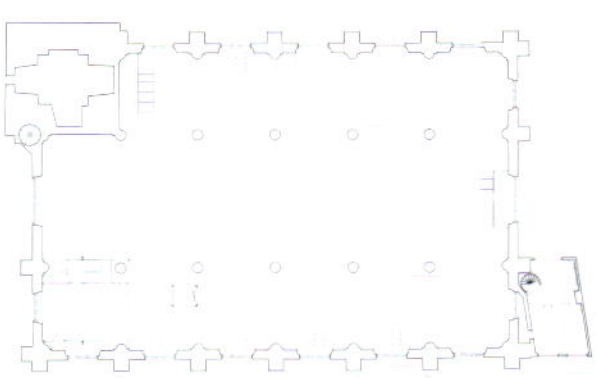

.ZdK

ZdK.first floor

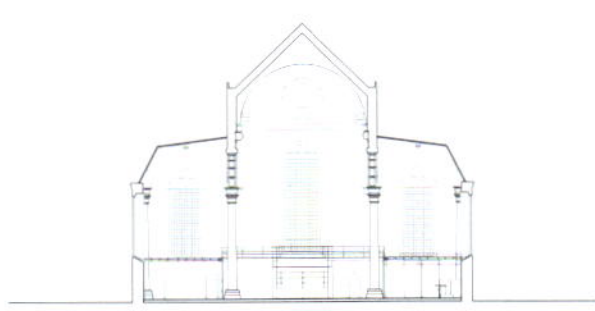

ZdK.section

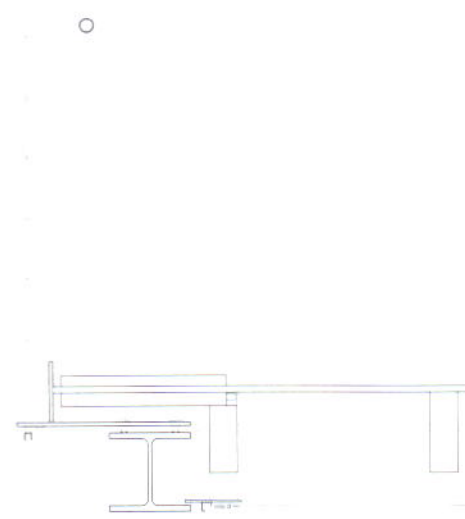

ZdK.detail banister

The church contains the exhibition space and information desk of the Department of Physical Planning (dRO), and the information and call centre of the Municipal Housing Agency. In addition, the remodelled church contains an auditorium, meeting rooms and office space.

. ZdK

To enhance the experience of the space and to distinguish old from new, all additions are in steel and glass and as light as possible. The furnishings are also light and open.

ZdK

7.ZdK

dienst Ruimtelijke Ordening
Grote kaart/maquette
Permanente exposities
Expo
'Amsterdam
1550/2000'
AMSTERDAM

ZdK

.ZdK

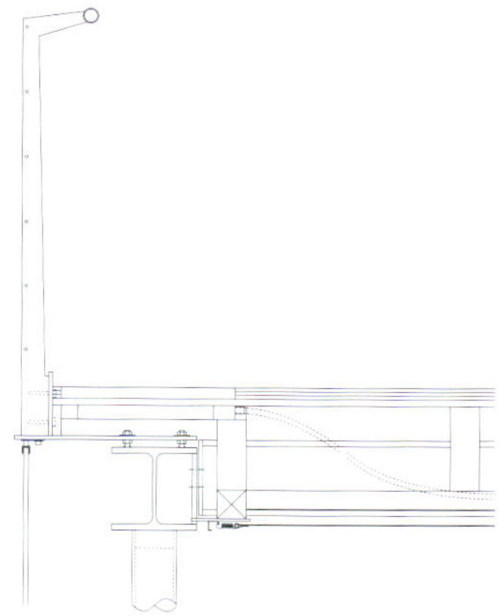

1:20

ZdK

Detail balustrade

Permanente
exposities

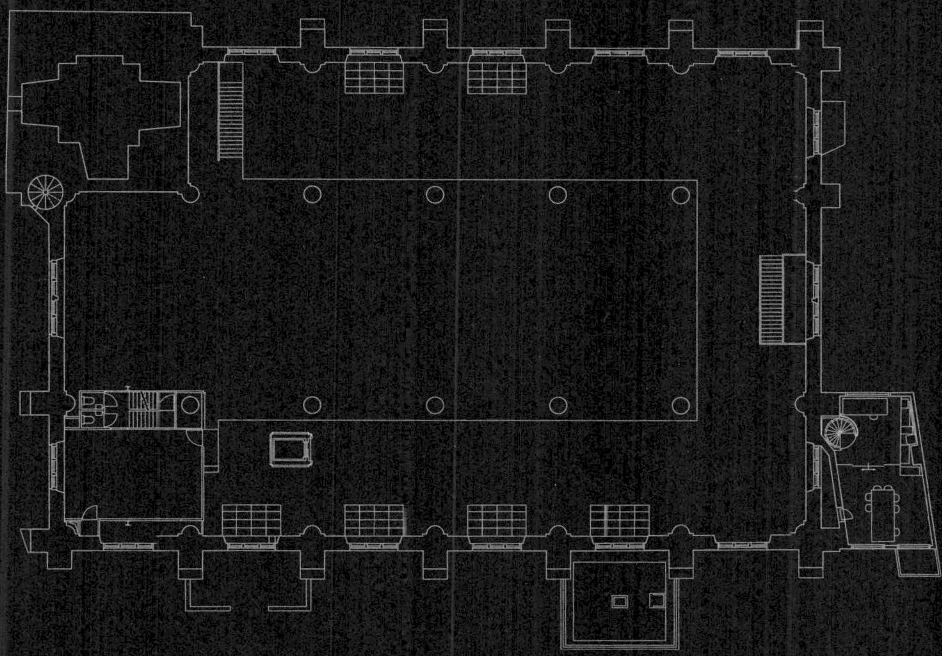

First floor

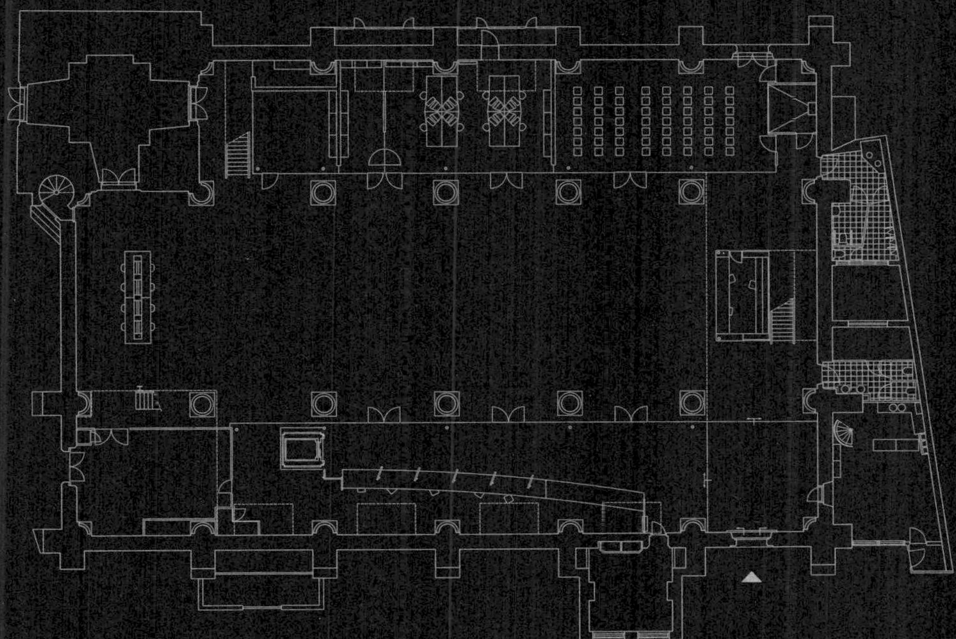

Ground floor
1:400

Section
1:120

.ZdK

Designing is a process of cleaning up, tidying, throwing away, analysing, ordering, sorting, choosing, selecting, classifying, composing, fitting, measuring, grouping, arranging, elaborating, refining and a little bit of styling. Good architecture results from searching for the ultimate solution and not stopping until it has been found. HvH

GoA.

name
Ganzenhoef Cultural
Educational Centre

project code
GoA

place
Bijlmerdreef 1245 t/m
1287, Amsterdam Zuidoost

client
SFB vastgoed bv,
Amsterdam

design
1999

construction
2000–2004

design team
Joris Berger
Peter Cammermans
Dick de Gunst
Stepanie Haumann
Hans van Heeswijk
Arjen Honig
Rob Hulst
Werner Kamp
Rutger van der Meer
André Meulenbelt
Arjan van Ruyven

The Ganzenhoef Cultural Educational Centre in Amsterdam-Southeast houses various social and cultural organizations. The largest part of the building is used as a Regional Training Centre. Other uses include a grand cafe, a conference centre and a sports hall. Above the centre are two floors of housing and below it is a basement car park.

The transparent multi-occupancy building is arranged around a publicly accessible atrium. The ready visibility of what is going on inside tempts passers-by to enter the building and take part in the activities. The heterogeneous programme is housed in a flexibly structured building: the clear separation between shell and contents means that it could in future be converted into a regular office building. As well as day-to-day activities, the atrium is suitable for events and exhibitions. From this covered plaza a central stair leads to the entrances on the upper floor.

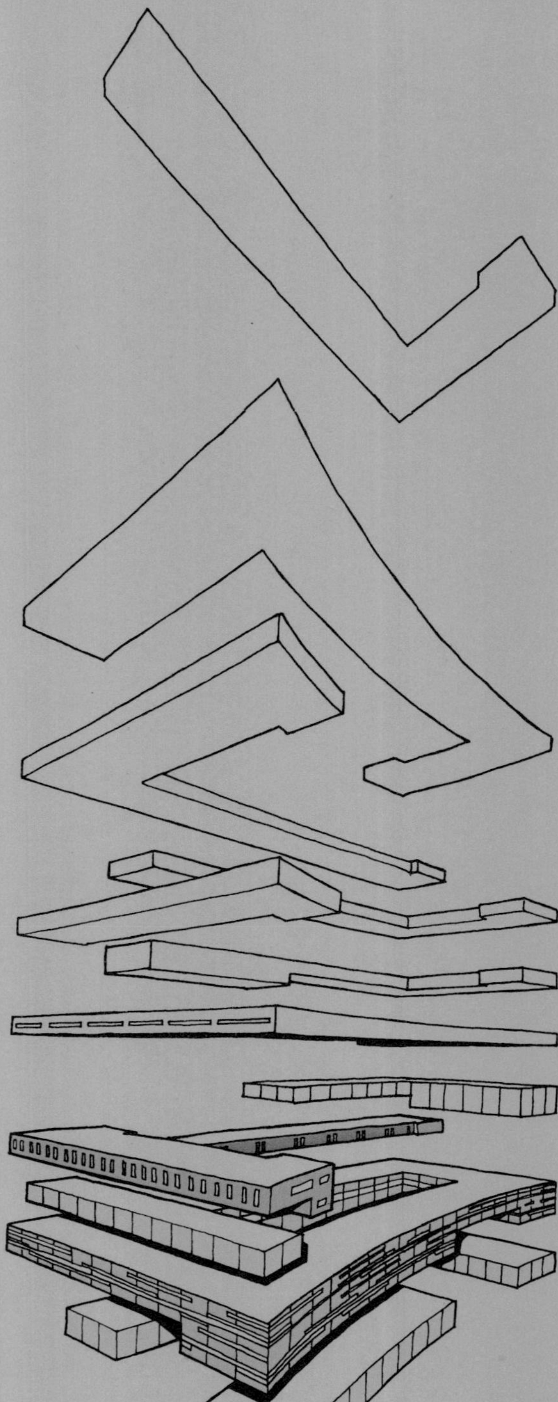

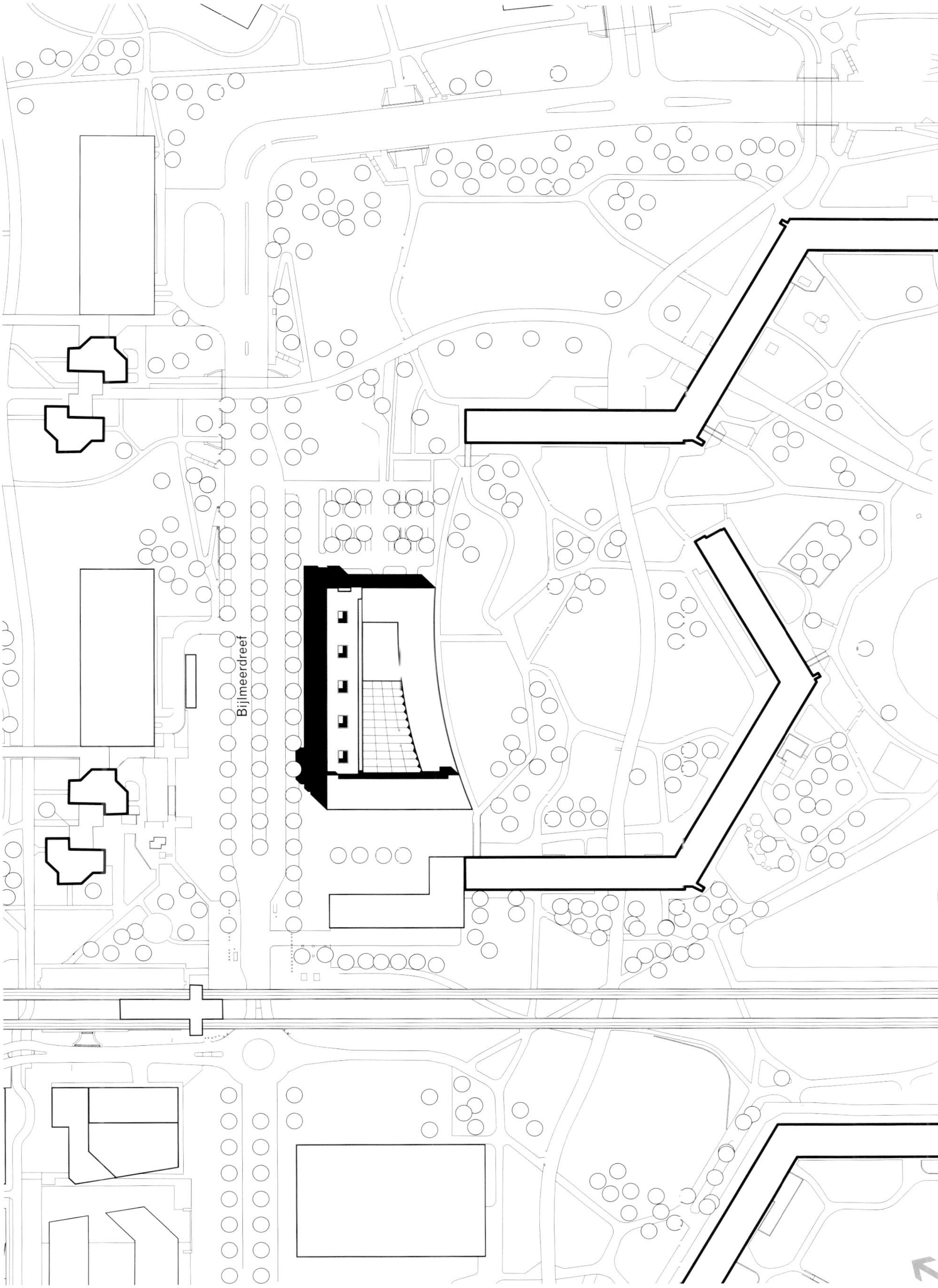

GoA

GoA

GoA.elevation 25.LK

GoA.elevation 26.LK

GoA.elevation 27.LK

GoA.elevation 14.LK

GoA.elevation 16.LK

GoA.elevation 17.LK

GoA.elevation 18.LK

GoA.elevation 19.LK

GoA.elevation 20.LK

GoA.entrance 29.DG

GoA.facade 12.HvH

GoA.facade 13.HvH

GoA.court 44.LK

GoA.entrance 46.LK

GoA.entrance 56.DG

GoA.atrium 35.LK

GoA.atrium 36.LK

GoA.atrium 39.DG

GoA.atrium 42.LK

GoA.desk 61.LK

GoA.desk 59.LK

GoA.desk 65.LK

GoA.interior 52.LK

GoA.desk 62.LK

GoA.interior 54.LK

GoA.interior 53.LK

GoA.interior 55.LK

GoA

GoA.gallery 74.LK

GoA.gallery 76.LK

GoA.dwelling patio 81.LK

.GoA

GoA.dwelling corner 80.LK

GoA.roof 06.LK

GoA.roof 09.DG

GoA.roof 04.HvH

GoA.roof 05.HvH

GoA.detail roof 01.HvH

GoA.detail roof 03.DG

GoA.stairs 67.LK

GoA.stairs 68.LK

GoA.stairs 70.LK

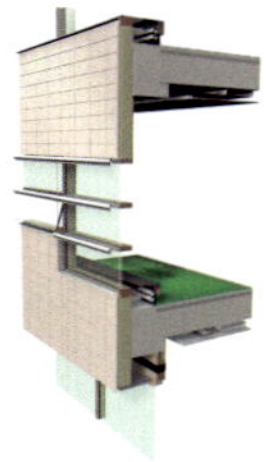

GoA.detail facade 30.HvH

GoA.detail facade 31.HvH

GoA.detail facade 32.HvH

GoA.detail facade 33.HvH

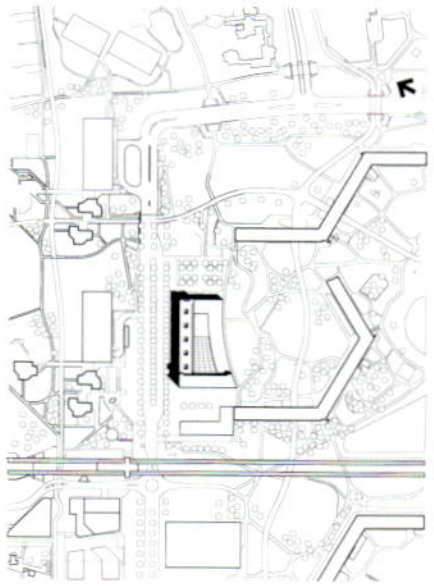

GoA.situation

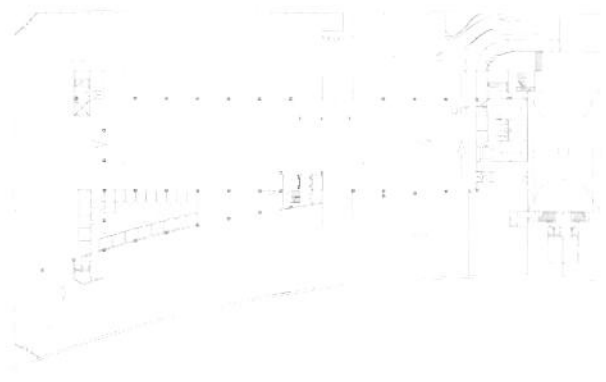

GoA.parking garage

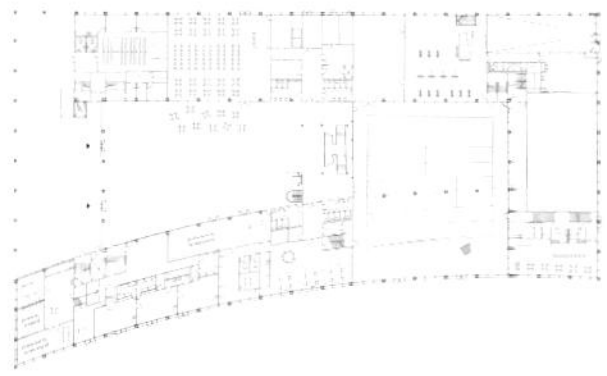

GoA.ground floor

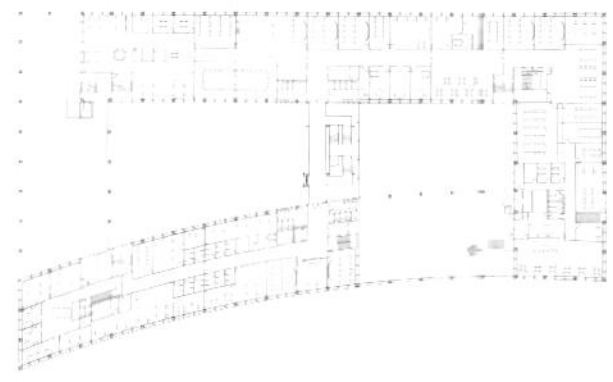

GoA.first floor

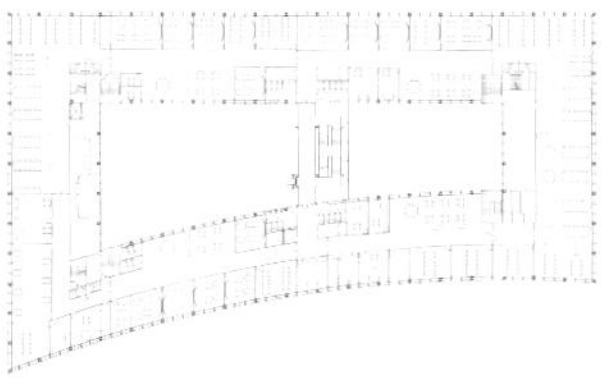

GoA.second floor

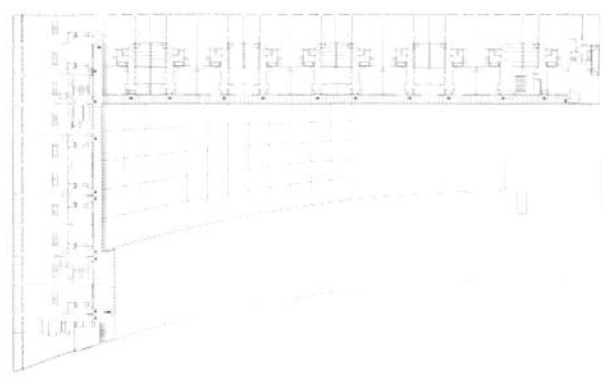

GoA.third floor

GoA.top floor

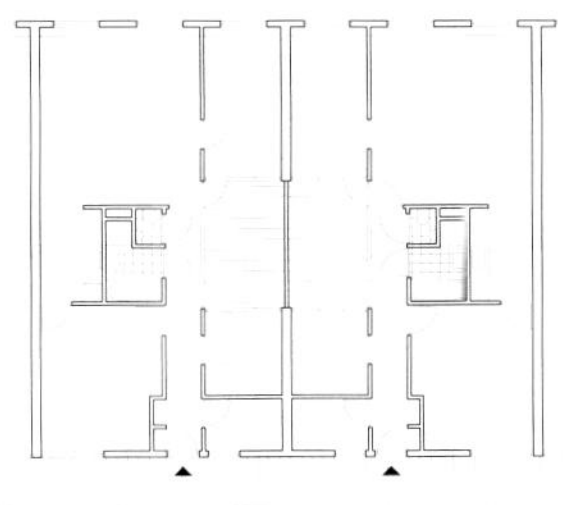

GoA.dwelling A

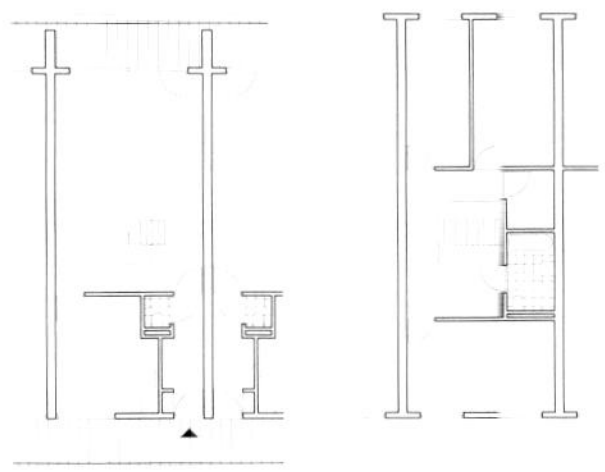

GoA.dwelling B

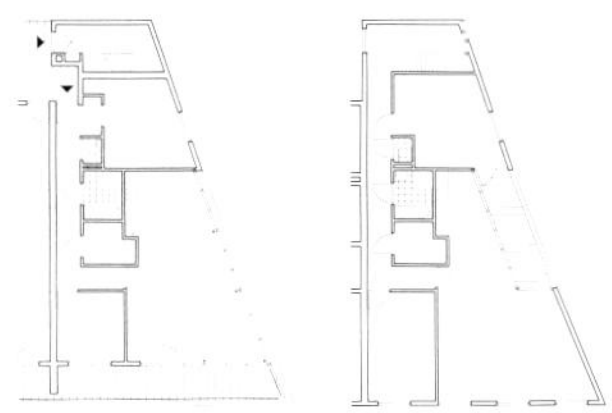

GoA.dwelling C–D

GoA.facade

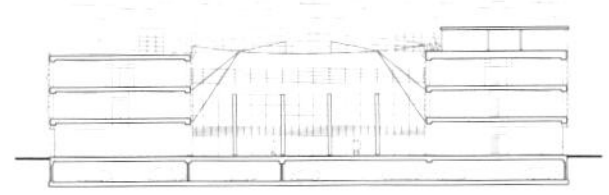

GoA.section 1

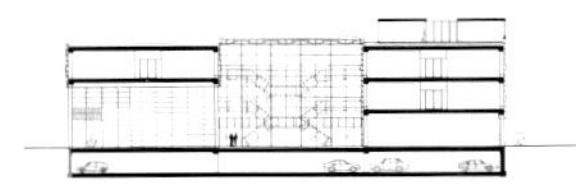

GoA.section 2

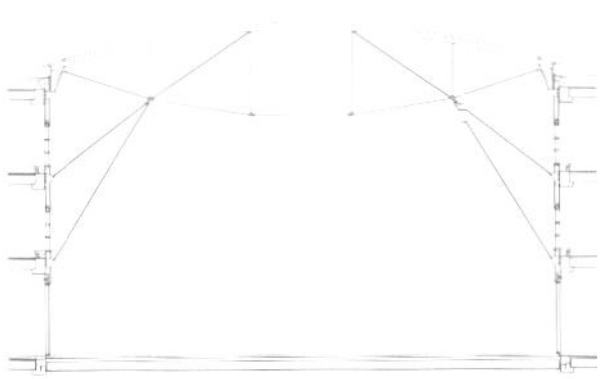

GoA.section inner court

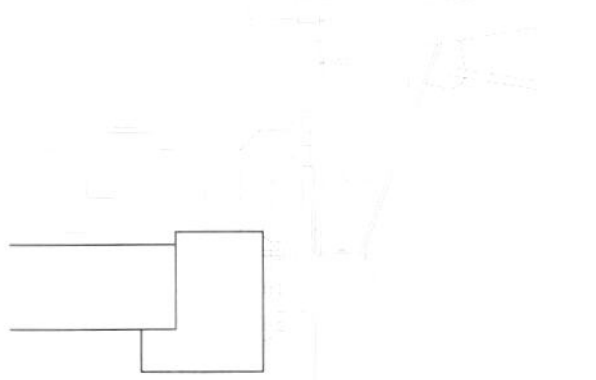

GoA.detail roof 1

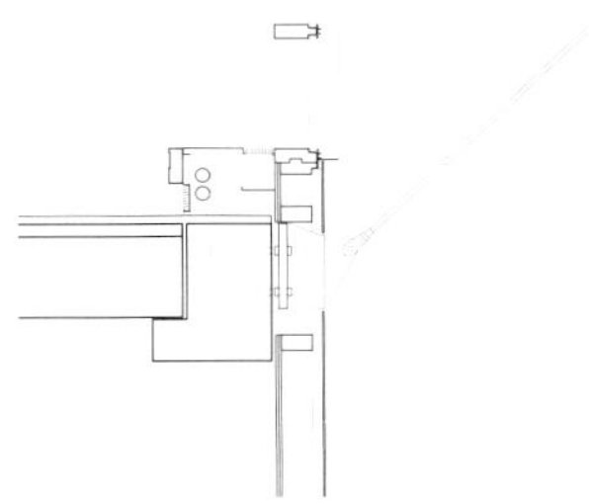

GoA.detail roof 2

GoA

The Bijlmer is a 1960s housing estate once promoted as 'the city of tomorrow for the people of today'. Consisting mainly of high-rise blocks in a park-like setting, the district was from the very beginning plagued by social problems, low occupancy rates and a high turnover of residents. Since 1992 the Bijlmer has been the subject of a radical makeover which has seen a lot of high-rise buildings demolished and replaced by high-density, low-rise housing. In addition, a host of amenities have been added, including this centre on Bijlmerdreef.

All the functions can be inferred from the outside of the building. From top to bottom: dwellings, training centre and community facilities. The largely closed facades of the top two floors of apartments are in sharp contrast to the rest of the volume which becomes progressively more transparent as one moves downwards.

In addition to its circulation function, the atrium can also be used as an auditorium or exhibition space.

GoA

The atrium has an air cushion roof of double ETFE film. This provides a transparent, lightweight roof with excellent thermal and acoustic properties. The skewed lines of the floor plan are reflected in a roof with a varied span. The steel structure, whose main purpose is to prevent the roof from lifting, was kept slender in the interests of maximum transparency.

GoA

3.GoA

So as not to detract from the open character of the public [illegible] stairs and lifts are executed in steel and glass.

The counters, bars and pantries provide a colourful contrast to the building's predominantly serene colour scheme.

GoA

.GoA

GoA

Patio dwelling

The rooftop dwellings are reached via a gallery on the inside of the block. Patios and skylights bring daylight into the heart of the very deep plans. As well as patio dwellings and apartments there are also maisonettes.

GoA

1.GoA

For the sake of speedy assembly, the facades of the training centre on the first and second floors are realized in timber-frame elements measuring 7.2 by 3.7 metres. On the outside they are finished with terracotta panels; on the inside with cement fibre board.

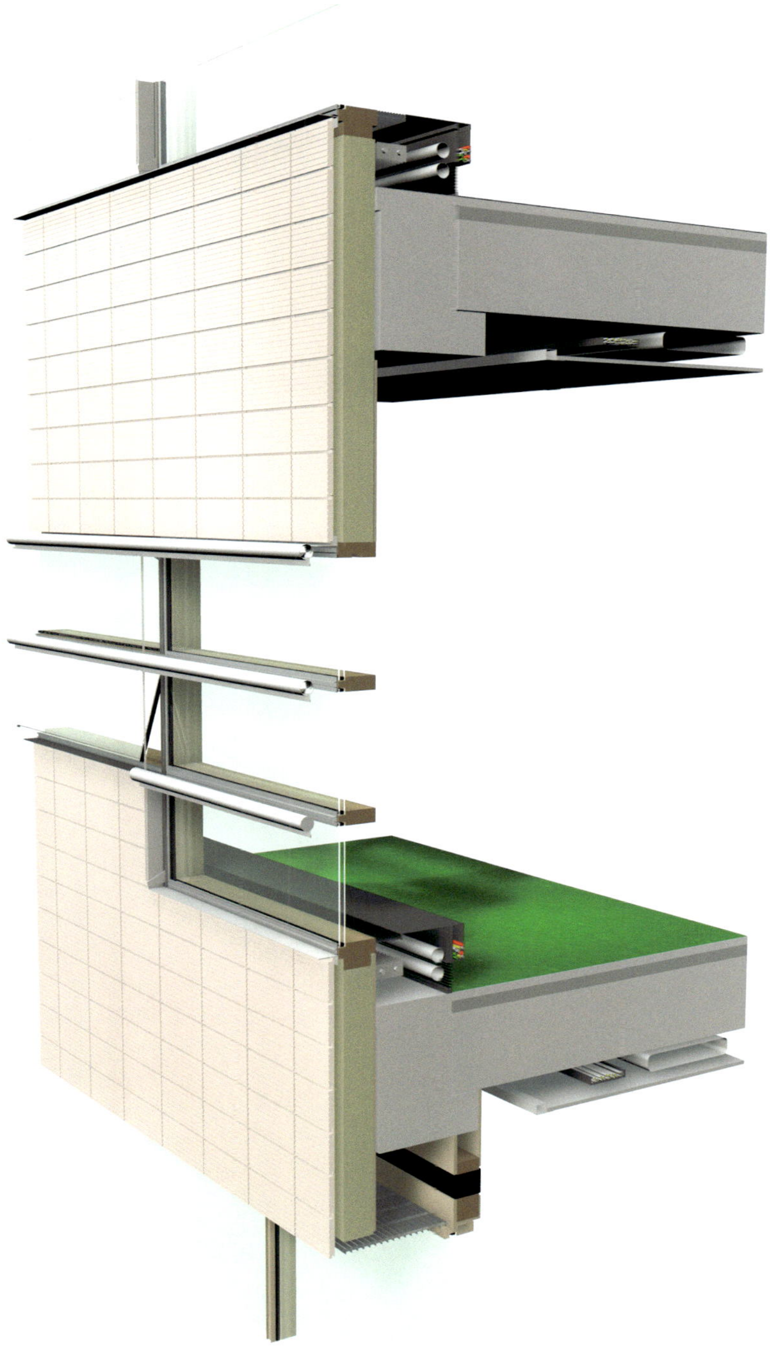

Detail facade

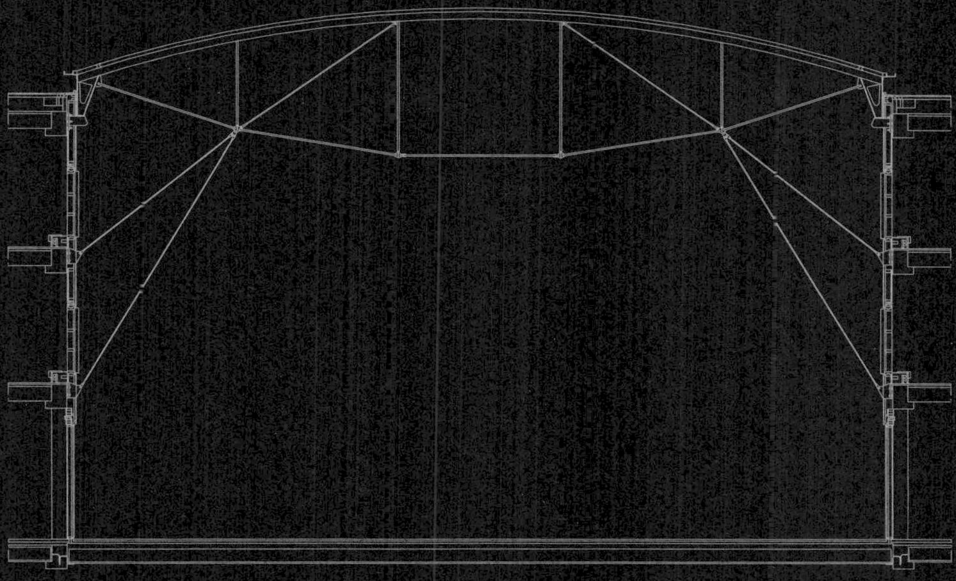

Section atrium
1:200

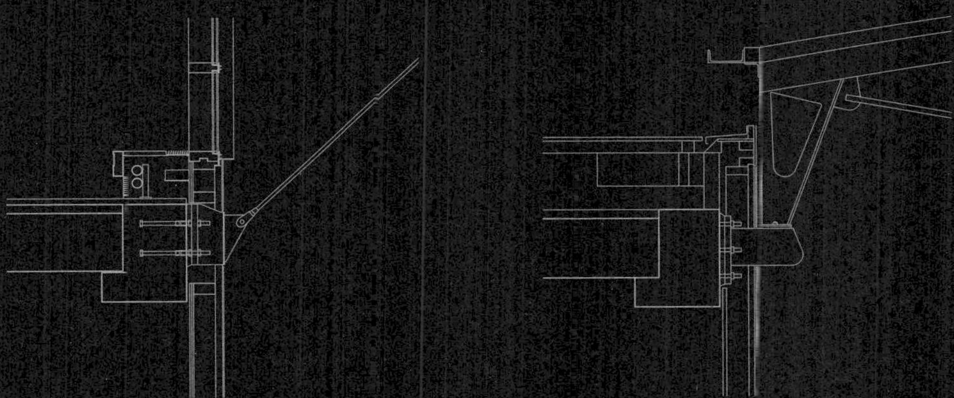

Details atrium roof fixing
1:50

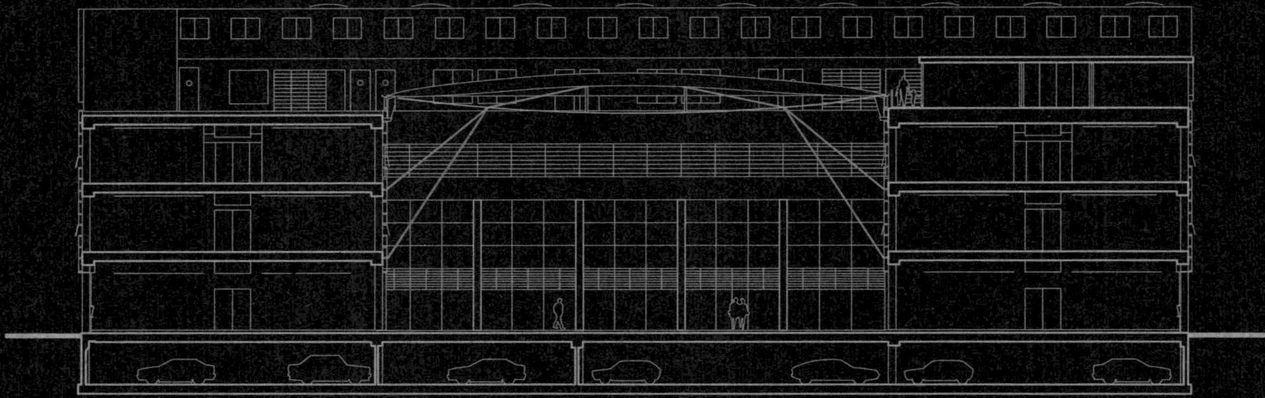

Section 1
1:400

Facade
1:400

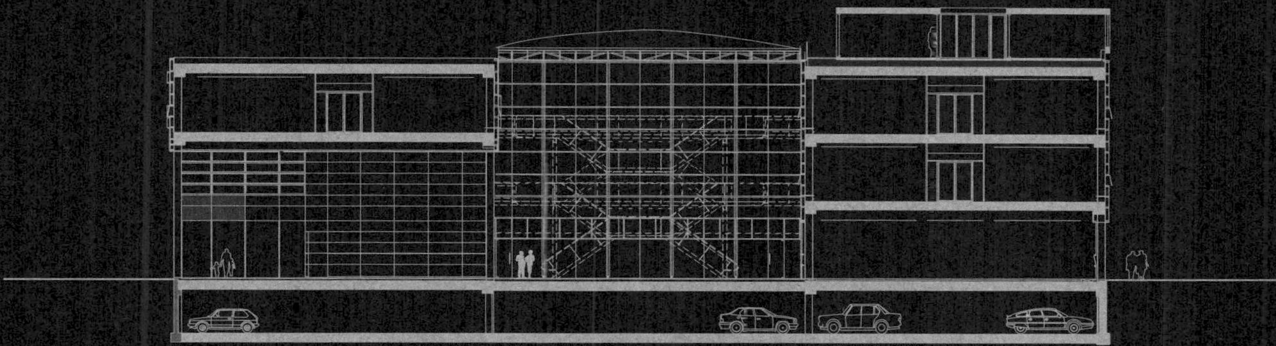

Section 2
1:400

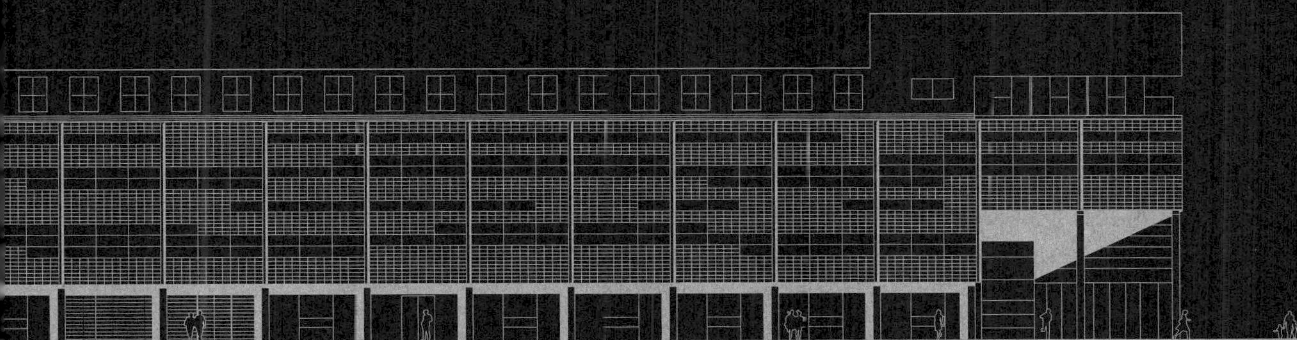

GoA

First floor

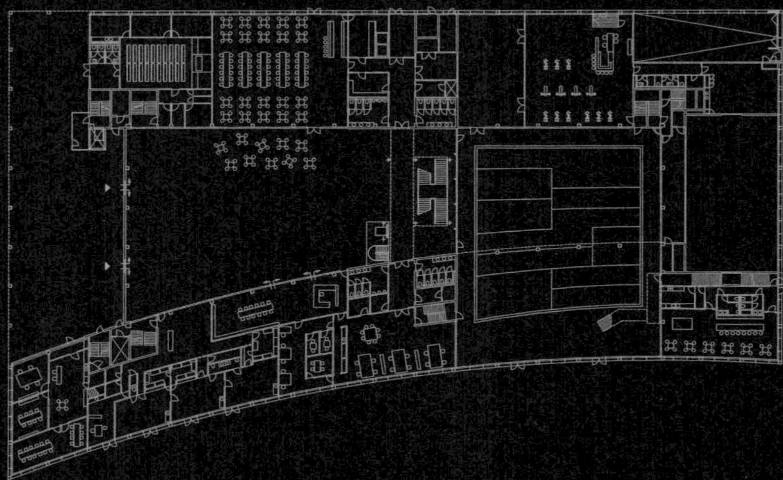

Ground floor

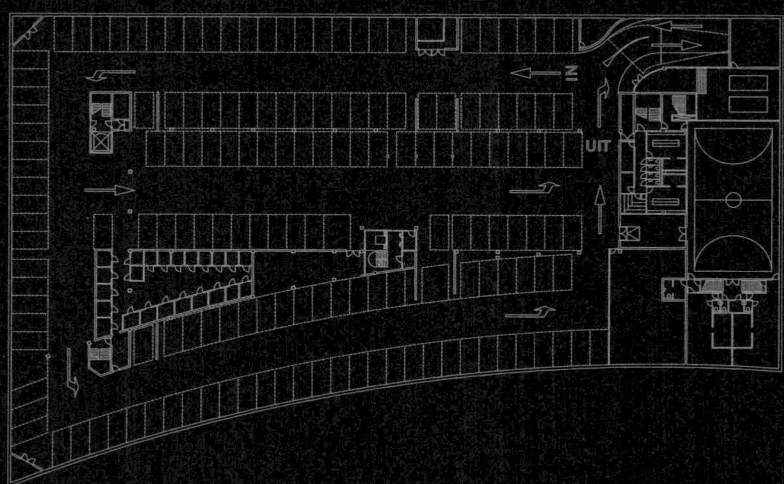

Parking
1:1000

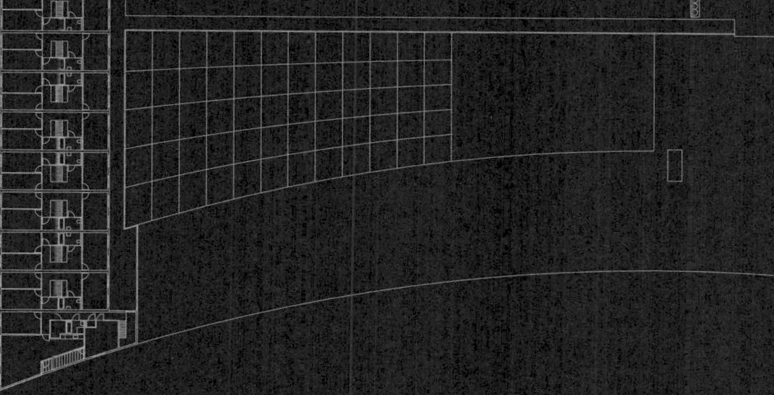

Fourth floor

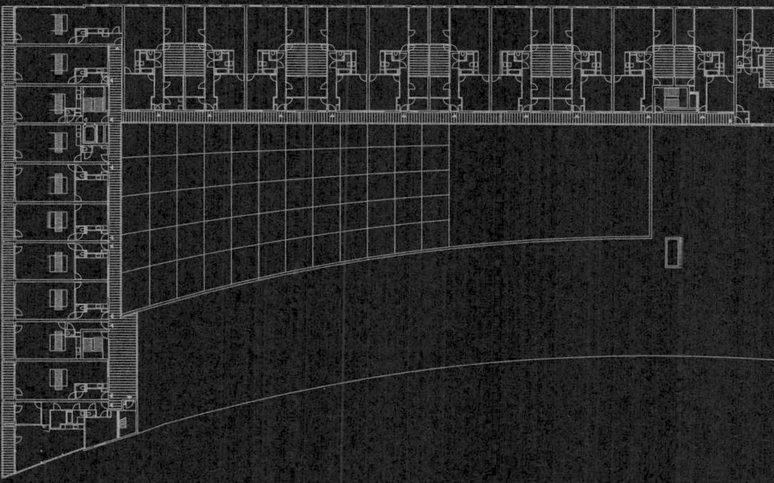

Third floor

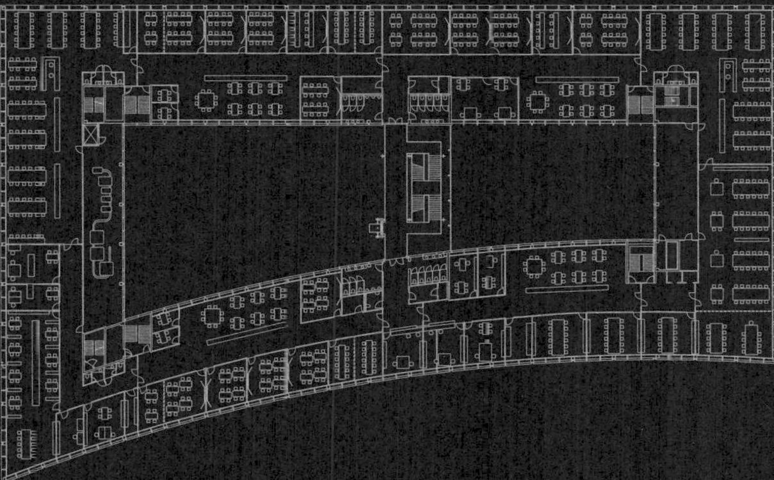

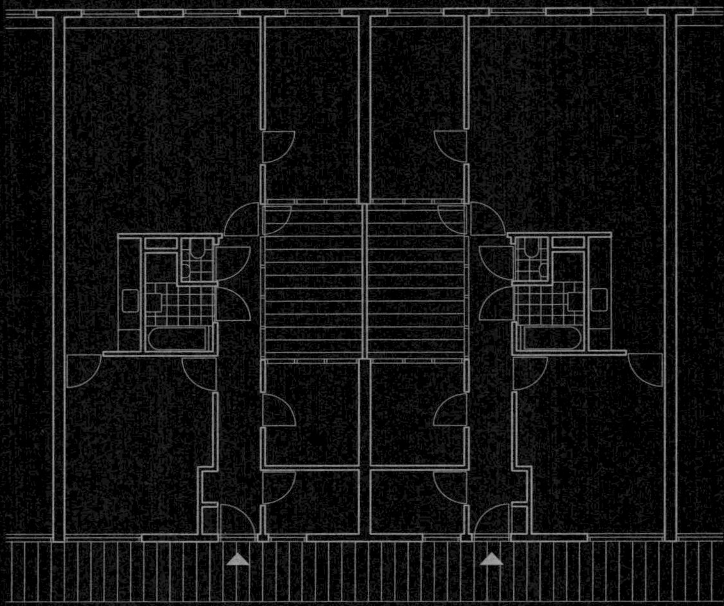

Dwelling A
1:200

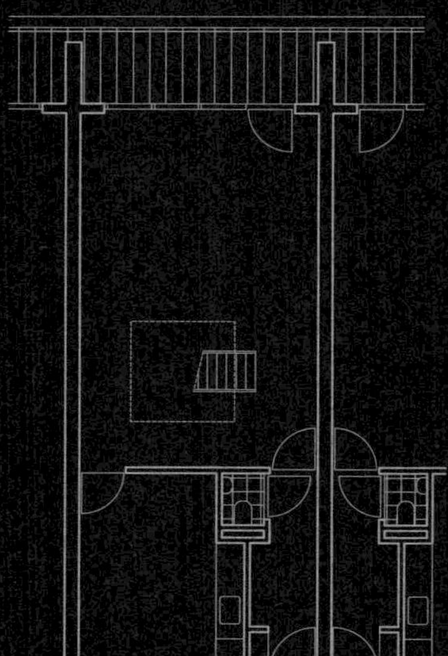

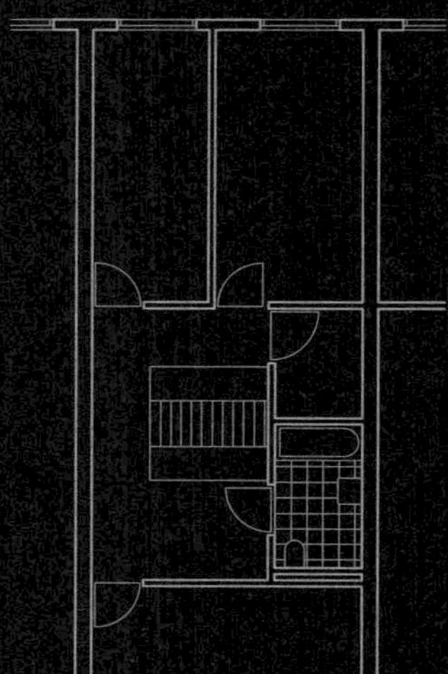

Dwelling B
1:200

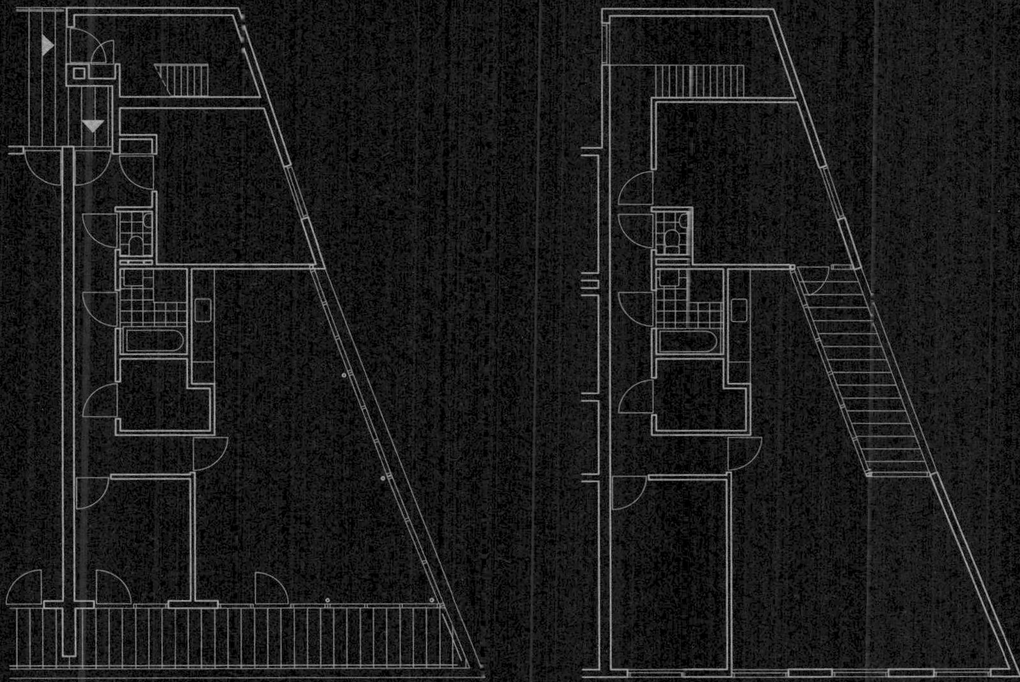

Corner dwelling (C-D)
1:200

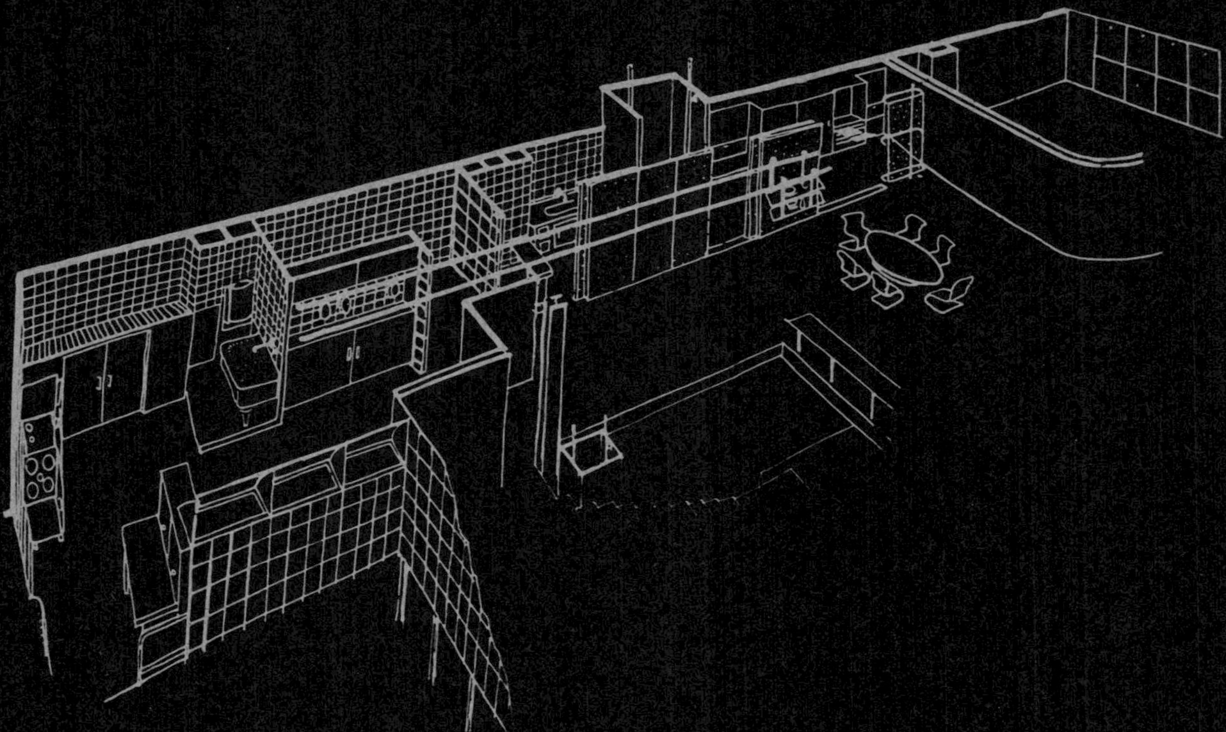

Ceiling-mounted system of rails for conveying meals from the kitchen to the dining room, Maison de Verre, Paris (unrealized)

KeI.

name
Renovation of interior of De Key directors' office

project code
KeI

place
Ertskade 1, Amsterdam

client
Woonstichting De Key, Amsterdam

design
2000

construction
2000–2001

design team
Ellen Baan
Hans van Heeswijk

The ground floor of Frits van Dongen's The Whale apartment block in the Eastern Docklands area of Amsterdam is taken up by offices and commercial premises. One of the offices is used by the directors of the De Key housing corporation. The rooms are rather low and fairly dark. The aim of the interior design was to make them as light and open as possible, with long sight lines, a clear layout and a restrained materialization.

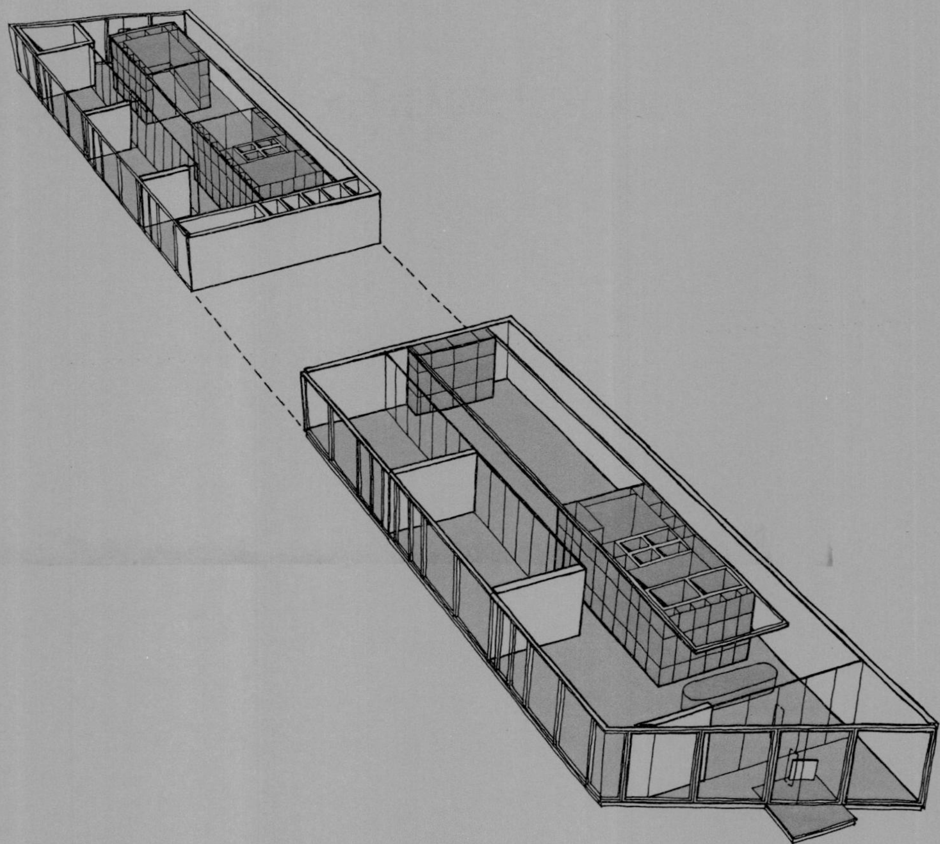

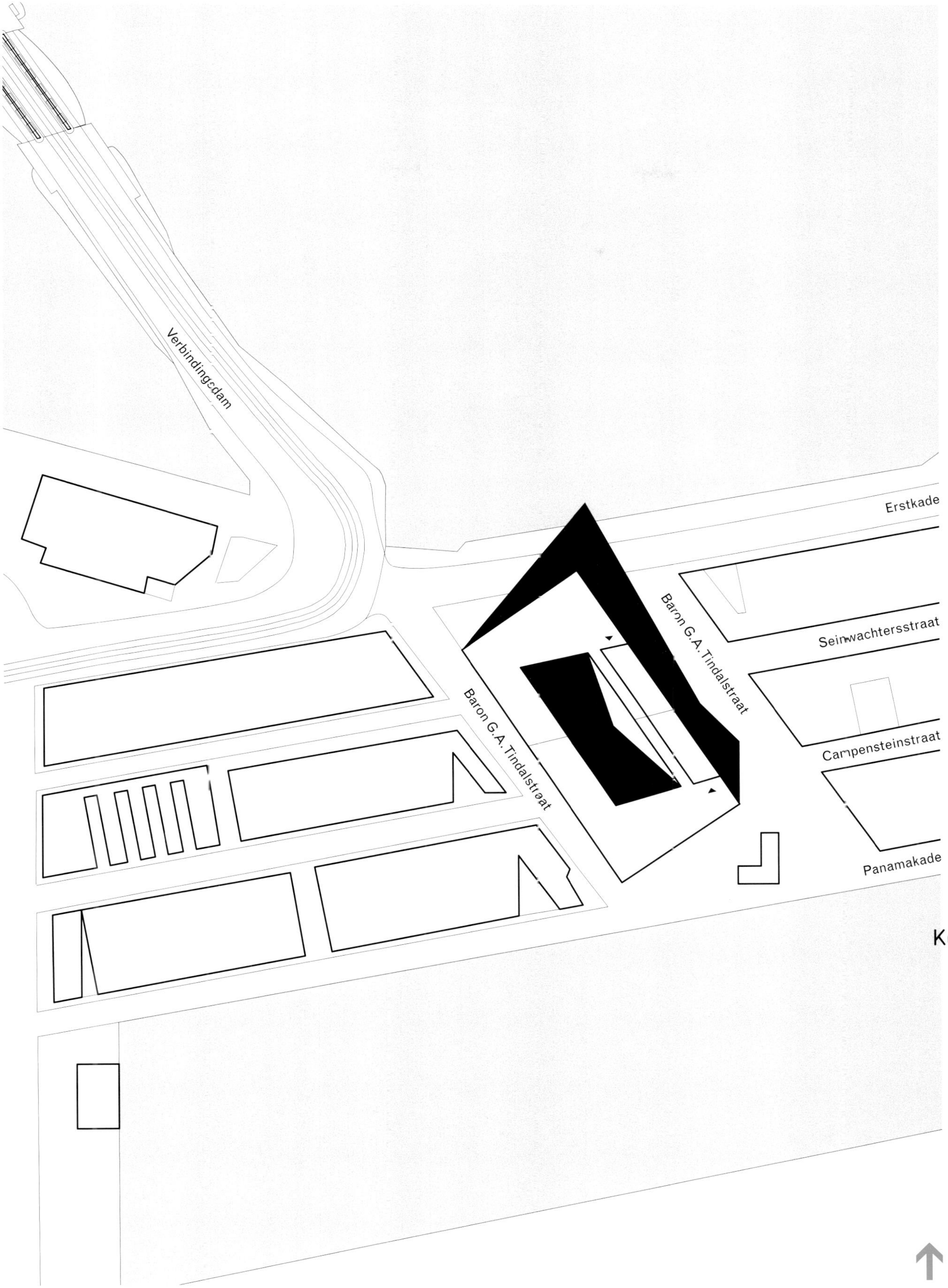
Verbindingsdam
Erstkade
Seinwachtersstraat
Baron G.A. Tindalstraat
Baron G.A. Tindalstraat
Campensteinstraat
Panamakade

KeI

KeI.elevation 08.LK

KeI.entrance 07.LK

KeI.pantry 04.LK

KeI.corridor 05.LK

KeI.meeting room 06.LK

KeI.meeting room 02.LK

KeI.corridor 01.LK

KeI.waiting room 03.LK

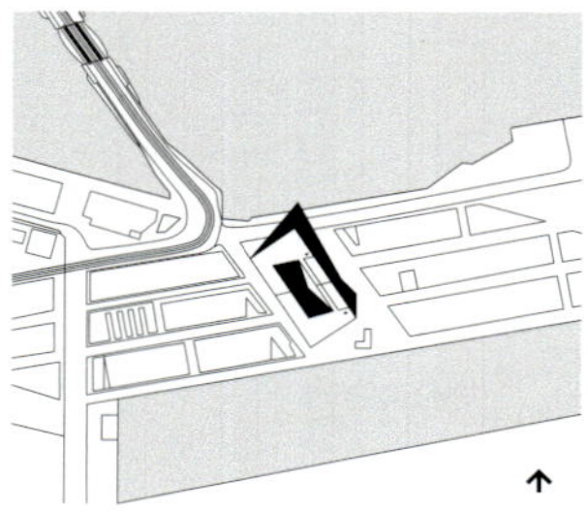

KeI.situation

KeI.floor plan

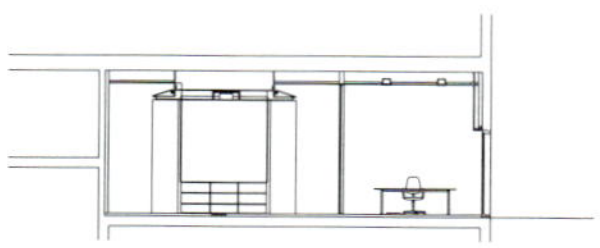

KeI.section

KeI

7.KeI

KeI

.KeI

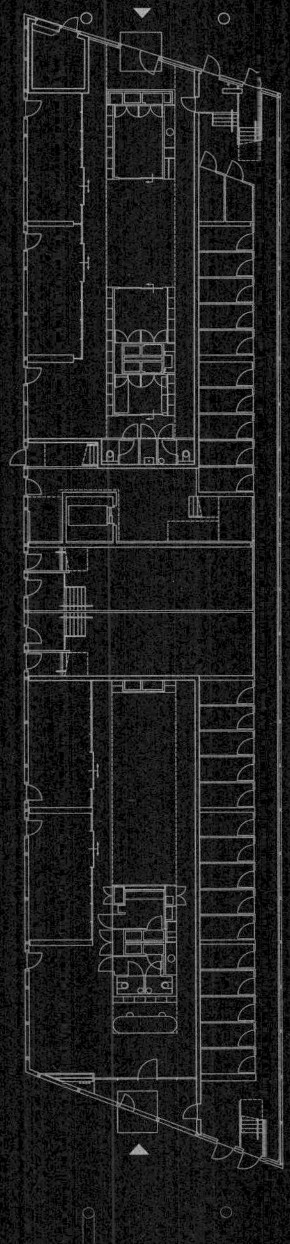

Floor plan
1:400

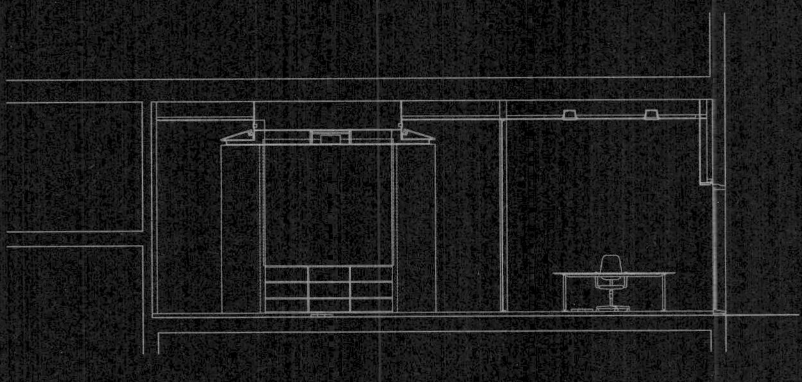

Section
1:120

However clearly and completely you see a building in your mind's eye while designing, actually experiencing the space for the first time is a unique sensation. It is always so much more spatial than you imagined, that for a few seconds you feel like a visitor in your own design. That moment alone makes the whole architectural enterprise worthwhile. HvH

AtT.

name
Beta Building,
Amsterdam Teleport

project code
AtT

place
Naritaweg 106–120,
Amsterdam Teleport

client
Montefiore Vastgoed bv,
Amsterdam

design
2000

construction
2000–2002

design team
Hans van Heeswijk
Jeroen Rademaker
Jochem van der Spek
Rick Thani

Among the office buildings at Teleport, the business district around Amsterdam-Sloterdijk railway station, stands this crisply-detailed, multi-occupancy building. It consists of a transparent entrance hall between two wings of different lengths. On top of this orthogonal building is an organically shaped roof structure. The building itself can be divided into variously sized offices. Dimensions and facilities are geared to heavy use, for example as a call centre.

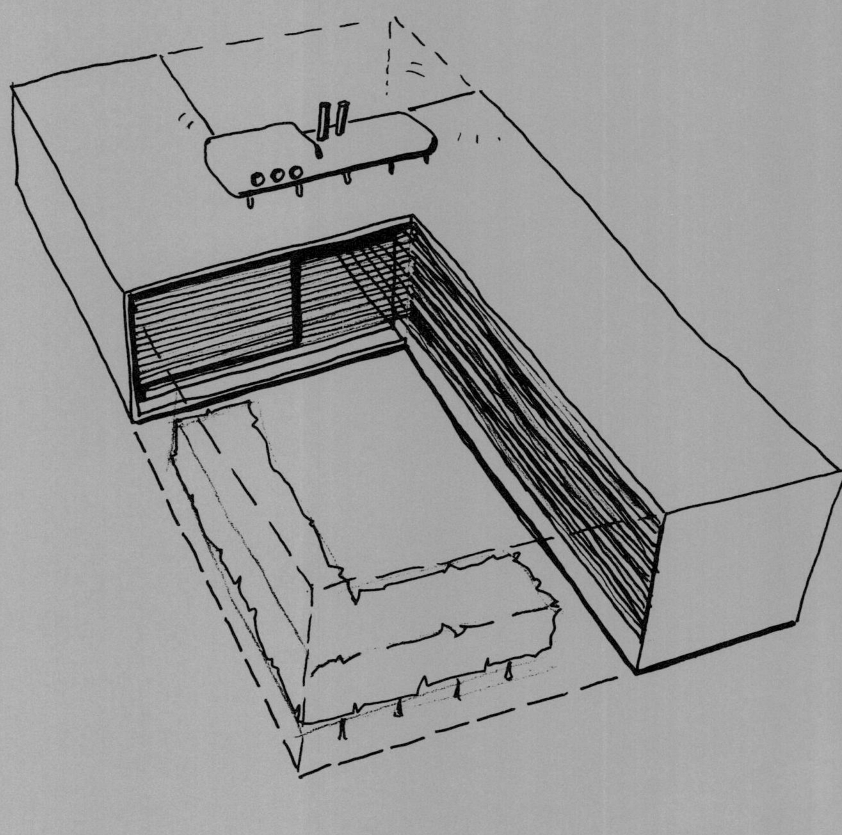

Het Betagebouw staat aan de Naritaweg, parallel aan de spoorlijn naar Haarlem.

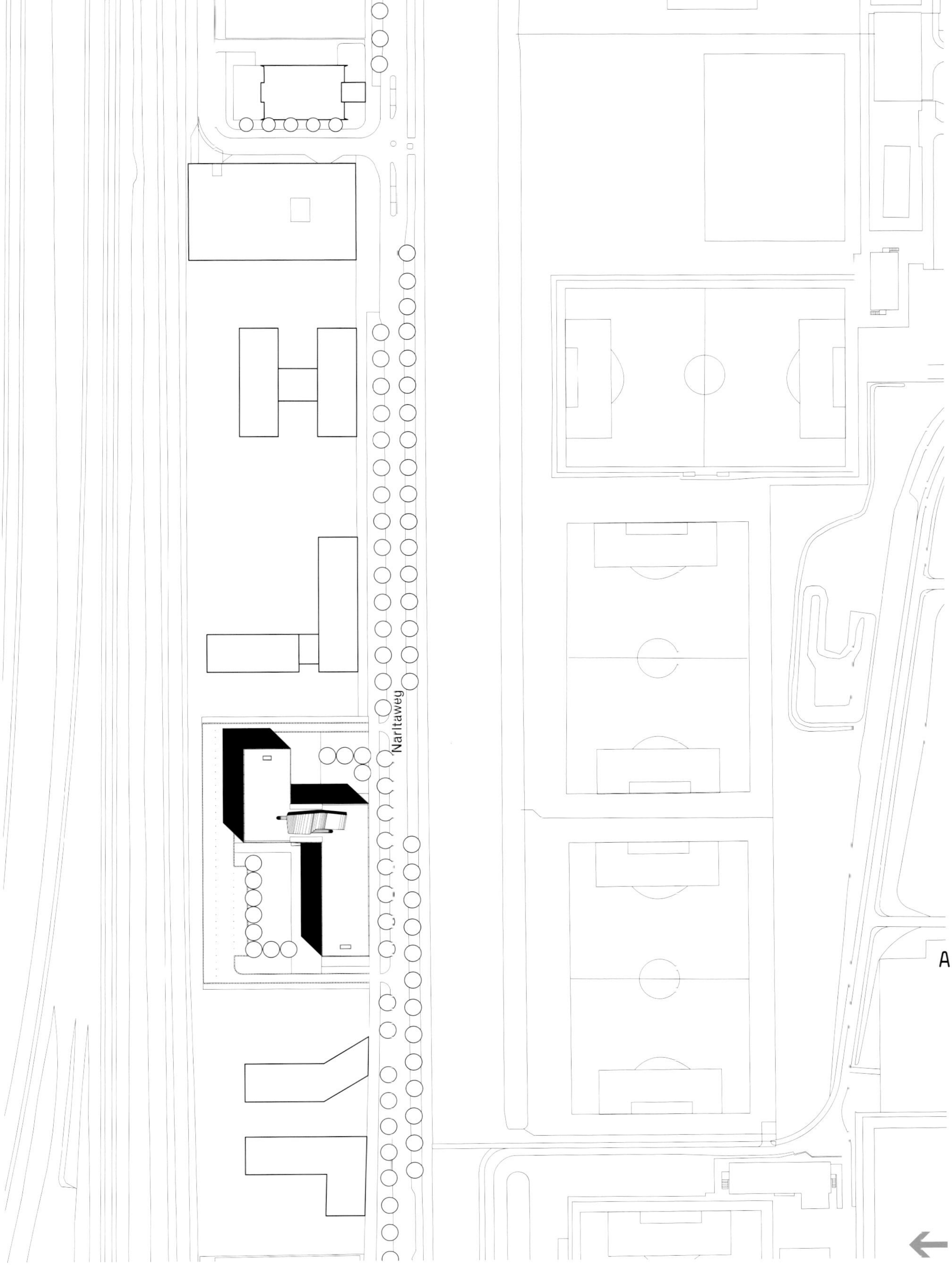

AtT.beta building 08.RR

AtT.beta building 09.RR

AtT.beta building 10.RR

AtT.beta building 11.RR

AtT.entrance 04.RR

AtT.entrance 05.RR

AtT.entrance 06.RR

AtT.entrance 07.RR

AtT.entrance 29.RR

AtT.facade 14.RR

AtT.facade 16.RR

AtT.facade 17.RR

AtT.facade 18.RR

AtT.lobby 13.RR

AtT.lobby 19.RR

AtT.lobby 20.RR

AtT.lobby 21.RR

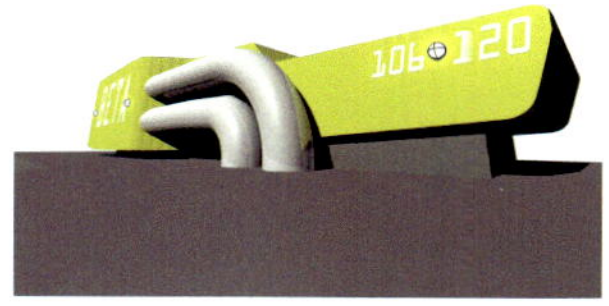

AtT.roof blob 22.HvH

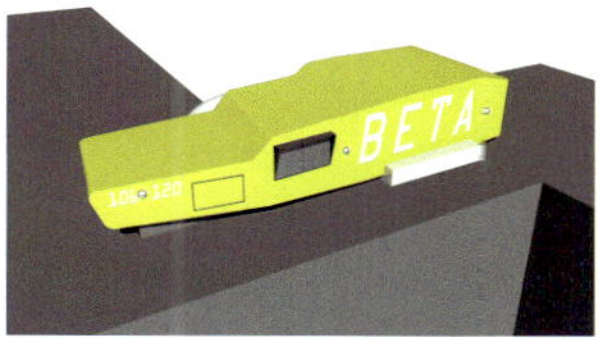

AtT.roof blob 23.HvH

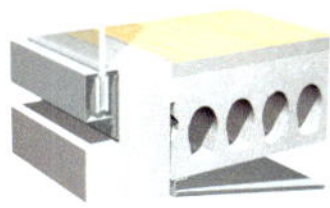

AtT.detail bridge 26.HvH

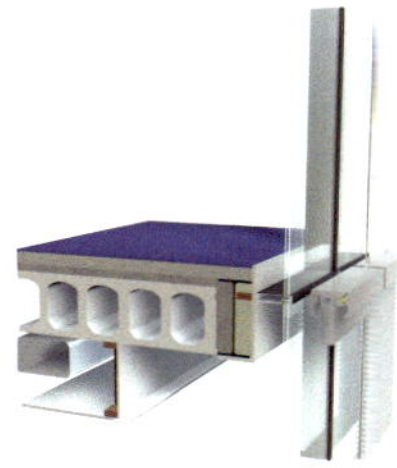

AtT.detail facade 24.HvH

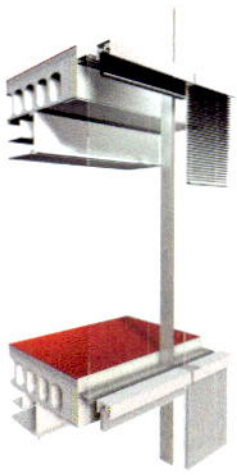

AtT.detail facade 25.HvH

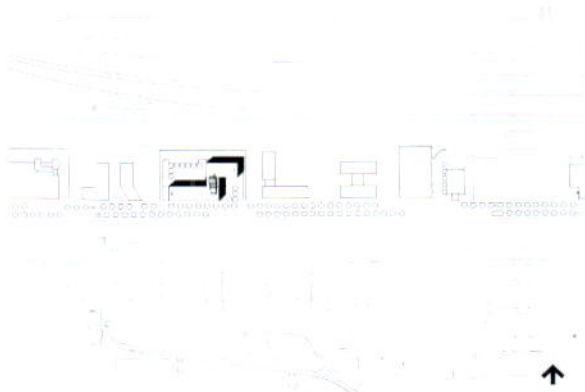

AtT.situation

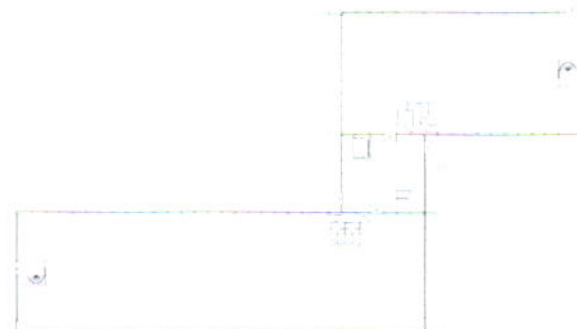

AtT.ground floor

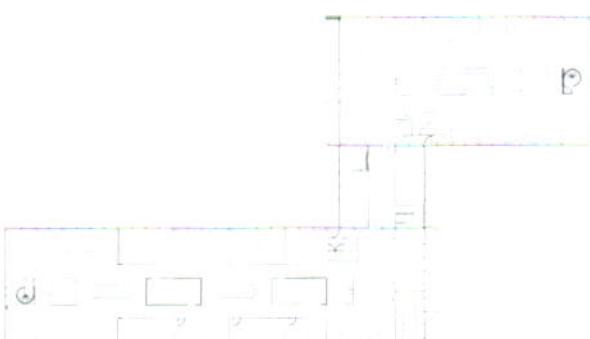

AtT.first floor

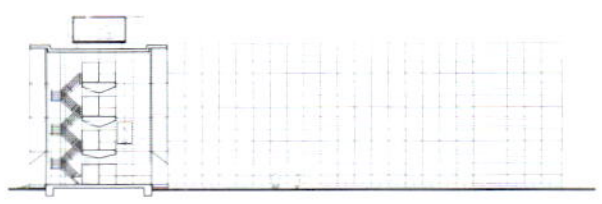

AtT.section

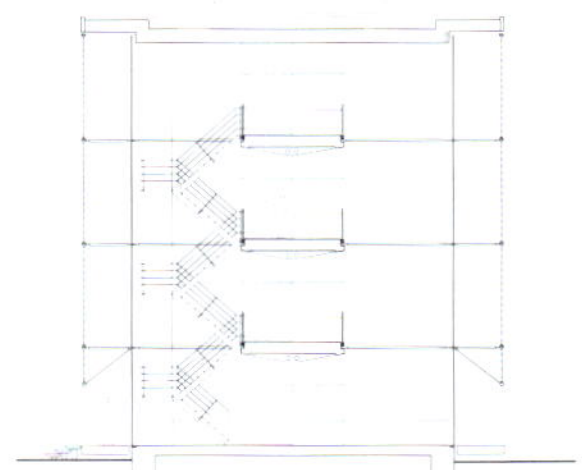

AtT

AtT.section fragment

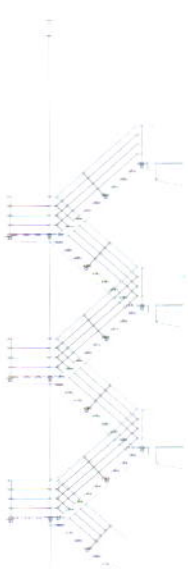

.AtT

AtT.stairs

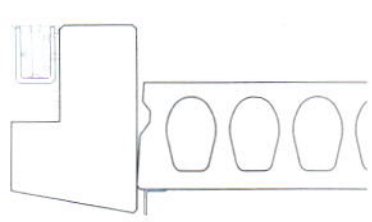

AtT.detail bridge

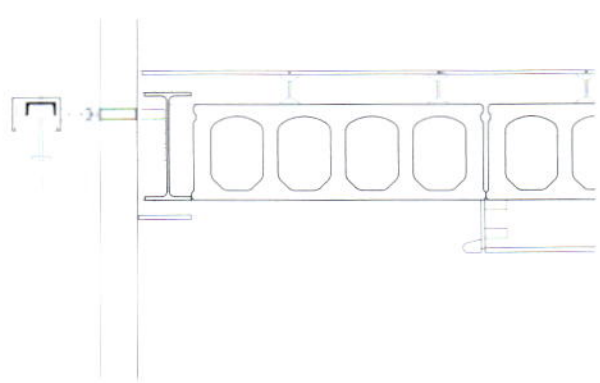

AtT.detail facade

Both the entrance hall facades and the ends of the office wings either side of this volume are completely transparent. Behind these transparent walls are the entrances to the office floors.

AtT

AtT

.AtT

The building is a predominantly closed volume with a transparent core. The entrance hall and adjoining facades are of glass; the remaining facades are covered with natural stone.

5.AtT

456.A

SYKES

The ground floor is half a metre above ground level, which has the effect of detaching the building from its surroundings and turning it into an autonomous object.

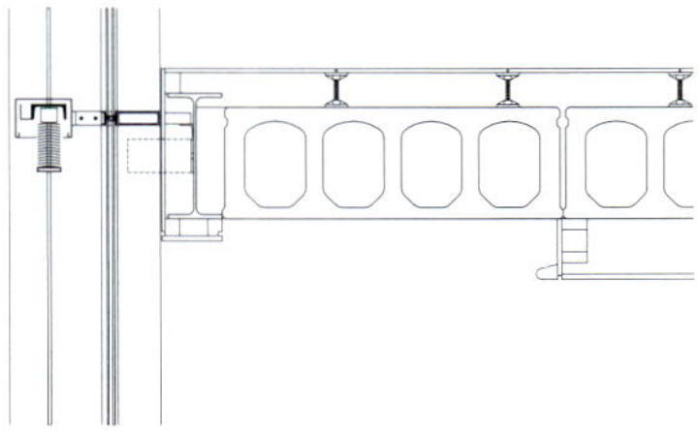

1:50

AtT

3.AtT

Detail glass facade

The stairs and the lift in the entrance hall are freestanding, open steel structures whose discrete, furniture-like presence serves to strengthen the sense of openness.

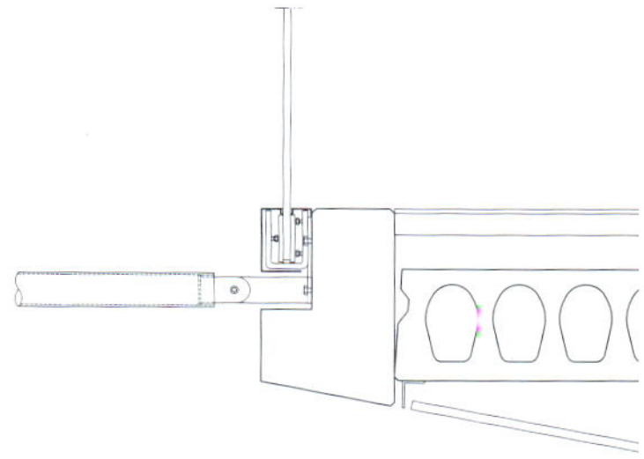

1:20

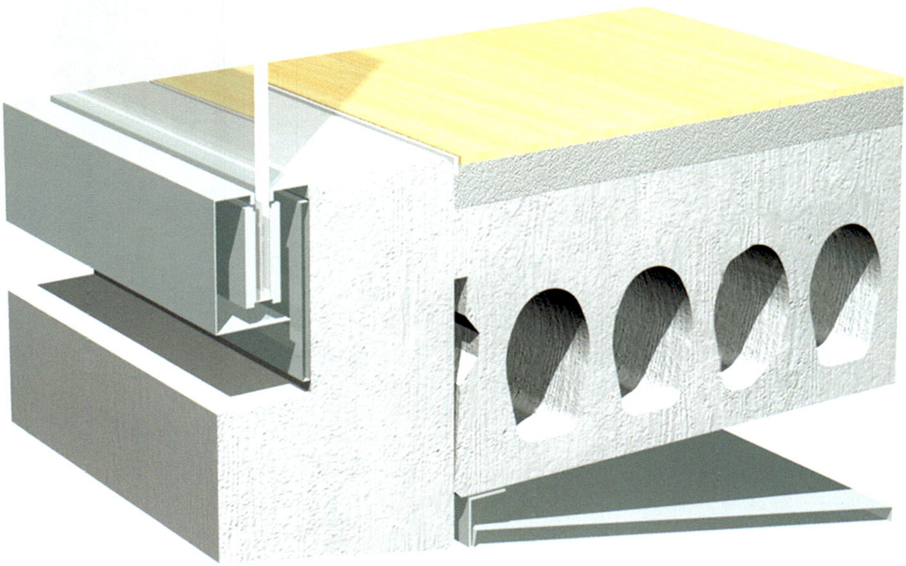

AtT

Detail walkway

The walkway soffits are finished with convex metal slats with integrated lighting and air ducts. The walking surface is laid with parquet.

.AtT

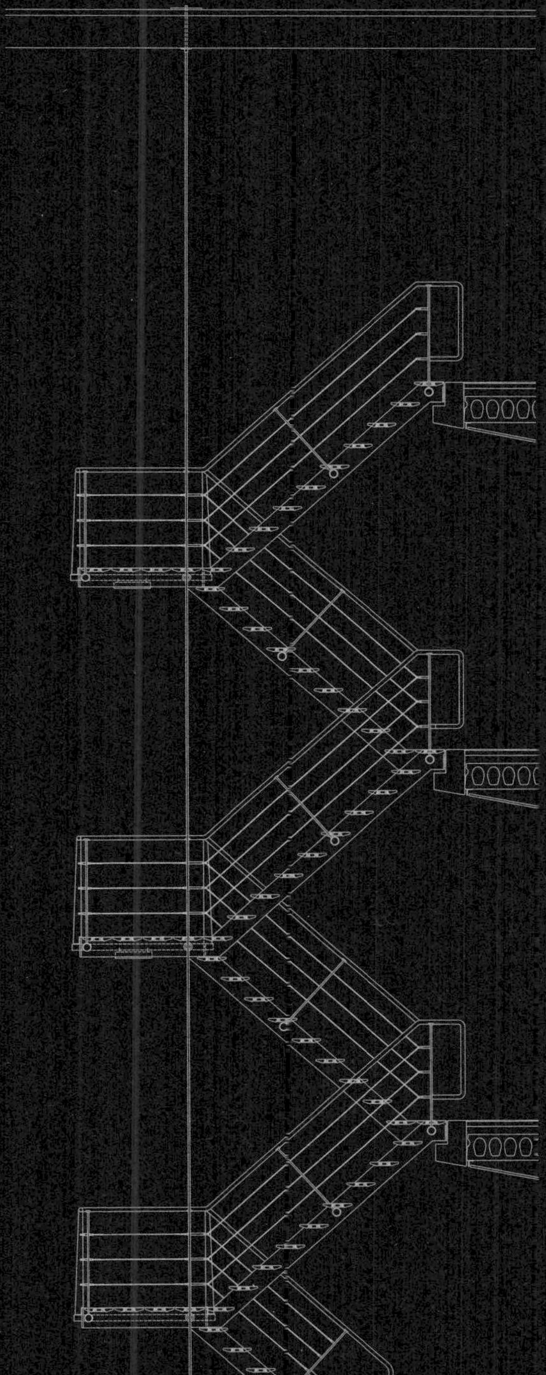

Stairs
1:50

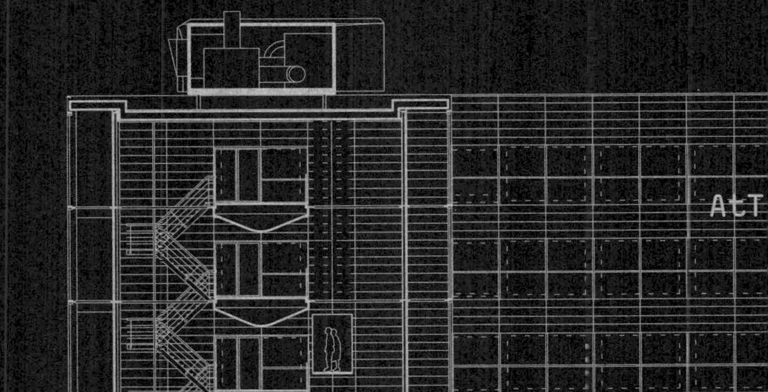

Longitudinal section
1:200

The office bays are 16.2 metres wide on a 1.8 metre grid. The column-free span accommodates a flexible layout.

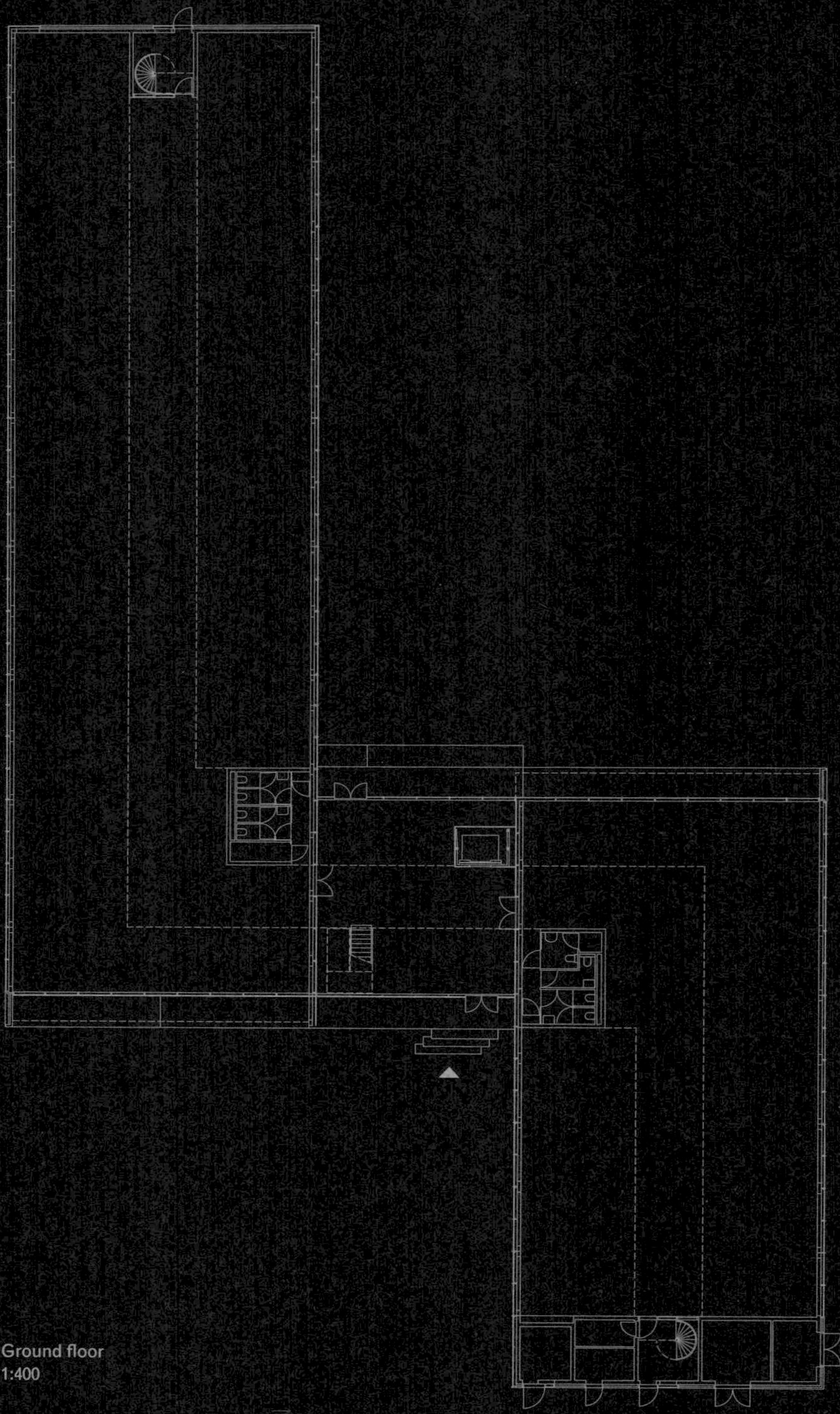

Ground floor
1:400

First floor

Watchtower, Prague

OhS.

name
De Schijf School and commercial space

project code
OhS

place
Oostelijke Handelskade 10, Amsterdam

client
Amplan Vastgoed BV, Amsterdam

invited competition
2000

design
2000 – 2001

construction
2001 – 2003

design team
Andrew Dawes
Dick Floris
Floris van Gennep
Stephanie Haumann
Hans van Heeswijk
José Kleeman
Edward Sorgeloose

This multi-occupancy building on Oostelijke Handelskade in Amsterdam, whose sturdy simplicity alludes to the harbour buildings of bygone days, contains primary schools, office space and a basement car park. The city council wanted a durable office building that could cater to the current demand for schools in the Eastern Docklands, an area with a high number of young children. The building houses the Piet Hein school and provides overflow accommodation for three other primary schools in the neighbourhood. As soon as school enrolments shrink the building can be put to other uses without the need for drastic renovation, thanks to the structural excess and the space allowed for changing and/or augmenting the building services. The high level of sound insulation and energy efficiency enhance the durability of this architecture.
Consultation with the schools resulted in the concept of a 'learning street' for the interior: a wide internal street flanked by classrooms. The street contains colour-coded toilet/cloakroom units for each classroom and can be used for teaching as well as for combined activities.

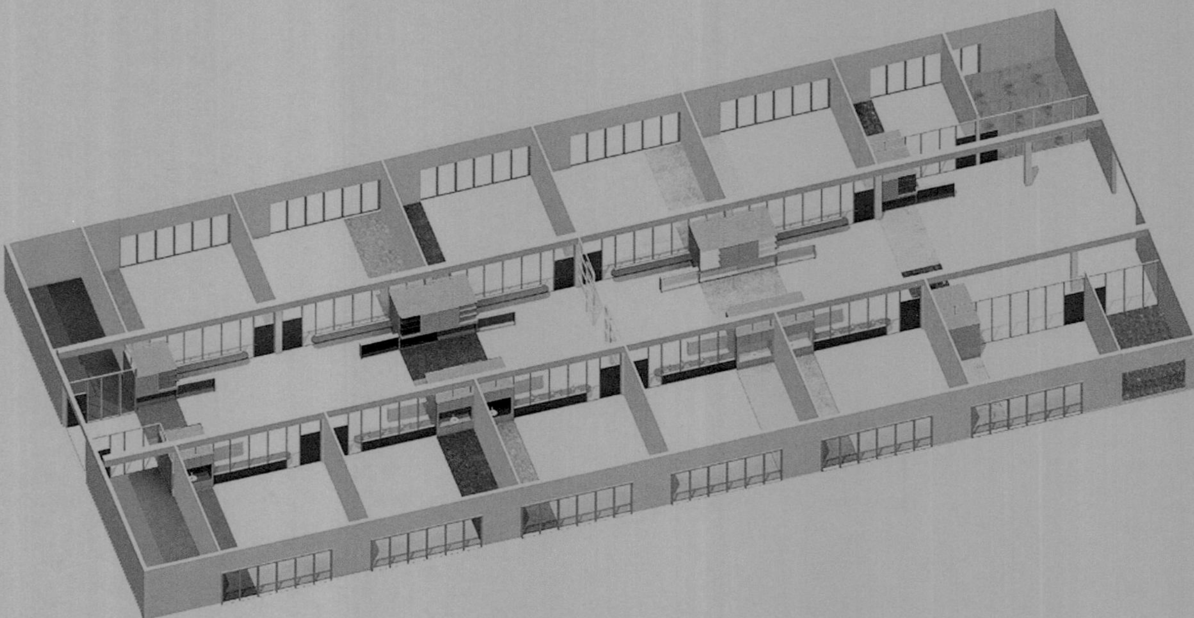

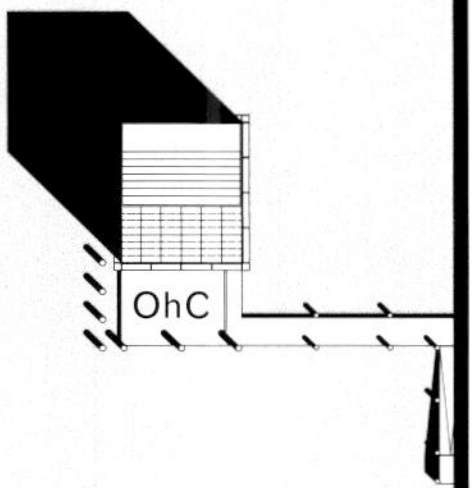

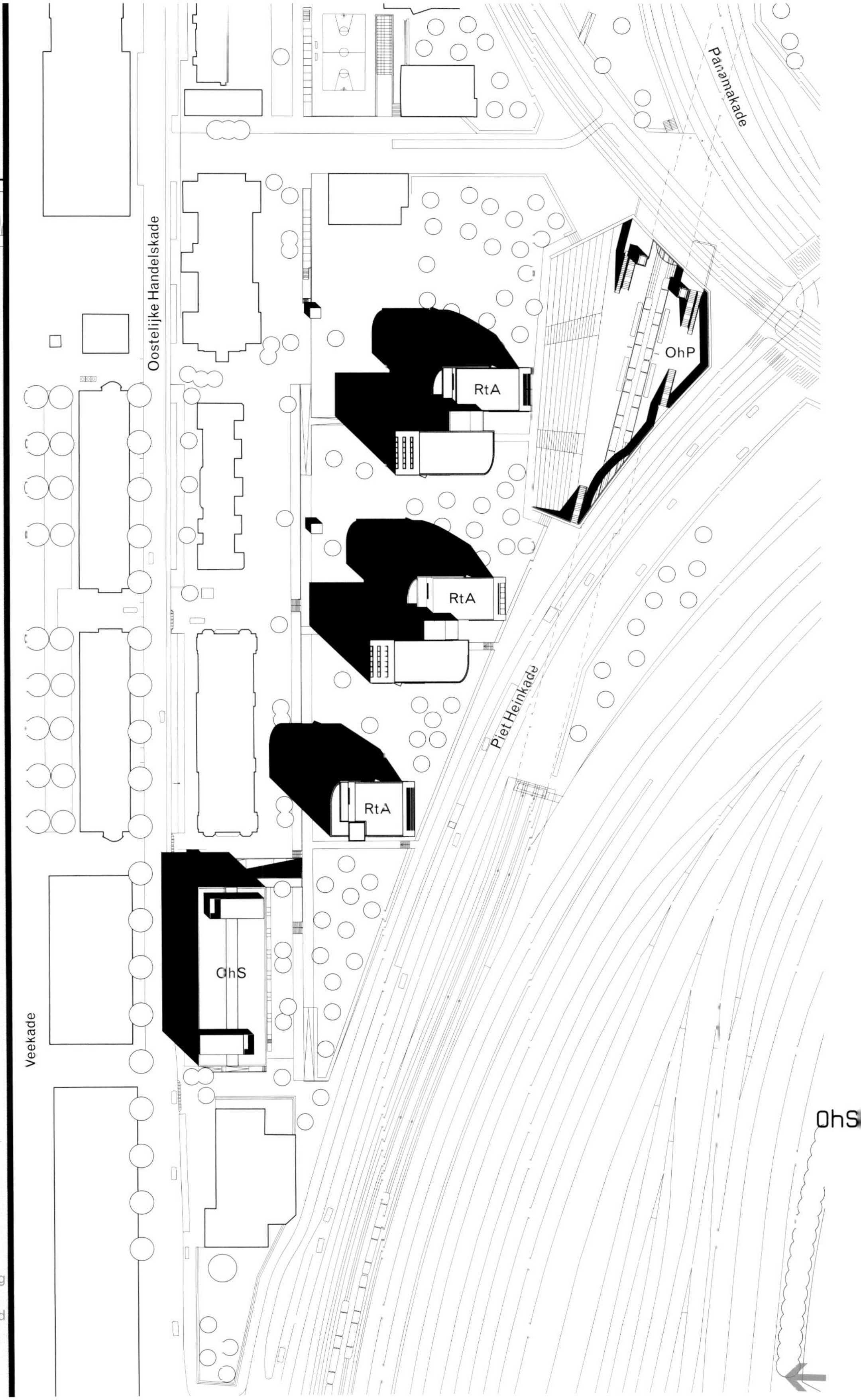

The multi-occupancy building is in a noisy location. On the south side the noise is caused by train, tram and road traffic on Piet Heinkade, on the north side by road traffic on Oostelijke Handelskade.

OhS.overview 01.LK

OhS.overview 07.LK

OhS.overview 02.LK

OhS.elevation 13.LK

OhS.bikes 01.HvH

OhS.bikes 02.HvH

OhS.overview 03.LK

OhS.overview 04.LK

OhS.elevation detail 14.LK

OhS.overview 36.RR

OhS.overview 05.LK

OhS.overview 06.LK

OhS.entrance 08.LK

OhS.entrance 09.LK

OhS.glass corner 10.HvH

OhS.glass corner 12.LK

OhS.stairs 31.LK

OhS.stairs 33.LK

OhS.stairs 34.LK

OhS.stairs 35.LK

OhS.middle zone 20.LK

OhS.middle zone 21.LK

OhS.middle zone 18.LK

OhS.middle zone 19.LK

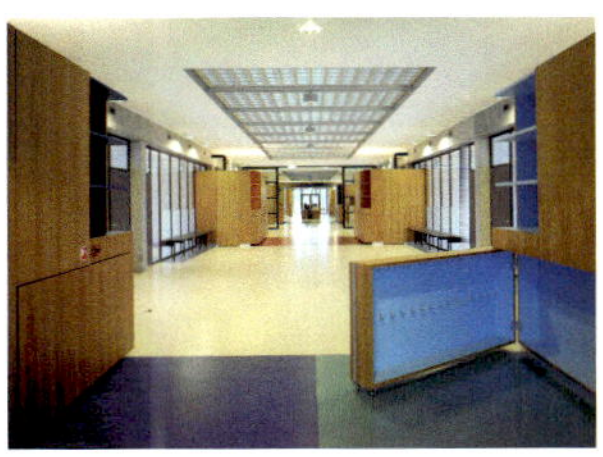

OhS.service blocks 25.LK

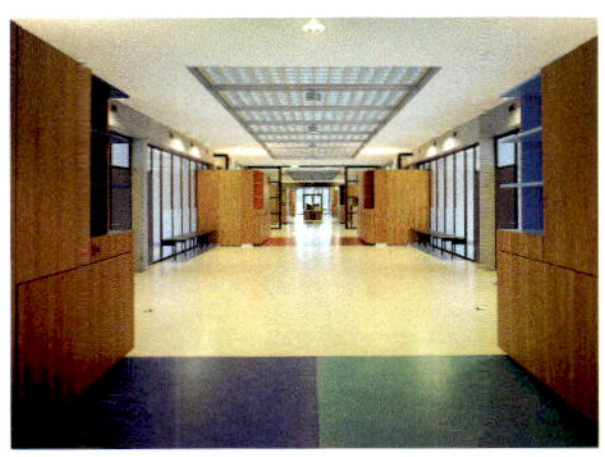

OhS.service blocks 24.LK

OhS.class room 23.LK

OhS.service blocks 27.LK

OhS.service blocks 28.LK

OhS.service blocks 29.LK

OhS.service blocks 30.LK

OhS.servic blocks 36.LK

OhS.servic blocks 37.LK

OhS.servic blocks 38.LK

OhS.elevation detail 15.HvH

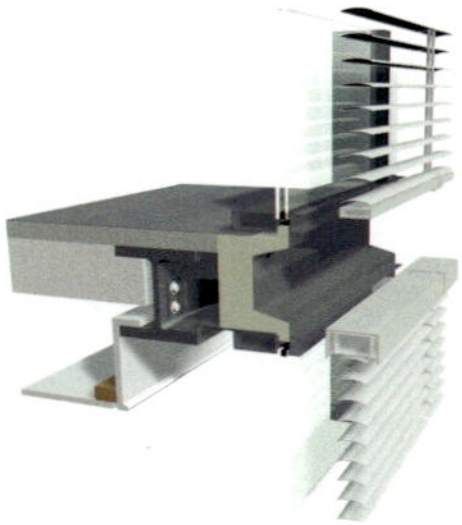
OhS.elevation detail 16.HvH

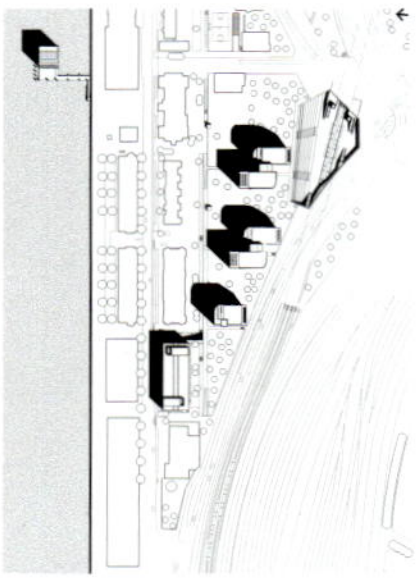
OhS.situation

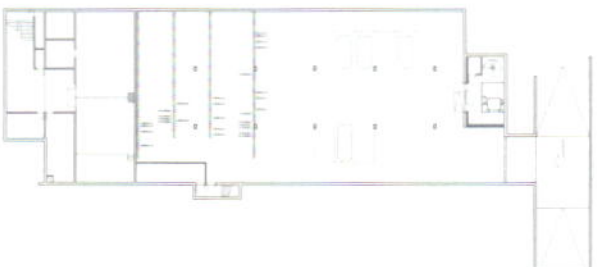
OhS.parking garage

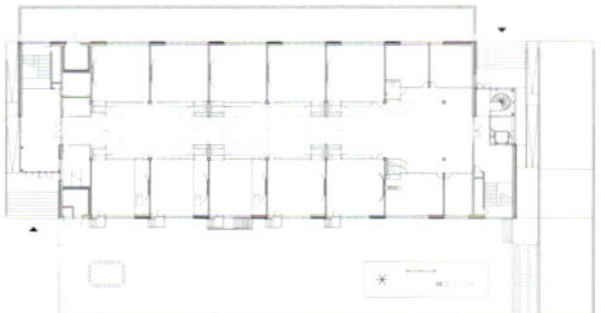
OhS.ground floor

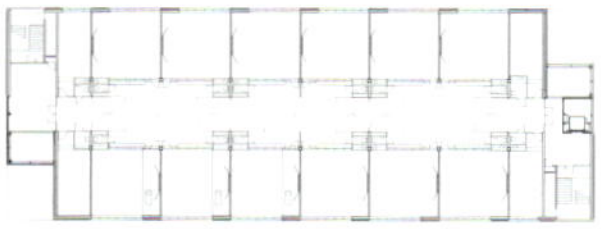
OhS.first floor

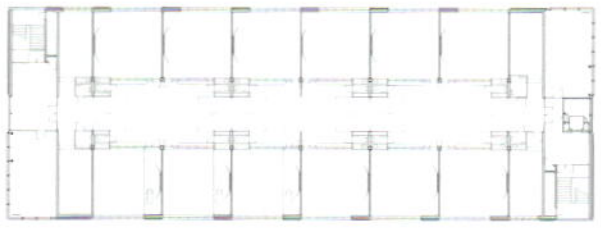
OhS.second floor

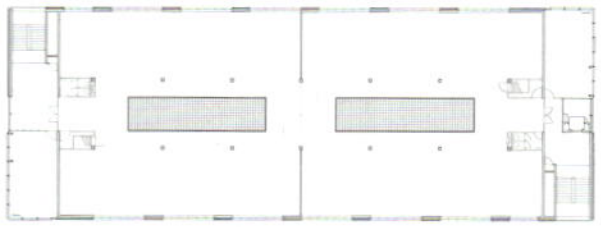
OhS.third floor

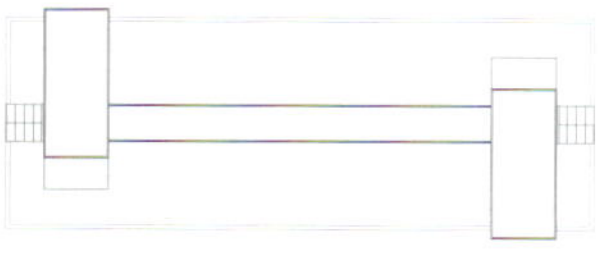
OhS.roof

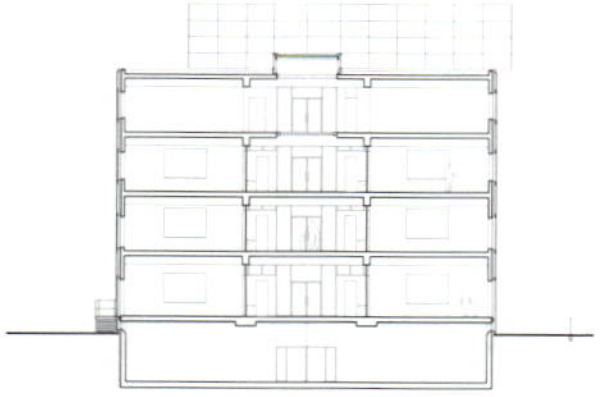
OhS.section

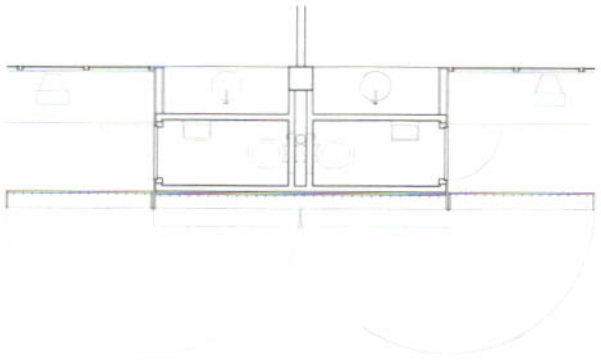
OhS.service unit

6

The building has identical entrances on the two short sides. For businesses the entrance is on the east side near the car park entrance, for the school on the sunny park side which is also where the playground is located.

The building is relatively deep. Rooms requiring daylight are located directly behind the facades, in the middle of the building there is a wide internal street that receives daylight via large glass partitions. The outwardly stern building makes a light and open impression on the inside.

6

The facades consist of a steel frame filled with ribbon windows and dark, hard-burnt bricks with a metallic sheen. At the short ends, large glass conference rooms are suspended from the steel construction. The staircase facades have an infill of glass blocks.

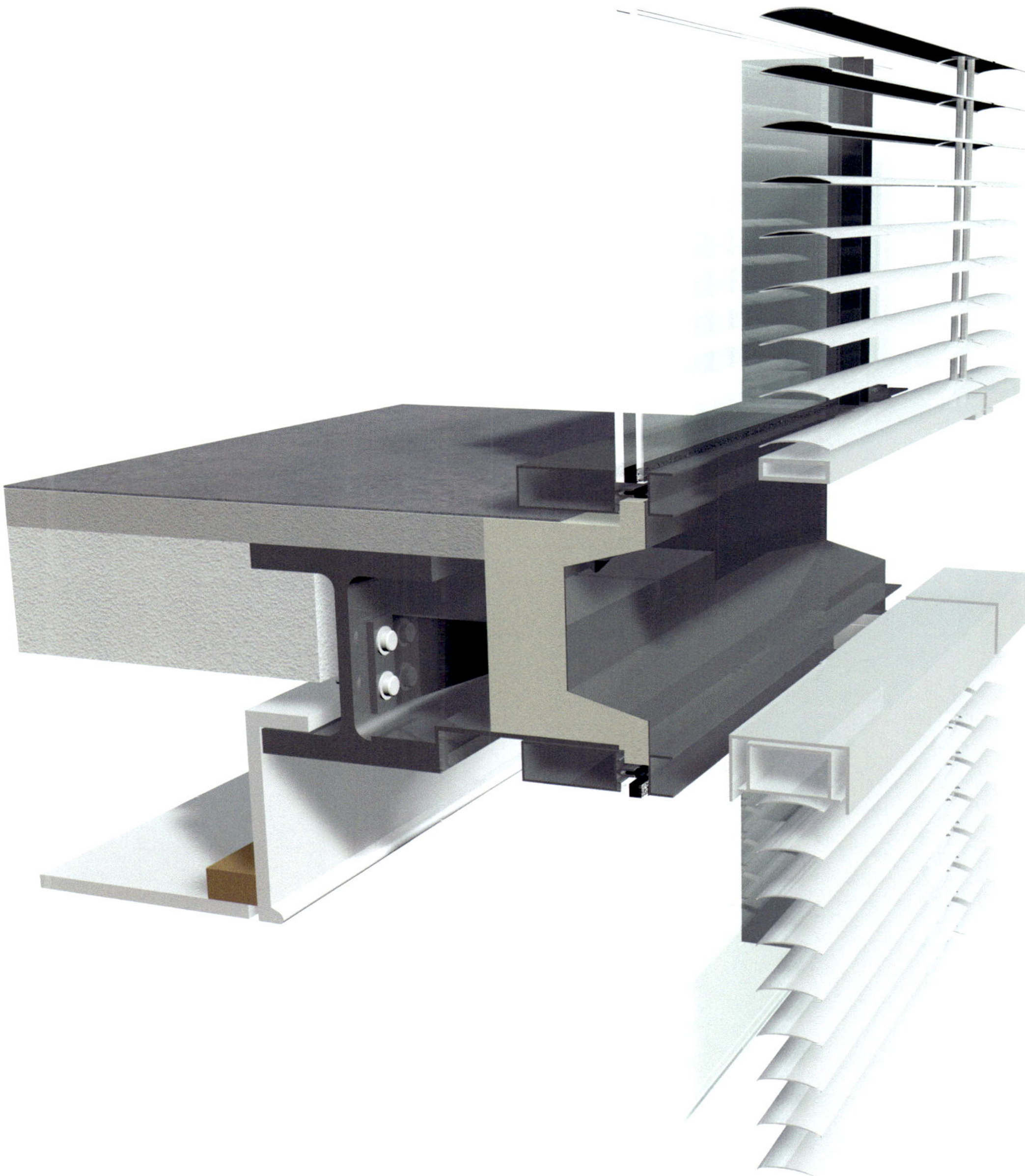

Movable cupboards can be used to divide the internal street into separate play areas.

The internal street for the schools is separated from the classrooms by large glass partition walls.

OhS

..OhS

The service units contain pantries on the classroom side and toilets, cloakrooms and cupboards with display shelves on the corridor side.

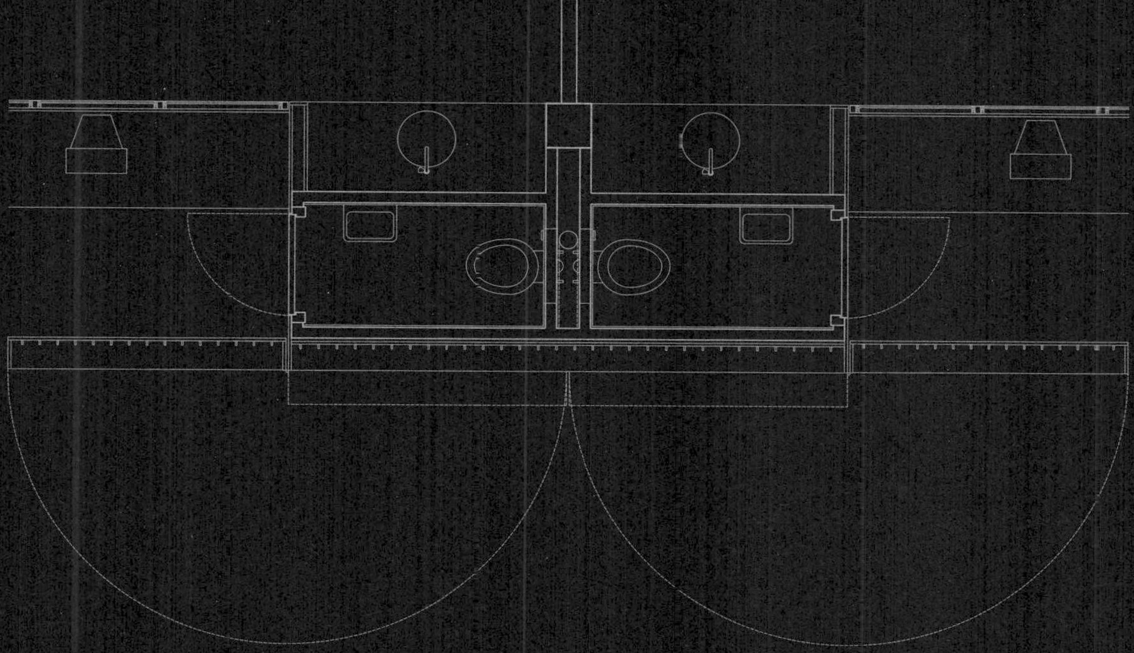

Service unit
1:50

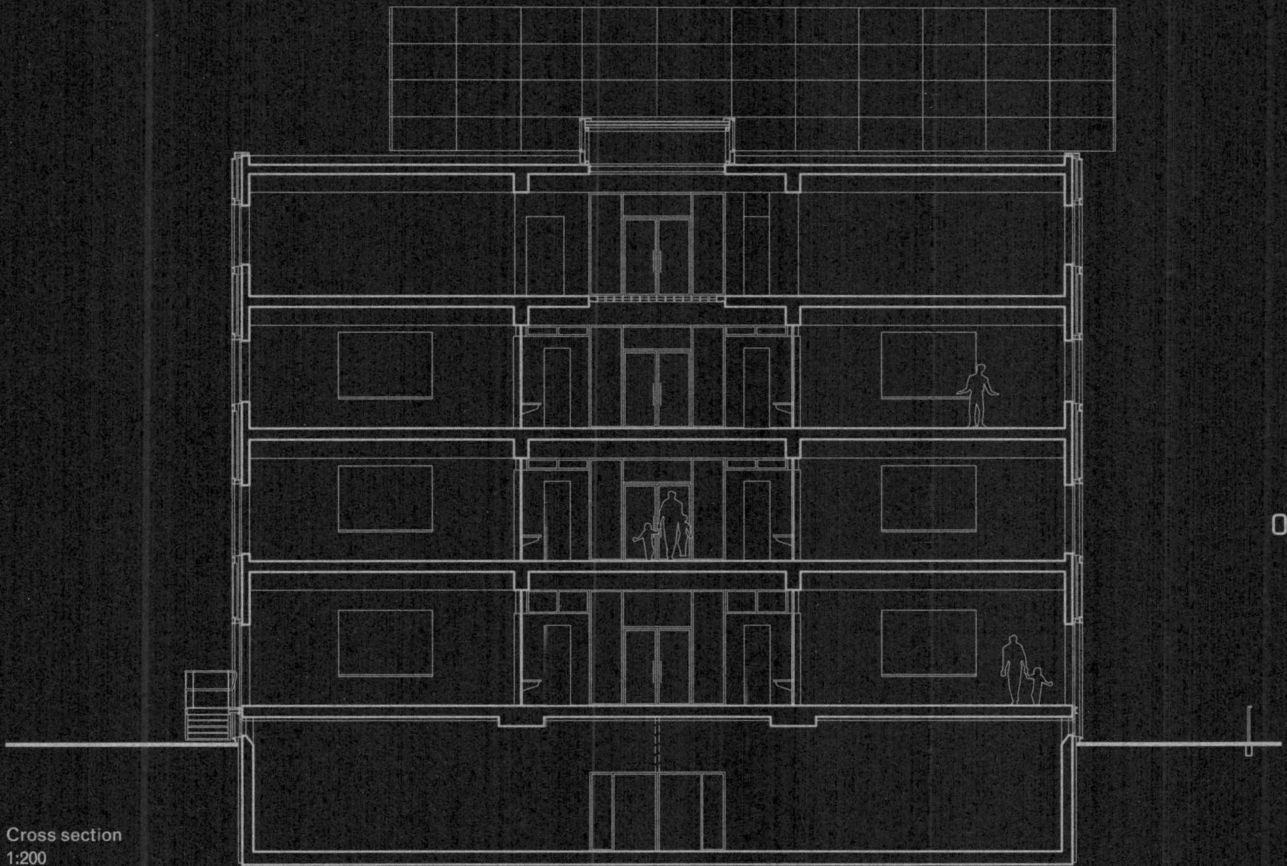

OhS

Cross section
1:200

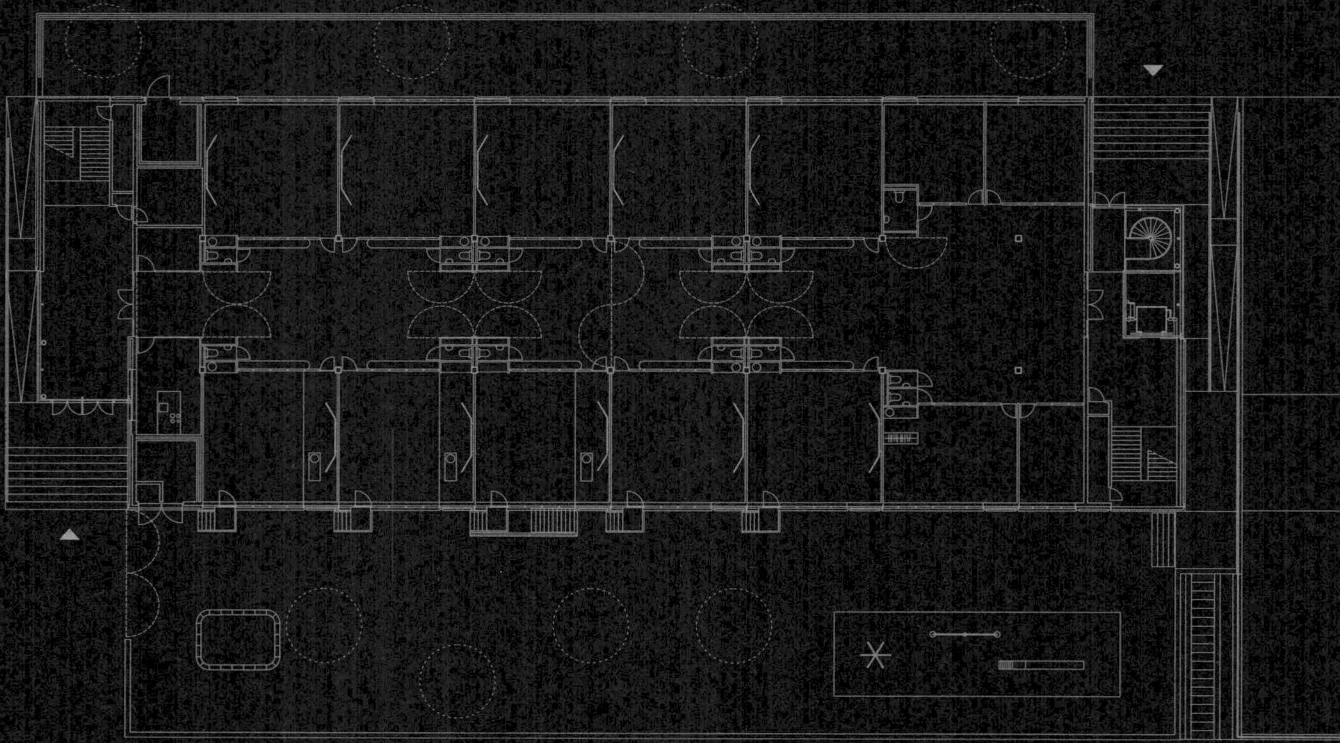

Ground floor

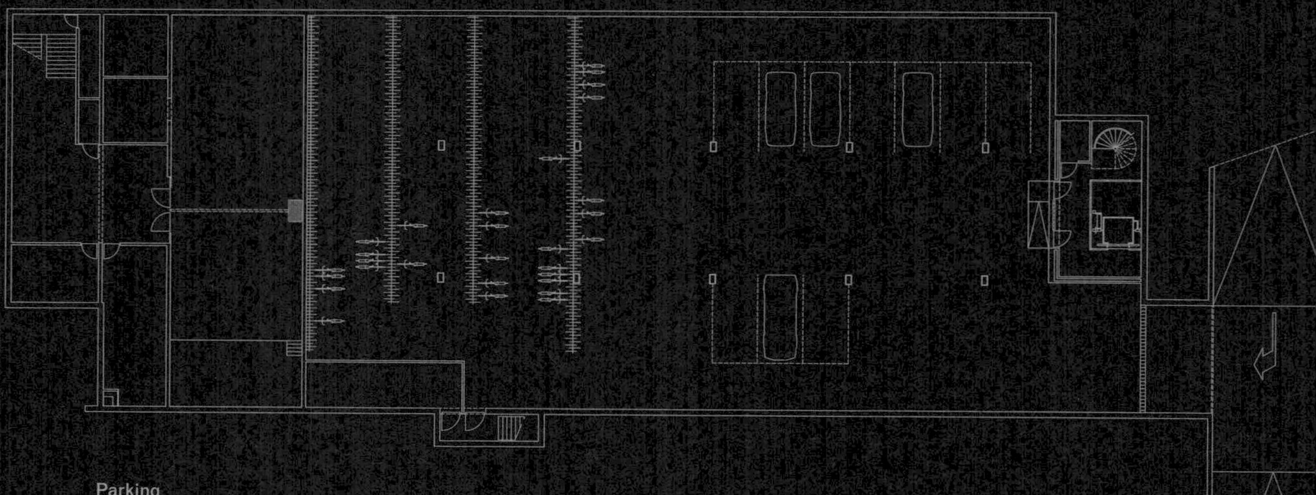

Parking
1:400

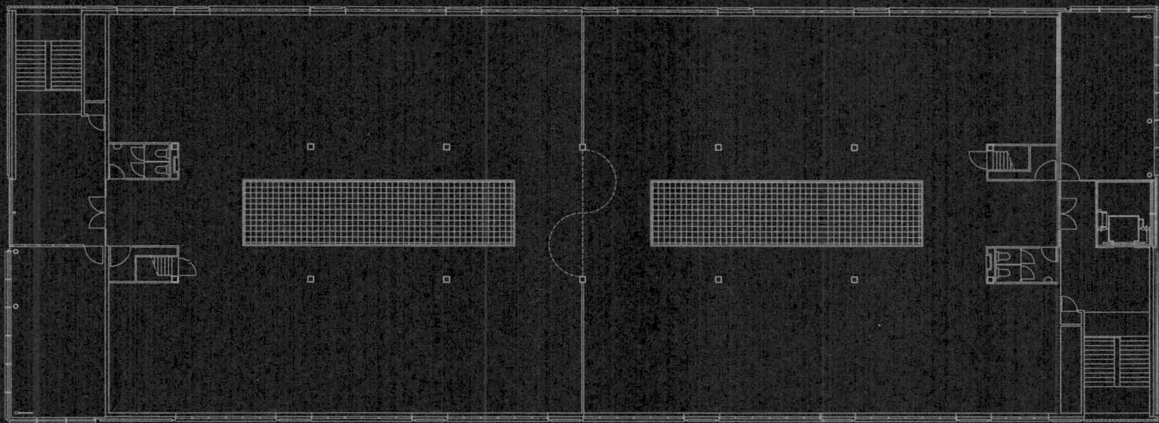

Third floor

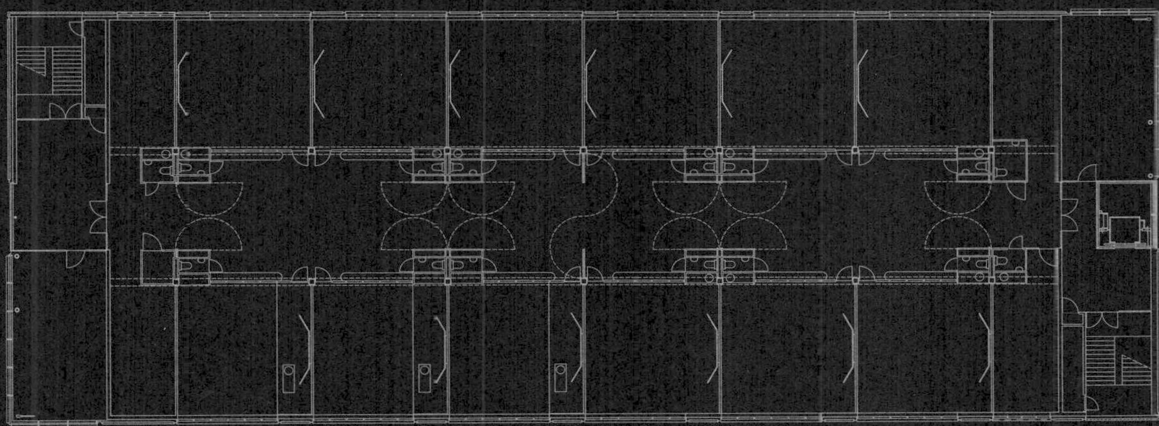

Second floor

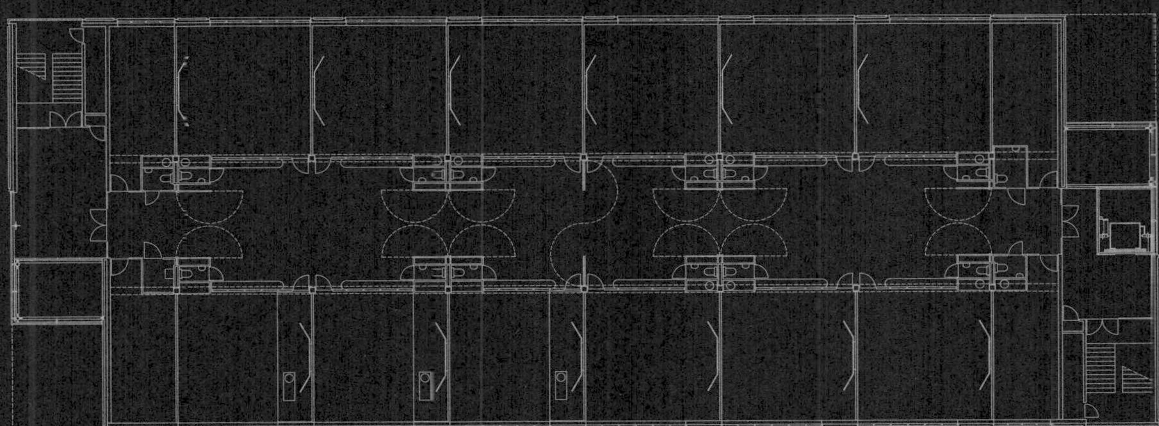

First floor

Amsterdam's Oostelijke Handelskade, circa 1950

OhZ.

name
Zouthaven Bridge

project code
OhZ

place
Oostelijke Handelskade, Amsterdam

client
Gemeentelijk Grondbedrijf Amsterdam

design
2000–2003

construction
2004

design team
Andrew Dawes
Hans van Heeswijk
Arjen Honig
Jeroen van Nieuwenhuizen
Arjan van Ruyven

The pedestrian bridge over the Zouthaven is the final piece in the redevelopment of Amsterdam's Oostelijke Handelskade, which includes the re-excavation of the Zouthaven dock. The bridge connects a new concert hall with a tram stop on the other side of the water.

The Zouthaven Bridge is over sixty metres long and weighs 120 tons. The bridge is made up of a flaring steel span structure with 21 cross-beams. The tension cables taper at the sides and beneath the bridge. They do not rise above the deck so they do not obstruct the view from the bridge. Owing to the difficulty of predicting how such a slender structure will vibrate, tests were carried out post-construction to determine where dampers were needed.

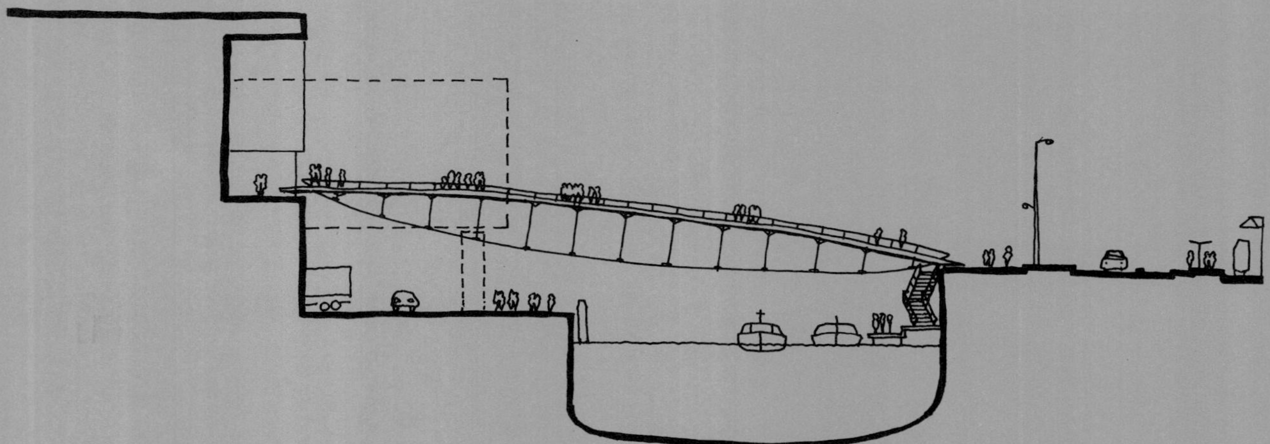

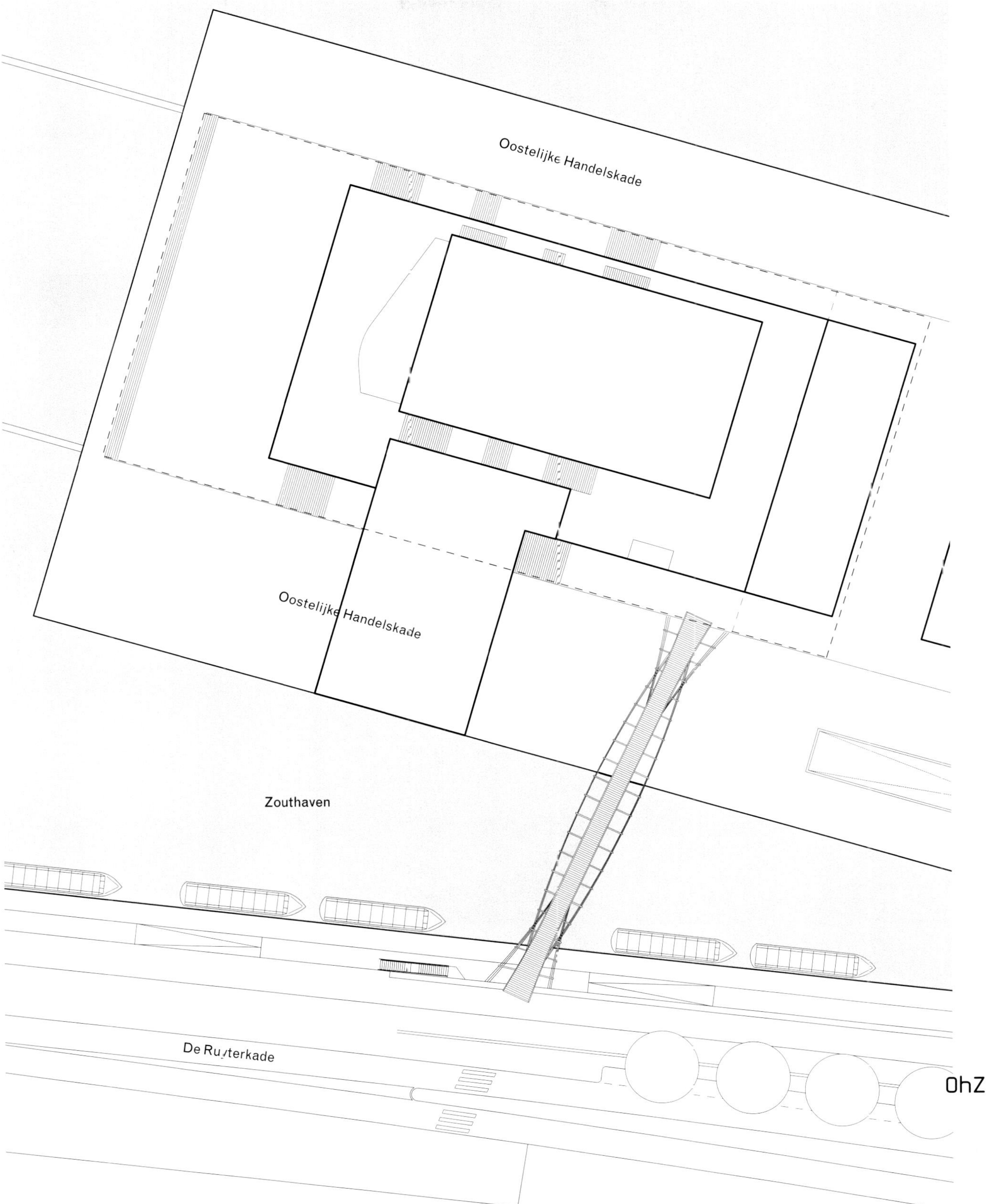

.OhZ

The bridge links the line 26 tram stop with the new Muziekgebouw concert hall. At the ends of the bridge the footway lies like a rolled-out carpet on the quayside and on the Muziekgebouw deck.

OhZ.overview 60.RR

OhZ.overview 61.RR

OhZ.night view 63.RR

OhZ.overview 62.RR

OhZ.overview 08.HvH

OhZ.connection Muziekgebouw 01.HvH

OhZ.connection Muziekgebouw 0388.JG

OhZ.silhouette 09.HvH

OhZ.detail 0365.JG

OhZ.detail 11.JG

OhZ.connection Muziekgebouw 0354.JG

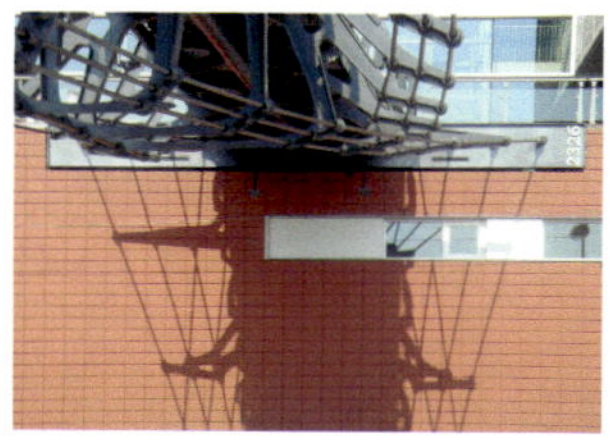
OhZ.underside 05.HvH

OhZ.side 04.LK

OhZ.underside 0364.HvH

OhZ.underside 06.HvH

OhZ.underside 07.HvH

OhZ.underside 03.LK

OhZ.shock dempers 10.HvH

OhZ.detail 02.HvH

OhZ.building site 41.HvH

OhZ.building site 48.HvH

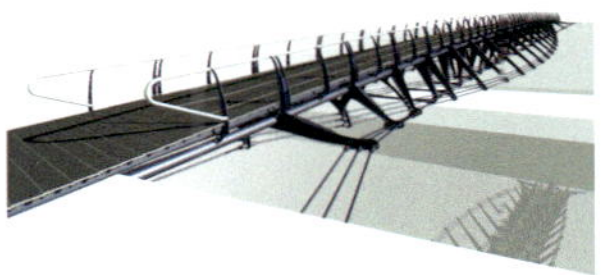

OhZ.3d 04.HvH

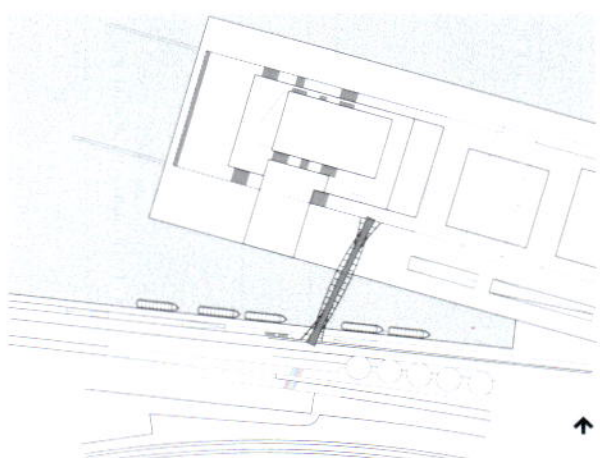

OhZ.situation

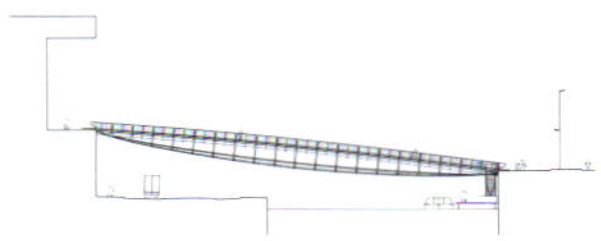

OhZ.side elevation

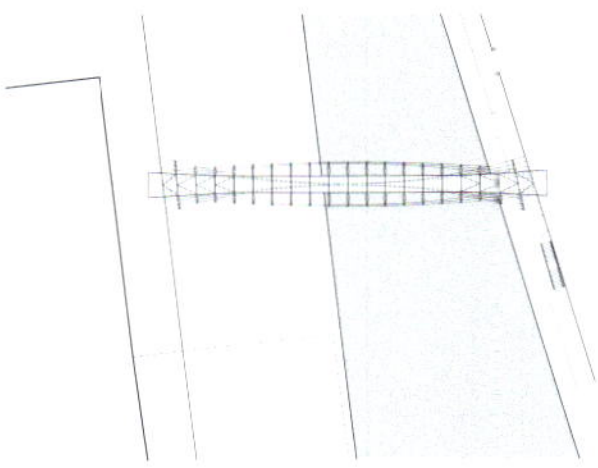

OhZ.top view

OhZ.connection Muziekgebouw

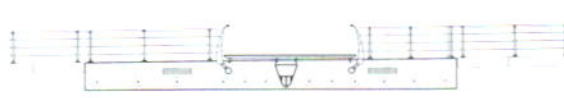

OhZ.connection Ruiterkade

OhZ

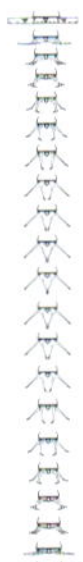

.OhZ

OhZ.frame

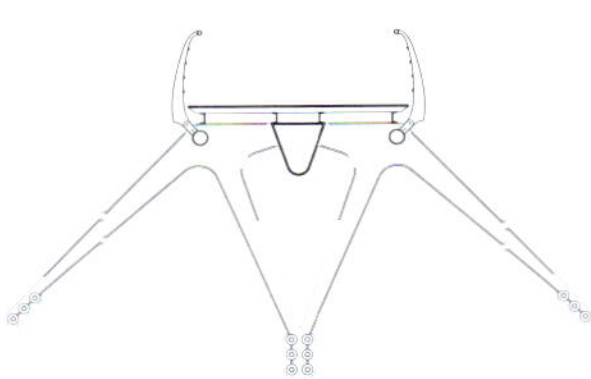

OhZ.truss 12

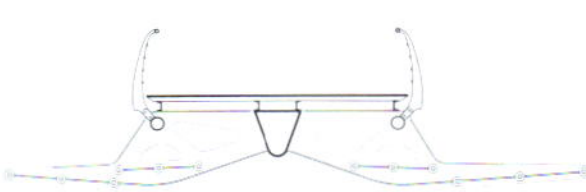

OhZ.truss 21

The sloping bridge connects with the publicly accessible deck of the Muziekgebouw.

OhZ

The bridge structure, beams, tension cables and railings are of steel, the bridge deck consists of aluminium trays filled with rubber granules.

MUZIEKGEB
WAA

The structure consists of a wedge-shaped gi-der down the middle of the bridge and 21 cross-beams connected to one another by 12 tension cables.

OhZ

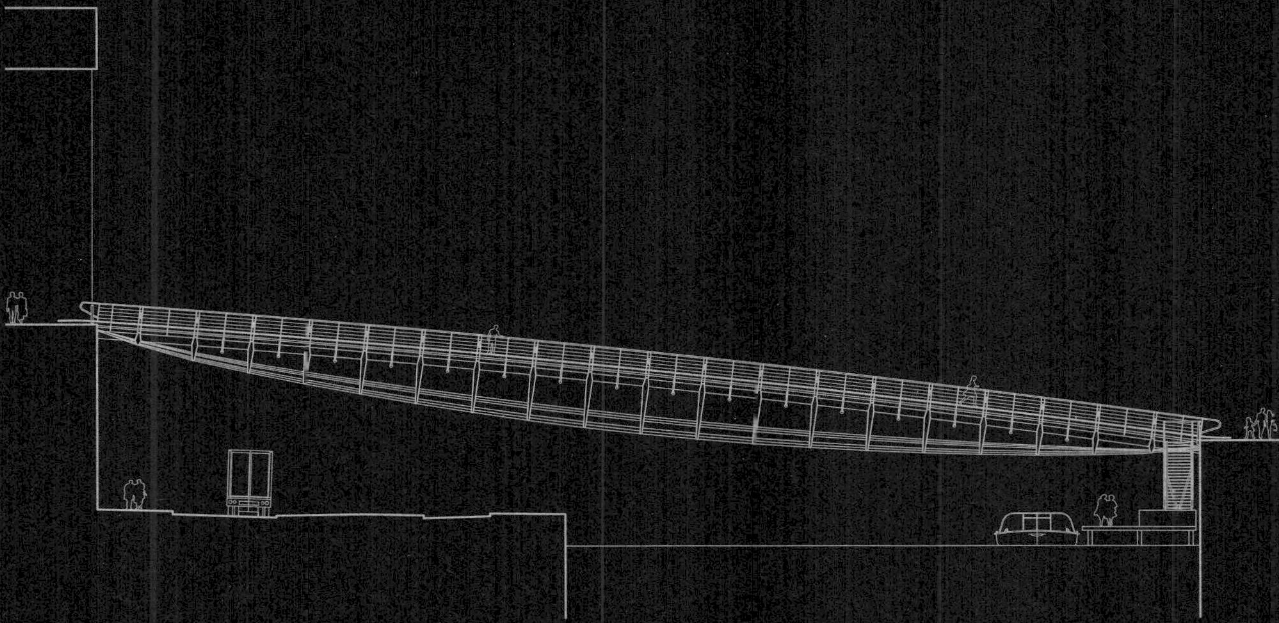

Side view
1:400

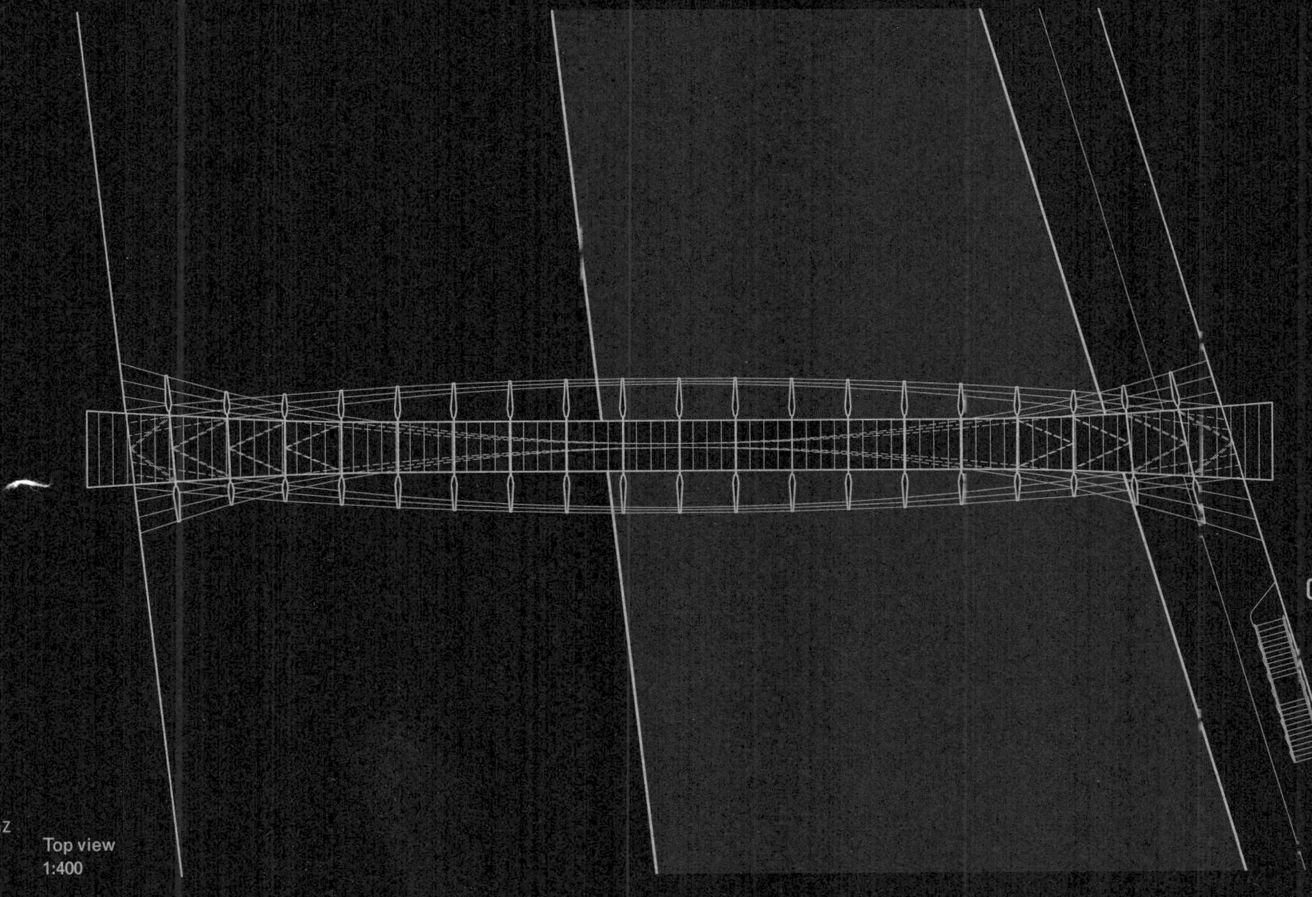

Top view
1:400

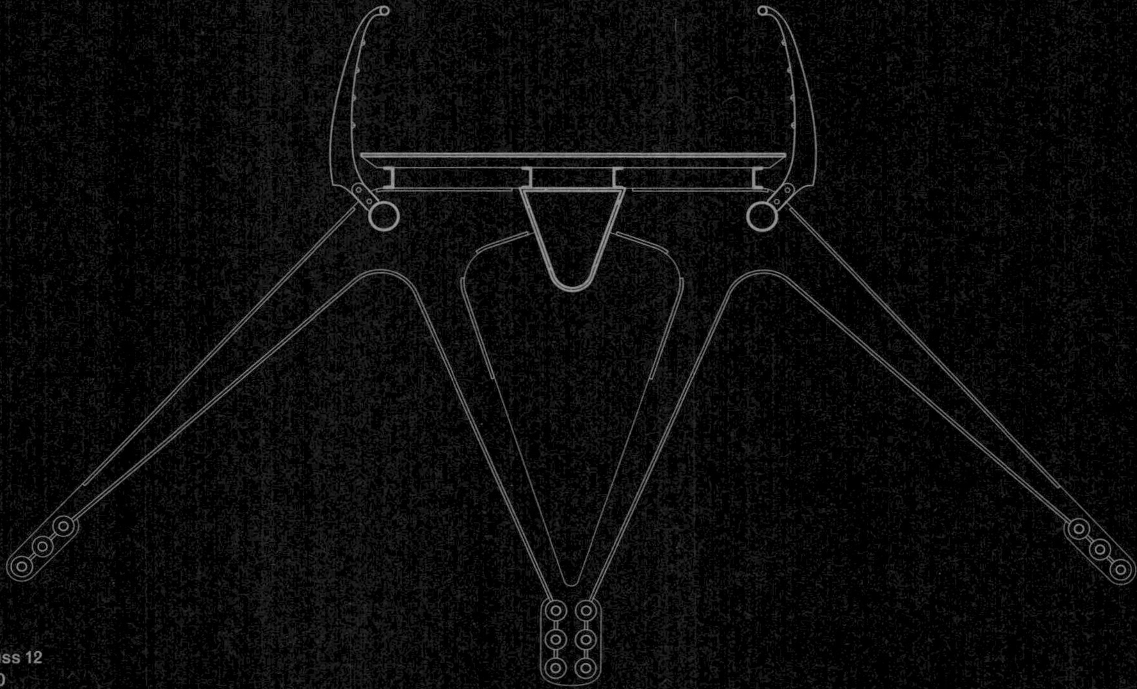

Truss 12
1:50

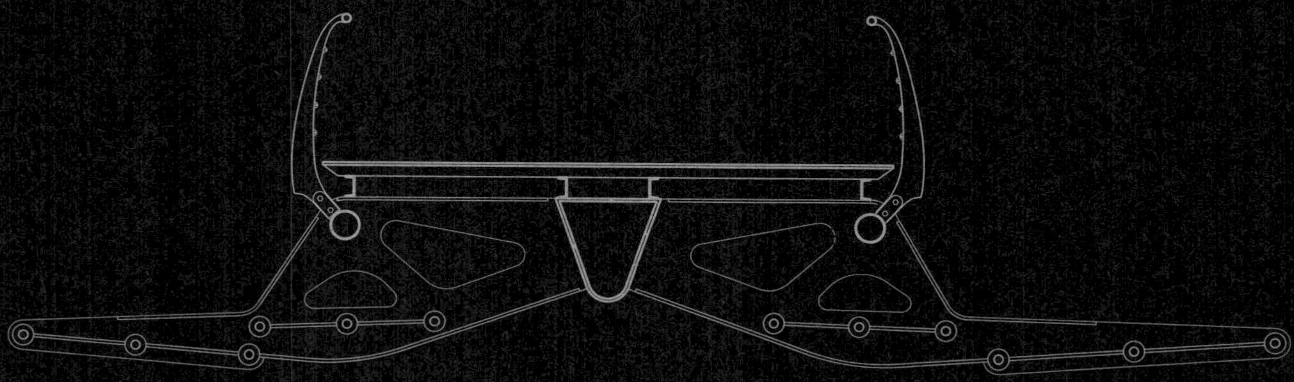

Truss 21
1:50

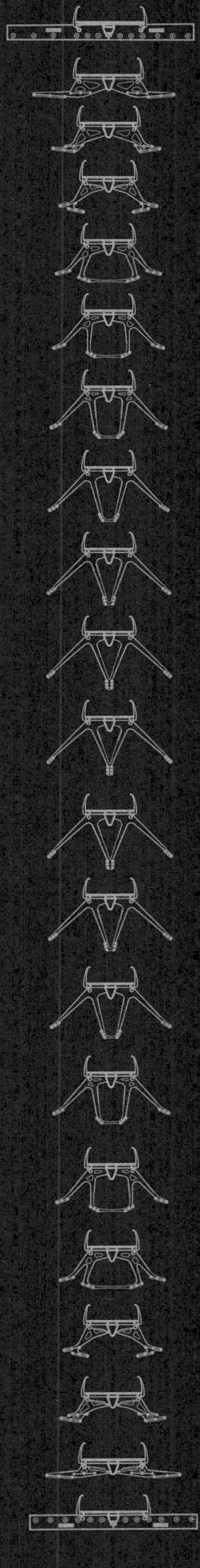

All 21 trusses
1:400

0hZ

..0hZ

OhP.

name
IJ-tram route design

project code
OhP

place
Tramline 26, between
Central Station and
IJburg, Amsterdam

client
Gemeentelijk Project-
bureau IJtram, Amsterdam

design
1998–2003

construction
2000–2004

design team
Floris van Gennep
Stephanie Haumann
Mirjam Heymann
Hans van Heeswijk
Arjan van Ruyven

IJburg, the big new residential development being constructed to the east of Amsterdam in the waters of the IJsselmeer, is connected to Central Station by the IJ-tram. Hans van Heeswijk architecten are involved in the design of all the bridges, tunnels, platforms, stairs and fencing of the IJ-tram route. The size of the project, which includes six kilometres of fencing, made it possible to develop special fencing with cast steel railings.

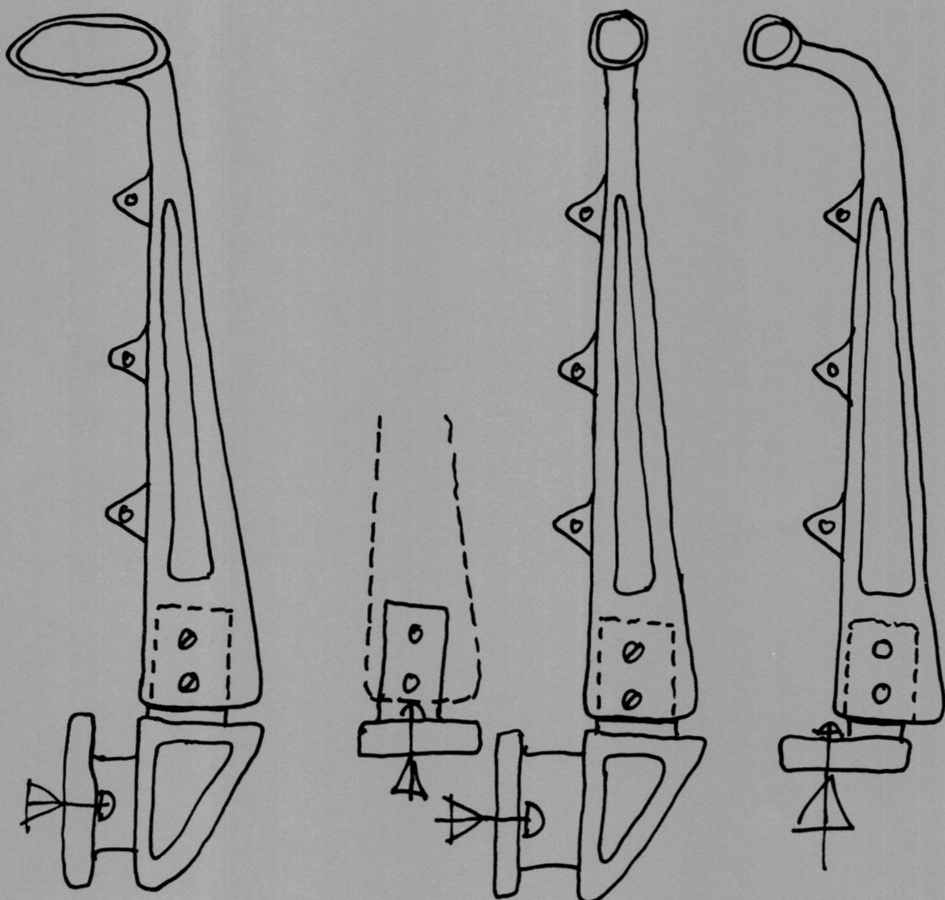

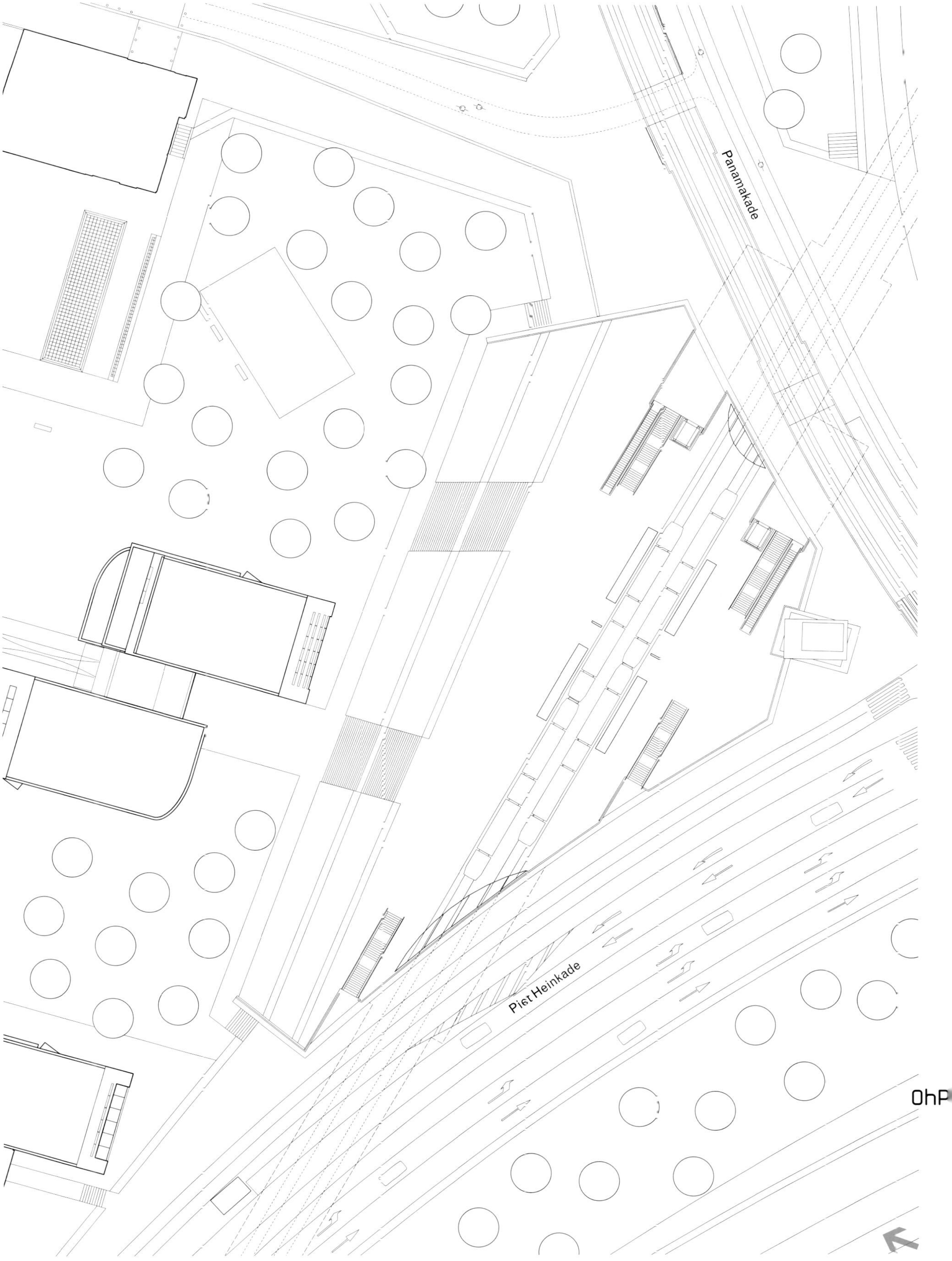

5.0hP

OHP.halte Rietlandpark 46.HvH

OhP.overview 0316.JG

OhP.overview 51.RR

OhP.overview 53.RR

OhP.overview 54.RR

OhP.overview 55.RR

OhP.overview 56.RR

OhP.elevator 50.RR

OhP.stairs and elevator 0294.JG

OhP.overview 0420.JG

OhP.stairs 0296.JG

OhP.stairs detail 0297.JG

OhP.banister 0287.JG

OhP.banister 0288.JG

OhP.banister 59.RR

OhP.bansiter stairs 0338.JG

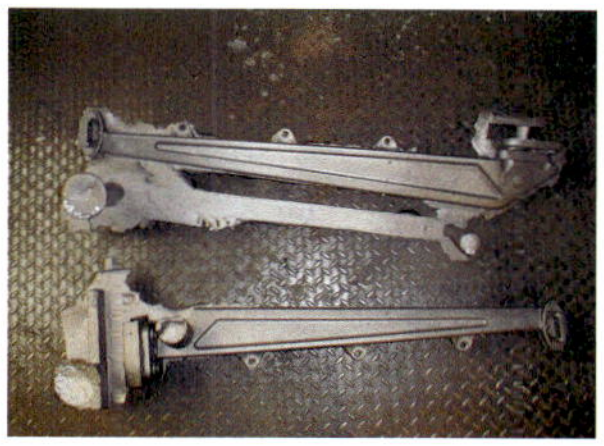

OHP.bansiter 02.HvH

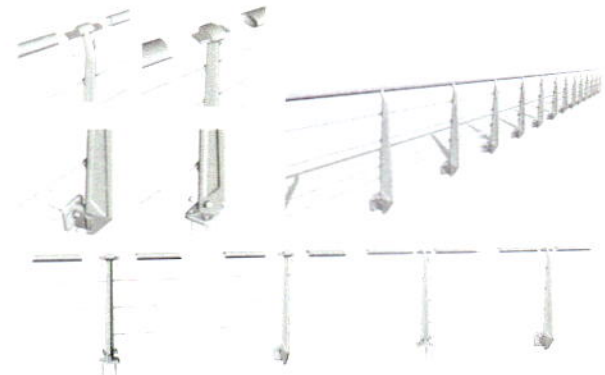

OHP.banister types 20.HvH

OhP.situation halte Rietlandpark

OhP.elevation tunnel

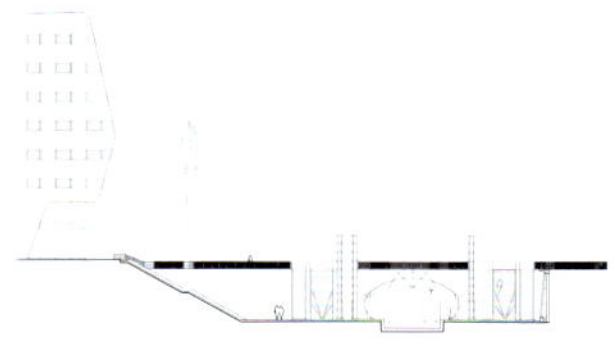

OhP.section 2

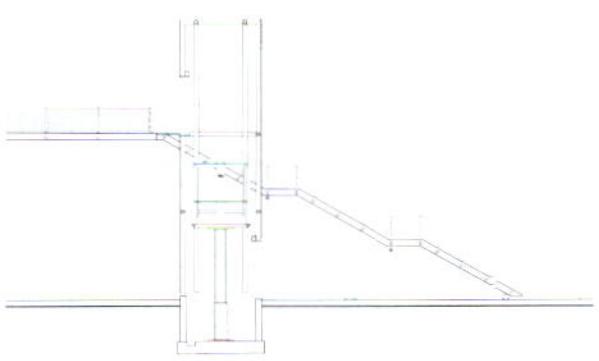

OhP.elevator and stairs

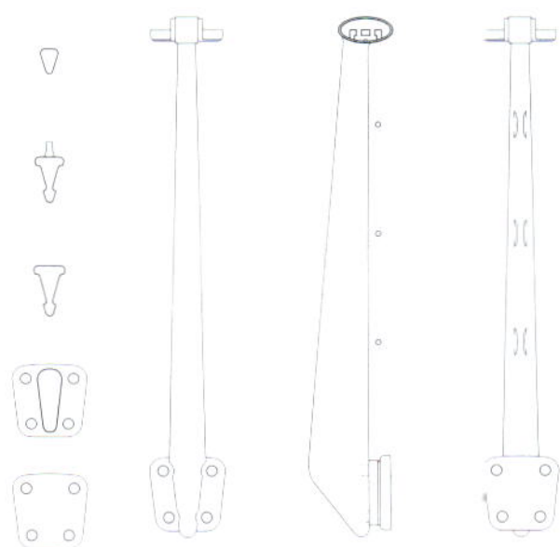

OhP.banister

OHP.station Waterfront 17.HvH

OHP.station Waterfront 15.HvH

OHP.station Waterfront 04.HvH

OhP.banister Muziekgebouw 0287.JG

OhP

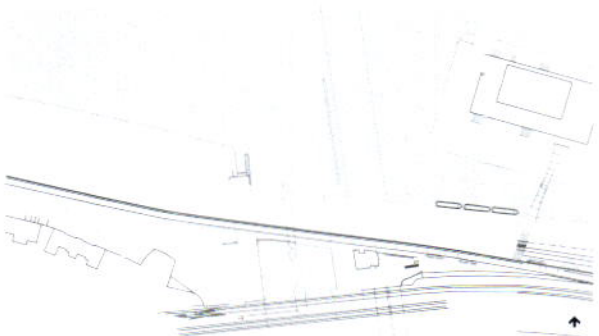

*.OhP

OhP.stop ohk

OhP.ground level

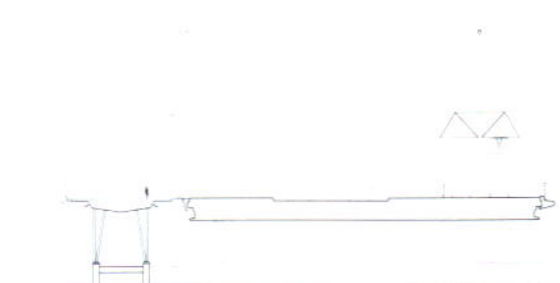

OhP.section 1

On the city side, just before the Piet Hein Tunnel, is the Rietlandpark stop, at the foot of office towers also designed by Hans van Heeswijk architecten. Because of the proximity of the tunnel, the stop is some six metres below street level. The sunken tram stop is a watertight container with a concrete floor and walls of anchored steel sheet pile.

OhP

Rietlandpark stop

1.OhP

OhP

OhP

3.OhP

Over 4500 railings were placed along the 6.7 kilometres of the tram route. Different types of cast steel railings were developed for the wide variety of fencing junctions along the tram route.

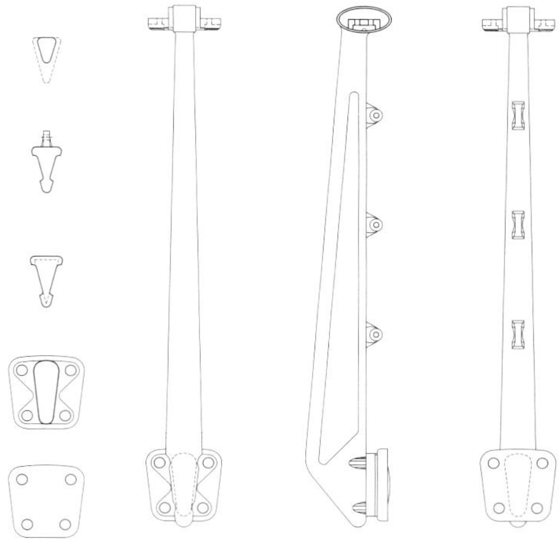

1:20

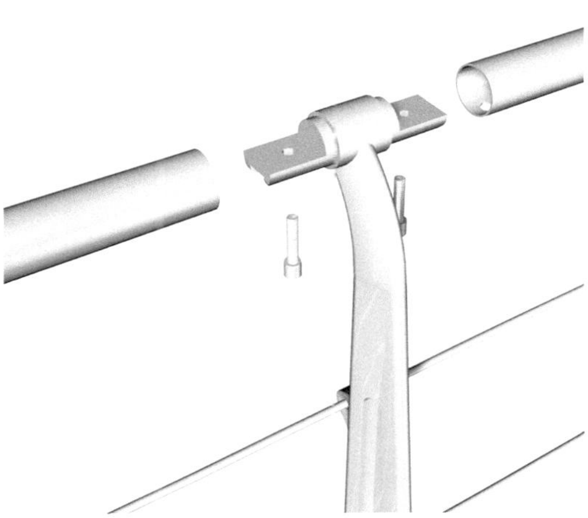

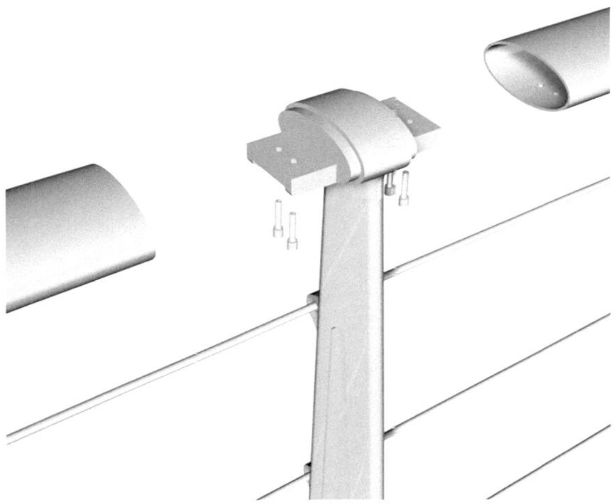

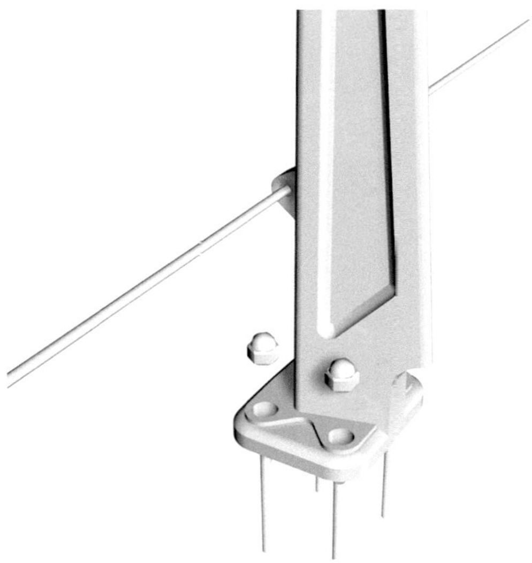

OhP

.OhP

Rietlandpark stop

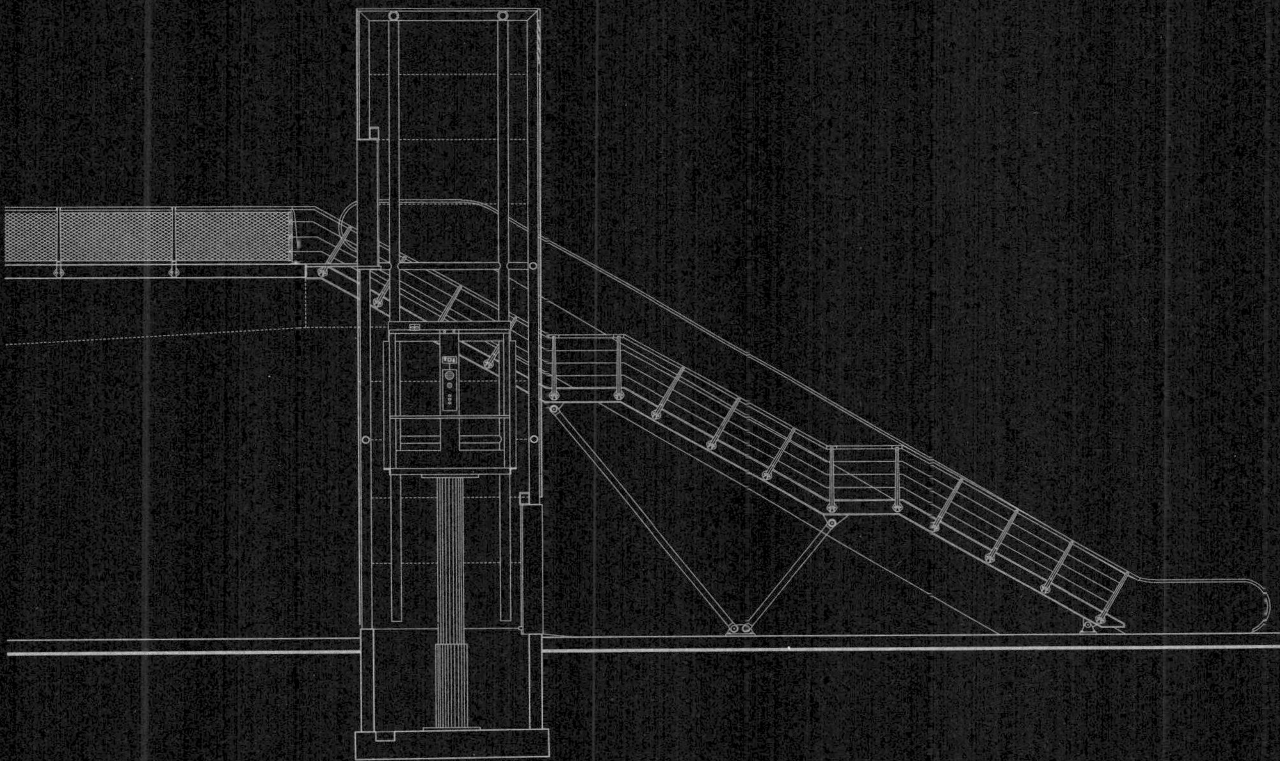

Lift and stairs, Rietlandpark stop
1:120

OhP

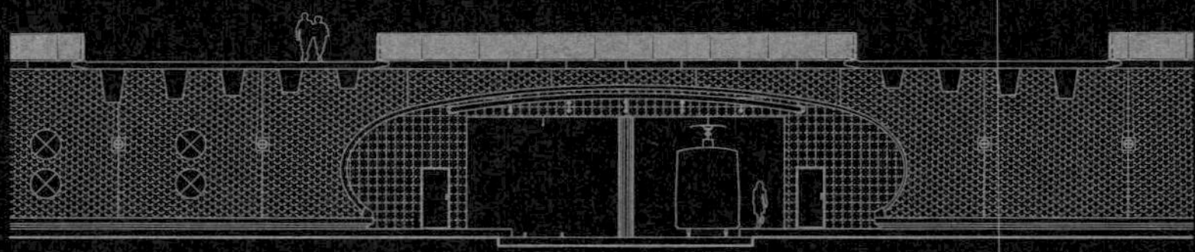

Elevation tunnel Rietlandpark stop
1:400

Section tunnel Rietlandpark stop
1:400

Rietlandpark stop

OhP

Muziekgebouw tram stop

The Muziekgebouw stop is on the bridge over the Oosterdoksdoorgang. To accommodate the tram stop, the bridge was widened by some six metres. This was achieved by adding a separate bridge for cyclists and pedestrians on the IJ side. This new bridge is a slender steel structure. As a contribution to the public safety of the area, retail spaces have been included underneath the bridge.

On the north side of the bridge over the Oosterdokstoegang, the area below the bridge is part of walking routes to the city centre and boarding stages for canal-tour boats. This area was fitted out with retail spaces. As part of the redevelopment of this area, the filled-in Zouthaven, parallel to the bridge, will be re-excavated and allowed to fill with water once again.

Tram stop level
1:2000

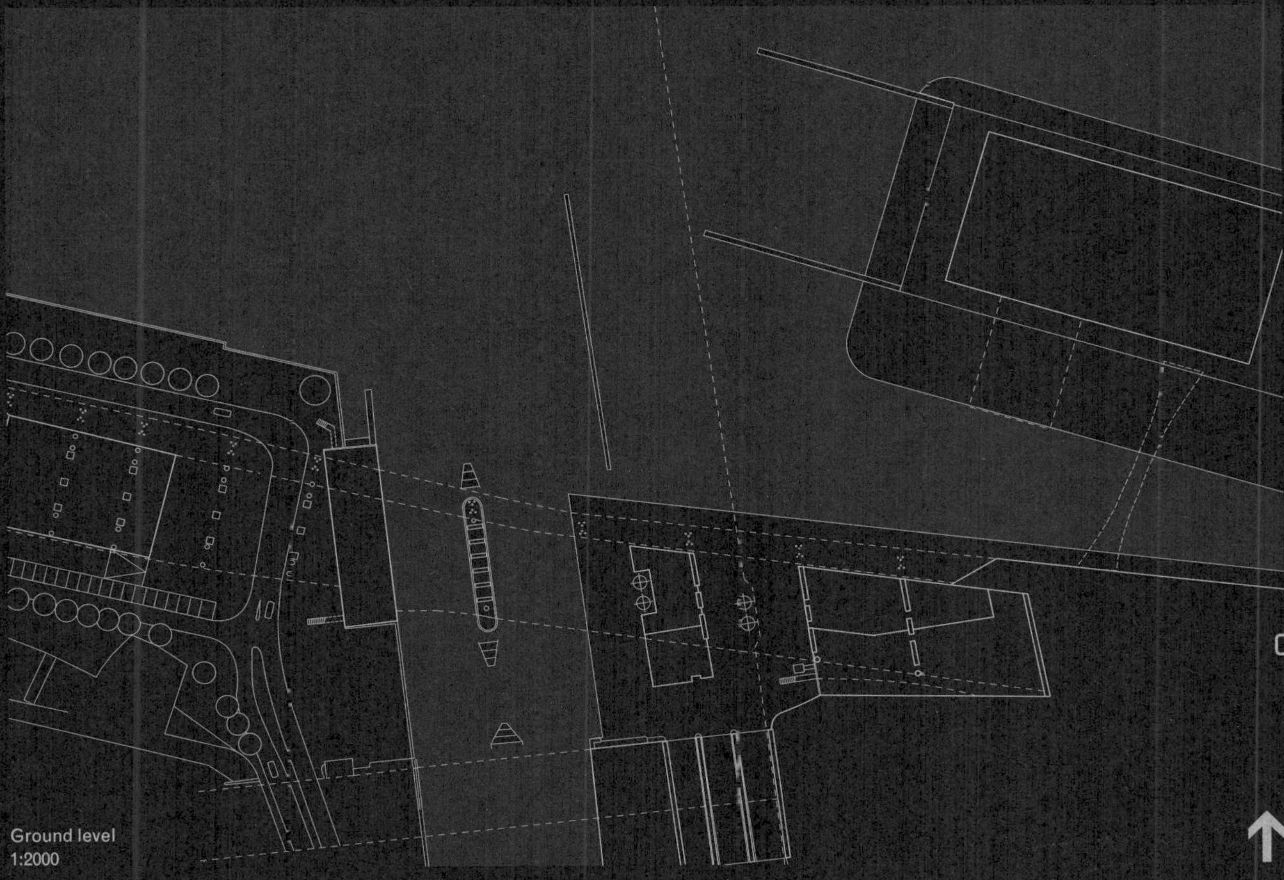

Ground level
1:2000

Section Muziekgebouw tram stop
1:120

OhP

.OhP

Kocher Canvas weekend house,
architect Albert Frey, 1934
The facades are clad with canvas
and painted aluminium

BrB.
MgV.

name
Art Lending Library
Breda

project code
BrB

name
Museum of Graphic Design

project code
MgV

place
Boschstraat 22, Breda

client
Gemeente Breda

design MgV
2002 – 2003

construction MgV
2005 – 2006

design team
Hans van Heeswijk
Arjen Honig
Werner Kamp
Annet Meijer
Jeroen van Nieuwenhuizen
Ellen Otte
Rick Thani

The transformation of the Beyerd arts centre into a Museum of Graphic Design is the most radical renovation that Hans van Heeswijk has designed since becoming the museum's 'in-house architect' in 1985. The design ensures a harmonious continuity between the original 1643 building by Laureys Drijfhout, the artotheek (art lending library) built in 1991, and the new exhibition spaces. Each part has its own identity; together they constitute a spatial whole. The old gateway building contains the entrance, a restaurant, cloakrooms and offices. The art library, an earlier design by Hans van Heeswijk architecten, has been reallocated and will contain spaces for workshops, conservation, documentation and knowledge transfer plus the museum shop. The extension behind the old gateway building, which dates from 1934, will be demolished and replaced by new exhibition spaces both above and below ground, and an auditorium underneath the courtyard.

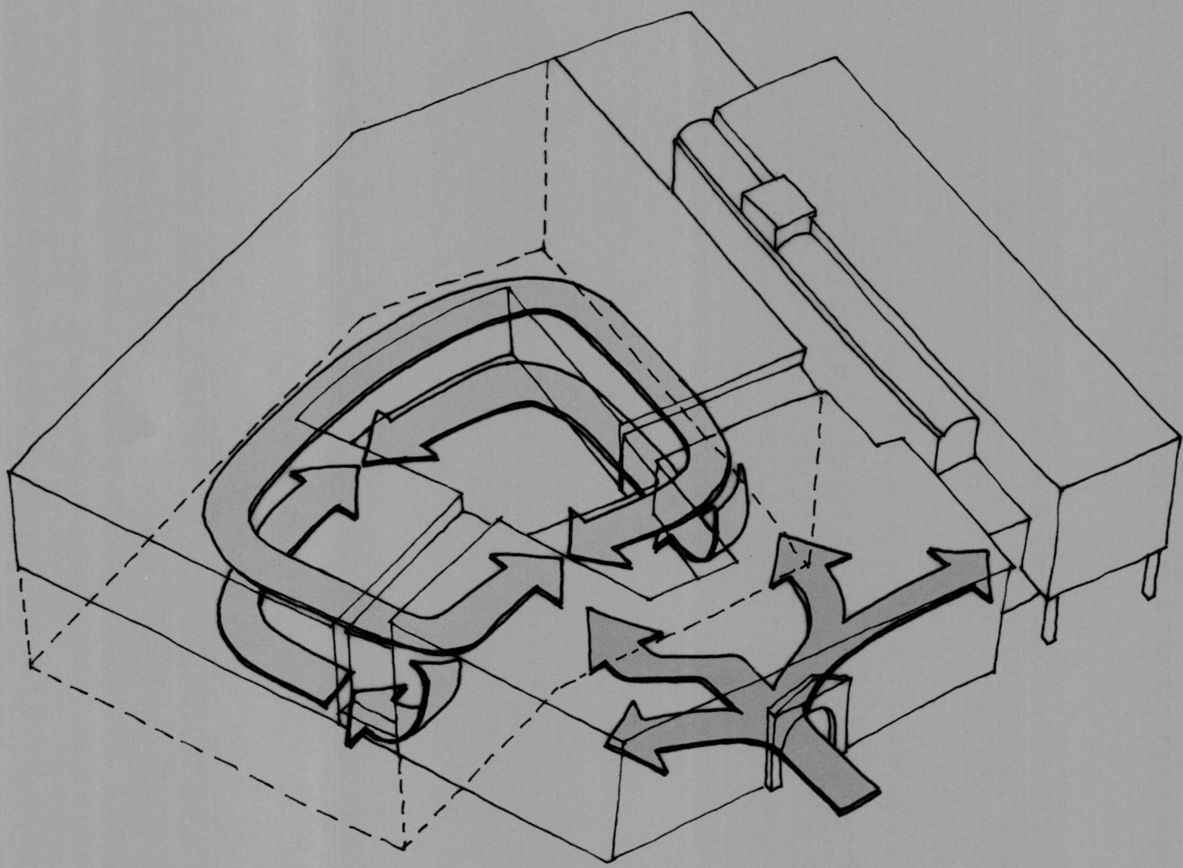

The museum consists of three sections: public functions in the historic gateway building, additional functions in the former art lending library and exhibition spaces in the new building.

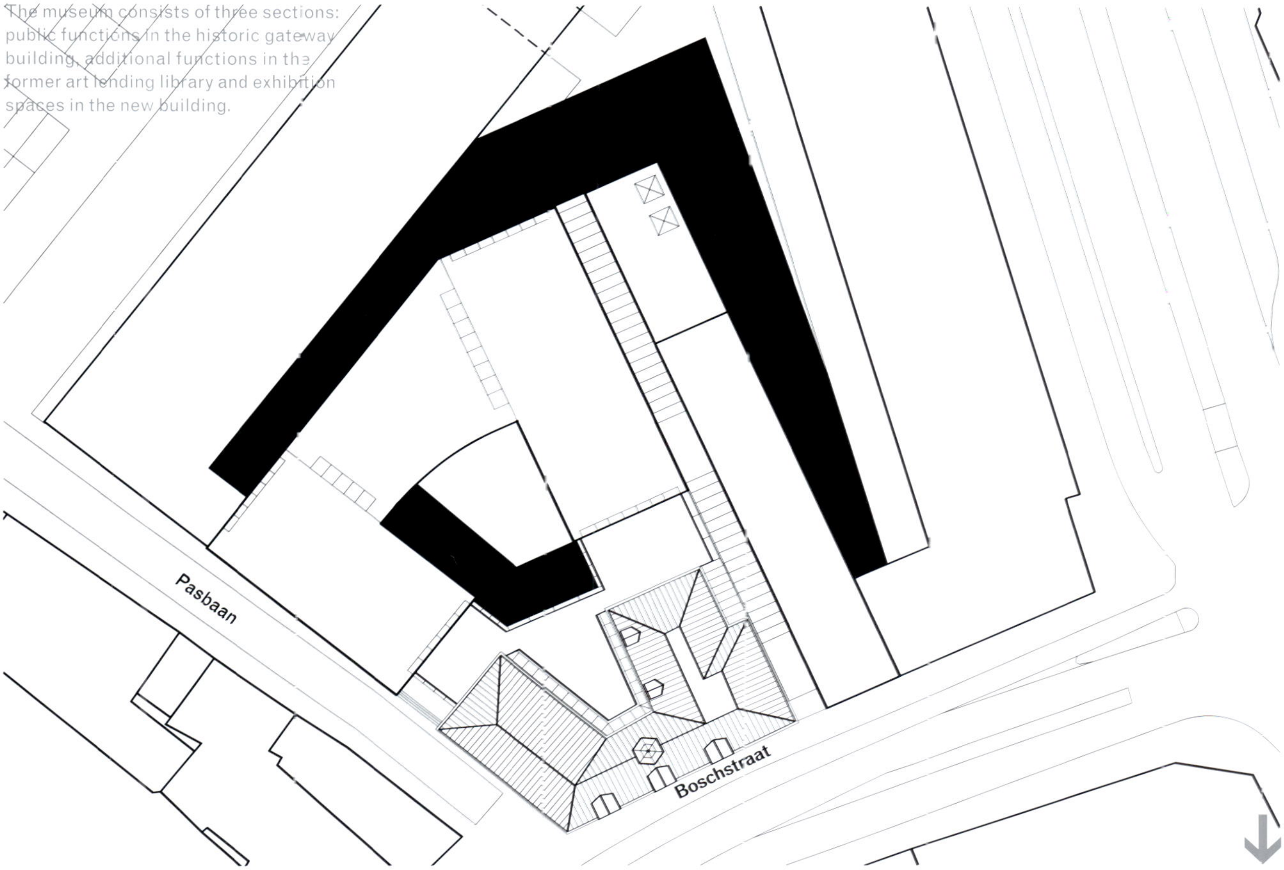

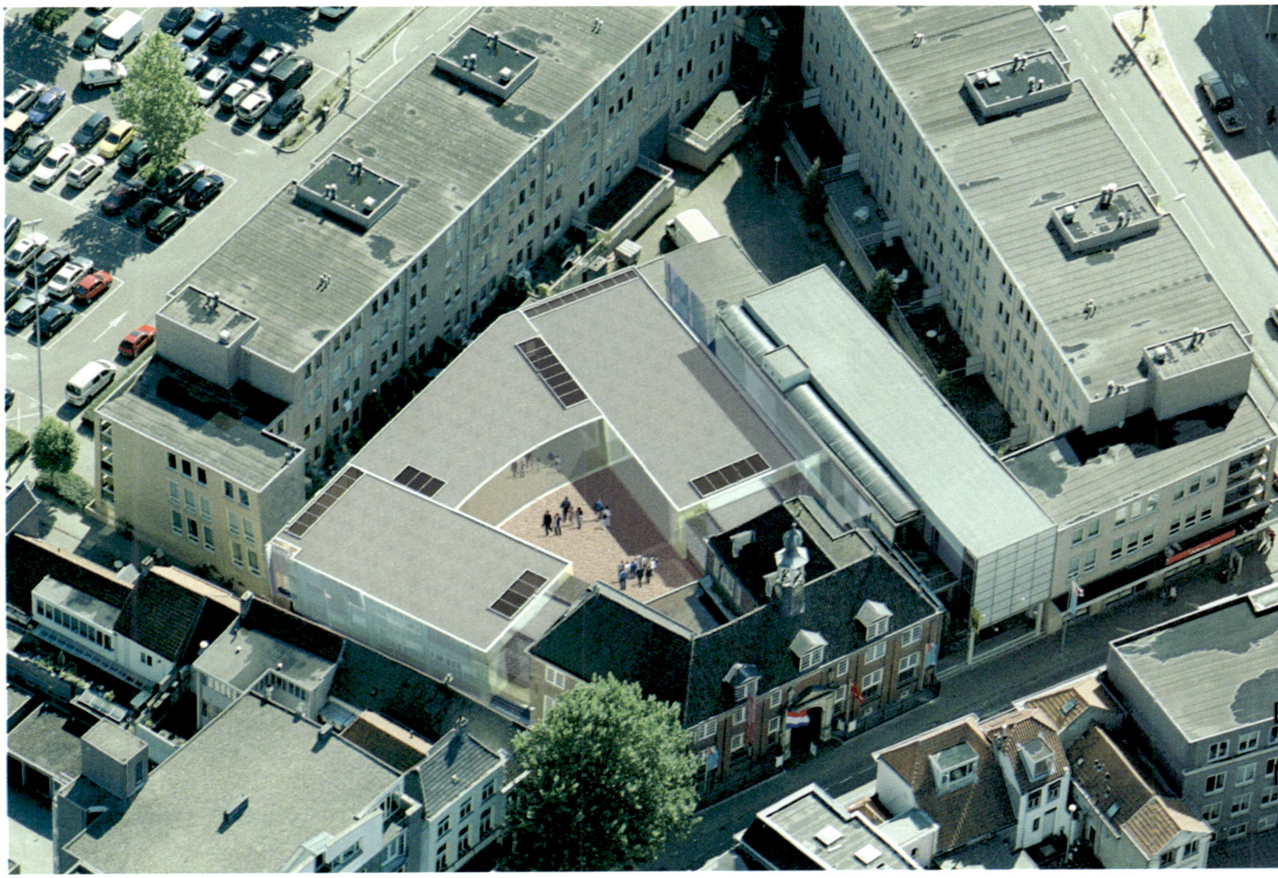

MgV.bird's-eye view 10.HvH

BrB.Artotheek elevation 09.SV

BrB.court 11.SV

BrB.entrance 01.SV

BrB.stairs 03.SV

BrB.elevator 19.SV

BrB.floor 02.SV

BrB.interior 20.SV

MgV.Artotheek 08.SV

BrB.detail 19.SV

BrB.detail 20.SV

MgV.streetcorner 18.HvH

MgV.side elevation 12.HvH

MgV.3D interior 05.PB

MgV.3D interior 04.PB

MgV.3D interior 07.PB

MgV.3D interior 06.PB

MgV.sketch elevation 13.HvH

MgV.sketch elevation 14.HvH

MgV.sketch facade 15.HvH

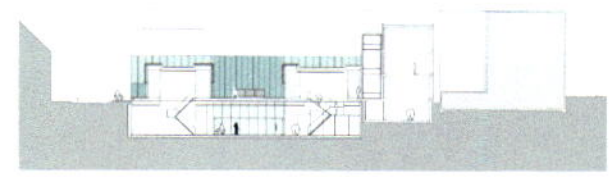

MgV.sketch section 16.HvH

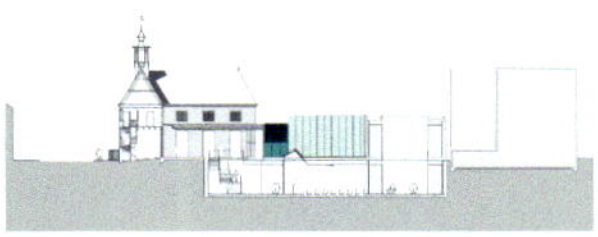

MgV.sketch section 17.HvH

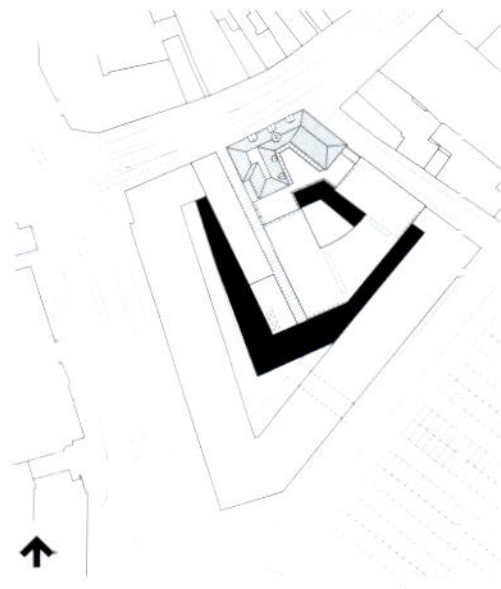

MgV.situation

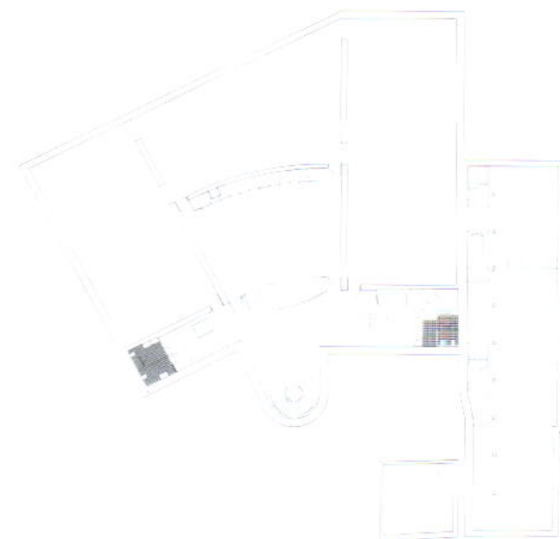

MgV.basement

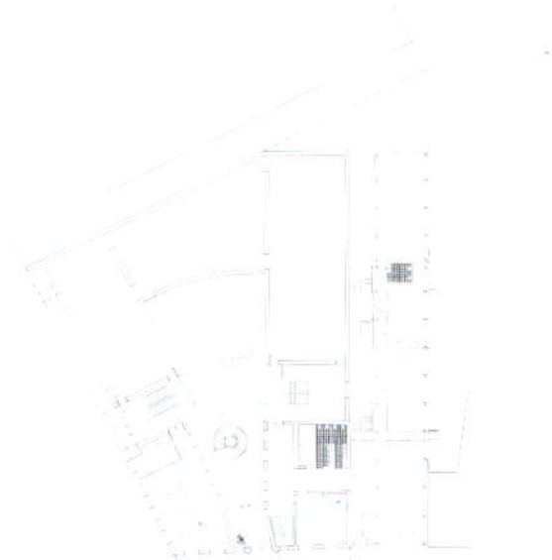

MgV.ground floor

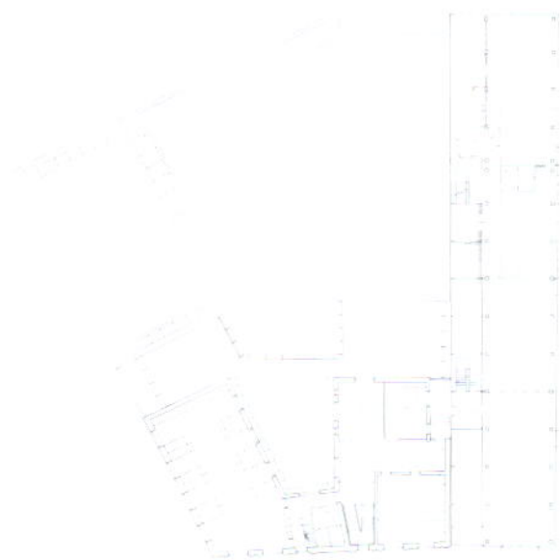

MgV.first floor

MgV.facade 1

MgV.facade 2

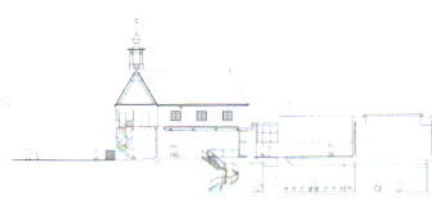

MgV.section

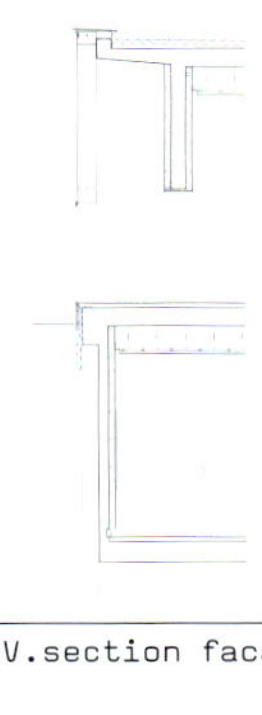

MgV.section facade

BrB
MgV

.BrB
MgV

The former art lending library consists of three concrete floors of 7 by 37 metres, a basement and a covered internal street almost three metres wide which allows light to penetrate deep within the building.

BrB
1.BrB

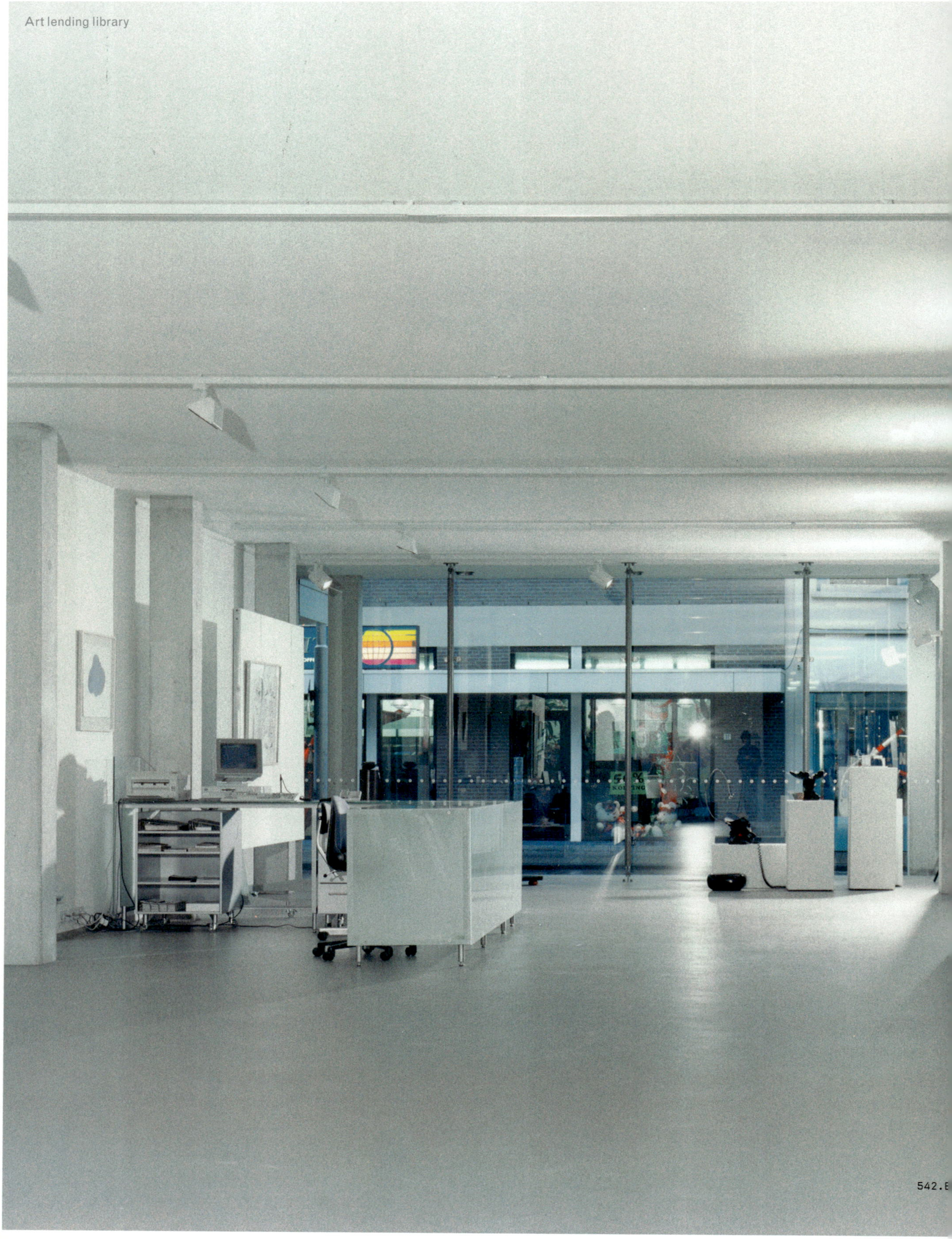

542.E

3.BrB

5.BrB

BrB

Museum of Graphic Design

De BEYERD
Terras geopend

Inside the building, detailing and colours are muted so as not to upstage the exhibited works, for the most part graphic designs. The walls of the exhibition spaces are largely imperforate; daylight enters via continuous roof lights at the ends of the rooms.

MgV

.Mgv

The facade along the side street (Pasbaan) is completely transparent. Behind it, running the full length, is a two-metre-deep space that is part of the exhibition circuit; from the outside this space acts as a kind of shop window.

Boschstraat elevation
1:400

Pasbaan elevation
1:400

Section
1:400

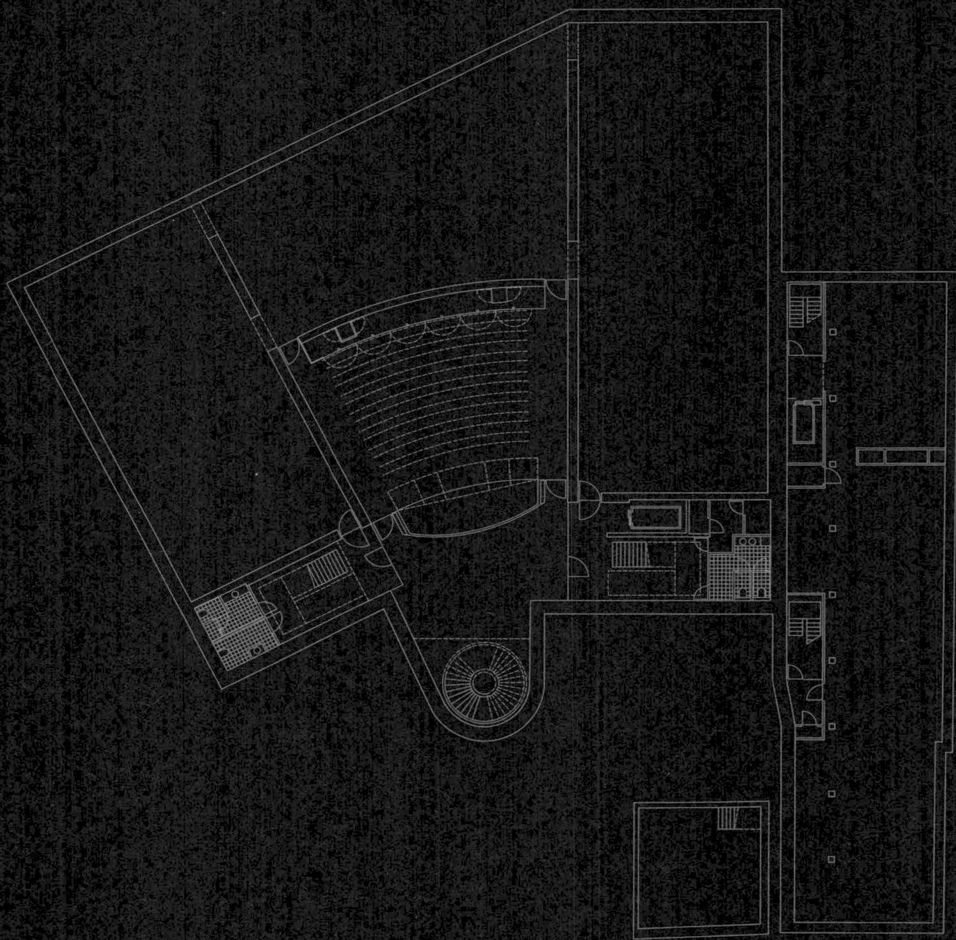

Basement
1:400

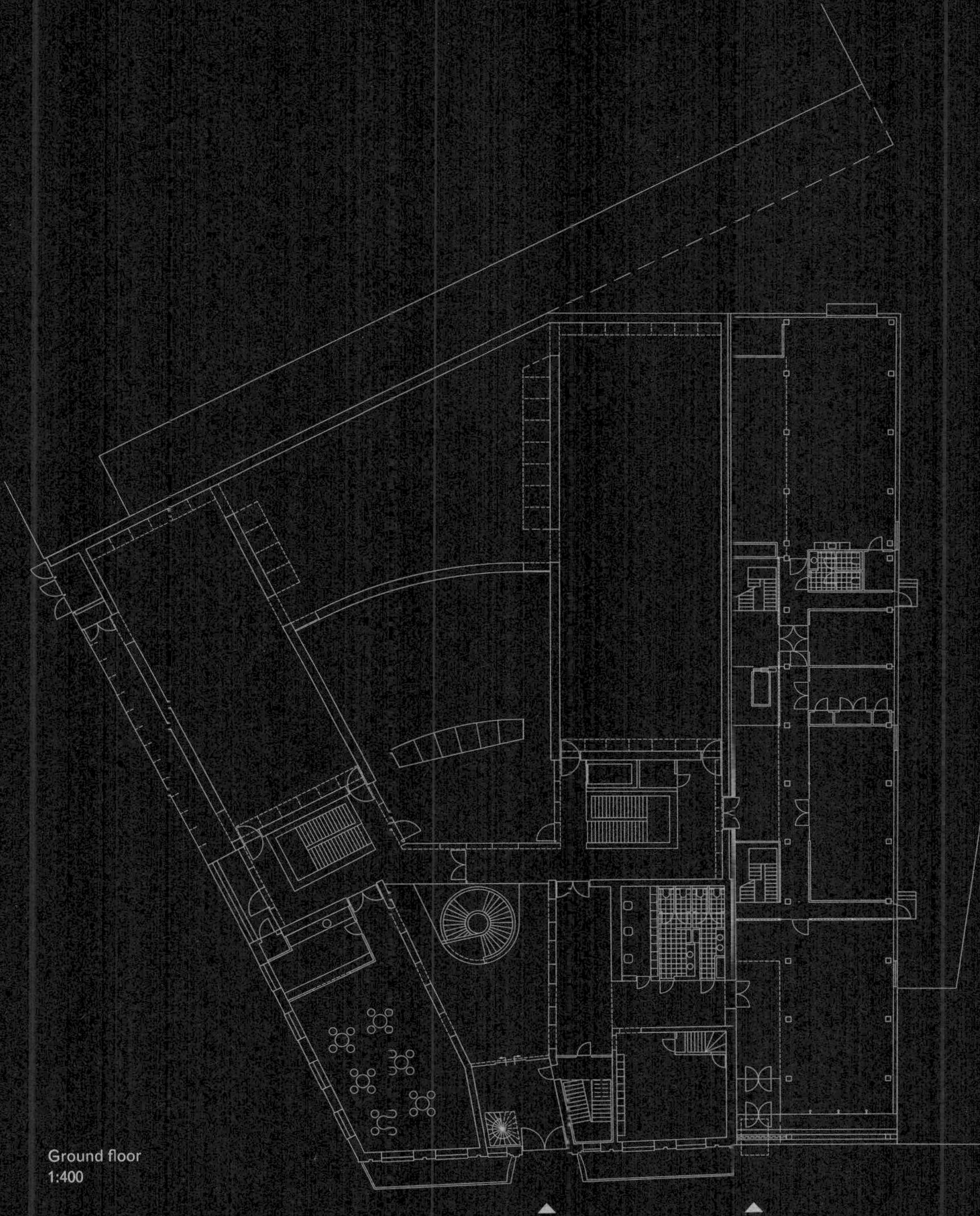

Ground floor
1:400

First floor
1:400

Section shop window

THE NATURAL HISTORY MUSEUM
Tinguely
Documenta11
MAC
SERRALVES
AVGVSTA EMERITA
Museu de les Ciències Príncipe Felipe. Valencia
Scotland Street School Museum
eames
CONHECIMENTO
FONDATION BEYELER
WATERLILIES
Space Needle
Seattle
The Lighthouse
THE BRITISH MUSEUM LONDON
neuesmuseum
MUSEI CIVICI VENEZIANI
Jüdisches Museum Berlin
KUB Kunsthaus Bregenz
PINAKOTHEK DER MODERNE
The J. Paul Getty Museum™
la Biennale di Venezia
MICHELANGELO
museoPICASSOmálaga
KUNSTMUSEUM
SEATTLE ART MUSEUM
SAN FRANCISCO MUSEUM OF MODERN ART
Royal Academy of Arts
This pencil is made from one recycled vending cup
Oakland Museum of California
NEUE PINAKOTHEK
THE MUSEUM OF TELEVISION & RADIO
TATE
MUSEE NATIONAL MESSAGE BIBLIQUE
Kimbell Art Museum
SCOTLAND STREET SCHOOL MUSEUM
HENRY ART GALLERY
NEANDERTHAL MUSEUM
MFA H The Museum of Fine Arts, Houston
motherwell heritage centre
expl( )ratorium
ART! INSIDE: SUPERSTAR B-LIST PIN-UP SOCIALITE EXCLUSIVE

HmA.

name
Hermitage Amsterdam

project code
HmA

place
Amstel 51, Amsterdam

client
Stichting de Hermitage Amsterdam

design
2005–2006

construction
2007

design team
Dick de Gunst
Johanna Günther
Stephanie Haumann
Hans van Heeswijk
Rinke Kluwer
David Künzel
Jeroen Rademaker

The State Hermitage Museum in St. Petersburg, Russia, is one of the most famous museums in the world. The Hermitage collection, begun by Catherine the Great and greatly expanded after her death, is so large that only a small portion can be exhibited in the museum's own buildings in St. Petersburg.
A satellite of the Russian museum is to be opened in the Amstelhof building in Amsterdam by Foundation Hermitage on the Amstel. Hermitage Amsterdam will hold temporary exhibitions sourced mainly from the Hermitage's collection. In addition to exhibitions, the Amstelhof will have a restaurant, auditorium, museum shop, a cultural institute and reception rooms.
Amstelhof, a courtyard building originally built in 1683 to house elderly female members of the Dutch Reformed Church, stands beside the Amstel River between the Muziektheater and the Royal Theatre Carré. The building was probably designed by the city carpenter, Hans Jansz. van Petersom, under the supervision of the city architect, Daniel Stalpaert.
What is now largely sequestered from the outside world as befits a rest home, will become an inviting public building. On the outside, Amstelhof will remain almost unchanged. Inside, the building will undergo a metamorphosis. The maze of corridors and small rooms will make way for a light and airy museum. The interior court with its Mien Ruys-designed garden will be open to the public. The west wing, along the Amstel, will be used for special gatherings. The north and south wings will contain exhibition rooms. The east (garden) wing will contain the entrance foyer, restaurant and auditorium. Service spaces and staircases will be located in the corners of the building.

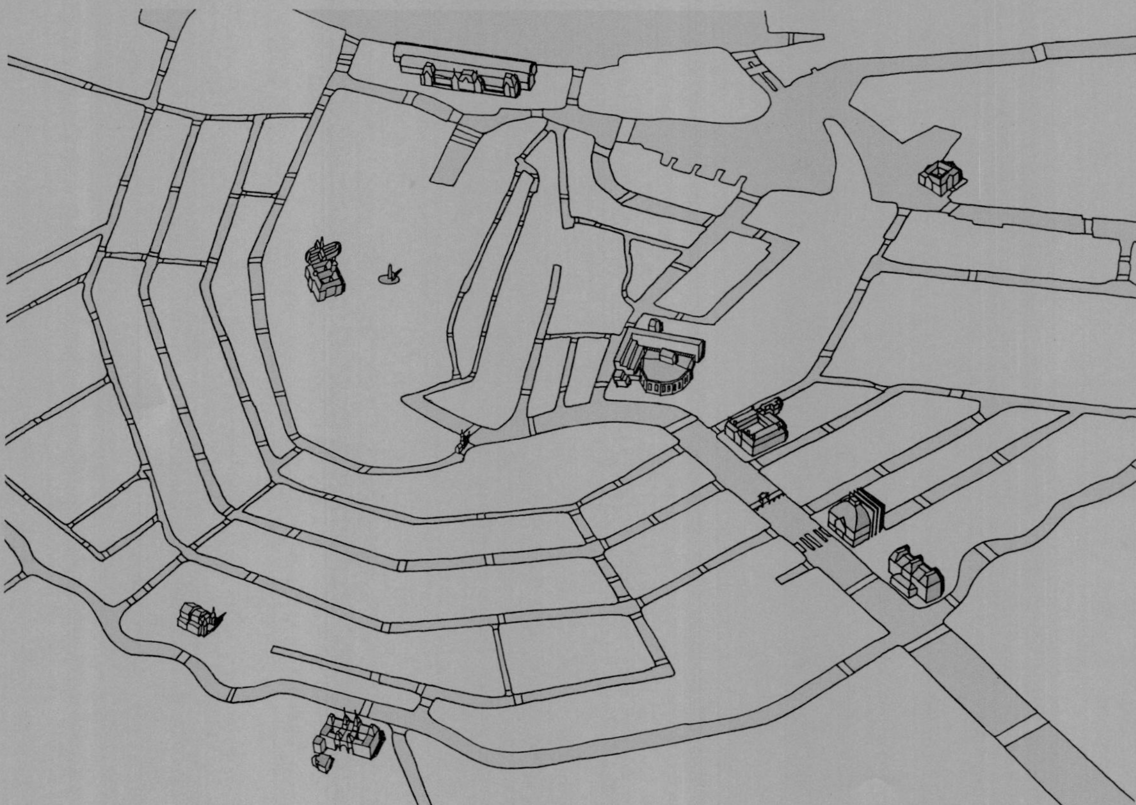

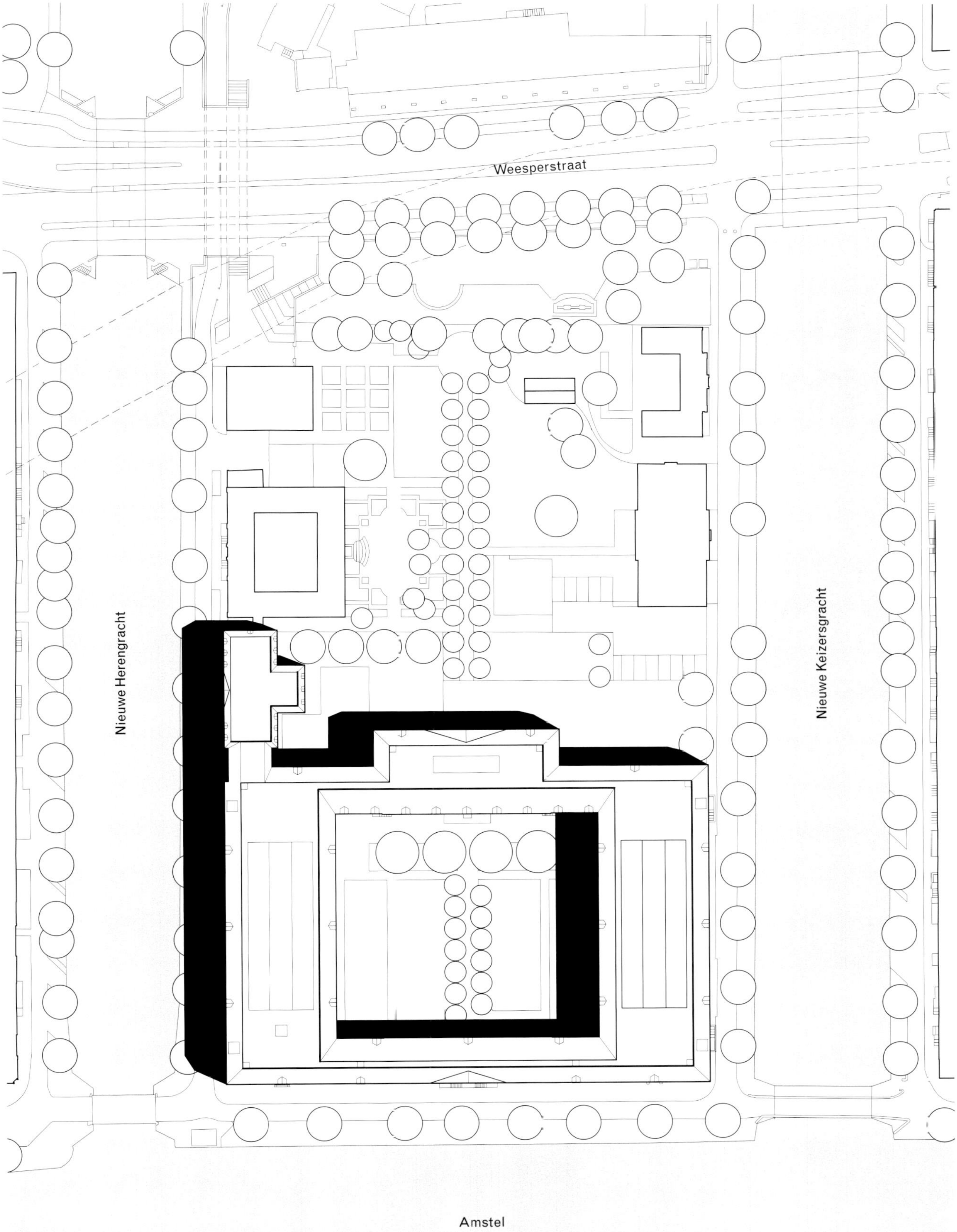
Weesperstraat
Nieuwe Herengracht
Nieuwe Keizersgracht
Amstel

9.HmA

HmA

HmA.overview 18.AS

HmA.overview 17.AS

HmA.overview 48.PB

HmA.new entrance Amstel 53.PB

HmA.new entrance Amstel 57.PB

HmA.foyer 51.PB

HmA.hallway 50.PB

HmA.exhibition space 58.PB

HmA.restaurant 49.PB

HmA.museumshop 55.PB

a

HmA.exhibition space 59.PB

HmA.section exhibition 56.PB

HmA.section 54.PB

HmA.side facing
Nieuwe Keizersgracht 05.PB

HmA.side facing Amstel 06.PB

HmA.west elevation 60.PB

HmA.north elevation 07.PB

HmA.garden elevation 08.PB

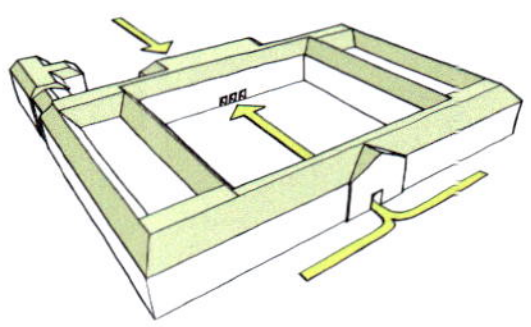
HmA.circulation 44.HvH

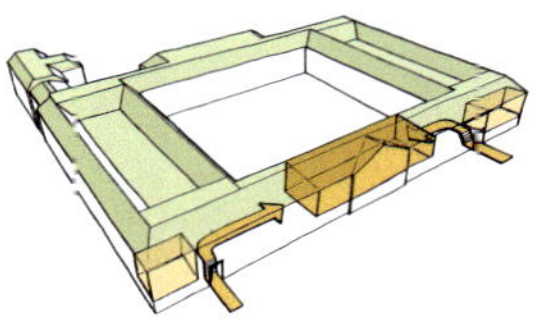
HmA.circulation 46.HvH

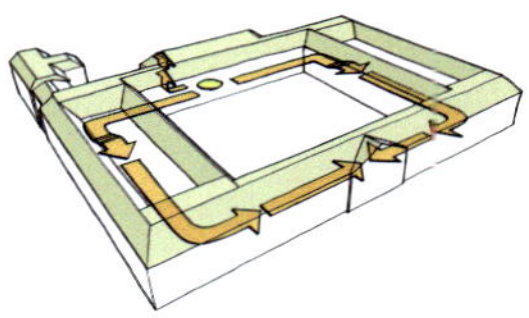
HmA.circulation 45.HvH

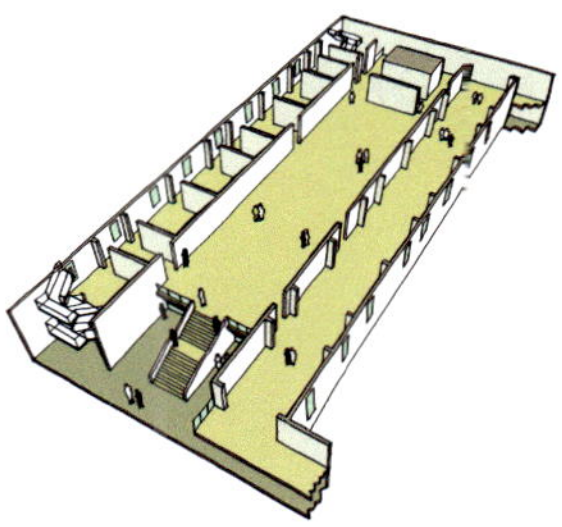
HmA.exhibition space 65.HvH

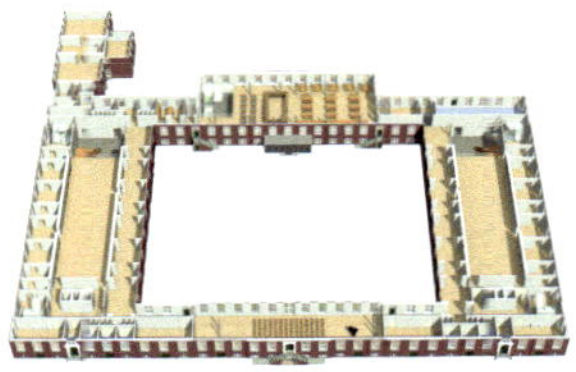
HmA.main floor 40.HvH

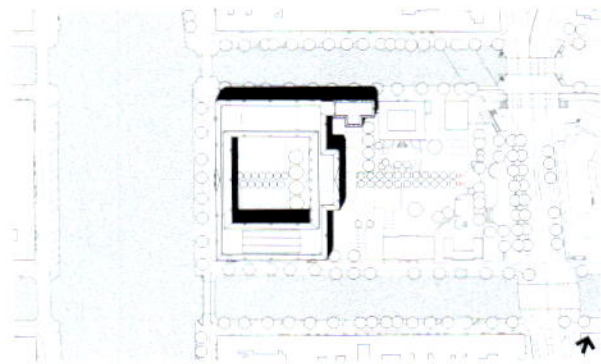
HmA.situation

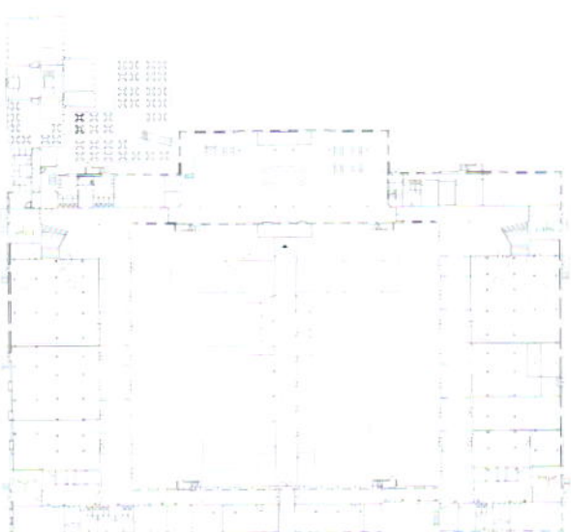
HmA.souterrain

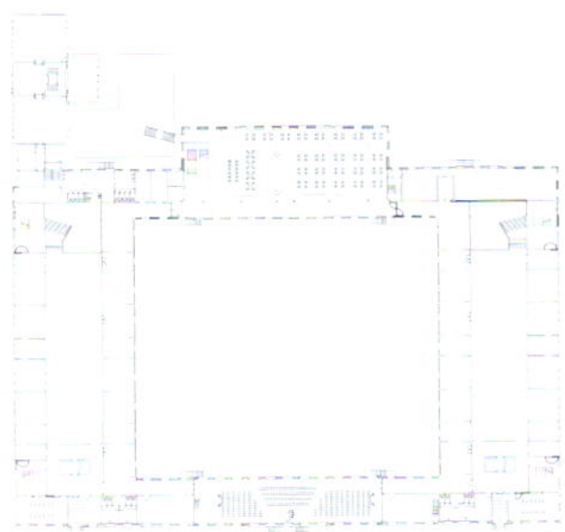
HmA.main floor

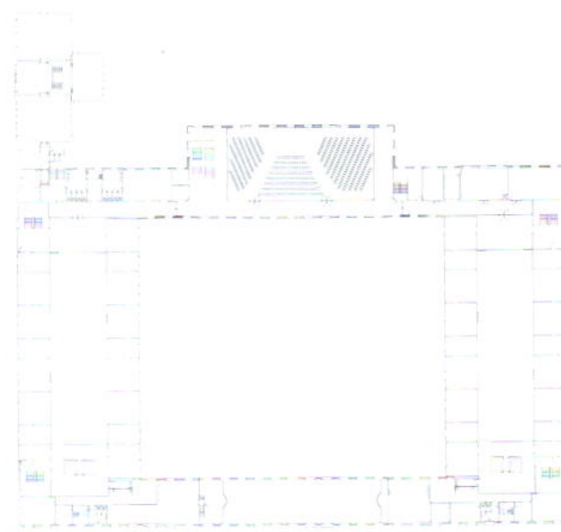
HmA.first floor

HmA.second floor

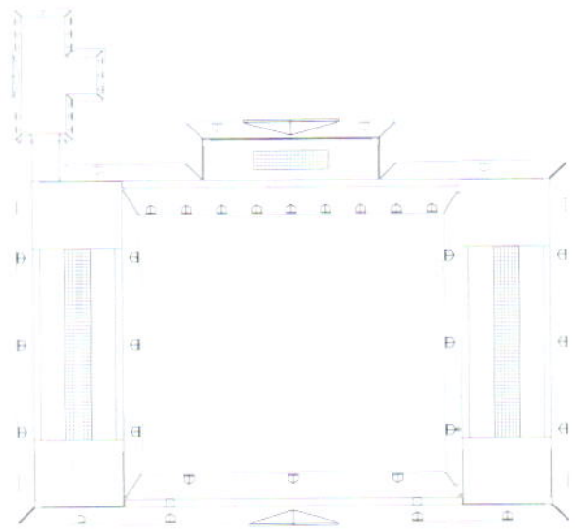
HmA.roof

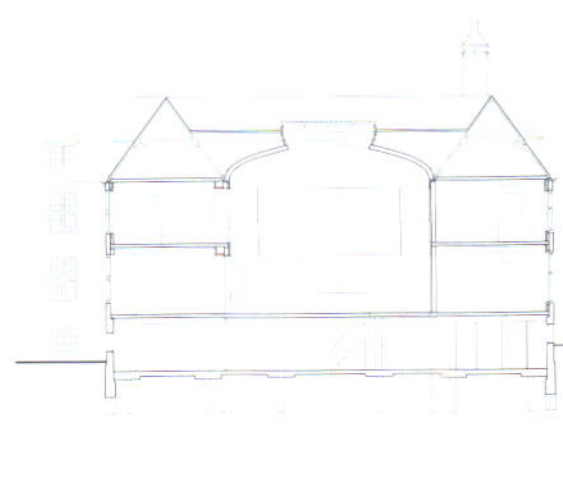
HmA.section

3. HmA

The main entrance of the building will be in the traditional tradesman's entrance beneath the main steps in the centre of the Amstel facade.

5.HmA

The foyer leads to both exhibition wings on the spacious and light interior court where the museum shop is also located.

Venezia!
Kunst uit de 18de eeuw

All the public functions such as the lobby, restaurant and auditorium are located one above the other in the garden wing on the east side of the building.

9.HmA

HmA

The exhibition spaces are in the north and south wings. What were once small courts will become the main rooms. Around these, over two floors, will be a succession of small side galleries.

71.HmA

HmA

The building will have a classical ordering of spaces with large reception rooms in the centre of each wing and at the outer corners.
On the first floor, the main floor of the museum, is a circuit of corridors linking all four wings. Stairwells are located at the corners, at the end of every corridor.

Section east and west wing

Section exhibition spaces

5.HmA

HmA

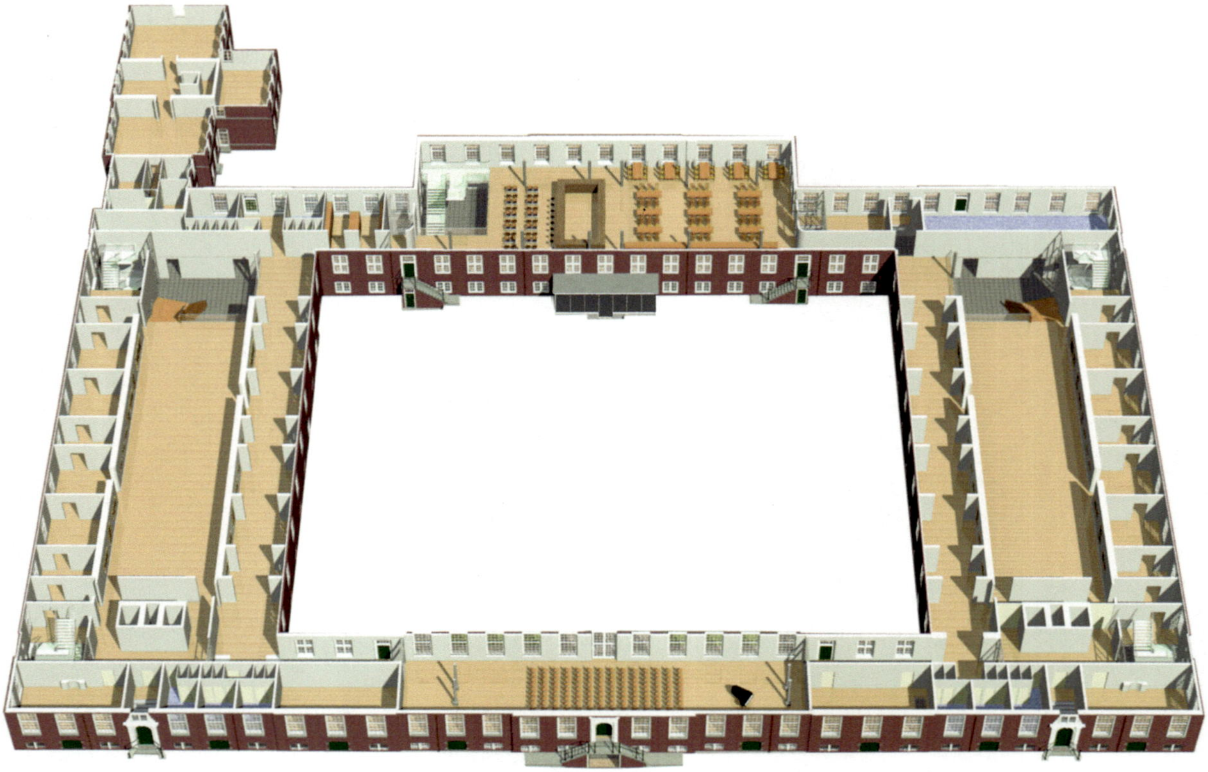

Main floor

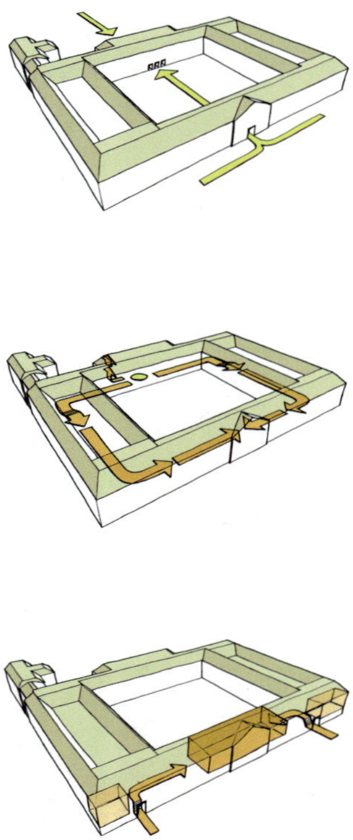

Circulation

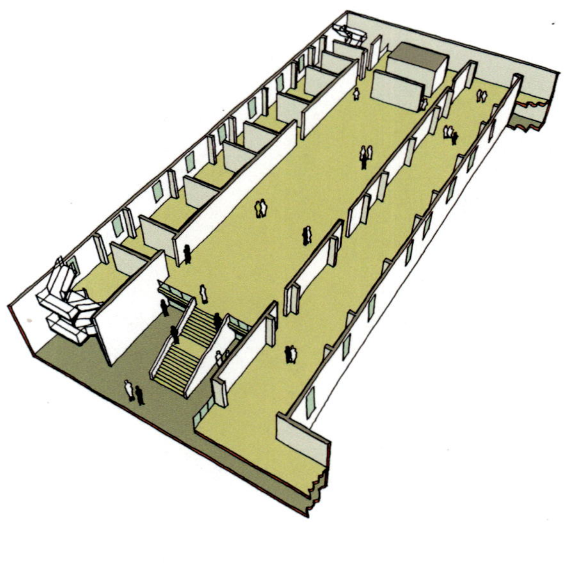

Exhibition space

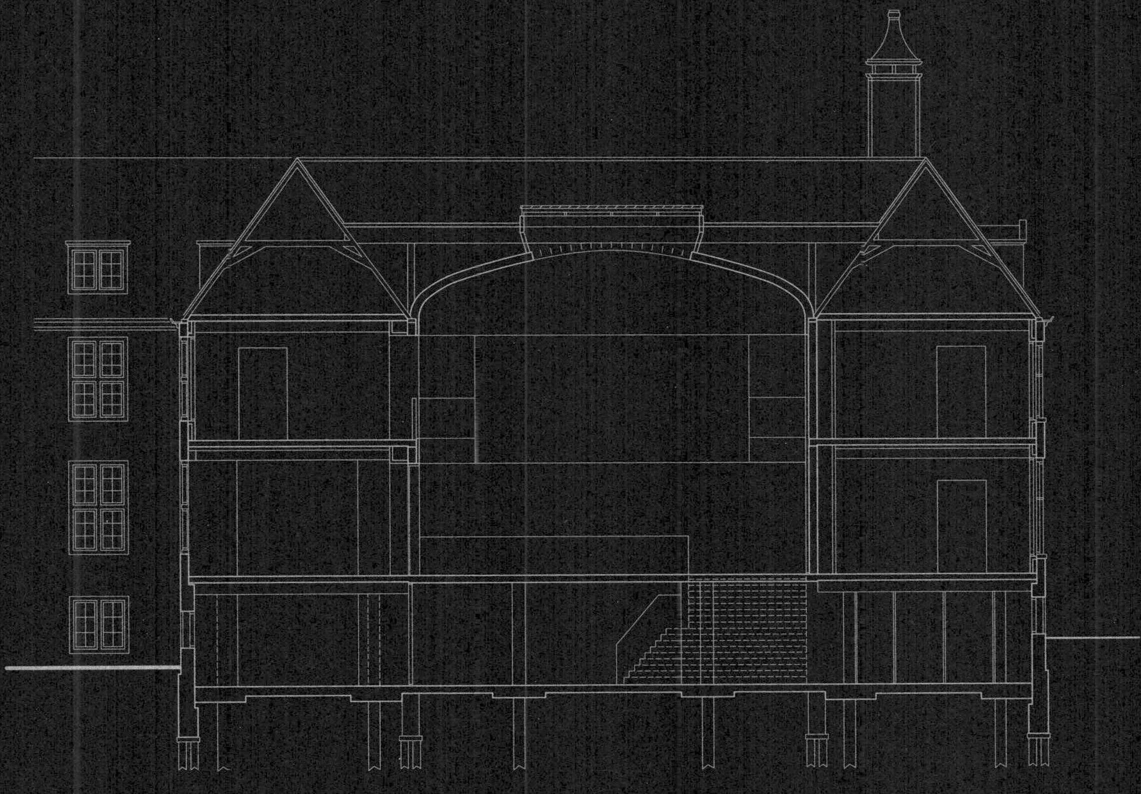

Section exhibition space
1:200

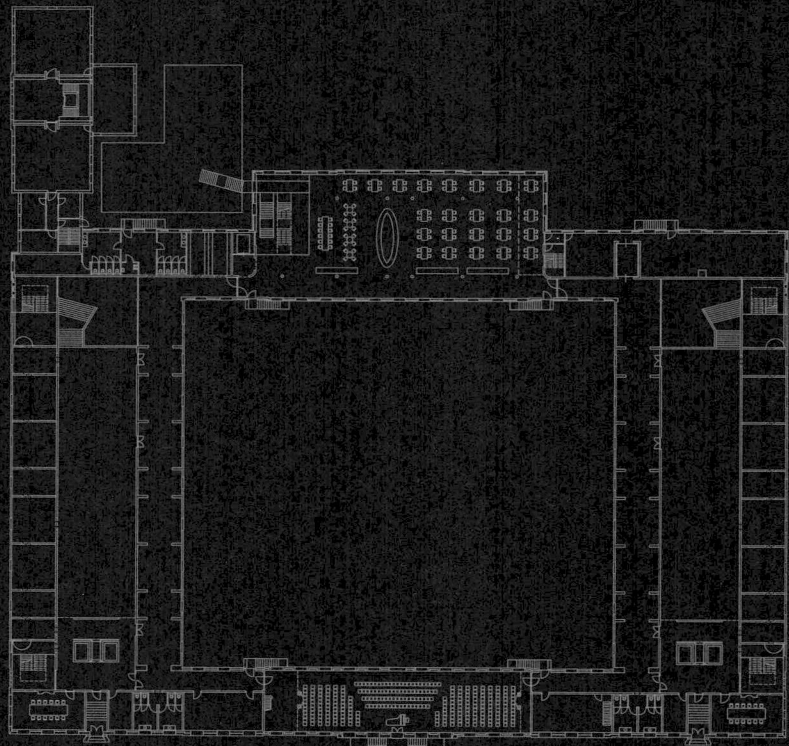

Main floor

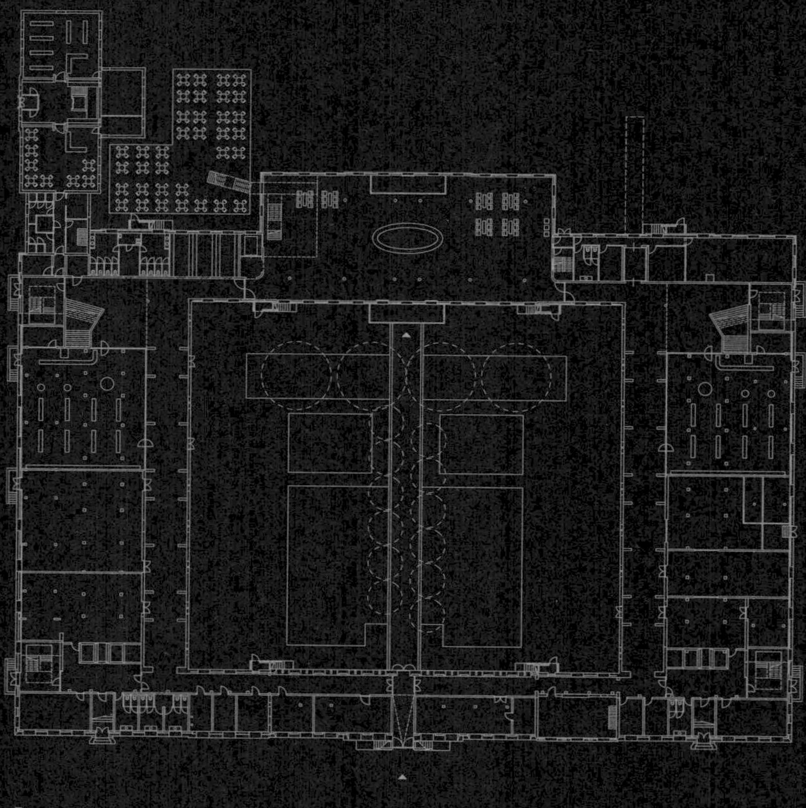

Basement
1:1000

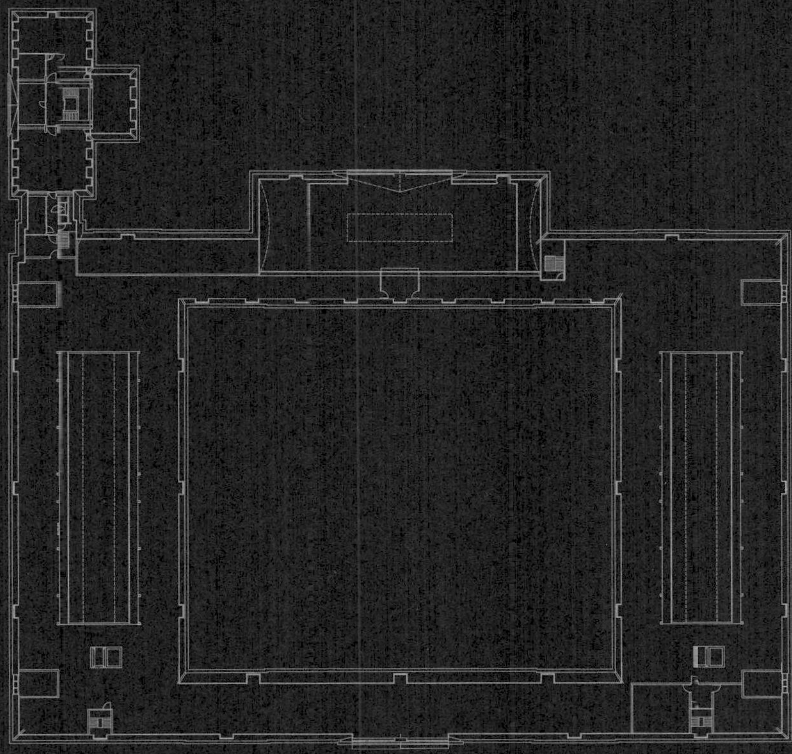

Roof

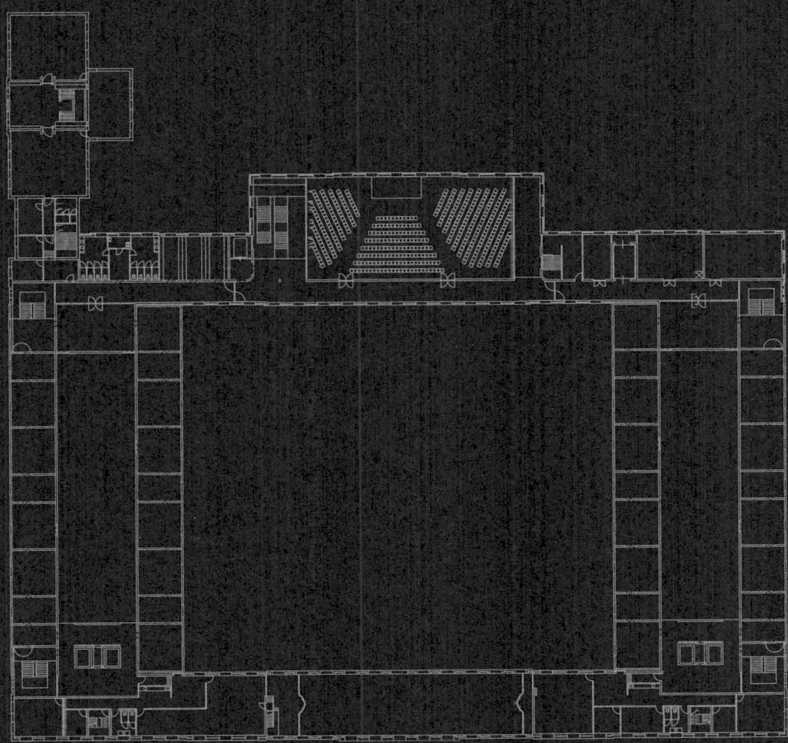

First floor

Hans van Heeswijk

in conver sation with Mels Crouwel

Hans van Heeswijk and Mels Crouwel have known one another since their student days in Delft. Immediately upon graduating in 1979, Crouwel founded a practice with Jan Benthem that is now called Benthem Crouwel. Van Heeswijk went to work for Aldo van Eyck before setting up for himself in 1985. Not only do both men belong to the same generation, but their work and area of activity also coincide to a large degree. Another notable similarity is their shared interest in the actual making of buildings.

Mels Crouwel
I don't know whether the 'making' of buildings is typical of our generation, but it is for those of our way of thinking within that generation, at least at the beginning.

Hans van Heeswijk
Maybe it has something to do with Delft, where we studied in the 1970s.

Mels Crouwel
Jo Coenen belongs to the same generation and he studied at Eindhoven. Yet he was very interested in it too. And we were all part of the first Young Dutch Architects Biennale in 1983.

Hans van Heeswijk
Most of the participants in that biennale were interested in making.

Mels Crouwel
Working out for yourself how to make something was more important then than it is today.

Hans Ibelings
Where did that interest in making come from? Because it didn't feature much in the architecture of the day.

Mels Crouwel
I always say it's because I attended Duiker's Open Air School.

Hans van Heeswijk
I grew up in a new suburb of Breda, so I saw the bricklayers laying bricks and putting in frames. I was fascinated by it all. But it's also got something to do with the attention devoted to it at Delft, by teachers like Jaap Bakema and Herman Hertzberger. Hertzberger spoke about such basic things as how a frame connects with a column and how that could become a meaningful place. And then there was the structural engineering side, taught by Tjeerd Dijkstra.

Mels Crouwel
And you also had the whole group of people preaching modern architecture. So our training involved a lot of Zonnestraal and Van Nelle Factory, the precise detailing, with all those slender steel frames and thermal bridges, and why it did or didn't work. And after that you had Aldo van Eyck and Hertzberger who kept harking back to it and showing how it was done.

Hans van Heeswijk
The course of study was more loosely organized in those days and you were allowed to take as long as you liked over it. In my case that was eight years.

Mels Crouwel
In mine five-and-a-half. But Jan Benthem took as long as you, he spent a lot of time tinkering with cars. And that's another source. You only have to see an English engine, and you can take it to pieces and put it together again. That sort of thing is important for you too Hans, wanting to understand how things fit together. That's how we wanted to do architecture back then. It proved to be very limiting and we're moving away from it a bit now, also because the firm is bigger and you don't do everything yourself anymore. But the idea of wanting to understand everything is always there in the background.

Hans van Heeswijk
It's the same for me, a building must be legible, comprehensible, logical. The examples we had at our disposal then were legible and understandable: there were lots of grid designs, both in the high-tech sphere and in structuralism. The one in steel and glass, the other in concrete.

Mels Crouwel
Do you still prefer to draw on squared paper too? I much prefer a squared pad to a lined one, even if I only use it for writing.

Hans van Heeswijk
The grid used to dictate your floor plan, your structure, and that's different now. Now it's spatiality that determines how I make a grid.

Mels Crouwel
We still place everything on a grid too, every time.

Hans van Heeswijk
Yes, but I approach it more loosely, which allows me to make a more spatial construction.

Mels Crouwel
Computers are very important of course. Things that used to be much too difficult, if you weren't good at maths, like me, are all possible nowadays. Back then you had to work it all out for yourself, so you just put it out of your head.

Hans van Heeswijk
But that very limitation meant that you kept it – had to keep it – simple.

Mels Crouwel
True. Our early work was much sharper than what we're doing now. If we were set on making a square box, that's what we did. Now we start thinking about all the things that can go wrong.

Hans van Heeswijk
When you're just starting out, the urge to make a mark is much stronger, I think, so you tend to look for unusual solutions and materials. I don't need

that anymore, nowadays I'm more concerned with the design itself. I've noticed that it's important whether a building lasts well, so I opt for a higher standard of detailing.

Mels Crouwel

That's obviously a matter of experience. There are some kinds of detailing we don't attempt, because we know it's risky. Besides, you're dealing with fairly big buildings nowadays, in other words a lot of money. The construction culture has changed. In the past if you made a mistake and things went wrong, it was annoying but not disastrous. Now you're immediately served with a claim. And rightly so.

Hans van Heeswijk

I'm not sure I agree there.

Mels Crouwel

If the client hasn't asked you to experiment but you go ahead and do it and it turns out wrong and costs him a fortune, he's entitled to hold you liable.

Hans van Heeswijk

Sure, but it's also true that buildings are prototypes. We need to get used to the idea that occupation is immediately followed by a period of follow-up care, during which growing understanding enables you to occasionally adjust elements that don't work or don't turn out as well as you'd hoped and expected.

Mels Crouwel

If you're able to reach an agreement about that with the client, well and good. But the client wants an object that is finished and that will last for as long as he has specified.

Hans van Heeswijk

They're much quicker to hold you to account now than fifteen years ago. I think architects should be given the opportunity to finish a job properly.
I think the expertise of architects has increased too. But there's been a steep decline in the skill of contractors with the result that poor buildings are still being made. I think things started to go wrong when building contractors were quoted on the stock exchange; they acquired other priorities, namely producing a return for shareholders rather than a good building. Only old-fashioned family businesses still seem to have a dedication to the job.

Mels Crouwel

I quite agree. In the past every foreman wanted to turn out good work, now they're hired to get the job done for the contractor as quickly as possible. So now it's a case of standing firm and pointing to the contract clause where it says that the contractor has to do this and this.

Hans Ibelings

Listening to this I get the impression that your position in the building process is under threat. That said, culturally speaking the status of the architect and architecture has continued to increase during the twenty-five years that you've been active.

Mels Crouwel

That's because the media play an important role in our profession; all very nice on the one hand, but on the other hand it's spawned a whole circle of architects who devote half their time to the media. Which is another way of procuring work.

Hans van Heeswijk

But isn't it also a kind of professional deformation that those architects are deployed for outward show, the design? Another possible problem is that the quality of those who write about architecture has declined. It's my contention that most architecture journalists are unable to distinguish craftsmanship, are unable to see whether a building is competently detailed. They concentrate on the general impression.

Mels Crouwel

I think precisely the same applies to the magazines as to the construction industry. Making a magazine pay has changed in exactly the same way as our profession. Architecture, fortunately, has become much more a part of life as a result of all the attention.

Hans Ibelings

The same goes for the interest in architectural and urban quality.

Mels Crouwel

And that has a lot to do with architectural policy in the Netherlands.

Hans van Heeswijk

Yet I have the feeling it's declined a lot in recent years. I see it at Rijkswaterstaat, which I've had a lot to do with, but also among developers. It seems as if economic interests are always being given precedence over cultural objectives.

Mels Crouwel

That's partly because of the economic recession.

Hans van Heeswijk

That's misused as an excuse for taking a routine approach and avoiding risks. The economic recession is the pretext for a return to cheaper and lazier building.

Hans Ibelings

Economic conditions were pretty bad when you started out, too.

Hans van Heeswijk

Very bad...

Mels Crouwel

...a genuine slump in the construction market.

Hans van Heeswijk

But it didn't affect me all that much because I started out with very small things, little buildings for relatives, a shop, a conservatory. These kinds of jobs gave me the opportunity to learn the profession.

Mels Crouwel

In our case it was partly at the expense of the client – I remember that well from those days. Dealing with a contractor wasn't something they taught you at Delft, so occasionally things went dramatically wrong.

Hans van Heeswijk

Of course, I started out at another practice, where I was able to explore the limits of the possible, and luckily for me it was a practice where the architects didn't rest until the last screw was in place. Quite different from Carel Weeber with whom I did six months' work practice when I was at Delft. He stopped after the preliminary design because he took the view that you should leave the detailing and elaboration to the real experts in this profession, and according to him that was the contractors. Van Eyck was the complete opposite. He had every lath in his building removed three times and screwed back slightly differently each time, then he'd step back to see how it looked, and then it had to be put back in its original position.

Mels Crouwel

So neither of those is the whole truth.

Hans van Heeswijk

And it doesn't happen like that anymore. Because there's been a shift in the construction industry away from making on site to assembling. It might be interesting to consider whether the same has happened in the design industry. Sometimes I get the feeling that a lot of young architects, when they make a design, model it directly with 3D, then overlay it with mappings and that's their design. You could call that a kind of assembling too.

Mels Crouwel

Of course, it's quite crazy to only do flat drawings. In big overseas engineering firms everything is done straight off in 3D nowadays and we're looking at introducing that too, so that you get a much better and more precise insight into your design.

Hans van Heeswijk

Weren't we expected to have more spatial insight in our day? You sketched in 2D, but you had the building in your head. Students with sufficient spatial insight were the ones who survived but now any student who can use a 3D program can become an architect.

Mels Crouwel

If you don't have to think about that aspect you can concentrate on other things. I wish I'd been able to do it back then. Jan and I are the only ones who don't sit at a computer now, of course.

Hans van Heeswijk

Neither do I. But what I want to say is that with the current tools there may be a greater risk that architects with less talent will manage to conceal this for longer, because of the sophisticated technology.

Mels Crouwel

You had that before, too, because mediocre architects simply operated on automatic pilot using standard details.

Hans Ibelings

Since that initial bad economic period you've actually had smooth sailing.

Mels Crouwel

Not at all, there have been two more slumps in-between times.

Hans van Heeswijk

There was another economic slump in the early 1990s.

Mels Crouwel

And again now, so we've experienced that cycle of seven or eight years twice already. It was only the last time that we had a bad year, but we came out of it all right.

Hans van Heeswijk

The nineties recession hit me hard. It took me about five years to get over that. Whereas this time I haven't been bothered at all. That's because of a shift in my work. Office construction suddenly came to a halt and then housing stagnated as well. But conversions, interiors and renovations simply continued. In retrospect I'm glad. Because after five or so years I was fed up with those speculative office buildings. You spend a couple of years on that kind of building and then two weeks before completion a big lorry drives up full of the wrong colour interior walls and the wrong furniture. That's pretty frustrating. Now we do conversions, interiors and buildings for organizations where the end user is known, which means that you can develop those projects down to the last detail, based on the same vision. That's much more satisfying. So in fact it's done me a favour, this recession.

Hans Ibelings

You've both had several commissions for museum renovations and extensions. How did that typecasting come about?

Mels Crouwel

You have architects whose output consists of buildings that are interesting in themselves. That doesn't necessarily mean they're always suitable for hanging art. We, I think, have always tried, certainly with an old building, to see what we wanted to retain and what we wanted to add. And if, like Hans with De Beyerd in Breda and like us with De Pont in Tilburg, you then make something that everybody considers a success, they'll keep on coming back.

Hans van Heeswijk

It also has something to do with the architectural outlook because our architecture – I think it's similar – lends itself to renovating and converting listed buildings because we generally make introvert designs and work with contrasting materials. That way you accept old buildings as they are.

Mels Crouwel

And in combinations of old and new the craft aspect of the profession is important; quite simply, that you know how to make a connection in an existing building.

Hans van Heeswijk

Quite so. These projects are not about architectural gesturing but about the pleasure of detailing. And that often entails a lot more skill and energy than a new building.

Mels Crouwel

You have to measure a lot because everything that looks straight is needless to say crooked and you have to solve that. One time you decide to make your own structure a tiny bit crooked without it being noticeable. Another time you think up some clever way of making the junction disappear from sight.

Hans van Heeswijk

It is certainly remarkable that we both have an order portfolio that doesn't leave us dependent on a single category of projects. We do offices, conversions, renovations, restorations, bridges and interiors.

Mels Crouwel

That's partly because that's what you yourself like, that spread.

Hans van Heeswijk

Yes, but I don't go looking for it, I'm asked to do it.

Mels Crouwel

But you could also say no.

Hans van Heeswijk

I'd refuse a commission for a villa with saddle roofs and shutters, but as soon as there's the hint of an architectural challenge I'm curious enough to want to see what I can make of it.

Hans van Heeswijk

Dimen sions in design ing

The raison d'être of every design is functionality, but there is obviously a lot more than that to a good design. Notions like spatial quality, scale, style, materialization and layeredness spring to mind. The design process, in which all kinds of factors play a role, and the designer's own perspective, can result in an architecture that transcends functionality, in form and content. Form and content should ideally be inextricably linked.

A design is only truly convincing when functionality, form and content are in balance, yet without being unnecessarily complicated. When it comes to the design of an everyday object like a fork, nobody needs the designer's perspective. In a simple design like this, a functional form is the best.

In designs for cities, buildings, interiors and furniture the same rule of a balance between form, content and function applies, be it that the designs of such things usually have greater significance than that of a fork. Functionality is no less important in this instance, but the significance of the form is usually greater. Moreover, the significance should relate to different aspects, which effectively make up the different layers of a design.

Just about every design, whether it be for an uncomplicated building or for a complete urban fragment, consists of more than a space, has several functions and forms of use, is made from several materials, has different scales and dimensions, and so on. And a design usually evokes more than one impression: for example, it may be simultaneously imposing and inviting, lucid and complex, surprising and familiar. In the same way, designs may feature oppositions like open and closed, light and dark, high and low, in various degrees and combinations.

Thus before long a design will comprise several layers, and with each design layer it acquires more significance and can be read and understood in more ways. The more layers a design contains, the more complex and rich it is. It should be the ambition of every designer to achieve maximum layeredness within a coherent, restrained visual form. Conversely, a busy visual form is not infrequently a sign of a one-dimensional design.

Layeredness is thus a fundamental design strategy. The various layers relating to functionality, tactility, spatiality, form, logistics and so on can in first instance be studied and elaborated in isolation before being linked to the other layers in a second stage. In this way a design can be built up and charged with significance. This pursuit of layeredness is not an argument in favour of increasingly complicated designs. The layeredness must serve a purpose and every layer should add something worthwhile to the whole, in the knowledge that designing is a process not of styling but rather of organizing, the visual manifestation of which is not the preconceived objective but the result.

It seems as though, in the course of history, there has been a negative evolution in the completeness of building design. In Antiquity, the Renaissance and Classicism, the architectural design was governed by a strict order that imposed a specific coherence on the different scales of a building. Modernism can be viewed as an emancipation from this rigidity. In the best cases it was replaced by a new, abstract coherence with a consistency comparable to that of Classicism. However, modernist abstraction has also given rise to a lot of one-dimensional superficiality. In combination with the ever-shorter lifespan of buildings, a by-product of the functionalist dogma that buildings should be tailored to their specific use, architecture has increasingly changed from a durable artefact into a consumer product that is simply demolished when it no longer serves its purpose.

Professional clients are particularly prone to take a cavalier attitude to buildings. Listening to them speak about them, you sometimes get the impression they are talking about second-hand cars. But even residents and users treat their buildings more and more like consumer goods these days. Very few people still ask themselves how a building was intended to be used. More often than not, they move into an office or house because the dimensions and location meet their needs. Architecture plays a subordinate role in their choice. In many cases residents and users will also have a preconceived idea of how they want to live or work, with the result that no sooner have they received the key than they start altering everything to make it conform to that preconceived image. And if, after a few years, they no longer like their home or office, they 'relocate'.

In short, a building has scarcely more value than a car or a suit that you swap for something different when they cease to please you. It is hardly surprising therefore that many builders, architects and consultants should have adapted to this 'off-the-peg' behaviour by expending less care on the product of their work. This is most apparent in housing and speculative office construction, which is rather awkward given that these types of buildings determine to a large degree the appearance of our daily environment.

None of this should be a reason for attaching less importance to the design, of course. It remains a breathtaking experience to enter a new building and to experience for the first time the reality of what at the beginning could only be represented in pictures and words.

Words and pictures are also of necessity the only means by which architecture can be approached in a book – a poor derivative of the built reality. Buildings can never be completely conveyed in either words or pictures. However extensive the documentation, only in reality can architecture provide a spatial experience which, if the architecture is good, is always more impressive and imposing than any two-dimensional representation. However superb the photographs of a building may be, they cannot compare with the spatial reality. The layeredness of buildings is difficult to record with a camera. A photograph can really only capture a fragment of the whole. And because of the perspective, which is almost inevitably distorted in a photo, the arrangement underlying the design is nearly always greatly obscured. A photo, moreover, is always just an incident, which almost inevitably fails to do justice to a building. Anyone wandering through a building will, unless they are wilfully blind, receive a great many impressions which should, ideally, acquire a kind of coherence. In richly designed buildings it is possible to walk through a building several times in succession and each time perceive different arrangements, layers or dimensions.

In short, architecture must be visited in reality. A book about architecture is nothing more than a reflection of reality. In one respect, however, a book can clarify something the built reality does not immediately reveal. A book can show the underlying relationship between unbuilt and built work and between structures that because of their geographical separation cannot be viewed simultaneously. I hope that, in addition to such relationships in the work, this book also reveals our daily passion, the ambition and pleasure involved in the enterprise and making of architecture.

Biography of Hans van Heeswijk

> 1952

Born in Breda

1980

Diploma of Structural Engineering, Architecture Department of Delft Technical College

1981–1983

Worked for Aldo van Eyck & Theo Bosch in Amsterdam

1983–1985

Worked for Aldo & Hannie van Eyck in Amsterdam

1985

Established Hans van Heeswijk architectural practice in Amsterdam

1985–present

Member of various juries and committees

1987–1999

Teacher at Amsterdam School of the Arts, Academy of Architecture

1987–present

Lectures in Amsterdam, Belo Horizonte, Breda, Delft, Dresden, Frankfurt, Ghent, 's Gravenhage, Graz, Haarlem, Leiden, Munich, Rio de Janeiro, Rotterdam, Stuttgart, Utrecht

> 1980

Archiprix for graduation design, 'Housing on Wittenburg in Amsterdam'

1982

Participant in final round of Prix de Rome 1982

1991

Merkelbach Incentive Prize for Architecture, awarded by Amsterdam Foundation for the Arts for office building at Stadhouderskade 84, Amsterdam

1999

Netherlands Concrete Prize for Tweede Stichtse Bridge along the A27 motorway at Huizen

2001

Netherlands Concrete Prize for bridge over Zuid Willemsvaart along the A50 motorway

2003

Netherlands Concrete Prize for the Eiland Bridge at Kampen

1985–present

Various prizes, awards and nominations for non-residential schemes, renovation projects and bridges

> 1983

Participant in first Young Dutch Architects Biennale

1992

Retrospective exhibition, Weissenhof Architectural Gallery in Stuttgart

2000

Retrospective exhibition 'Samples', ABC architecture centre, Haarlem

Staff members past and present

Jerome Adema, Ellen Baan, Marieke Bekirov, Jan van de Berg, Joris Berger, Jens Böhm, Eelco Braakman, Peter de Bruin, Peter Cammermans, Nikki Carman, Sjuul Cluitmans, Bart Commandeur, Rob van Dam, Sebastiaan van Damme, Andrew Dawes, Milos Dimitrijevic, Dick Floris, Floris van Gennep, Valerie Gorissen, Hélène Gros, Dick de Gunst, Johanna Günther, Eddy 't Hardt, Dennis Hartman, Stephanie Haumann, Remko van Heummen, Mirjam Heymann, Arjen Honig, Remco de Hoogh, Rob Hulst, Jonts van Itterson, Khalid Jamaludin, Werner Kamp, Maartje Kaper, José Kleeman, Rinke Kluwer, Anneli Kramer, David Künzel, Evelijn Léon, Sasja Maes, Rutger van der Meer, Anèt Meijer, Fanny Melis, André Meulenbelt, Geert Mol, Annette Molenaar, Holger Mührmann, Jeroen van Nieuwenhuizen, Dorieke Olde Weghuis, Ellen Otte, Luís Pires, Thijs Postma, Jeroen Rademaker, Joost Rademaker, André de Ruiter, Arjan van Ruyven, Paul Seuntjes, Mart Smits, Edward Sorgeloose, Ton Span, Betty Speelman, Jochem van der Spek, Leen Stapper, Meike Stoetzer, Hugo Suidgeest, Wilbert Swinkels, Lai-Man Tang, Brigitte Tenback, Rick Thani, Jurgen van Tiggelen, Claudia Tjon Soei Len, Rob Torsing, Bart van der Velde, Mariette de Vries Robbé, Nadine Warmer, Derk-Jan Wentink, Joost Woertman

Texts by Hans van Heeswijk

Heeswijk, H. van, *Vanzelfsprekend bruikbaar, het werk van Lucien Lafour*, *Forum* 1980/1982 no. 4, pp. 40-41
Heeswijk, H. van, 'Architecten over hun werk: Paul De Ley', *Forum* 1983 no. 1/2, p. 28
Heeswijk, H. van, 'Theo Bosch', *Biënnale de Paris Architecture 1985*, Paris 1985, pp. 82-85
Heeswijk, H. van, 'Einfaches Bauen mit Glas', *Detail* 1995 no. 3, pp. 394-399
Heeswijk, H. van, *Hans van Heeswijk architect*, 010 publishers, Rotterdam 1995
Heeswijk, H. van, 'De culturele component' in *Bruggen – Visie op architectuur en constructie*, Matrijs, Utrecht 2004

Texts about Hans van Heeswijk

Oosterman, A., 'Posities, Hans van Heeswijk', *Archis* 1995, no. 12, pp. 70-75
Huisman, J., 'Onopvallend opvallend', *De Volkskrant* 13-01-1996
Spits, P., 'Vormgeving van bruggen en viaducten', *Cement* 2003, no. 1, pp. 4-7, 10-13, 54-58, 67-71

Texts about projects by Hans van Heeswijk architecten

Student urban renewal plan for Wittenburg, Amsterdam

Zwinkels, C., 'Studentenplannen 1980', De Architect 1980, no. 12, pp. 65-69
Studentenplannen 80/81, Ministerie van Volkshuisvesting en Ruimtelijke Ordening, The Hague 1982, pp. 49-69

Katendrecht community centre, Provinciehuis Rijnmond Prix de Rome 1982

Architecture International Rotterdam, Rotterdamse Kunststichting, Rotterdam 1982, pp. 73-74
Graaf, R. de, 'De Prix de Rome verdient een winnaar', *WONEN TA/BK* 1982, no. 24, pp. 2-4
Brouwers, R., 'Ook debat over Prix de Rome zonder winnaars', *WONEN TA/BK* 1983, no. 1, p. 6
Maas, T., 'Prix de Rome, geen talent ontdekt', *De Architect* 1983, no. 1, pp. 56-65
Cate, G. ten, 'In het land der blinden?', *Bouw* 1983, no. 12, p. 7
Barbieri, U. (ed.), ' Architectuur en Planning Nederland 1940–1980 / De jonge generatie', *Items* 1983

Young Dutch Architects Biennale 1983

Dijk, H. van (ed.), 'Biënnale Jonge Nederlandse Architecten 1983', *WONEN TA/BK* 1983, no. 17-18, pp. 8-17

AmH Architecture Museum Holland, competition 1984

Polin, G., 'Alcuni giovani architetti olandesi', *Casabella* 1984, no. 504, pp. 16-17

StL Bus passenger shelter, Leiden 1984–1985

Moerman, I. (ed.), *Niet gebouwd Leiden*, Utrecht 1987, p. 63

PrB Development of taxation department site, Bergen op Zoom, Competition 1987

Heuvel, W. van, 'Ideeën voor een stadsfragment', *Architectuur & Bouwen* 1987, no. 11, pp. 37-39

StK Office building, Stadhouderskade, Amsterdam 1989–1991

De Kunstprijzen Amsterdam 1991, Stichting Amsterdams Fonds voor de Kunst, Amsterdam 1991
Koster, E., 'Wedijver in doorzichtigheid', *De Architect* 1991, no. 11, pp. 99-103
Krewinkel, H.W., 'Bürohaus in Amsterdam', *Glasforum* 1992, no. 3, pp. 21-26
Dijk, H. van, *De herovering van de transparantie, Architecture in the Netherlands Yearbook 1991–1992*, Rotterdam 1992, pp. 158-165
Koster, E., 'Duell um Tranzparantz', *Bauwelt* 1992, no. 4, pp. 164-169
'Gevel, vide en lifttoren kantoorgebouw, Amsterdam', *Bouwen met Staal* 1992, no. 10, pp. 82-83
Peterse, K., 'Licht en luchtig in de moderne traditie', *Bouw* 1993, no. 4, pp. 32-34
Kloos, M. (ed.), *Amsterdam architecture 1991–1993*, Arcampocket, Amsterdam 1994, pp. 96-97, p. 141
Soest, M. van (ed.), 'De beste in zijn vak', *Vrij Nederland* 08-04-1995
'Eingangshalle eines Bürohauses', *Baumeister sonderheft Erschliessung* 1995, pp. 42-45
Evers, H., 'The constructional detail', *Amsterdam in Detail*, Amsterdam 1996, pp. 117-127
Schittich, C., *Glasbau Atlas*, Munich 1998, pp. 224-227
Dijk, H. van, *Architectuur in Nederland in de twintigste eeuw*, Rotterdam 1999, pp. 143, 166

BrB Art Library, Breda 1989–1991

Mens, R., 'Stipendia '85/86, individuele subsidies voor architecten nader belicht', *De Architect* 1987, no. 3, pp. 49-55
Koster, E., 'An und für sich', *Bauwelt* 1992, no. 14, pp. 786-789
Krewinkel, H.W., 'Artotheek in Breda', *Glasforum* 1992, no. 4, pp. 21-26
Koster, E, 'Flexibel en transparant', *De Architect* 1992, no. 6, pp. 68-73
Rutten, J. (ed.), *Meer dan mooi alleen*, The Hague 1992, p. 23
Dijk, H. van, 'De herovering van de transparantie', *Architecture in the Netherlands Yearbook 1991–1992*, Rotterdam 1992, pp. 158-165
Zunino, K.M.G. (ed.), 'Olanda Musei / Netherlands Museums', *Abitare* 2002, no. 417, p. 96

HpH Regional office, VSB Bank, Haarlem 1992

Krewinkel, H.W., 'VSB Bank in Haarlem (NL)', *Glasforum* 1993, no. 5, pp. 27-30
'Bankgebouw te Haarlem', *Bouw* 1994, no. 2, pp. 21-22
Isphording, S. & P. Lorenz, 'Transparentes Bindeglied – VSB Bank Haarlem, Niederlande', *Banken und Geldinstitute*, Verlagsanstalt Alexander Koch, Leinfelden Echterdingen 2003

DpA 53 dwellings in the Dapperbuurt, Amsterdam 1992–1995

Oosterman, A., 'Woonblokken in Nederland, voorbeeldige architectuur van de jaren negentig', *Woningbouw in Nederland*, NAi Publishers, Rotterdam 1997, pp. 94-95

VdA Bridge 163 in the Verbindingsdam, Amsterdam 1993–1996

Bos, L. & H.J. van Kleef, 'Nieuwe toegang voor eilandbewoners', *Bouwen met Staal* 1997, no. 6, pp. 52-55

PwS Parkweg metrostation, Schiedam 1994–2002
Rietveld, B., 'De zes gezichten van de Beneluxlijn', *Architectuur & Bouwen* 1995, no. 12, pp. 10-15
Pieters, D., 'Sociale veiligheid domineert techniek', *De Architect* dec. 2002, pp. 58-61
'Entree en lichtkoepels metrostation Parkweg', *Bouwen met staal* 2002, no. 168, p. 55
Hoogewoning, A. et al., *Architecture in the Netherlands Yearbook 2002>03*, NAi Publishers, Rotterdam 2003, pp. 44-45
Gelder, J. van, 'Stalen stationskappen onderscheiden metrostation Beneluxlijn', *Bouwen met staal* 2004, no. 174, pp. 35-47

RwS Eiland bridge, Kampen 1994–2003
'Tuibrug N50', *Bouwen met Staal* 2004, no. 180, p. 125
Bakker, M.M., B.H. Coelman & H.P. Klooster (eds.), 'Eilandbrug over de IJssel bij Kampen' in *Bruggen, visie op architectuur en constructie*, Uitgeverij Matrijs en de Nederlandse Bruggenstichting, Utrecht 2004, pp. 186-187

AcB Cable-stayed bridges for AC Restaurants, Woudenberg & Nieuwegein 1995–1999
Askes, J.T et al., 'Sprong over snelweg verhoogt omzet', *Bouwen met staal* 2000, no. 157, pp. 14-19
Bakker, M.M.; B.H. Coelman & H.P. Klooster (eds.), 'Voetgangersbruggen over de A12 bij Veendendaal en over de A27 bij Nieuwegein' in *Bruggen, visie op architectuur en constructie*, Uitgeverij Matrijs and Nederlandse Bruggenstichting, Utrecht 2004, pp. 198-199

KwD New premises for Geo-information and ICT Department, Delft 1995–2003
'Büromaschine, Verwaltungsbau in Delft / NL fertiggestellt', *Baunetz* 28-07-2004
'Centrale hal kantoorgebouw AGI', *Bouwen met staal* 2004, no. 180, p. 39
Koster, E., 'Kantoor Adviesdienst Geo-informatie en ICT van Rijkswaterstaat, Delft', *Bouw* 2004, no. 8, pp. 22-25

ScB Convair office building, Schiphol Oost 1996–2000
Motta, F. (ed.), 'Amsterdam', *Area* 2002, no. 60

PdD Conversion of 6 car parks to offices, Amsterdam 1996–2000
Kloos, M., 'Het beest getemd. De Bijlmermeer en de eisen van de tijd; Bijzondere projecten', *Archis* 1997, no. 3, p. 81
Mulder, M., 'De Bijlmer bloeit op', *Bouw* 1997, no. 6, pp. 50-51
Kolkmeijer, M., 'Opwaarderen parkeergarages', *Bouwwereld* 2000, no. 15, pp. 24-27
'Behouden huis', *Bouw* 2002, no. 5, pp. 52-53

PlR Papendorp Bridge, Utrecht 1997–1998
Krijgsman, A., 'Een brug te ver?', *Bouwen met staal* 1999, no. 147, pp. 14-19
Jong, C. de & J.J. ter Poorten, *Bouwen met water*, Blaricum 2003, p. 226

NbZ Renovation of Noordwachter, Brandaris and IJdoorn apartment buildings, Zaandam 1997–1999
Kruit, C. (ed.), 'Glazen serregevel met messcherpe facetten', *Detail in architectuur* 2000, no. 4, pp. 24-27

RwS Bridge over Zuid Willemsvaart, Veghel 1997–2000
'Verkeersbrug Zuid Willemsvaart, Nominatie nationale staalprijs', *Bouwen met staal* 2002, no. 168, p. 136
Jong, C. de & J.J. ter Poorten, *Bouwen met water*, Blaricum 2003, p. 235
Bakker, M.M.; B.H. Coelman & H.P. Klooster (eds.), 'Brug in de A50 over de Zuid-Willemsvaart in Veghel' in *Bruggen, visie op architectuur en constructie*, Uitgeverij Matrijs and Nederlandse Bruggenstichting, Utrecht 2004, pp. 188-189

RtA Rietlandpark office towers, Amsterdam 1997–2002
Buurman, M & M. Kloos, *Amsterdams Architectuur 2000–2002*, Arcampocket, Amsterdam 2003, pp. 68-69, p. 133
Abrahamse, J.E. et al., *Eastern Harbour District Amsterdam. Urbanism and Architecture*, NAi Publishers, Rotterdam 2003, pp. 190-191
Nieuwenhuizen, J. van & J. Renckens, 'Onderzoek: de ontwikkeling van vlakdoek klimaatgevels', *Architectenweb* 06-10-2004

SbT Constellation office building, Schiphol Oost 1998–2000
Motta, F. (ed.), 'Amsterdam', *Area* 2002, no. 60, p. 39
'Gevel kantoorgebouw Constellation Building', *Bouwen met staal* 2002, no. 11, p. 61
ZdK Renovation of Zuiderkerk, Amsterdam 1998–2000
Motta, F. (ed.), 'Amsterdam', *Area* 2002, no. 60, p. 38

OhP IJtram route design, Amsterdam 1998–2004
Abrahamse, J.E. et al., *Eastern Harbour District Amsterdam. Urbanism and Architecture*, NAi Publishers, Rotterdam 2003, p. 194
Andriese, A.; W. Schipper & H. Warning (eds.), 'Lijntekeningen De aanleg van de IJtram in elf persoonlijke schetsen', Dienst Infrastructuur Verkeer en Vervoer, Amsterdam 2005

GoA Ganzenhoef Cultural Educational Centre, Amsterdam 1999–2003
'Instellingen in Zuidoost onder één dak – Ultramodern gebouw van 41mln', *Het Parool* 21-12-1999, p. 5
Debets, C., 'Luchtkussens voor een licht atrium', *Bouwwereld* 2002, no. 20, pp. 48-51
Lebesque, S. & J. Luwema (eds.), 'C.E.C. wonen op het dak', *Projectdocumentatie 2003/2004 Woningbouw*, Amsterdam 2004, p. XI, pp. 98-99

OhB Nieuw Europa office building, Amsterdam 2000–2006
Abrahamse, J.E. et al., *Eastern Harbour District Amsterdam. Urbanism and Architecture*, NAi Publishers, Rotterdam 2003, p. 221

OhC Watertheater facade, Amsterdam 2000–2006
Jong, C. de & J.J. ter Poorten, *Bouwen met water*, Blaricum 2003, p. 5
Abrahamse, J.E. et al., *Eastern Harbour District Amsterdam. Urbanism and Architecture*, NAi Publishers, Rotterdam 2003, p. 189

WwC Bebouwingsstudie Wuhu city, China
Buurman, M.; Kloos, M. (red.), *Dutch Architects in Booming China*, Arcampocket, Amsterdam 2005, pp. 256-283, 359

Oeuvre 1977–2005

PkE
Housing Kerkstraat
Pingjum
client Woningbouwvereniging Wymbritseradeel
competition 1977, first prize
construction 1979–1980

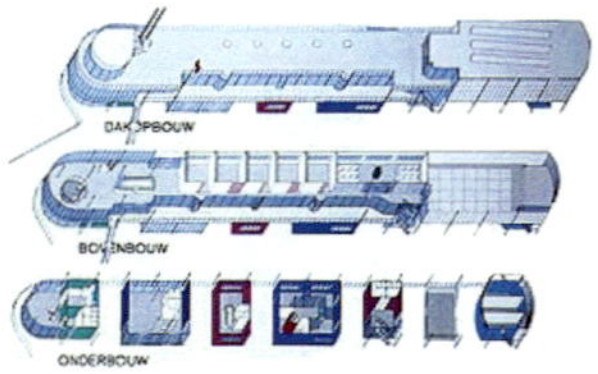

KaR
Katendrecht community centre
First round Prix de Rome (Architecture)
Prix de Rome 1982

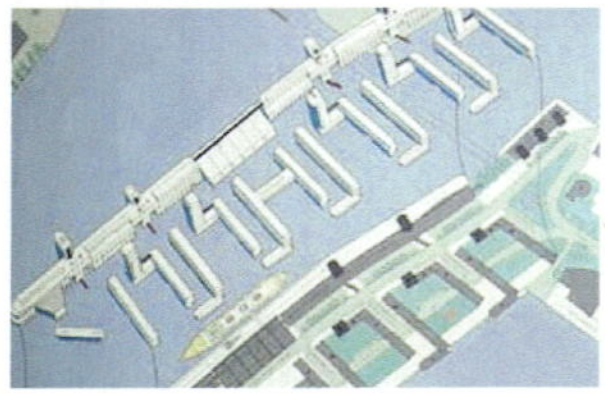

PrR
Provincial government office, Rijnmond
Final round Prix de Rome (Architecture)
Prix de Rome 1982

ObP
Opéra de la Bastille, Paris
competition 1983

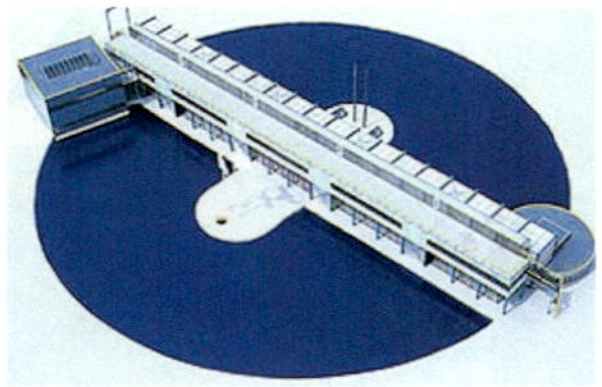

AmH
Architecture Museum Holland
competition 1984

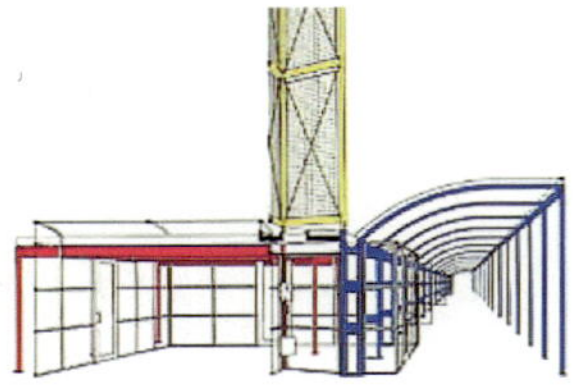

StL
Bus passenger shelter
Stationsstraat, Leiden
client City of Leiden
design 1984–1985

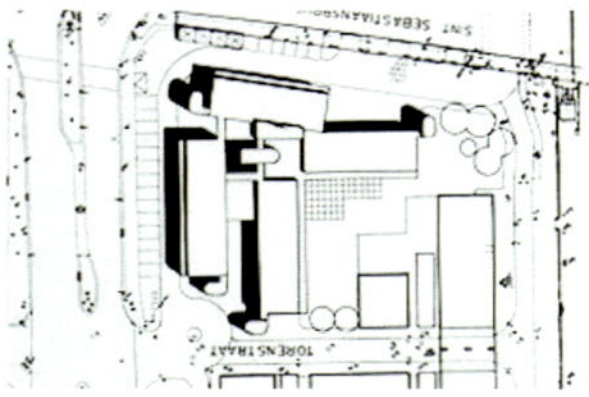

SuD
Youth hostel, Delft
competition 1985

GfR
Advertising agency: renovation and
interior design
client Commotion, Rotterdam
design and construction 1985

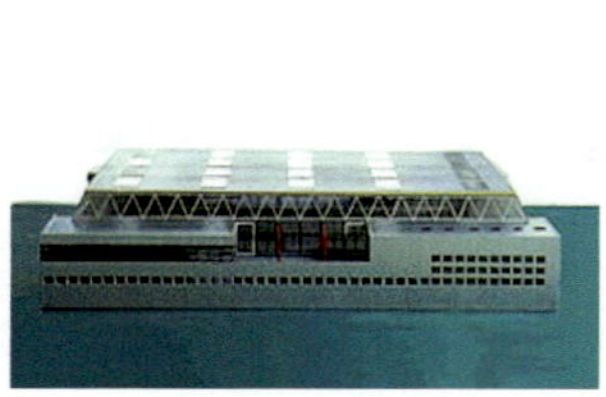

EsN
Estec Services Centre
Zuidlaan, Noordwijk
client ESA-ESTEC, Noordwijk
invited competition 1986

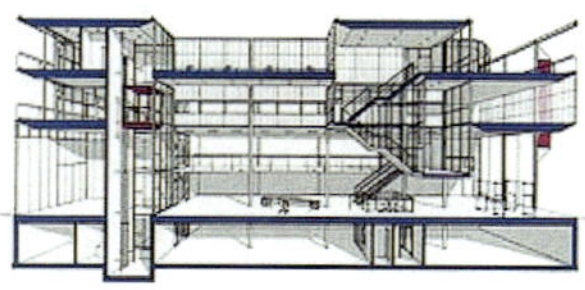

BrB
Breda Art Library
Boschstraat 22, Breda
client City of Breda
invited competition 1986

PrB
Development of taxation department land,
Bergen op Zoom
competition 1987

RijV
Police Station
De Meent 7, Volendam
client Government Buildings Agency
design 1987
construction 1988

BrI
Various renovations and interiors
for De Beyerd
Boschstraat 22, Breda
client De Beyerd, Breda
design and construction from 1987

BrE
De Beyerd entrance
Boschstraat 22, Breda
client De Beyerd Breda
design and construction 1988

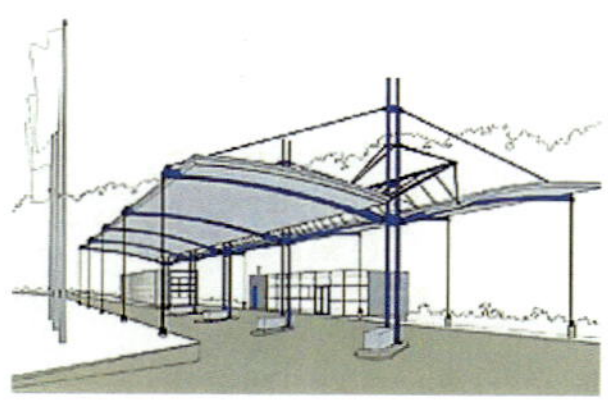

OcH
Aral Service Station
client Aral Nederland NV
design 1988

StK
Office building Stadhouderskade
Stadhouderskade 84, Amsterdam
client Nationale-Nederlanden VastGoed
design 1989
construction 1990–1991

BrB
Art lending library
Boschstraat 22A, Breda
client De Beyerd Breda
design 1989
construction 1990–1991

RhO
Office building
Hoofdweg 7, Rotterdam
client Heijmans Rosmalen
design 1990
construction 1992–1993

MbE
Study of redesign for De Markiezenhof Museum
Markiezenhof, Bergen op Zoom
client De Markiezenhof Museum Bergen op Zoom
study 1991

HpH
Regional office, VSB Bank
Houtplein 7, Haarlem
client VSB Bank, Haarlem
design 1991
construction 1991–1993

BsH
Housing and shops
Bussumerstraat, Naarderstraat, Hilversum
client De Bussumer Poort bv Loosdrecht
design 1991–1994

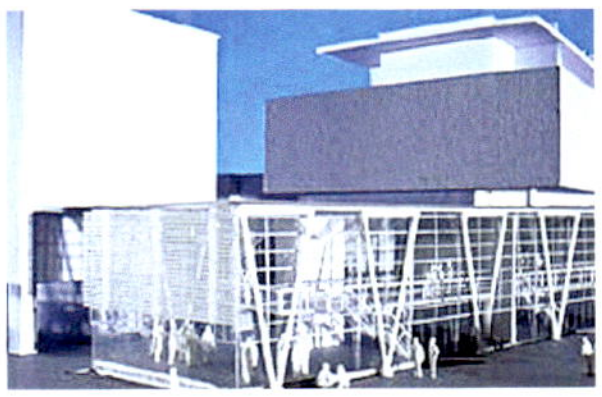

WkA
Multi-occupancy building
Westerdokskade Amsterdam
client Amsterdam Waterfront
design 1992

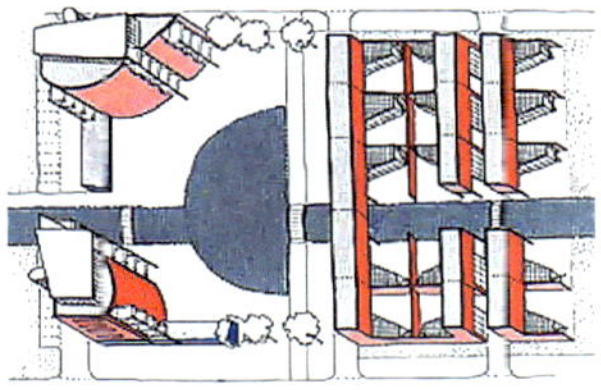

WdN
Housing study
Diemen Noord
client Verwelius, Weesp
invited competition 1992

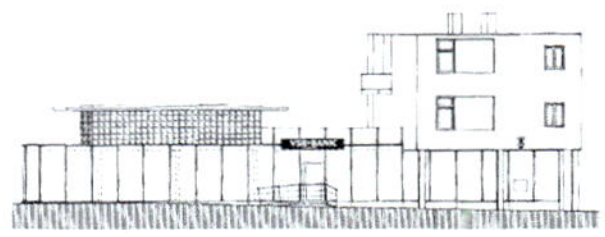

HpZ
Renovation of VSB Bank
Grote Krocht, Zandvoort
client VSB Bank, Haarlem
design 1992

RnW
Office park services centre
Bedrijvenpark Rotterdam Noordwest
client City of Rotterdam
invited competition 1992

DpA 📖
53 Dwellings in the Dapperbuurt
Linnaeusstraat, Von Zesenstraat,
Dapperstraat, Amsterdam
client Lieven de Key, Amsterdam
design 1992–1993
construction 1994–1995

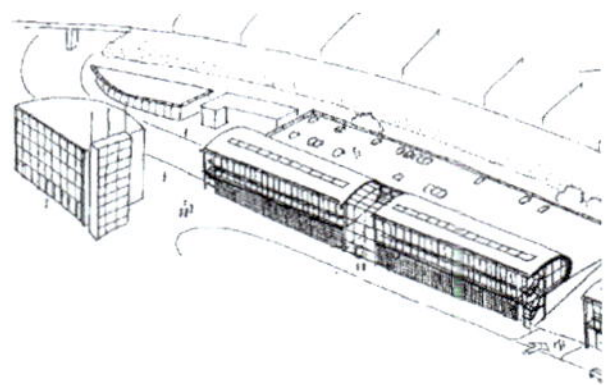

CrA
Study for Parks & Gardens service building
Cruquiuskade, Amsterdam
client Dienst Parkeerbeheer Amsterdam
design 1993

VdA
Bridge 163 in the Verbindingsdam
Amsterdam
client Grondbedrijf Amsterdam
design 1993
construction 1995–1996

GvA
GVB terminus facilities
client GVB Amsterdam
design 1993
construction 1997

RwS
Design of Rijkswaterstaat engineering works
client Bouwdienst Rijkswaterstaat
1993–1998

KsA
Preliminary study of Voorwerf naval barracks
Kattenburgerstraat, Amsterdam
client Government Buildings Agency
invited competition 1994

VmA
Interior of De Principaal office
Veemarkt, Amsterdam
client De Principaal, Amsterdam
design and construction 1994–1995

GsD
Noise barrier along the A16
A16 motorway at Wielwijk, Dordrecht
client Bouwdienst Rijkswaterstaat
design 1994
construction 1995–1997

LnA
Bridges, Nieuwevaart Lozingskanaal
Cruquiuskade, Amsterdam
client Grondbedrijf Amsterdam
design 1994
construction 1995–1997

BgB
Service building
Julianastraat, Borgharen
client Bouwdienst Rijkswaterstaat Utrecht
design 1994
construction 1996–1998

PwS
Parkweg metro station
Parkweg, burg. Honnerlage Gretelaan, Schiedam
client RET, Rotterdam
design 1994–1995
construction 1997–2002

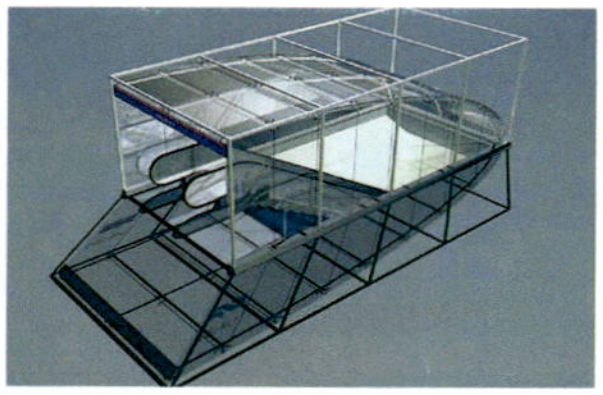

NzL
Study for Noord/Zuidlijn
client GVB, Amsterdam
invited competition 1995

NbA
NIBRA extension
NIBRA, Schaarsbergen
client Government Buildings Agency
invited competition 1995

BrA
Renovation of BKVB offices
Brouwersgracht 276, Amsterdam
client Fonds BKVB, Amsterdam
design 1995
construction 1996–1997

AcB
Cable-stayed bridges for AC Restaurants
Rijksweg A12, and Veenendaal and Nieuwegein
client AC Restaurants & Hotels, Breukelen
design 1995–1998
construction 1999

KwD
New premises for Geo-information
and ICT Department
Derde Werelddreef, Delft
client Government Buildings Agency, The Hague
design 1995–1999
construction 2000–2003

CpB
Interior of mayor's office, Breda
Claudius Prinsenlaan 10, Breda
client City of Breda
design and construction 1996

SpR
Dispatch building
Industriepark Schiphol Zuidoost
client Schiphol Real Estate, Schiphol
design 1996

KeA
De Key office interior
Loods 6, KNSM-eiland, Amsterdam
client De Key, Amsterdam
design 1996
construction 1996–1997

ApW
31 market sector dwellings, De Aker
De Aker, Amsterdam
client SFB Vastgoed, Haarlem
design 1996
construction 1997–1998

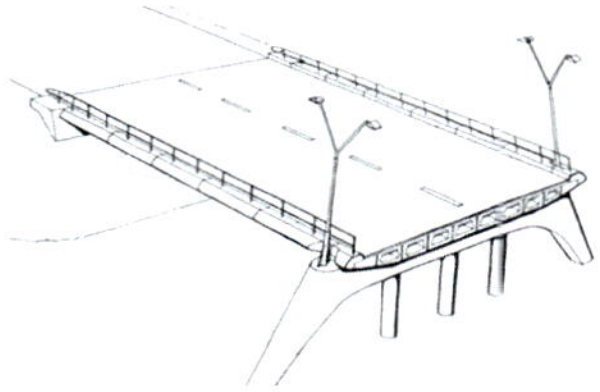

NvZ
Bridge with movable section
Nauernasche vaart, Saendelft, Zaanstad
client Zaanstad city council
design 1996
construction 1998–1999

PdD
Conversion of 6 car parks to offices
Daalwijkdreef, Amsterdam Zuidoost
client Dienst Parkeerbeheer, Amsterdam
design 1996
construction 1997–2000

ScB
Convair office building
Stationsstraat, Schiphol Oost
client KLM Facility Services, Schiphol Oost
design 1996
construction 1999–2000

SoD
New premises for Sports Medicine Clinic
Olympiaplein, Amsterdam
client stichting Fysiotherapie Amsterdam
design 1996–2002
construction 2002

IJdL
Heightening housing blocks and construction
of new dwellings
IJdoornlaan, Amsterdam Noord
client Algemene Woningbouwvereniging Amsterdam
design 1996–1999
construction 2001–2003

CwA
Port Authority Building
Westelijk havengebied, Amsterdam
client Havenbedrijf, Amsterdam
invited competition, 1997

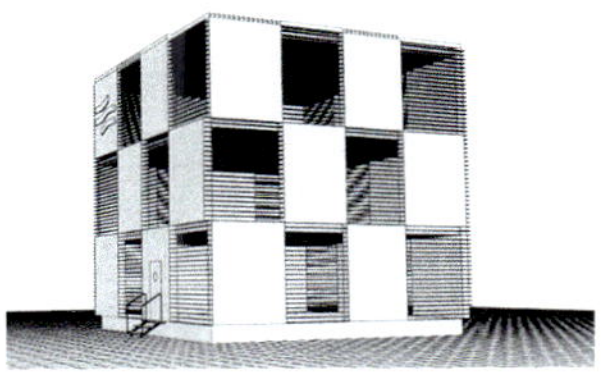

GvZ
GVB Depot
Station Zuid Amsterdam
client GVB Amsterdam
invited competition 1997

EpB
Erasmuspark pedestrian bridge
Amsterdam
client Stadsdeel Bos en Lommer, Amsterdam
design 1997
construction 1999

PlR
Papendorp Bridge
client Ontwikkelingsbedrijf
Leidsche Rijn Utrecht
invited competition 1997–1998

OkD
Bolkesteijn Bridge
Bolkesteijnlaan, Deventer
client City of Deventer
design 1997
construction 1998

NbZ–N
Renovation of Noordwachter and IJdoorn
apartment buildings, Zaandam
client Patrimonium Housing Corporation,
Amsterdam
design 1997
construction 1998–1999

NbZ–B
Sustainable renovation of Brandaris
apartment building, Zaandam
client Patrimonium Housing Corporation,
Amsterdam
design 1997
construction 1998–1999

RwS–V
Bridge over the Zuidwillemsvaart
Veghel
client Bouwdienst Rijkswaterstaat
design 1997
construction 2000

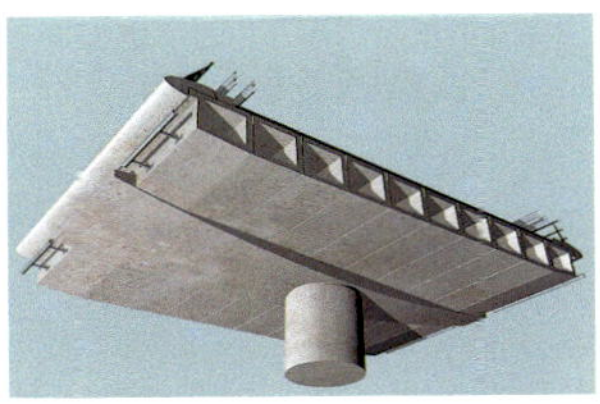

AtN
Arch viaduct A2/A9
A2–A9 intersection, Amsterdam
client Grondbedrijf Amsterdam
invited competition 1997
construction 1999–2000

TrS
Truck Service Centre
Industriepark, Schiphol Zuidoost
client Truckland Amsterdam
design 1997
construction 2000

SpA
Office premises and gymnasium on Sporenburg
Ertskade 105, Amsterdam
client New Deal, Amsterdam
design 1997
construction 1999–2000

RtA
Rietlandpark Office Towers
De Rietlanden, Amsterdam
client Amplan Vastgoed, Amsterdam
design 1997
construction 2000–2002

GhH
Heerhugowaard Town Hall and Library
Stadsplein, Heerhugowaard
client Heerhugowaard city council
design 1997–2003
construction 2004–2006

WvN
Design for theatre, cultural centre and housing
Wantveld, Golfbaan, Noordwijk
client Noordwijk city council
invited competition 1998

AzW
Study for office building
Various locations, Amsterdam Zuidoost
client Van Namen & partners, Hoofddorp
design study 1998–1999

AtC
Study for Teleport offices
Naritaweg, Amsterdam
client Van Namen & partners, Hoofddorp
design 1998–1999

SbT
Constellation office building
Stationsstraat, Schiphol Oost
client Schiphol Real Estate, Schiphol
design 1998
construction 1999–2000

ZdK
Renovation of Zuiderkerk
Gravenmakersplein Amsterdam
client Stedelijke Woningdienst, Amsterdam
design 1998
construction 1999–2000

BlK
Jacob van Lennepkanaal Bridge
Amsterdam
client Stadsdeel Oud-West, Amsterdam
design 1998–1999
construction 2004

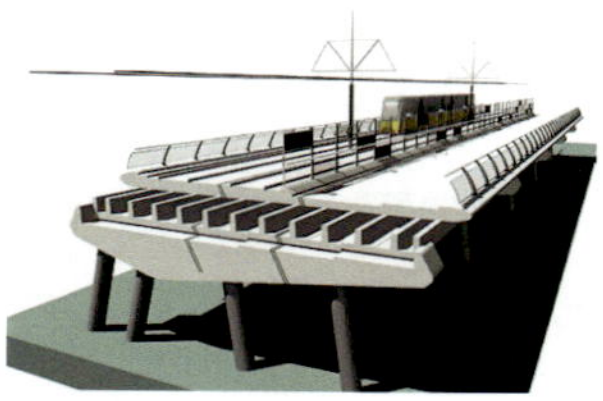

BlV
Two viaducts over the A4
A4, Leidschendam
client Ontwikkelingsbedrijf Leidschenveen
design 1998
construction 2004–2006

SoC
Olympiaplein maintenance building
Olympiaplein, Amsterdam
client Stadsdeel Amsterdam Zuid, Amsterdam
study 1998–2002

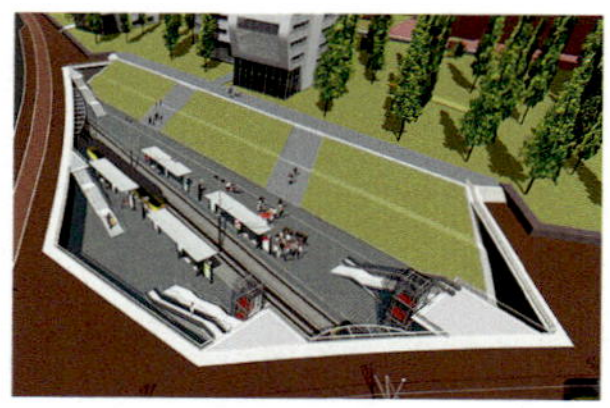

OhP
IJ-tram route design
Centraal Station–IJburg line, Amsterdam
client Projectbureau IJtram, Amsterdam
design 1998–2003
construction 2000–2005

BdW
Design of cycle and pedestrian bridge
Wilhelminakanaal, Dongen
client Dongen city council
design 1999

RsP
Study for office development
Rhijnspoorplein, Wibautstraat Amsterdam
client Steenhart Vastgoed Advies, Amsterdam
Design study 1999

AtL
Study for Amsterdam office building
Teleport, Amsterdam
client Leaflock SE, Brussels
design study 1999

BoG
Design for Haarlemmertrekvaart bridge
client Oegstgeest city council
invited competition 1999

OkT
Snipperlings Bridge, Deventer
Deventer
client City of Deventer
design 1999
construction 2000–2001

AtF
Cycle viaduct over A2
A2, Amsterdam
client Grondbedrijf, Amsterdam
design 1999
construction 2002–2003

GoA
Ganzenhoef Cultural Educational Centre
Bijlmerdreef, Amsterdam Zuidoost
client BPF bouw invest BV Amsterdam
design 1999–2001
construction 2002–2003

BlX
Meerweg Viaduct
Meerweg, Zoetermeerse rijweg, Leidschenveen
client Ontwikkelingsbedrijf Leidschenveen
design 2000
construction 2000–2001

KeI
Redesign of De Key office interior
Ertskade, Amsterdam
client De Key, Amsterdam
design 2000
construction 2000–2001

AsT
Renovation of NS station
Almelo
client NS Rail Infrabeheer, Zwolle
study 2000

AtT
Beta Building, Amsterdam Teleport
Naritaweg, Amsterdam
client Van Namen & Partners, Amsterdam
design 2000
construction 2000–2002

OhS
De Schijf School and commercial space
Oostelijke Handelskade 10, Amsterdam
client Amplan Vastgoed BV
design 2000
construction 2002–2003

BkD
Amstelwijk cycle bridge
Kilweg, Dordrecht
client City of Dordrecht
design 2000
construction 2003–2004

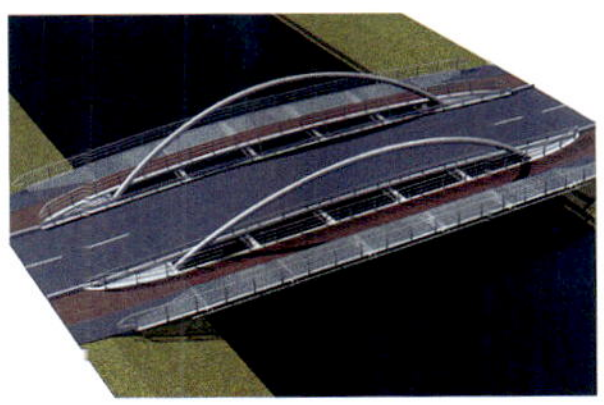

BgD
's Gravendijkdreef Bridge
Amsterdam Zuidoost
client Stadsdeel Amsterdam South East
design 2000–2001
construction 2003–2004

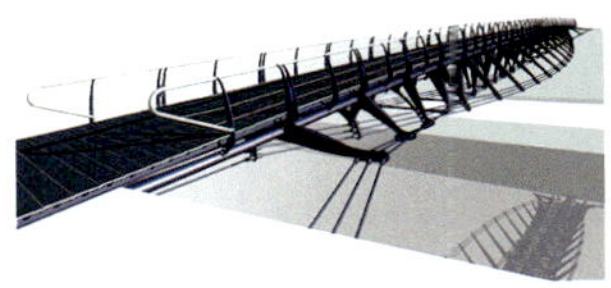

OhZ
Pedestrian bridge over the Zouthaven
Oostelijke handelskade, Amsterdam
client City of Amsterdam
design 2000–2003
construction 2004–2005

OhB
Nieuw Europa office building
Oostelijke Handelskade, Amsterdam
client Amplan Vastgoed, Amsterdam
design 2000–2003
construction 2006–2008

OhC
Watertheater facade
IJ haven, Amsterdam
client Blauwhoed Amsterdam
design 2000–2004

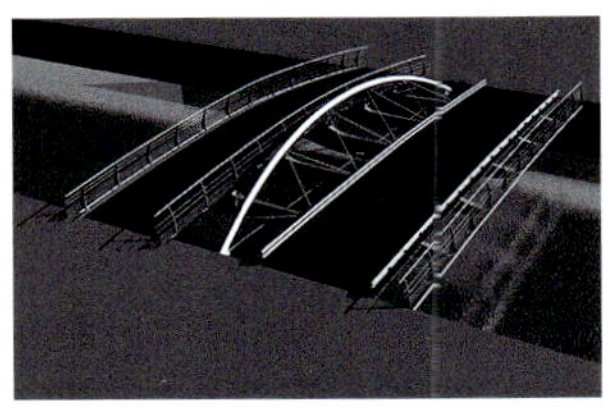

BrG
Competition for two city bridges
Neerschelde, Ghent
client City of Ghent
competition 2001

AdH
Design for Art Library renovation
Denneweg 14a, The Hague
client Artotheek, The Hague
invited competition 2001

LdS
Design for Lindodduin apartments and
new sheltered housing complex
Scheveningen
client Vestia Den Haag, Scheveningen
design 2001

BsT
Centraal Station Island bridges
De Ruyterkade, Amsterdam
client Dienst IVV, Amsterdam
design 2001
construction 2003–2005

AbB
Renovation of De Boelelaan housing
and office blocks
De Boelelaan, Amsterdam
client Patrimonium Amsterdam
design 2001–2003
construction 2005–2006

GvC
Extension of Amsterdam tram depot
Havenstraat, Amsterdam
client Gemeentevervoerbedrijf
design 2002

NbO
Study for extension and renovation
of Oostdorsch housing complex
Poelenburg, Zaandam
client Patrimonium Amsterdam
feasibility study 2002

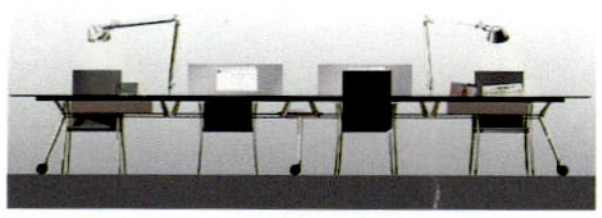

ZdG
Renovation of Zuiderkerk gravedigger's dwelling
Amsterdam
client City of Amsterdam
design 2002
construction 2003

GvT
Parnassusweg transformer shed
Amsterdam
client Gemeentelijk Vervoerbedrijf Amsterdam
design 2002
construction 2003

GoA
Interior of CEC Ganzenhoef
Amsterdam Zuidoost
client ROC Amsterdam
design 2002
construction 2003/2004

GsT
Krispijn Noise Barrier, Dordrecht
client Bouwdienst Rijkswaterstaat Tilburg
design 2002–2004
construction 2006

MgV
De Beyerd Museum of Graphic Design, Breda
Breda
client City of Breda/De Beyerd
design 2002–2005
construction 2006–2008

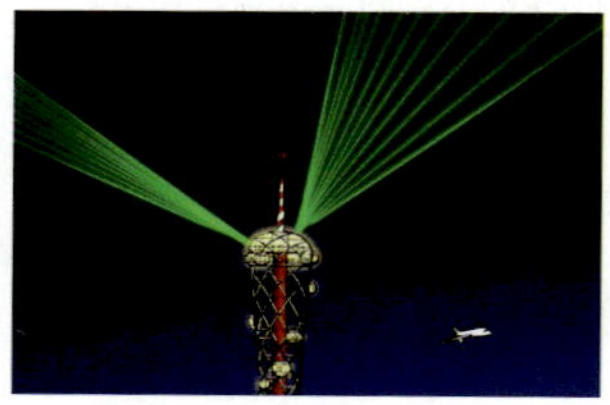

WwC
Development studies for Wuhu city, China
WuHu, China
client Niek Roozen landscape architects
study 2003

GwZ
Saenwonen/Parteon Housing Corporation Offices
Van Goghweg Zaandam
client Saenwonen/Parteon
design 2003–2005

AvP
Vondeltuin Restaurant
Vondelpark Amsterdam
client R. van Dantzig
design 2003–2004

JsA
Marina in the Spoorweg Basin
Amsterdam Zeeburg
client Nautiek Vaaropleidingen, Amsterdam
design 2003–2004
construction 2005

IF I MET AN ICE AGE ANIMAL

IF I PLAYED RING TOSS WITH A WOOLLY RHINOCEROS

by Jenna Lee Gleisner
illustrated by Michelle Simpson

GRASSHOPPER

Tools for Parents & Teachers

Grasshopper Books enhance imagination and introduce the earliest readers to fiction with fun storylines and illustrations. The easy-to-read text supports early reading experiences with repetitive sentence patterns and sight words.

Before Reading

- Discuss the cover illustration. What do readers see?
- Look at the picture glossary together. Discuss the words.

Read the Book

- Read the book to the child, or have him or her read independently.
- "Walk" through the book and look at the illustrations. Who is the main character? What is happening in the story?

After Reading

- Prompt the child to think more. Ask: The main character imagines playing ring toss with a woolly rhinoceros. If you could play a game with any animal, what game and animal would you choose? Why?

Grasshopper Books are published by Jump!
5357 Penn Avenue South
Minneapolis, MN 55419
www.jumplibrary.com

Library of Congress Cataloging-in-Publication Data

Names: Gleisner, Jenna Lee, author.
Simpson, Michelle (Illustrator), illustrator.
Title: If I played ring toss with a woolly rhinoceros
by Jenna Lee Gleisner; illustrated by Michelle Simpson.
Description: Minneapolis, MN: Jump!, Inc., 2023.
Series: If I met an Ice Age animal | Includes index.
Audience: Ages 5-8.
Identifiers: LCCN 2021060814 (print)
LCCN 2021060815 (ebook)
ISBN 9781636909486 (hardcover)
ISBN 9781636909493 (paperback)
ISBN 9781636909509 (ebook)
Subjects: CYAC: Woolly rhinoceros–Fiction.
Rhinoceroses–Fiction. | Prehistoric animals–Fiction.
LCGFT: Picture books.
Classification: LCC PZ7.1.G5885 Ifj 2023 (print)
LCC PZ7.1.G5885 (ebook)
DDC [E]–dc23
LC record available at https://lccn.loc.gov/2021060814
LC ebook record available at https://lccn.loc.gov/2021060815

Editor: Eliza Leahy
Direction and Layout: Anna Peterson
Illustrator: Michelle Simpson

Printed in the United States of America at Corporate Graphics in North Mankato, Minnesota.

Table of Contents

Horns and Rings

Today is the school fair. My favorite game is ring toss. I got the ring around the woolly rhinoceros's horn!

What if I played ring toss with a real *woolly rhinoceros?* I wonder.

If I played ring toss with a woolly rhino, I'd have to go back to the Ice Age. Woolly rhinos have been extinct for more than 10,000 years!

Everything is covered in ice and snow. I'd have to dress warm. But the woolly rhino has thick, shaggy hair. She is built for the cold.

I try to get the rings around the rhino's two horns. But she is tall. Her front horn is *even* taller!

She sweeps away snow with her horns. She looks for food. Woolly rhinos were herbivores.

When she stops to graze, I toss a ring.
Extra points for the tall horn!

If I played ring toss with a woolly rhino, her calf would want to play, too. Its horns are shorter. This is tricky!

In the distance, two males fight for the female's attention.

They come over. They want to play, too!

Just then, we hear something. A saber-toothed cat is coming our way!

The mom fights the cat.
She uses her horns.
She protects her calf.
She protects me, too.

Phew! We are safe.

“Thanks for playing,” I say.
“But I think I’ll stick to normal ring toss.”

Parts of a Woolly Rhinoceros

Woolly rhinoceroses were about 12 feet (3.6 meters) long and six feet (1.8 m) tall. They weighed up to 6,000 pounds (2,720 kilograms). Take a look at the parts of a woolly rhinoceros.

Picture Glossary

calf
A young woolly rhinoceros.

extinct
No longer found alive and known about only through fossils or history.

graze
To feed on grass and other plants that grow close to the ground.

herbivores
Animals that eat plants.

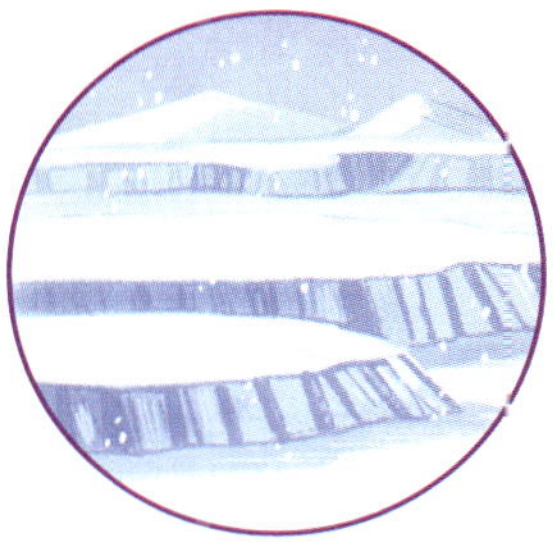

Ice Age
A period of time, about 10,000 years ago, when a large part of Earth was covered with ice.

sweeps
Clears away.

Index

To Learn More

FACT SURFER

Finding more information is as easy as 1, 2, 3.

1. Go to www.factsurfer.com
2. Enter "**ifIplayedringtosswithawoollyrhinoceros**" into the search box.
3. Choose your book to see a list of websites.